A Royal Duty

A Royal Duty

PAUL BURRELL

MICHAEL JOSEPH
an imprint of
PENGUIN BOOKS

MICHAEL JOSEPH

Published by the Penguin Group

Penguin Books Ltd, 80 Strand, London WC2R ORL, England

Penguin Putnam Inc., 375 Hudson Street, New York, New York 10014, USA

Penguin Books Australia Ltd, 250 Camberwell Road, Camberwell, Victoria 3124, Australia

Penguin Books Canada Ltd, 10 Alcorn Avenue, Toronto, Ontario, Canada M4V 3B2

Penguin Books India (P) Ltd, 11 Community Centre, Panchsheel Park, New Delhi – 110 017, India

Penguin Books (NZ) Ltd, Cnr Rosedale and Airborne Roads, Albany, Auckland, New Zealand

Penguin Books (South Africa) (Pty) Ltd, 24 Sturdee Avenue, Rosebank 2196, South Africa

Penguin Books Ltd, Registered Offices: 80 Strand, London WC2R ORL, England

www.penguin.com

First published 2003

I

PICTURE CREDITS

Section 1 – Plate 3, top: Shelley/Carraro/Rex; Plate 6, top and bottom: Nils Jorgensen/Rex
Section 3 – Plate 2, top: Tim Rooke/Rex; Plate 3, top: Today/NI Syndication; Plate 3, bottom: Kelvin Bruce; Plate 4, top: Mirrorpix; Plate 4, bottom: Camera Press London; Plate 5, top left: Rex; Plate 5, top right: PA Photos; Plate 5, bottom: Mirrorpix; Plate 6, top right: Mirrorpix; Plate 6, bottom left and bottom right: PA Photos; Plate 7, top: Robin Nunn; Plate 7, bottom: PA Photos; Plate 8: PA Photos

Every effort has been made to trace the copyright holders and the publishers apologize for any unintentional omission. We would be pleased to insert the appropriate acknowledgement in any subsequent editions.

Set in 11.75/14.25pt Monotype Bembo
Typeset by Rowland Phototypesetting Ltd, Bury St Edmunds, Suffolk
Printed in Great Britain by Clays Ltd, St Ives plc

A CIP catalogue record for this book is available from the British Library

ISBN 0–718–14720–0

To my wife, my children and the princess –
you will always be with me

THANK YOU. 'They are two small words which mean so much, and people don't say them often enough these days,' the princess always used to say.

I doubt there was a more prolific writer of thank-you letters than the Boss. She must have sat for hours at her desk in the sitting room at Kensington Palace, penning endless notes in her fountain pen, taking time to sit down and thank someone for their help, kindness, generosity, hospitality, advice or friendship.

If there was one thing I encouraged her to do, it was to put down her thoughts on paper. If there was one thing she encouraged in me, it was the never-to-be-forgotten importance of writing a thank-you letter, something her father, the late Earl Spencer, had instilled in her as a child.

This is my written thank-you to the team who have supported me in the compiling of *A Royal Duty*, my own tribute to the life and work of the princess.

So, thank you:

First and foremost, to my wife, Maria, and my sons, Alexander and Nicholas. We have all shared a traumatic time, and your constant love, support and understanding continue to make me the proudest husband and father, supported by relatives on both sides of our family.

To my friend Steve Dennis, for working your magic and being with me every step of the way on this literary journey; and for sharing with me the passion to enshrine the memory of the princess.

To my agent Ali Gunn, for your invaluable advice, never-ending encouragement and laughter along the way. I am for ever indebted to you.

The production of *A Royal Duty* has illustrated to me the mammoth effort required to make books such as this possible, and I believe I have had the best team in the industry: a huge thank-you to my publisher Tom Weldon, for your vision, judgement, and for believing in me and this book in the first place; and to everyone else on the team at Penguin in London and New York, especially my editor Hazel Orme, for your expert eye, Genevieve Pegg, Sophie Brewer and Kate Brunt, for your tireless efforts and patience behind the scenes; and American publishers Carole Baron and Jennifer Hershey who have been 'awesome'.

To the people of Naas in the Republic of Ireland, especially Mary Elliffe, Laura and Kevin, and everyone else at the Town House Hotel, for making Steve and me feel at home, and for keeping us sane over these past few months with your songs and hospitality.

To my brilliant legal team, who fought the injustice of my trial at the Old Bailey: Lord Carlile QC, Ray Herman, solicitor Andrew Shaw, and their able assistants Lesley and Shona. Words fail me for how much you believed in me during that nightmare time.

To the close friends of the princess: you all know who you are, and I will never forget your unstinting support in being prepared to take the witness stand in my defence. I know we stand as one in defending the memory of a remarkable woman, whose warmth and friendship touched us all.

What you are all about to read is a legacy that certain people wanted to destroy from a man they tried to silence.

Paul Burrell
October 2003

Contents

Preface xi

1. Growing Up 1

2. Buckingham Palace 17

3. A Princess in Love 51

4. The Queen and I 74

5. The Other Royal Wedding 90

6. Deceit at Highgrove 108

7. Caught in the Crossfire 149

8. KP 169

9. 'The Boss' 198

10. Handling the Divorce 225

11. A Matter of Trust 243

12. Side by Side 261

13. Goodbye, Your Royal Highness 284

14. A Very Strange Business 299

15. A Knock at the Door 324

16. Cloak and Dagger 342

17. Regina v. Burrell 366

Preface

The princess died at four a.m. in a hospital in Paris on Sunday 31 August 1997. The last time I saw her was when she was waving goodbye from the back of her BMW, being driven away from the front door of Kensington Palace on Friday 15 August.

The previous day, we had been to Waterstones bookshop in Kensington High Street. We drove because time was tight, and we didn't fancy walking back with what she called her 'heavy reading matter': half a dozen books, hardback and paperback, on spirituality, psychology and healing. She put them in the boot and got into the front passenger seat, and we headed back to the palace so she could finish packing with assistance from her dresser, Angela Benjamin.

As we turned into the palace drive, she was in a relaxed mood. 'I'm looking forward to a quiet holiday, good company and lots of light reading!'

Her friend Rosa Monckton had hired a yacht with a crew of four to sail her and the princess around the Greek islands on a six-day Mediterranean holiday. When she returned, the princess was due to go on holiday with another female friend, Lana Marks, for a five-day break to Italy, staying at the Four Seasons Hotel in Milan. She had not intended to spend that final week of August with Dodi Al Fayed. Reservations had been made and flights booked for her to be with Lana. That holiday was cancelled at the last minute because Lana's father died suddenly, which left the princess at a loose end until the boys returned to Kensington Palace on 31 August. She accepted Dodi's offer to spend more time with him on the *Jonikal*, cruising around the French Riviera and Sardinia.

Before she flew out to join Dodi, she would be back at the palace for one day, on 21 August, but I wouldn't be there because I had deliberately booked my family holiday to Naas, in the Republic of Ireland, to fit in with the princess. As she finalized her packing on 15 August to head off to the airport, I was sharing that demob-happy feeling as I waited with Rosa inside KP. 'We must do something about this one. He's not right for her, you know that. Will you do what you can?' I asked her. I knew that the princess would listen to Rosa, and I sensed that Rosa shared my concern, because 'this one' was Dodi. Rosa nodded and smiled. She understood.

The princess had been fussing around in the sitting room, tidying her desk, putting the wastepaper bin out in the landing to be emptied, checking her shoulder-bag. As the two friends came down the stairs to leave, she stopped half-way down and went through her cross-checking routine, thinking aloud: 'Passport, phone, Walkman . . .'

I was leaning on the wooden banister, looking up at her. She was wearing a simple Versace shift dress. 'Do you know?' I said. 'I've never seen you looking as good. You look perfect. You don't need the sunshine – look at your tan already!' and she skipped down the stairs, smiling.

We went through into the inner hallway. 'Hang on to that a minute.' She thrust her shoulder-bag into my hands and disappeared into the ladies' room. Within minutes, she was ready to go. She stepped out into the sunshine and into the rear passenger seat of the BMW as the chauffeur started the engine. I pulled out and stretched the seatbelt, then leaned across her to fasten it. 'If you have a chance to ring me, you will, won't you?' she asked me.

'Of course,' I said, having arranged that week for her mobile telephone to be allocated a new number that only a handful of people would know.

'Have a nice time, Paul.'

I walked back to the doorstep, and the princess waved. I watched the BMW turn left and out of sight. She was heading for Heathrow and an aeroplane to Athens.

The Burrells joined Maria's side of the family, the Cosgroves, on a four-day holiday in Naas. We visited Kilkenny Castle and then the village where the BBC series *Ballykissangel* was filmed, visiting the famous Fitzgerald's pub. I was under strict orders from Maria to forget about work and the princess. 'This is a family holiday and family time,' she said.

The only problem was that I had promised the princess I would ring. Four days of no contact would be noticed by the Boss, so I found myself making excuses to go for long walks.

The princess was on the deck with Rosa when I rang. She told me how sunny and hot it was. I told her how wet and miserable the Republic of Ireland was. She had completed a book on spirituality and was tackling a new one already, she said. I hung up, promising to speak to her again when I was back at my home in Farndon, Cheshire, and she was on the *Jonikal* with Dodi. I told Maria that the long walk had done me a power of good.

On 21 August, she made a flying return to Kensington Palace then dashed off to Stansted Airport for a flight to Nice to meet up with Dodi and head back to the *Jonikal*. While she had been away, the refurbishment of the sitting room had been finished so she saw the reupholstered sofas and sky blue curtains.

The refurbishment was ironic because, after flicking through the property brochures from America, the chance had arisen to purchase a clifftop property in California: the home of British actress Julie Andrews. The princess was seriously considering a new future there, but it would not have been a permanent move. She wanted to buy a holiday home where she could spend up to six months of the year, while she kept KP as her London base.

A move to America had been on the cards since the spring. In August, between holidays, she had spread out the brochure and said, 'America is where my destiny lies, and if I decide to do this, Paul, I would like you, Maria and the boys to join me.'

As we knelt on the sitting-room floor, she pointed at the Julie Andrews property, featured on several colour pages and floor plans. 'This is the main reception area. This is where William's room will be, and Harry's. And that annexe is where you will live with Maria and the boys. This can be a new life. Isn't it exciting? It is a land where anyone can achieve,' she said.

I had longed to live in America but it all seemed too sudden. 'I think you should slow down. Even I'm finding it impossible to keep up with you,' I said, trying not to burst the bubble.

That afternoon the princess peppered me with questions. 'Well, if we don't live there, what about Cape Cod? It's nearer to London. We can travel the world, Paul, and seek out all those people who need help.'

We sat there imagining the American lifestyle: the jogs along the beach, the constant sunshine, the sense of freedom. And there was one more thing. Something she had always talked about. The one thing she had always wanted at Kensington Palace but felt was not possible. 'And we can get a dog,' she said. The princess had always longed for a black labrador. The thought of America made her so happy. 'I always said we would end up living in America, didn't I?' she said.

The princess was making clear-cut decisions. Many things were discussed. Secrets that I cannot mention here. Secrets that will go away with me. But surprises would be coming, and the prospect of all that excited her.

After the holiday in Naas, I spoke to the princess nearly every day, but I never rang her from home. When we spoke, she was either lying on the deck of the *Jonikal* or relaxing out of the sun in her cabin. From the first call, I knew she was getting restless in that environment. 'It's roasting on the deck, it's like a fridge downstairs – I'm crawling the walls here!' she said.

Dodi had given her a silver photo frame, inscribed with a poem. She read it to me.

'That's a bit deep and meaningful, isn't it?' I jested.

'No!' She laughed. 'It's sweet and romantic.'

He had also given her a necklace and a pair of earrings. 'He's got it bad, hasn't he?' She giggled.

I could see what was happening. The Boss had enjoyed the frisson of a new liaison, the excitement of the chase, the flattery of an attentive man who had fallen head over heels. As they all did. But for her the novelty was wearing a bit thin. She knew that Dodi had fallen in love. He had told her so over dinner. But she hadn't reciprocated. It was too early, she said.

'So what did you tell him?' I asked curiously.

'I told him, "Thank you for the compliment."'

In the mythology that has been peddled since the princess's death, there have been two ludicrous claims: that she and Dodi were going to get married, and that she was pregnant. The monstrous suggestion of pregnancy is not true.

As for marriage, which seems to have been a story that emerged from Dodi's friends, he might well have told them that he was *planning* to pop the question, but the princess was in no mood to accept. Happy she might have been. Hasty she was not.

In another call from the boat, she speculated about whether the next gift would be a ring. She was excited at the prospect but becoming increasingly worried about what it all meant. 'What do I do, Paul, if it's a ring? I want another marriage like I want a bad rash,' she said.

'It's easy. You accept it graciously and slip it on to the fourth finger of your right hand. Don't put it on the wrong finger if you don't want to send the wrong signals!' I warned light-heartedly.

Fourth finger. Right hand. We kept saying it.

'That means it will become a friendship ring,' I said.

'What a clever idea. I will. I will,' she said.

We never had another conversation about a ring, or whether one was actually produced.

There was another nagging doubt in the princess's mind about Dodi. 'He keeps going into the bathroom and locking the door behind him. He keeps sniffing, blaming the air-conditioning system, and it disturbs me. Maybe I can help him, Paul.' The conversation switched to how much she was looking forward to spending time with William and Harry. She couldn't count the days fast enough until she was with them. She was so desperate to come home that she wanted to cut short her time with Dodi and return to London two days early. She had considered rearranging her flight, but Dodi persuaded her to stay.

'I'm just ready to come home now,' she said. 'I need to go to the gym.'

'You've had enough of all that pampered luxury, then?' I asked.

There was a sigh. I did what I often did and tried to second-guess what she was thinking. 'Don't tell me. You're feeling trapped on the boat and he's controlling your every move?'

'Right again. I need to come home.'

She told me about the last-minute diversion to Paris on Friday 29 August. She spoke to me from the deck of the *Jonikal*. It was one of the last six phone calls she made in the final twenty-four hours of her life, as recorded in the call-register of her mobile telephone.

I was on the telephone, sprawled on the sitting-room floor at my brother-in-law Peter Cosgrove's house in Farndon, two doors down from our first house, bought that spring as a holiday home. The family – Maria, the boys, Peter, his wife Sue, and their daughters Clare and Louise – had all given me privacy, but were growing impatient in the kitchen because I must have been on the telephone to the princess for around forty minutes.

In that call, the timetable for her arrival had changed. Originally she had been due to come back to London direct from the Mediterranean, arriving on Saturday 30 August ahead of the boys' arrival on the Sunday. But Dodi had told her he needed to go to Paris for 'business reasons'. She seemed reluctant to go but, again, Dodi had persuaded her.

'We've got to go to Paris, but I promise I will be back on Sunday,' she said. 'Now, I bet you can't guess where I am.'

I tried Sardinia.

'No. Monaco. And I bet you can't guess where I'm going tonight.'

I hazarded a fine restaurant.

'No. I'm going to visit the grave of Princess Grace. It will be a special moment.'

It would be the first time she had returned to the grave since she attended her funeral in 1982. 'I'm going to lay some flowers and say a few words,' she added.

Then, her mind was back on land. She was thinking ahead and making plans, giving me instructions: remember to book Mr Quelch at Burberry (the boys' tailor) for the following Monday. The Armani fitting for 4 September. She asked what was in the diary. I told her lunch with Shirley Conran, and an appointment with aromatherapist Sue Beechey. Otherwise she had plenty of free time with William and Harry.

As that marathon call neared its end, the princess told me: 'I'm looking forward to catching up with friends and I can't wait to see the boys. There's a lot we have to talk about, so don't be late! I'll tell you everything else when I see you.'

In the background, an impatient family was calling me from the kitchen.

'Paul?' the princess asked. 'I want you to promise me something.'

'Of course,' I said.

'Promise me you'll be there,' she said, in a chirpy voice, and I laughed at her worrying about me being late or not being on the front doorstep.

'Say it!' she demanded. 'I want to hear you say those words!'

I started to laugh. 'Okay, okay, if it makes you feel happier, I promise I'll be there.'

The princess laughed. The family guffawed behind the kitchen door. The poignancy of those final words only hit me later but they have stayed with me ever since. I will carry on that responsibility of being there for her – even when others object.

'Good!' said the princess. 'I'll see you when I get back.'

It was the last time I spoke to her.

1. Growing Up

The late-night double-decker bus crawled sluggishly up the hilly back roads of the colliery communities of God's own country: Derbyshire. Like an inebriated miner weaving his way home after last orders, it seemed in no rush to make its final destination. The familiar smell of sulphur and tar from the coalface hung in the air, mixed with a whiff of burned wood. It was around eleven p.m. on Bonfire Night 1956.

On the bus, a lone, rather stout woman, wearing black, round-rimmed spectacles, cut a sober figure on the lower deck. Sarah Kirk sat with a handbag perched on her knee and a black cloche hat on her head, counting down the number of stops left until she alighted in the pit community of Grassmoor. Once there, she would cross the main road cutting through the village, walk down a cobbled slope into Chapel Road, turn right at the bottom, and be home at No. 57. She had enjoyed her night out and several half-glasses of mild at the Elm Tree pub three miles away in Clay Cross.

Saturday nights were a chance to catch up with Dolly, her eldest daughter of eight children. They offered respite from caring for her sick husband William, a miner, whose lungs were congested with coal dust from a lifetime spent underground at the neighbouring Grassmoor Colliery. Sarah always left before last orders to catch the Chesterfield bus home. Come eleven fifteen, William was keen to see his wife. As the bus slowed, Sarah gathered her gloves, pulled them on and stood up. Home. Almost. She stepped out on to the pavement, turned left and began to walk along beside the bus, her breath like cigarette smoke in the raw air. Blinded by the back of the bus to her left side, she didn't see the motorbike that struck and tossed her into the air. It was shortly after eleven fifteen.

Sarah Kirk was the grandma I never got to meet. She died there and then on the pavement at the top of the cobbled street that would become my childhood playground. She had suffered massive head injuries. She was sixty-three.

I

In one of life's cruel twists, that awful tragedy, two years before my birth, was a defining moment. It led my parents into marriage and, in turn, shaped the world into which I was born.

Grandad William Kirk, struck down by terminal pneumoconiosis, heard a woman's footsteps on the cobbles, then the latch lifting on the back door. His prized possession, a gold pocket watch, told him it was ten past eleven. Sarah was five minutes early.

The footsteps trotted up the wooden stairs and a face he adored peeped round the door. It was his youngest daughter – my mum. Beryl Kirk sat at the foot of Grandad's bed, telling him of the pleasant date she had enjoyed with a local man from neighbouring Wingerworth. She was Graham Burrell's first girlfriend.

Dad, then twenty-one, was on the two-mile walk home, down unlit back roads. A double-decker bus passed him on its way into Grassmoor.

The frantic knocking on the back door of No. 57 Chapel Road startled father and daughter. A male neighbour grabbed Mum. 'There's been a terrible accident. Come quick – come quick!'

Then only twenty, Mum leapt up and half walked, half ran to the brow of the hill. There, a friend saw her and headed her off. No one wanted her to witness such a scene, yet everyone heard her hysterical screams when she was told.

It was a loss from which she never truly recovered. She cried often throughout my childhood, reminiscing. Every Sunday, for the rest of her life, she visited Hasland cemetery, polished the headstone and laid fresh flowers. I often went with her. If ever there was a time when I began to believe in 'the other side' it was in childhood. Mum was spiritual: she talked to Grandma in the kitchen, and beside her gravestone, updating her on the latest events. Grandma was still with us, she said.

'What shall I do? Have a twenty-first birthday party or get married? We can't afford to do both,' Mum said to Dad. In the weeks of mourning after the road accident, it seemed romance had died too. It was as if Dad had been given a choice of what to eat for dinner – or tea, as we called it in the north of England. Meat and potato pie or stew and dumplings?

Dad's reply was nonchalant. 'Well, s'pose we'd better get married, then.'

Had Grandma Kirk not died, my parents would not have married so soon. According to Dad, anyway. Circumstances shoehorned him into wedlock and fatherhood. Grandma's passing elevated Mum to the woman of the house at No. 57 as she nursed Grandad, sharing the duty with her elder sister, Auntie Pearl, who lived in the same street at No. 16.

Four months after Grandma was killed, Beryl Kirk and Graham Burrell tied the knot on 25 March 1957. It was a sombre occasion, remembered for the one person absent and not for those present. Afterwards, Mum went in her bridal dress and laid her bouquet of red roses on the grave.

It had been four years since Mum and Dad shared their first date – a romantic stroll down Mill Lane, which linked Grassmoor with Wingerworth, two villages dissected by the Sheffield–London railway line. Mum, although she was only seventeen, pulled pints in the Miner's Arms, where Auntie Pearl was landlady with husband Ernie Walker, and also had a day job as an assistant cook at the colliery. The pub and the colliery sat at opposite ends of Chapman Lane, which runs parallel to Chapel Road, equidistant from home. The two streets formed a tight-knit huddle of back-to-back terraces. Every home housed a miner, and every drinker in the pub was either a miner or his wife. It was one night in 1952 – the year Queen Elizabeth II ascended the throne – that Dad and his brother Cecil wandered in. Mum remembered him 'staring at her half-baked'. Dad remembers 'a very attractive lady pulling pints'.

Dad, then eighteen, was young, shy and naïve and had never had a girlfriend. Mum and I remained convinced that alcohol had given him the Dutch courage to ask her out. She accepted – and never looked at another man. He was one of five children from a small homestead, and grew up surrounded by pigpens, chicken-runs and an apple orchard. He never became a miner but worked for the National Coal Board on the locomotives shunting full coal-wagons into the carbonization and coking plant at Wingerworth. He had always feared the caged drop into the shaft, but he also wanted to escape everyone's expectations that he would be a miner. One day, I, too, would know that feeling. National Service had provided his escape route: two years away from home, serving Queen and country, was a far more attractive option than a lifetime in darkness, and he went to RAF Warrington as an airman. He told us he swept the runway for Vulcan bombers to take off, but in fact, he was on guard duty for air-traffic control. He returned to Derbyshire in 1954.

June 6, 1958 was not a remarkable day for most people, but it was for my parents. On a beautiful sunny summer's evening, I was born in Scarsdale Maternity Hospital, Chesterfield, and brought with me a surprise. Mum and Dad had anticipated the arrival of a daughter and had already chosen her name, Pamela Jane. It was the midwife who broke the news on my delivery. 'Well, Mrs Burrell, it's not a Pamela,' she said, 'it's a boy!' So I became Paul.

From the moment Mum walked down the aisle, all she ever wanted was a child. Dad was not convinced. It became an immediate source of friction in the early days of their union. Mum had given up work at the pit canteen and pub to care for Grandad Kirk, and pleaded with Dad: 'I'm stuck here twenty-four hours a day. It would make little difference having a baby to feed and wash as well.' Mum always waited until Grandad was asleep before she raised the subject with Dad in the front bedroom. Eventually, she wore him down. When she announced that she was expecting, one night in November 1957, she did so with some trepidation, but Dad was as delighted and excited as she was.

Mum continued to care for her father right up until my birth, heaving him into a more comfortable position in bed, washing and shaving him, bringing him meals up and down stairs. It took its toll. As the due date for my arrival approached, she was admitted to the maternity hospital suffering from exhaustion and high blood pressure. Dad accompanied her in the ambulance on the six-mile journey into town. He left her that night in hospital and promised to be back the next day.

When he returned, Mum was not there. He walked down the corridor and heard her cries of pain in the delivery suite – she was screaming for her mum. Fear of fatherhood gripped him, and he ran down the corridor and out of the front entrance. He didn't stop until he reached his parents' home in Wingerworth, six miles away.

His own mum had little sympathy. 'What on earth's the matter? She's only having a baby,' she told him. 'Pull yourself together.'

Back at the hospital, I was a tiny bundle wrapped in blankets. By eight o'clock that night, news reached Dad that Mum and his son were fine. I had arrived in the world, born on the Queen Elizabeth II ward.

Six months after I arrived at No. 57 Chapel Road, Grandad Kirk moved into No. 16 with Auntie Pearl. She had recently been widowed and was forced to relinquish the tenancy of the Miner's Arms. She took on the burden of caring for Grandad because Mum found it increasingly difficult to cope with both of us. Within two years, Mum was pregnant again – this time at Dad's insistence. They both pictured a little girl running around the house.

Elsewhere in the country, in a world vastly different from ours, another family was desperate for a child. At Park House, on the Sandringham Estate in Norfolk, the Spencers had already produced two daughters, Jane and Sarah. A son, John, had also been born but died within a few hours. It was deemed a must that the next should be a boy, an heir to the then Viscount Althorp.

In 1961, the hopes of both sets of parents were dashed.

My brother, Anthony William, was born on 30 March. Mum didn't make it to hospital this time so he was delivered in the front room by next-door neighbour Annie Tunnicliffe. She and Dad were proud to have a healthy second son. But there was bitter disappointment at Sandringham: an heir was not produced. Instead a third daughter was born four months later on 1 July, named Diana Frances. I was three years old.

Three months before Anthony's birth, in December 1960, Grandad Kirk succumbed to his terminal illness. I vaguely remember his funeral: a coffin placed in the front parlour, a room packed with adults, everyone in black, me crying, unable to see Grandad. Mum told me later the whole street turned out that day and every house drew its curtains as a mark of respect. It was customary for a dead relative to spend a final night in their candlelit front parlour for relatives, friends and neighbours to file past the open coffin and pay their respects. Some called it a wake. In our village, it was called 'coming home for the last time'.

I was too young to remember much else of life at No. 57. My

only other vivid recollection is of bathtime in the back room. A tin bath was dragged in from the wash-house and filled with tepid water before the roaring coal fire. As I soaked, Mum held a towel to the fire to warm it. The house was constantly cold. Bathtime wasn't so good if Mum was in a hurry: she would stand me in the white ceramic Belfast sink in the corner of the back room, scrubbing me clean with what felt like a scourer as I held on to the single cold-water tap, its vertical lead piping rattling in its brackets on the wall.

Shortly after Grandad's funeral, we moved five doors down to No. 47. Chapel Road was cobbled, with black, wrought-iron lanterns. Both of our homes were on the bottom row of the L-shaped street and faced west with rear yards backing on to open fields that sloped down to the east and the colliery's perimeter. There were shops in Chapel Road: Hartshorn's haberdashery where Mum, a knitter, bought her wool; 'Auntie Hilda's', with its tin-plate signs on the outside wall, advertising Bovril, Cadbury and Oxo above a green-striped awning; and Fletcher's betting shop, where Dad never went. At the bottom of the road, just round the corner, was Monty White's ice-cream parlour, my favourite, where dollops of freshly made dairy ice-cream were trowelled on to cones in exchange for a threepenny bit. I haven't tasted ice-cream like it since. Bang opposite our new home was Eldred's Bakery. I woke each morning to the smell of freshly baked bread and, on Good Friday, cinnamon-spiced hot-cross buns – soon chased away by the waft of sulphur and tar from the colliery.

From my bedroom window I looked out across open fields that ran into mountainous slagheaps, behind which towered twin head stocks. In the foreground, every August, ninety pit ponies were let out from the darkness into the fresh air to graze during the miners' fortnight's holiday.

The back-to-back houses were all identical in size and construction, single-fronted with sash windows; the brick-red had dulled over time with grime. Each had a wash-house, outside toilet and coal-house in grassless backyards where flapping white sheets hung out to dry. From the top of the main road, grey-slated roofs slanted into the distance, broken up by red battlement-style chimney pots. The streets swarmed with the vigour of working-class life: mothers, in pinnies with headscarves knotted into turbans, scrubbed the doorsteps, scurried to the shops, 'canted' over the front gate with neighbours; fathers, heavy-booted and flat-capped, traipsed to and from the coalface, sharing banter; children yelled and screamed, playing hide-and-seek or tag.

We moved into No. 47 using a fleet of wheelbarrows. Mum said it was the most desirable of properties: it had a bathroom. The rent went up to twelve and six, but the extra financial burden was worth the luxury of being able to go to the loo indoors, and Dad worked more overtime. It was goodbye to tin baths in front of the fire and the potties whose contents froze under the bed at night. With no central heating, my bedroom was so cold that, each morning, I woke to find condensation frozen on the inside of the windows.

I suppose the bathroom was our *only* luxury in a home where life revolved around the back room. There was no such thing as fitted carpets: we had wall-to-wall linoleum, scattered with home-made rag-rugs. A black-and-white television sat on the sideboard and Dad rigged up a frying-pan with wire as an aerial and strung it to the wall. Miraculously it caught the signal, even if the picture was hazy and rolled occasionally. This crude invention allowed me to enjoy the BBC's *Watch With Mother*, with the Wooden Tops or Bill and Ben. Later in childhood, we sat around as a family and watched *Saturday Night at the London Palladium*, with the country's best-paid entertainer Danny La Rue often top of the bill.

Chores were part of childhood. Even before we started school, at five, we were expected to chip in. On 'washday Monday', I helped Mum with the weekly load and watched her at the 'dollypeg', twisting dirty clothes in the tub as she plunged into the soapy water with the 'ponch'. I turned the handle as she fed drenched garments through the mangle. Tuesday was 'Brasso Day', when the brasses were laid out on a tablecloth of newspaper in the kitchen. Mum's hands and fingernails went black and I helped her rub ornaments and polish them up. One day, I would make Georgian silver shine for royalty, not horse brasses for Mum. There were two prized possessions in our home: a wooden mantel clock, whose 'Westminster Chimes' struck on the quarter-hour throughout my childhood. Then there was the monstrous upright piano, which filled the back wall in the front parlour. We had a sing-song once a week, when local seamstress and Mum's friend Gladys Leary came round with her friend Winifred

Lee. They performed songs from music halls for me and my brother.

Mum was fastidiously houseproud. She raked out the grate every morning, scrubbed the doorstep with carbolic soap, wiped the front windows with water and vinegar, and washed the net curtains.

Money was always tight. We only ever had fresh fruit when someone was ill. A bout of yellow jaundice at the age of eight brought me oranges, grapes and bananas for the first time. Folks with a fruit bowl on their sideboard were considered posh. Fresh flowers in a vase were unheard-of unless someone had died.

Visits from the gas and electricity men brought the prospect of extra cash. The utilities were paid for with a coin-operated meter. When the officials came round, the money was tipped out on to the kitchen table, counted and piled into pound stacks. Mum watched the counting process like a hawk, hoping there was more money than the bill required – meters were viewed as bonus moneyboxes.

Every Friday night, Dad brought home his wages, and Mum dived in first. She put some aside in a teapot for the rent, then Dad would go to the fish-and-chip shop and queue for an hour: fish and chips was every family's end-of-week treat. We often ran out of cash in our household so Mum had a slate at the corner shop and an account at the Co-op, which rewarded her with a dividend: it was a sort of Dark Ages shopping loyalty scheme and the 'divis' were saved as an emergency or summer-holiday fund, for a trip to Skegness, Scarborough or Newquay.

As I grew up, it seemed my family was the poorest of all our relations. Uncle Bill, Mum's eldest brother, sold petrol and cars. A huge, illuminated red and blue sign dominated his garage forecourt advertising Regent petrol. He had so many cars that I thought he must be a millionaire. It was thanks to Uncle Bill that Dad had a succession of second-hand motors. Our first was a black Morris Minor, and then we moved up in the world with a 1957 Ford Zephyr, two-tone blue and cream. Both had leather seats too hot to sit on in the summer for boys wearing shorts.

Uncle Bill's second wife, Auntie Marge, was a slim, immaculately dressed woman with tailored tweed suits trimmed with fur. I remember thinking she looked like a film star. Mum wore cardigans over pretty floral frocks. Auntie Marge brought with her a ready-made family, with her two daughters, Sandra and Sheila. The family was so well-to-do that the girls could afford to buy *Photoplay* magazine every month, with its glamorous pictures of film stars: Elizabeth Taylor, Jean Simmons, Bette Davis and Jayne Mansfield adorned the front covers. The magazines were stacked high in a corner.

'You can have some if you want. We've read them,' said Sandra.

I couldn't believe my luck and grabbed as many as I could carry before they could change their minds.

I pored over them in my bedroom and tore out my favourite pictures to stick over the blue and cream floral wallpaper.

My youngest brother Graham, named after Dad, was not planned, and when Mum found she was pregnant, the name Pamela Jane came up again – but there was a more poignant hope. Mum and Dad knew their third child was due in November 1965, and Mum prayed for it to be born on the ninth anniversary of Grandma Kirk's death.

When November arrived, Mum's waters broke on the fourth. Aged seven, I bawled to see her in pain and carried into an ambulance. Before the doors closed, I heard her say: 'Please, Jesus, not on this day.' I feared she was going to die. Of course, she just wanted to hang on for a few more hours. A guardian angel must have been with her that night because the labour dragged on well into the next day. Eventually Graham was heaved into the world by forceps and suction at eleven p.m. on 5 November – ten minutes before the exact anniversary.

I had an ordinary happy childhood in a community where toil provided a wage for people who were the salt of the earth, and whose values revolved around the family unit. Our street was open house, warm and friendly. I was my mother's son: Dad said I hung off her apron strings.

Dad was born on 2 August 1935, son of Cecil Burrell, a farrier who shod pit ponies and horses at Bonz Main colliery outside Chesterfield. Grandad was the last farrier in the north-east Derbyshire coalfields. Dad was nicknamed Nip because he was small, thin and the youngest: the nipper of the family. Not much scared Dad – apart from a life down the pit. He was hard-working, and after the locomotives arrived, he became a coal-delivery driver. He was strong-willed and a strict disciplinarian, very smart, and his hair was slicked back with that Brylcreem sheen. I remember him pressing his trousers into knife-sharp creases down the leg, a habit from his days in the RAF. He taught me how to press trousers expertly – my first lesson in valeting, I suppose. When he left home each morning in his flat cap and donkey jacket, he seemed to be gone for ever. He was back just in time to say goodnight as we three brothers got into our shared bed. Mum's running joke was that we saw more of the family doctor than we did of Dad. He worked all hours in an effort to better our futures.

Mum was born that same leap year, on 29 February. For three years her birthday was celebrated on 28 February but every four years on the twenty-ninth we celebrated her proper birthday. At thirty-six, she joked she was really only nine. She was not a woman who wanted or asked for much. Whatever she earned or saved, she ploughed back into the home. A tall, angular lady, she wore horn-rimmed glasses and often had a cigarette between her fingers.

Grandma Kirk was always with her in spirit. Whenever she lost anything in the house – a piece of jewellery, a knitting pattern or her purse – she sat down and called out: 'Come on, Sarah, help me find it.' She always found what she was looking for and never put it down to coincidence. Her kindness and generosity knew no bounds, and I can't remember her once raising her voice. She always had a kind word and a sympathetic ear for the troubled, a gentle touch for the ill, a gesture for the needy, a gift for those poorer than ourselves. When there was a fire in our street, one family lost everything, and Mum knocked on every door for an item of clothing or a cash donation. At the pit canteen before my birth, her specialities were meat and potato, and cheese and onion pies, and Yorkshire pudding. She was famous for them, so much so that after she left miners would knock on our door and ask her to rustle one up. Then she would cook our meals, make extra helpings and carry plates of dinner up the road to order. She also made meals for poorer neighbours who didn't ask, and visited elderly men, bedridden or in wheelchairs, who lived in the street. She shaved them, washed them and carried away their dirty linen. She also went twice weekly to clean the house of a woman dying of cancer.

One woman came to the house in tears because she had four children under the age of five and was pregnant again. Mum sat with her and calmed her down with a dose of common sense. Everyone seemed to bring their problems to our house because Mum always had an answer. In the rare moments when her world stood still – often when we were tucked up in bed – she would knit cardigans, jumpers and baby clothes for all the neighbours' children. She was the community grandma, nurse, cook and agony aunt rolled into one, known to all as Auntie Beryl.

One day I saw the upright piano being wheeled out of the front door. Mum had given it to a boy eager to play whose family could not afford such a luxury.

'Mum, that's our piano,' I protested.

'It will have a better home with him, Paul,' she reassured me.

The Victorian-built Grassmoor Junior School, with its huge paned windows, high ceilings and echoing corridors lined with white ceramic tiles, was situated off the main village road and faced an expanse of green, which was home to the cricket club. Pupils sat in rows at slanted wooden desks and scrawled with a nibbed wooden pen, dipped into an inkwell. It was 'real writing' and my duty each morning as 'ink-well monitor' was to fill the tiny porcelain pots with fresh supplies of Quink. Watching the princess write at Kensington Palace reminded me of those days. She always used a gold-nibbed fountain pen, but instead of filling its cartridge, she dipped it into a bottle of Quink. She wrote all her correspondence – personal letters, thank-you notes and memos – in that way.

Mr Thomas, who taught me all subjects, stood before the class. In his deep, booming voice, hardly softened by a Welsh twang, he said: 'Write an essay on what you want to do when you leave school.'

In silence, the minds of thirty children began to tick. Most boys mapped out a future that followed in their father's footsteps to coalmining, but even at ten, I was sure that I wasn't going to do that. Mining seemed a punishing future of coal dust, damp and darkness. Too much like hard work. 'When I Grow Up I Want To Be A Vicar' was the title of my essay. A life in the ministry, for me, was then the perfect solution. Maybe such thoughts were spawned by my mother's sense of spiritualism and the importance she had drilled into me of helping those less fortunate.

I was a painfully shy, quiet boy. It was not a pleasant experience, therefore, to be singled out by Mr Thomas, who read out my career plan to the rest of the class. I turned beetroot red as the class broke into a fit of sniggering. I never thanked Mr Thomas for that moment but, in time, there was much to thank him for. I could never profess to be an intellectual but I was eager to learn and he saw in me a desire to break the mould cast for each generation of each local family. Grandad Burrell was a colliery farrier, Grandad Kirk a miner, Dad worked for the National Coal Board, and his brother Cecil was a miner. Mum worked in the pit canteen, while her three brothers – Uncle Stan, Uncle Bill and Uncle Keith – had all started out as miners. My brothers Anthony and Graham also went on to work down the pit.

The normal educational path was from Grassmoor Juniors to Danecourt Secondary School in neighbouring North Wingfield. It was there that boys turned into men in recruitment drives for the mines. It seemed I was destined for such misery after failing my 11-plus examination for a place at Chesterfield Boys' Grammar. Then Mr Thomas stepped in. He told my parents that he saw potential in me that would be wasted at Danecourt and lobbied for me to gain a place at William Rhodes Secondary School for Boys, Chesterfield. It was not the grammar school but it was the next best thing, and Mum and Dad were delighted. The mould had been broken.

Acceptance to William Rhodes was a big thing in our street. I was to have a *new* uniform, not second-hand. It was an expensive purchase, which sent me on my first-ever train ride, to Sheffield, with Mum. The tie and badge were the colours of Wolverhampton Wanderers Football Club, black and gold, and Mum knitted a grey pullover. She was so proud that she walked me to the school bus that first day in September 1969, ensuring that the black cap stayed on my head.

I boarded the double-decker bus packed with children and sat next to the first boy I spotted wearing the same uniform. 'Take off the cap – you look like a twat,' he said. So I did. Kim Walters, harder than me, bigger than me, better at art than me, became my close friend and protector for the next five years.

William Rhodes was an all-boys school where masters wore black gowns. It was a strict regime ruled by the cane. Headmaster Mr Crooks, who always wore a mortar-board and put the fear of God into me, administered it frequently to bring into line the insubordinates. He was a stickler for manners and pristine appearance. There was an emphasis on competitive sport, but English language and literature were my forte. Kim excelled in every outdoor pursuit, and became a professional footballer with Blackburn Rovers.

History was another of my strong points. I collected PG Tips historical tea-cards of the greatest sailing ships, Brunel's engineering feats, flags of the world and kings and queens of England and Scotland. It kick-started my fascination with royalty and heritage, going back to the Norman Conquest of 1066. When other boys played out after school, I stayed in and completed my homework, which Kim would copy on the bus the next day. When I had finished, I remained at the desk in my bedroom and read book after book about kings and queens. I went on to pass English literature O level with an essay on Richard III, much-maligned, misunderstood and wrongly portrayed as a hunchbacked, twisted and wicked man: in truth he was courageous and passionate in his reign, which lasted just two years. It should have taught me that members of the Royal Family whose faces don't fit can be cruelly judged by history.

I was nearly twelve when we went to London as a family for the first time in the spring of 1970. We walked down the Mall, and the imposing, blanched-stone frontage of Buckingham Palace came into sight. Mum and Dad wanted 'to go and see where the Queen lives'.

'I wonder if she's in, lads?' mused Dad.

Anthony and I were mesmerized by the awesome building before us. We stood with our faces between the black railings on the front gates, hands gripping a rod either side as we watched the Changing of the Guard. It was the most incredible scene I had witnessed as a child. It was also a world away from the life we lived. I still don't know why I said it but I looked up and said: 'One day I want to work there, Mum.' It was the sort of thoughtless, dreamy remark that children make – they want to be a pilot if they see a plane flying over or, when Neil Armstrong became the first man to walk on the moon, an astronaut.

Dad ruffled my hair affectionately. 'Sure you do, me duck.'

It was impossible for either him or me to know that, within the same decade, I would stand behind Her Majesty the Queen, as her footman, on the Irish State Coach as it swept out of those palace gates in a full state procession.

But my first 'royal role' came later that year in the autumn. I was in the Grassmoor village production of *Aladdin*, produced by family friend Margaret Hardy. My part? A servant to Princess Sadie, played before an audience at Grassmoor Working Men's Club.

I left William Rhodes Secondary School aged sixteen with six O levels. My application to High Peak Catering College in Buxton, Derbyshire, had been accepted and, in September 1974, I took up residence in digs in the town. It was a two-year course in hotel and catering. In that time, I learned everything from cooking the perfect meal to making up the neatest bed, and became a housekeeper, bookkeeper and chef rolled into one. I won a British catering award for sculpting Chesterfield's famous crooked spire from margarine. It was expert training and knowledge, and all I needed next was experience.

I drew up a list of places where my skills could be best utilized: Trusthouse Forte, Travco Hotels, Pacific & Orient, for its cruise-liners and container ships, Cunard, for the most famous cruise-liner in the world, the *QE2*, and then Buckingham Palace, which needed an army of staff. That summer I dispatched several letters offering my services and expressing eagerness to work.

The first response came from Travco Hotels, offering a job at the three-star Lincombe Hall Hotel, Torquay. This meant leaving college early to begin work in June 1976 as assistant manager in time for the summer season, which would take me away from home for months. It was a job but it was not ideal. I accepted it, and asked Mum to open all mail addressed to me at home. Trusthouse Forte came back with a rejection, as did P&O, but then I had an interview with Cunard in Southampton, and another at Buckingham Palace. I went home from Torquay and we drove, with brother Graham, to the capital.

I entered Buckingham Palace via a side entrance, wearing a dark suit. I was in awe of the place, walking down those same red-carpeted corridors into a history I had only read about after school. I felt like a serf entering a world where my face and class would never be accepted.

When I reached the first-floor office of Mr Michael Timms, the Master of the Household's assistant, Mum's reassuring voice spoke in my mind: 'Just be yourself and you'll be fine.' It wasn't the best advice she had ever given me because I walked in for that interview, sat down without being asked and failed to call the prospective boss 'sir'.

'Do you always sit down before you are asked?' said Mr Timms, in an officious, pompous manner. 'Do you respect your seniors?'

'Of course I do.'

'Then why don't you address them as sir?'

Within two weeks, a follow-up letter had informed me I had been rejected 'on this occasion' but all details would be kept on file. There was no word from Cunard. Both dream jobs seemed out of reach.

Torquay was where a shy, quiet boy grew into a more outgoing, confident, assertive member of management with status. I became convinced I could go a long way in the hotel industry. Senior management recognized my potential and transferred me that October as assistant manager to the group's flagship hotel, the Wessex in Bournemouth.

Bournemouth was totally different. I hated every minute of my time there, living in a shoebox room. Homesickness crept in and Mum and Dad were so worried that they drove down to visit me. Mum wanted to take me home, but that was no solution: this was my one opportunity to carve out a career.

Bournemouth went from bad to worse. I was relegated to the basement as storeman, sent into the kitchen to be breakfast chef when the main chef was off, shunted into the dining room as a waiter at functions. I had no friends and was going nowhere.

It was a cold November morning at No. 47 Chapel Road. Dad had left for work and Anthony, then fifteen, was on a milk round. Mum, preparing breakfast in the back room for the still dozing Graham, heard the letterbox rattle. She dried her hands on a tea-towel, walked into the front room and picked up the post. There were two letters for Mr Paul Burrell.

She didn't recognize the C-logo on the first cream envelope but on the rear it said 'Cunard, Southampton'. The second letter was like one she had received before: its white envelope bore the black frank mark of Buckingham Palace. On the rear was the Queen's red-embossed coat-of-arms. They had arrived with a gas bill.

Mum tucked both letters into the pouch at the front of her pinny where they remained for half an hour as she busied herself in the kitchen. Graham came downstairs to get dressed in front of the fire. Mum told him: 'There's two letters for our Paul. One from Cunard. One from Buckingham Palace.' She sat down and took a knife from the kitchen table. She slit open the royal envelope carefully. It was from Mr Michael Timms, offering me a position of under-butler in the silver pantry. The other letter was from Cunard's personnel department and offered the post of steward aboard the QE2. Mum stared at both letters. She knew I would jump at the chance of a life at sea, and thought long and hard about what to do next.

Then she snapped into life. 'He'll chuff off on that boat and we'll never see him again,' she told Graham, and tossed the Cunard letter, in its envelope, on to the fire. Graham and she watched my potential career at sea go up in smoke. 'As long as I live, Graham, you must never tell him what I've just done,' she said. Then she propped the letter from Buckingham Palace in the centre of the mantelpiece.

She hurried across the road to Eldred's Bakery to use the telephone.

I was in the storeroom at the Wessex when I was called to the phone.

'Paul. You've had a letter from Buckingham Palace offering you a job. You are going to take it, aren't you?'

She didn't need to ask. It was a dream offer, and disbelief overrode euphoria.

Without me knowing, Mum had made for me the biggest decision of my life and steered me towards land and Buckingham Palace. Graham kept his promise and never uttered a word. Not for nineteen years. Not until we were standing by Mum's grave at Hasland cemetery. He told me moments after her coffin had been lowered into the ground, in 1995, near the plot of Grandma and Grandad Kirk.

At the time, I was working for the most extraordinary woman in the world, the Princess of Wales. It was all down to my wonderful mum and I never got the chance to thank her.

When everyone had drifted away, I did what she always did with Grandma Kirk: I spoke to her at the graveside. And said thank you.

2. Buckingham Palace

I could not believe the regal sight before me.

The Queen, who was in deep concentration in her sitting room at Buckingham Palace, looked up and caught me staring, smiling. She stopped what she was doing. 'Why are you smiling, Paul?' she inquired, a hint of amusement in her voice.

'If you could only see what I can see, Your Majesty.'

We both grinned broadly. It was late at night, not long before bedtime, and there she sat, in a smart silk dress in her chair at the desk near the window. She was wearing the Imperial State Crown. And her pink mule slippers. It was an incredible sight: the Queen of England in crown and slippers, looking both majestic and motherly, a picture of state without ceremony. It was as charming as it was incongruous, and as humorous as her smile acknowledged.

I had caught her by surprise when I entered the room to say goodnight after completing a final duty: ensuring that the nine corgis were comfortable in their beds further down the plush, red-carpeted corridor. A tall, folding screen shields the room on the left of the doorway. On entry, you must walk a few steps across the wooden floor then on to a huge rug and emerge into full view. I had stopped and stood still.

The Queen, wearing her half-moon, rimless spectacles, sat at her desk where a flexible table-lamp's lowered arm cast bright light on to the red government dispatch boxes, and the papers she was working on. In the half-light, a thousand facets flashed back from the crown. I had often seen the Queen in her slippers, but never matched with the most glorious and priceless of the Crown Jewels. However, it was the eve of the State Opening of Parliament and the Queen, as she does every year, needed to get used to the weight of the crown, the equivalent of two bags of sugar, on her head.

As she smiled at me, I asked, 'Will there be anything else, Your Majesty?'

'No, thank you, Paul.' She lowered her head to carry on with her paperwork.

I bowed. 'Goodnight, Your Majesty.' I never again saw the Queen in her crown in private. It happened just that once.

Life, and living quarters, had changed for the better on 20 December 1976: from the claustrophobia of the Wessex, Bournemouth, to the vastness of Buckingham Palace, London.

I trembled as I walked into the palace on that first day, wearing my best dark suit, and carrying a small suitcase. I had wondered if it would be like working in a grand hotel. It was nothing of the sort: hotels have narrow corridors; palaces have carpeted avenues. The baroque décor and anachronistic job titles made it feel more like a museum.

If old schoolfriend Kim Walters thought a William Rhodes school cap looked ridiculous then he should have seen my uniform. In my room I stood for several minutes in front of the full-length mirror on the inside of the wardrobe door. It was pantomime season. Staring back at me was a reflection from the past, a stranger dressed in royal livery as if he was about to serve King George III, not Queen Elizabeth II. A navy blue velvet riding cap; a white starched ruff frilled out round the neck over a collarless shirt; a black embroidered waistcoat with gold threaded stripes and a plain silk back, fastened tight at the front with gold buttons embossed with the royal crest; red, coarse-velvet breeches tied below the knee with gold buttons and a tassel; pink silk stockings and black, patent leather, buckled pumps. At my left side hung a sword and scabbard. I slipped on the white cotton gloves.

For a few minutes I felt silly, then a huge sense of pride as I pulled on the final piece to complete the full state livery: a scarlet tailcoat with thick gold edges running down the buttoned front and gold hoops around each arm. It was a uniform that had been handed down over at least two hundred years. Repaired, stitched and musty but with a magnificence that hadn't faded over time. Only one thing had changed: the insignia stitched to the upper arm of the left sleeve bore the initials 'EIIR' encircled by the royal garter, 'Honi soit qui mal y pense' – which means 'Shame on him who thinks evil of it' – topped with the embroidered Imperial State Crown.

I had first tried on those clothes in the livery room in the palace basement, with floor-to-ceiling wardrobes and a broad table running down its centre. It took all day to kit me out with the essential uniforms. All had been owned and worn by others before me. At Buckingham Palace, as well as at Grassmoor, second-hand garments were commonplace. Even the shirts, trousers and suits of the boy Prince Andrew were altered and passed down to Prince Edward.

Deputy sergeant footman Martin Bubb handed me five different uniforms: the full livery, for state occasions, to be worn inside and outside the palace; the scarlet, a tailcoat with top-hat for semi-state occasions and Royal Ascot; the epaulet, a double-breasted, high-neck tailcoat only worn aboard the Royal Yacht *Britannia*; the tropical, a white, safari-like jacket worn in hot climates; and the everyday livery, a black tailcoat worn with white shirt, black tie and scarlet waistcoat. I was also handed a red felt coachman's cape, boxes of shirts and hangers with extra pairs of trousers.

The palace was empty, save for a skeleton household staff. The court had moved to Windsor Castle for the holiday and its newest recruit was ready to commence royal duty. In terms of being dressed, at least.

Nothing had prepared me for my first ever task on Christmas Eve after I had been shuttled by train to Windsor. I was standing on the octagonal-shaped first floor in a stone tower on the north-east corner of the castle, overlooking the East Terrace with its panoramic views of the gardens and the golf course. The monogrammed demi-tasse coffee cups rattled and clinked on a large silver salver as my clammy hands shook with nerves. My stomach churned. I fretted about making a mistake and felt painfully self-conscious in the uniform. Would I stand out like a sore thumb? Would I drop the salver? Was I good enough? Was it going to be a disaster? I was about to enter the formidable presence of the entire Royal Family for the first time.

I was waiting in the Octagon Room, with a high Pugin-style ceiling and oak-panelled walls. A short, red-carpeted corridor led to the room I was about to enter – the cavernous state dining room where the Windsors were having dinner by candlelight. For two hours, I had watched an endless stream of uniformed footmen, under-butlers, pages and wine waiters come and go up and down that corridor. It was a human conveyor-belt, stacked with plates, silverware, glasses and dishes of food; a non-stop movement from first course to main course to the pudding. Then it was time for dessert – a pear, banana, some pineapple or a peach, to be tackled with a gold-plated knife and fork. One doesn't eat a banana like a monkey in a royal residence: one uses a knife and fork, as if it were a skinny melon.

Everything about the Royal Family, even private mealtimes, is planned, scripted and orchestrated to perfection. Many people, like me that day, stand nervously with small, insignificant parts; like the cast of a musical waiting in the wings in strict formation. Behind the door, the backstage line-up goes into position. Liveried footmen stand stiff-backed, holding dishes of food in an orderly queue. First the meat. Then potatoes. Vegetables. Salad. A voice always prompts the procession to begin. 'Meat . . . Go.' Thirty seconds pass.

'Potatoes and gravy . . . go.' Thirty seconds pass.

'Vegetables . . . go.'

'Salad . . . go.'

It was some time before I was trusted to handle meat or potatoes. Empty china cups were the sum total of my early responsibilities.

Then I realized coffee was about to be served, and my big moment had arrived. Through the half-open door, with the tray weighing heavy in my arms, I caught a glimpse of the room's grandeur. Laughter and loud after-dinner conversation spilled through to me. Mr Dickman, the palace steward in charge of the slick operation, sensed my nerves. 'Don't worry, there's nothing to be concerned about,' he said.

It was the simplest of tasks, given to me deliberately. It was meant for me as an introduction to royal service, and for the Royal Family as an introduction to a new face.

'Just go into the dining room, stand in the corner and the footman will come to you to replenish the tray. All you have to do is stand there. The footman will serve the coffee,' Mr Dickman explained.

Not a line to say. Just a walk-on part. But the smile I returned must not have been very convincing. 'They won't eat you!' said my new boss. He gave me a gentle push on the back. 'Off you go, then, there's a good lad.'

As lead feet dragged me into that room, I remembered the words Mr Dickman had spoken much earlier. 'Don't stare or look at anyone in the eye. The Royal Family does not like to be watched when eating.' My eyes were fixed on the shaking china cups. Carefully. Ever so carefully. All I needed to do was walk ten paces to the corner of the room.

Got there. Looked up. In front of me was the biggest table I had ever seen: an oval of polished mahogany, around twenty feet long, with a central line of candelabra interspersed with extravagant floral arrangements. Crimson velvet curtains with gold tassels were drawn across the huge Gothic windows. Queen Victoria's colossal portrait stared down on her ancestors from above the Victorian stone fireplace.

Then my eyes did what they were not allowed to do, and stared. I scanned the table for the Queen among the thirty members of her family, all in evening dress. The Queen Mother came into view: she was sitting in the middle, in the largest, gilded, throne-like chair, engrossed in an animated conversation with her favourite grandson, Prince Charles. The Queen was on his other side, in a much smaller chair like everyone else, opposite Prince Philip, the Duke of Edinburgh, listening intently to a conversation.

Most people struggle to see beyond the one-dimensional image of a woman whose real character and personality remain diluted by the duty she must perform. But here she was relaxing at home with her family. It was my first view of the monarch behind closed doors. I noted her natural smile, and thought how small she looked in real life. I remember thinking how close I was. I remember thinking of Mum. If only she could have seen me. If only the whole village of Grassmoor could have seen me.

Jewels glinted in the candlelight. The footmen worked quickly and efficiently in serving the table, and I was glad to be doing nothing more than impersonating a statue holding a tray.

I could see the young Princes Andrew and Edward, Princess Anne and her husband of two years, Captain Mark Phillips. Princess Margaret was dominating the conversation, with her high-pitched shrill voice. The talk was all so loud, I thought.

I looked away before I was found staring. My salver was suddenly empty and I walked slowly out of the room, unnoticed.

'See? Wasn't that bad, lad,' said a smiling Mr Dickman, on the other side of the doors. I felt as proud as Punch.

Normally at New Year, our family brought in a lump of coal through the door to bring good luck all year round. The arrival of 1977 would be different. I spent it at Sandringham House and, as the youngest footman, it was my awesome responsibility to let in the New Year on behalf of the Royal Family. I stood inside the front doorway, awaiting my cue. Through the glass-panelled windows, as I shook with cold and nerves, I saw the champagne being served by the other footmen. The Windsors were all gathered, and the countdown to midnight had begun. On the stroke of midnight, the door was opened and I strode in to do my duty: I had to weave my way through the drawing room towards the fireplace, pick up a log from the pile and throw it on to the burning embers. As the new log sizzled, a round of applause broke out. And as a reward for performing that tradition, I had the privilege to be the first member of staff to approach my new employer with the appropriate greeting.

'Happy New Year, Your Majesty.' I beamed.

I should never have been a footman in those days. After all, the letter Mum had opened offered the post of under-butler – someone who works in the china and glass pantry, working elbow-deep in soap suds, scrubbing plates and cups until they squeak clean in the wooden sinks. But a last-minute vacancy had arisen in the footmen's room so I joined their number, under the stewardship of sergeant footman John Floyd, ranked number fourteen out of fourteen with a salary of £1,200. The top two slots of the Queen's personal footmen seemed light years away.

Staff living quarters were of standard hotel-room size, basic and sparsely decorated. Each one had a corner sink, single bed, desk, chest of drawers, wardrobe and green carpet. They were gloomy, with high-set windows that let in little daylight.

Before the official livery fitting, the deputy sergeant had shown me to my room on the all-male 'Pages' Lobby', which hides behind that series of narrow windows on the Buckingham Palace east-facing frontage; the top-floor windows situated just beneath the pediment. I was not senior enough to have a room looking down on the Victoria Monument and the Mall, so my room was on the other side of the corridor, overlooking the inner quadrangle, the red-gravelled courtyard encompassed by all sides of the palace. I often stood on the radiator to look down on the stone-pillared, glass veranda of the Grand Entrance where everyone arrived, from heads of state to garden-party guests. Adjacent to that was the black double-fronted 'King's Door', used by those having a private audience with Her Majesty, such as the Prime Minister arriving for the weekly Tuesday evening briefing.

There was an overwhelming amount of information about palace life to absorb. There was a maze of underground corridors, and a labyrinth of interconnecting rooms and hallways linking more than six hundred rooms. Buckingham Palace is a foreign village on the mainland. Its people speak the same language but live in a different world. It has its own police station and a twenty-four-hour fire brigade, a post office, doctor's surgery, laundry, electricians, a chapel and chaplain, carpenters, gilders and plumbers. It also has its own bar, run by the Naafi.

A bewildering collection of posts from the eighteenth century covers a multitude of household jobs: Master of the Household and Palace Steward; Page of the Presence, Page of the Backstairs, Page of the Chambers; Mistress of the Robes (who has to be a duchess), Woman of the Bedchamber and ladies-in-waiting; Yeoman of the Silver Pantry, Yeoman of Glass and China, and equerries-in-waiting. Not to mention the Keeper of the Privy Purse and the Gentleman Usher to the Sword of State. Buckingham Palace is run by the royal household, headed by the Lord Chamberlain. Beneath him is a family tree of six offices: Private Secretary's Office, Privy Purse and Treasurer's Office; Lord Chamberlain's Office, Master of the Household's Department, Royal Mews Department and the Royal Collection Department. Staff like me worked to the Master of the Household, whose department was then split into three groups: H-branch for housekeeping, F-branch for food, and G-branch for general. Footmen worked in G-branch, reporting to Palace Steward Cyril Dickman.

Then there were procedures: the rules, protocols and traditions one must never forget. For the first year, I carried a pocket notebook to jot down the names and titles of colleagues and superiors, log the short-cuts to different places, draw mini diagrams of how to set a dining-table. Even a tray had a layout plan: cup and saucer with handle and spoon pointing towards five o'clock; plates and saucers turned so the royal crests were at twelve o'clock; salt on right, mustard on left with the pepper behind; sugar basin with cubed white sugar, never granulated, and sugar tongs; toast always in a silver toast rack and never on a plate; no more than three balls of butter in the dish. And never forget the linen napkin.

Even the communal bathroom threw me. It had several baths set in narrow cubicles with a chrome, overhanging shower head. I had never seen a shower before, and it was a cause of slight embarrassment that I needed to ask how it was operated.

In the corridors, with the silk-papered walls, housemaids were not allowed to use vacuum cleaners before nine a.m. to avoid disturbing the Royal Family. Instead, stiff yard brushes were used to sweep the deep-red of the shagpile upright. It was never wise to walk down the middle of the carpet because it was, apparently, 'far too presump-tuous for a footman to do so'. A freshly brushed carpet was fit only for royal feet. Staff had to walk along its foot-wide border. The red carpets were treated like the wickets of the proudest cricket groundsman. If a footman saw a member of the Royal Family approaching down a corridor, the protocol was to stop walking, stand to attention, turn with back against the wall, and bow as they passed, without saying a word.

The art of being a good servant, I learned, was to perform as many of my duties as possible without being seen. A servant's life was spent in the shadows and, at best, he or she should be invisible. At its most extreme, this requirement led a scurrying army of maids or footmen to hide until the coast was clear. At Sandringham House, maids would dart into a walk-in cupboard under the stairs so as not to be seen when the Queen was coming down into the main hall. This 'hide without seek' led to many bizarre situations as staff lurked behind a closed door of a back passageway leading to a bedroom, ear pressed to the door to listen for a quiet that signalled it was safe to proceed. From a shadowy recess, staff watched a drawing room until the last guest had left, then cleared empty glasses, stoked the fire, plumped the cushions and brushed up the carpet.

When it came down to snobbery, I found there were more noses stuck in the air in the royal household than in the Royal Family. There was a pecking order in everything, down to something as simple as staff mealtimes. It was a class-system straight from the decks of the *Titanic*, encouraged by the hierarchical household masters, whom the Princess of Wales referred to as 'the men in grey suits'.

The most junior members of staff – from under-butlers to footmen, chefs to maids, porters to postmen, grooms to chauffeurs – all sat at white-clothed tables with a self-service menu and beakers of cold water in a ground-floor room with plastic seats and linoleum floors, rather like a workplace canteen. The atmosphere was loud, raucous, and down-to-earth.

The Stewards' Dining Room was on the first floor with upholstered chairs and carpets. The mood was more businesslike. It was reserved for senior staff who had served twenty years or more or who had been decorated for loyalty – pages, Pages of the Presence, Pages of the Backstairs, Yeomen of the Pantries, sergeant footmen, the Queen's dressers, her chauffeur – and presided over by the Palace Steward. One notable treat was that they had a selection of bread, a varied cheeseboard and crackers.

Next door, another rung up the ladder, was the Officials' Dining Room, reserved for personal secretaries and assistants, clerks, press officers, typists and administrative personnel.

Then came the far grander Lady Barrington's Room with its high ceiling and a central chandelier. Here, small-talk and serious conversation occupied the assistants to the Master of the Household, the Chief Housekeeper and the Paymaster. So senior were these staff that they were allowed a pre-meal sherry or whisky and to have wine with their meal.

Then, beside the Bow Room, was the grandest room of them all, reserved for the *crème de la crème* of the household. Royal Collection portraits hung on the walls above the Chippendale and Sheraton sideboards. Food was served on fine china plates, eaten with silver cutlery, and wine from the royal cellars was poured into crystal glasses. This splendour was the sole preserve of ladies-in-waiting, senior Women of the Bedchamber, the Mistress of the Robes, private secretaries, press secretaries, the Keeper of the Privy Purse, the Queen's chaplain, equerries-in-waiting and the Lord Chamberlain. It had a prim, stiff atmosphere akin to a Conservative private members' club. Oddly, it was four times larger than Her Majesty's dining room, and more grandly decorated.

The higher echelons of the dining system became a training

ground for green footmen such as me. Before being entrusted with the responsibility of waiting at a royal table, I had to learn and polish my craft in the presence of the Lord Chamberlain, which was nerve-racking in those early days. I had to become expert at setting the perfect dinner-table – placing knives and forks one centimetre from the table's edge and ensuring that every setting mirrored the next with faultless uniformity. Or how to fold a napkin into the shape of the Prince of Wales's feathers. Or how to ensure that vintage wine and champagne never filled a glass more than half-way up.

For three months, I shadowed a senior footman and needed to learn quickly the intricacies of duty: from ensuring the Queen's dinner was carried from the kitchen to her dining room hot and on time, to spit-and-polishing the boots of an equerry. It was important to be inconspicuous in this shadowing role but I needed to be ultra-observant. Away from the dining room, another string to a footman's bow was to become a gentleman's valet.

Standing in complete darkness in the corner of one bedroom where a visitor was sound asleep, I watched and learned as my mentor, Martin Bubb, showed off the skills required: the art was to be hush-quiet, swift, and have night vision. Alarm clocks are not provided in royal palaces and castles. The footman or valet – or maid – enters a room on the stroke of a designated time to call his master or mistress. Treading deftly in the dark, Martin placed a small wooden 'calling tray' of freshly brewed tea and a glass of orange juice with one digestive biscuit on a chair at arm's length from the bed. If that didn't have any effect, then the subsequent task usually did. Martin picked his way across the carpet and drew the curtains to flood the room with daylight. I had an odd feeling that I was invading as the light revealed me, utterly redundant, standing in the corner as still as a coat-stand.

As the gentleman stirred, Martin picked up discarded clothes from the previous night and took a wooden hanger from the wardrobe for the trousers, shirt and dinner jacket, then placed it outside the door, along with the shoes, which needed polishing, and the socks and underwear for washing. For the day ahead, he chose fresh clothes and laid them out in a way I needed to rehearse: pressed and folded trousers flat across a chair seat with a pocket corner turned back so they could be easily picked up; a folded shirt, as if fresh from a box, placed at a vertical angle on the trousers, every button open and cufflinks inserted; a clean pair of undershorts on top; shoes with laces undone beside an easy chair; socks on top. Martin then approached the dressing-table and opened the top drawer to select some ties (a valet must always leave a choice, never pick out a single tie). He left out a clean, pressed and folded handkerchief too.

Then he beckoned me to follow him into the adjoining bathroom. The man still slept. On closing the door, he explained the 'bathroom procedure'. He turned on the taps and ran a lukewarm bath, laid a mat on the floor and pulled towards it a bathroom chair. 'This is how you lay out a towel,' said Martin. He draped it lengthways over the chair so that when the gentleman sat down he could pull it around him and stand up as if he was wearing a robe. Martin's job was done and we both left the bedroom.

This was exactly the same procedure adopted by dressers and valets not only for guests but for all senior members of the Royal Family. It was valuable training – in theory, at least. The first time I valeted alone to a rather elderly gentleman, I panicked. I couldn't find his discarded clothes on the floor, and wondered where on earth he had left them. Then his arm stretched out from under the duvet. He was still fully clothed.

Later I learned that the Prince of Wales had meticulous needs, which his valets, from the late Stephen Barry to Michael Fawcett, had to observe. A silver key, bearing his feathers, was attached to the end of a toothpaste tube like a sardine-tin key and turned to squeeze enough to fit on the brush. His cotton pyjamas had to be ironed each morning.

It was a footman's duty to man all doors and entrances to the palace and carry the red government boxes, delivered from the Home Office, Downing Street and the Foreign Office, along the corridors to the Queen's apartment.

To the outsider, the level of subservience may seem odd but the monarchy could not function or survive without the huge machine that is the royal household. It provides both the engine room and the first impression of the Royal Family. Every cog, from an under-butler to the Lord Chamberlain, turns at every minute and hour of every day to ensure the smooth running of royal lives and duties.

The Queen is on friendly terms with most staff, and the relationship between employer and employee is one of mutual respect; the formality of duty is mixed with informality on staff occasions.

On a day of engagements, a lift door opened and, as if by magic, the Queen appeared on the ground floor, sending ladies-in-waiting into a curtsy and private secretaries and equerries into respectful nods. It was all extremely formal and subdued. On the party's return, though, the Queen often hovered near the lift and wanted to engage in conversation. Perhaps there had been an amusing incident or eccentric gesture during the day and Her Majesty would smile and talk, then thank her staff for an enjoyable day. As she turned to go back into the lift, the formality kicked back in, and the curtsies and bows would be more heartfelt. Some such gestures were a little exaggerated: I remember one particular lady-in-waiting, whose knee-cracking curtsy was so deep that I wondered if she would seize or topple over.

From the moment I began working at the palace, I had – and still have – enormous respect for Her Majesty. She is a remarkable, kind, Christian lady, but it would be a little while before I got to know and understand her better. I was the footman who earned the nickname 'Buttons'. Martin Bubb and fellow footman Alastair Wanless christened me as such because I was assigned to the livery room to polish and stitch gold-embossed buttons on to dozens of uniforms. It was a tedious task that filled hours of my time during my three-month probation period.

As Britain prepared to celebrate the Queen's Silver Jubilee, palace staff had never worked so hard, with receptions and banquets held almost every week. For that momentous year, I remained of junior status and had no major role to play. From the vantage-point of my room, I watched, that June, as the gilded Coronation coach, built for King George III, carried the Queen from the quadrangle courtyard in state procession through the streets of London to St Paul's Cathedral. Fellow footmen walked alongside the carriage in full state livery surrounded by the Yeomen of the Guard (commonly called Beefeaters) and the Household Cavalry. In the distance, I heard the thronging crowds cheering.

It was only the second time the Queen had ever ridden inside that impressive but not very comfortable carriage, the first being her Coronation in 1953. On her return, I heard her remark at a cocktail reception: 'I had forgotten how uncomfortable that ride could be.'

Silver medals with white ribbons were awarded to everyone in the palace who had served a year on 2 June 1977. I was the only footman not to receive one because I had only served six months. I could only wonder how many years I would have to languish as the fourteenth footman. As it turned out, I didn't have long to wait.

Word swept through Windsor Castle about 'an accident' in one of the bedrooms, but the evidence pointed elsewhere. A half-consumed bottle of gin stood on the bedside table beside an opened container of pills. A man who had been suffering from depression lay unconscious in bed. There was the strange sight of an ambulance at the Augusta Tower Door on the south side of the castle. It arrived with no lights or sirens so as not to create a fuss. The ambulancemen went to a second-floor room. The Queen's personal footman – one of the two who shadowed the monarch wherever she was in the world – was stretchered away, critically ill after a suicide attempt in the middle of the day. It was April 1978. The footman in question survived but never returned to duty and retired on grounds of ill-health. Around the same time, the Queen's page (more senior in rank than a footman) Ernest Bennett, retired after an impeccable service that dated back to the end of the Second World War. Those two events brought about a restructuring of the Queen's immediate household in which I gained an unlikely promotion.

Amid the relaxed repartee of the footmen's room at the palace, speculation was rife about who would be elevated to the privileged position of Queen's personal footman, a role that included looking after the nine corgis. Colleague Paul Whybrew was the first to be promoted, and one other was required. Unknown to me, the Queen had been conducting a subtle reconnoitre of the footmen at luncheon and cocktail parties, observing from the corner of her eye their attention to detail, their manners, appearance and overall performance. We had all been in the 'shop window' without knowing it.

Days later, I was summoned to the office of the sergeant footman, John Floyd. 'Would you like the opportunity to become the Queen's footman?' he said.

There was only one answer and, within the space of sixteen months, I had what was considered to be a dream job – a powerful one in the household: any position so close to the Queen is considered a special, privileged one. Only an exclusive band of people surround the monarch and therefore have automatic access to her. The key people around her are not the officials who share her administrative and state duties and diaries but her dressers, pages and footmen who share her most intimate, private world. I was suddenly on the informed inside. It was not unknown for a private secretary to 'test the water' with me to gauge the Queen's mood or reaction to a certain event before having an audience with her. Members of the household did valuable homework by gleaning snippets of information from her personal staff. My word began to carry some weight.

Having two Pauls as footmen made life easier for the Queen because whenever she called the name, one of us would always appear – but it did nothing for our confusion. So, for the sake of clarity, Her Majesty dreamed up nicknames: I became 'Small Paul', at five foot ten, and he became 'Tall Paul', at six foot two.

It helped the Queen, if not Princess Margaret. On the telephone, height was of no use to tell us apart: 'Which one is it? Small Paul or Tall Paul?' she would say, in her unmistakable articulate drawl, which was far more grandiloquent than her sister's voice.

It pained me to have to reply, 'It's Small Paul, Your Royal Highness.'

For a decade, the entire Royal Family called us by those names.

There was one considerable perk to becoming Queen's footman. I moved across the corridor of the Pages' Lobby and into a front room with a magnificent view down the Mall. Mine was the fourth window from the end on the left, beneath the pediment.

Every morning, at seven a.m., my day began as it ended – walking nine corgis: Brush, Jolly, Shadow, Myth, Smokey, Piper, Fable, Sparky and Chipper, the only male in the pack. After their walk, they were allowed into the Queen's bedroom. The dogs – and a cup of tea – were her eight a.m. wake-up call.

At nine, it was time for a second walk. The Queen opened her bedroom door, where I waited and lassoed each head as it came out.

Nine corgis on nine leads had some pulling power, and I discovered their true force at Sandringham House. Corgis are determined little creatures and each dog wanted to be first to exit the front door. One morning, there had been a sprinkling of snow, and the steps, like the drive, were notoriously slippy in winter.

As the doors opened, and I turned to shut them with one hand, nine leads yanked me the other way. I fell, banged my head on the steps and was knocked unconscious as the corgis scurried off into the snow. The next thing I knew I was waking up with the faces of the Queen and Princess Anne above me. 'Paul, are you all right?' said the Queen. I had been lying there for around ten minutes when they found me. They helped me to my feet. I felt a huge lump on my head and had wrenched a muscle in my back. The pain was excruciating. The Queen called Sandringham GP Dr Ford, and instructed me to take bed rest for the remainder of the day. Thankfully, someone had rounded up the corgis.

Feeding them was less trouble. It was a canine state banquet, but the Queen liked to feed her cherished pets personally whenever she could. I chatted most naturally with Her Majesty at these times either at Buckingham Palace, Windsor Castle, Sandringham House or Balmoral Castle. Dog-feeding time became my one-on-one time with the Queen, the one chance I got to speak with her with no one listening or interrupting, and we had some good conversations over the years.

I got used to the sight of the Queen, with a silver spoon and fork, taking great delight in dishing out portions of Pedigree Chum mixed with fresh rabbit and dry biscuit, and topped with gravy. Sometimes, as a special treat, leftovers of pheasant from the previous evening's dinner were added. It was my duty to place nine yellow plastic bowls on individual mats as she called their names one by one. At these times, the Queen was at her most jolly, talkative and relaxed. She would recount stories from her day, injecting humour into them, and it was not unknown for me to share with her a hearty laugh.

She often began with 'Do you know? The most extraordinary thing happened . . .' Or if she had met an old friend, she would say: 'Do you know who I saw yesterday?' Or if there had been a comical incident: 'The funniest thing happened . . .' Even better was when one of her horses had been first past the post. 'Did you know that one of my horses won at . . . ?'

31

It was during one of our many conversations at dog-feeding time that the Queen told me a remarkable story about another monarch, King Charles I, and took me back in time to his execution on 30 January 1649 when Oliver Cromwell rode into London on a wave of anti-royalism. 'Do you know? The most extraordinary thing happened the other day. I received a letter from someone whose ancestor had been in the crowd when King Charles I was executed,' the Queen started. She relayed the story of the monarch's final moments outside the Banqueting Hall in Whitehall before he was beheaded. As Her Majesty mixed the dog food, she continued, 'As they chopped off his head, a piece of his collar-bone splintered into the crowd and it was picked up by their ancestor. It has passed down through generations of their family ever since, and I have been sent that piece of bone.'

I was ignoring the corgis at my feet by that stage. 'What are you going to do with it, Your Majesty?'

'There was only one thing to do, Paul,' she said, 'and that was to return it to its rightful owner. I asked for it to be placed inside the coffin of King Charles I.' She went on to explain that when the coffin was opened, they had seen that the King's severed head had been sewn back on to his neck. 'And, do you know, because of the air-tight coffin, his beard was still intact – totally preserved,' said a rather astonished Queen to an even more astonished footman.

'Can you imagine it, Your Majesty – staring at the face of history?' She chortled at the thought.

The Queen's sense of humour comes to the fore with her skill for mimicry, which she displays in private. Then her forte was regional accents. She had a fondness for the vernacular of the East End, Ireland, Yorkshire, Merseyside and Australia, which she impersonated with affection because she admired the characters, her people, whom she met on royal tours. The monarch in full mimicking flow is not quite what one might expect, but ladies-in-waiting and private secretaries have been reduced to fits of laughter by her on many occasions.

I shall never forget the Royal Ascot race meeting when, as I rode behind Her Majesty in scarlet livery in an open landau, a Cockney voice from the cheering crowd bellowed: 'Gi' us a wave, Liz.'

Such a natural, spontaneous greeting made the royal party smile, but Prince Charles, opposite his mother, had not heard what the man had said. 'What did he say, Mummy?' he asked.

With a perfect East End accent, the Queen replied: 'He said, "Gi' us a wave, Liz."' Charles and his father laughed as the Queen continued to wave.

If only more people could hear the Queen's natural laughter or see her smile more often. Behind the pomp and pageantry, the tradition and protocol, and the sense of duty she puts above all else, there is a warm, natural woman with a lighter side that would melt the austere, severe, cold caricature the country has built up. The man in the street sees only this misleading image. The Queen is one of the easiest people to converse with, and is not at all grand or pompous. We would chat about her observations of the gardens, the wildlife and fellow household staff. She is fascinated by people and would chat about those she had met, and those she was looking forward to meeting. Her Majesty is like a country lady who just happens to be the monarch.

She is also the most caring dog-owner you could meet. When a corgi had a coughing spasm, she was on her hands and knees to hold it down and prised open its jaws while I squirted Her Majesty's recommended dose of cough mixture down its throat with a syringe. The corgis though, however cute they appeared, could fight. Once at Windsor, when the Queen was out to dinner, I had watched *Dallas* on BBC1 and was about to take them for a final walk. As I put on my coat, they raced down the corridor to the door, and all hell broke loose. Jolly, Princes Andrew and Edward's corgi, was being attacked like a fox snared by hounds. She was the smallest and weakest, being literally savaged by the others. As I turned the corner, the poor little thing's stomach had been torn open and there was blood and mess everywhere. Christopher Bray, the Queen's page, had heard the growling, yelping commotion and, together, we managed the mayhem by snatching each dog from the mêlée and locking it behind a closed door. In the process, we were both bitten and nipped but I was shaking: I was convinced little Jolly was going to die. Then a terrible thought dawned on me: the Queen would be furious.

The vet was called for the corgi and the doctor to treat Christopher's and my bites. It was nothing a tetanus jab and sticking plaster couldn't mend but Jolly was taken away and underwent emergency surgery. She survived, but only after twenty stitches to her abdomen.

When the Queen returned from dinner, I broke news of the incident with some trepidation. It was then that I first discovered Her Majesty's tolerance. She was aghast but understanding. She went into her dressing room and came back with two homeopathic arnica pills for me to take. 'Here, Paul, this will help the healing process,' she said. Unknown to me at the time, the dogs fought regularly. When they snapped and snarled at feeding time, the Queen shouted at them: 'Oh, do shut up. They can be *so* recalcitrant!'

While we were feeding the corgis, conversations often revolved around the subjects most important to the Queen: horses, dogs, Prince Philip and her children. It was the joke among staff that such topics came in that order of importance. That is a little unfair. It is just that she is perhaps *more passionate* about horses and dogs. Wherever the Queen went, the dogs followed. The noise of scampering paws and panting breath became an early radar signal that Her Majesty was close at hand.

The Duke of Edinburgh needed no reminding of their omni-presence. As the Queen sat at her writing desk with government dispatch boxes open, the corgis slept as doorstops at the several entrances into the sitting room. They nearly always blocked his path and he had to nudge the door open. In his husky voice, he once said: 'Bloody dogs! Why do you have to have so many?'

The Queen never did understand his frustration. 'But, darling, they're so collectable,' she replied. In the outside world, people collect stamps. The Queen collects corgis. (Although she is a phil-atelist, too, and owns the country's largest private collection, started by her grandfather King George V.)

Those dogs always greeted strangers with a chorus of growls and barks, but a short, sharp 'Oh, do shut up' from the Queen was enough. Even the dogs obeyed her.

Feeding them was easy. Walking them was the chore. Her Majesty was adept at dropping the hint that it was time for a walk when the weather was foul. 'Outies,' her voice called to the corgis. When I looked out of the window at Balmoral it was always the same: sheets of rain. Oh, God, I thought, because a walk had to be at least forty-five minutes. 'Come on, Chipper, Piper, Smokey . . .' I attached nine red leads and trudged outside into the driving rain. In those bleak Scottish hills, I soon found shelter from a downpour in dense woodland near the river Dee, a short walk from the castle, as the corgis ran about.

Each dog's collar had a round disc that carried the words 'HM The Queen' in case any got lost, which was the worst possible prospect when I was charged with looking after them. I shall never forget the day I came back with eight, not nine. After forty-five minutes outside, I traipsed back, tired and wet, with the drenched corgis.

'Oh, there's only eight,' the Queen said, with alarm. Shadow was missing.

Horror must have registered on my face, but the Queen just looked at me.

'Don't worry, Your Majesty, I'll go back and find her.' Still sheets of rain.

Half an hour later, I found her by the river Dee and I could breathe again.

Chipper became my firm favourite and the Queen sensed the affinity between us. After I had been in service by her side for a year, she allowed him to sleep in my room, but only at Balmoral, Sandringham and Windsor, never at Buckingham Palace because my living quarters were too far away on the top floor. Whenever we were away, though, Chipper slept at my feet at the bottom of a single bed until he died nine years later.

Routine governs the monarch's life and must run like clockwork. The Queen's dresser entered the bedroom at eight with the 'calling tray' and a china pot of Earl Grey tea. The corgis rushed in and greeted her as the curtains were drawn back.

The royal milkman delivered his crate from Windsor long before anyone was awake. A herd of Jersey cows in Windsor Great Park provides the Queen and the Royal Family with a daily supply of full-fat milk in wide-necked bottles stamped in blue EIIR Royal Dairy, Windsor, and sealed with a green and gold top. Cream arrives in waxed cartons emblazoned with a similar cypher.

At nine, Her Majesty walked through her sitting room and into her dining room, carrying her old-fashioned Roberts radio tuned permanently to BBC Radio 2. Minutes earlier, I had set a small dining-table with a frugal breakfast: one slice of granary toast, a smear of butter and a thin layer of dark, chunky marmalade. The room was used for family meals, but the Queen often ate here alone. The round table, big enough to seat four, was in the centre as the sunlight cast a silhouette of the large panelled window on to the huge rug that covered the floor. Gold-framed landscape paintings from the Royal Collection hung from chains on the walls, which were decorated with panelled blue silk.

It became a familiar sight to watch the Queen standing at the sideboard, waiting for the electric kettle to boil so that she could brew herself some tea in a silver teapot. She sat down and scanned the British newspapers, laid out in required order in a neat, flat file that showed each masthead: from the bottom, *The Times*, the *Daily Telegraph*, the *Daily Express*, the *Daily Mail* and the *Daily Mirror*, with the full front of a folded *Sporting Life* horse-racing paper on top. Her favourite magazines were *Harpers & Queen*, *Tatler* and *Horse and Hound*. She never read the *Sun* or the *Daily Star*, but was always informed of every royal story, thanks to a detailed summary compiled each morning by the press office and laid out next to the newspapers.

The *Daily Telegraph* was folded so that the crosswords faced out. The Queen always *had* to complete both puzzles. She sometimes fell weeks behind, but the daily crosswords were saved in an ever-growing pile and travelled with her to be tackled wherever she was in the world.

The first newspaper she picked up was the *Sporting Life* to scan the day's race meetings and read the form. Her small pocket racing diary was constantly updated by her racing manager, with the dates, meetings and types of race her horses would be competing in. On those days, when the Queen's colours were on any racecard, she was even more eager to read the form and size up the rest of the field. If the Queen ever had an escape from duties of state, it was her passion for horses. She was fascinated with the 'Sport of Kings', from horses to trainers, jockeys to stable-hands, winners and losers.

If you are going to engage in small-talk with the Queen, the subject of horses is a sure-fire winner. But be sure to know your subject: her knowledge is expert and vast, from the winners of classic races to the structure of handicaps or weights, to the intricacies of breeding. I never dared take on such expertise but did, occasionally, hint towards a cheeky tip from the top when one of her favourite horses ran.

'I see that Highclere is running today, Your Majesty. Does it stand a chance?' I said one day.

'It depends, Paul,' she replied, then launched into a scientific explanation of weights, rivals, class and going, which left me none the wiser.

A royal tip never came my way but, loyal to the end, I always backed the Queen's horses at Royal Ascot and Epsom, for the Derby, the one classic flat race that continues to elude her stable.

At ten, the day's business began. The Queen sat at her desk in the sitting room, side-on to the large window, with an old-fashioned switchboard-style speaker system in front of her. She pressed the thick, square button marked 'Private Secretary' and said, ever so jolly, 'Would you come up, please?'

'Of course, ma'am,' enunciated like 'jam', not 'farm'.

Seconds later, the private secretary – Sir Martin Charteris, in those days – walked briskly along the corridor, carrying a small square basket of letters. With a gentle tap on the door, he entered and, for around an hour, stood beside the seated monarch to sort the queries, engagements and dilemmas of the country and Commonwealth. (Private secretaries, or anyone else for that matter, never sit during an audience with the Queen unless invited to do so.)

The Queen is used to a day working alone at her desk or eating in her own company. There was no speakerphone to summon a footman or page: instead, she pressed a bell and a little red circular disc dropped into a small round window of a wooden box on the wall in the pantry opposite her apartment. Each hole was labelled to indicate which room the Queen was in: SITTING ROOM, BEDROOM, DINING ROOM, AUDIENCE ROOM, DRAWING ROOM, and so on.

The hours between eleven o'clock and one o'clock were always allocated for private audiences at the palace or pre-lunch engagements. It was also when government ministers, privy councillors or ambassadors were presented to the Queen in the splendour of the Bow Room or the Eighteenth-century Room to mark their appointment to office in a ceremony dictated by ancient tradition, called 'kissing hands'. Each appointee would kneel and, with his right hand, take her extended right hand – fingers slightly closed – and brush it with the lightest of kisses.

Throughout all these engagements, the Queen remained standing, sometimes for two hours at a time. It was little wonder that on her return to her sitting room she would ask: 'Is the drinks tray ready, Paul?' I would have pre-empted her enquiry. She often made herself a large glass of her favourite pre-luncheon tipple, gin and Dubonnet, in equal half measures, with two lumps of ice and a slice of lemon. Lunch was always at one o'clock and lasted approximately an hour.

If there was no engagement, the corgis and the Queen went on long walks in the gardens for up to two hours. As she donned headscarf and overcoat, she often turned to me and said: 'Would you mind recording the race?' an instruction to set the video-recorder for a televised meeting at Epsom or Ascot, York or Goodwood some time between two thirty and five. If a race meeting was not televised, a special live-link – the same audio service fed into betting shops nationwide – was boomed into Buckingham Palace. She listened intently to a specific race for the name of one of her horses. Footman and pages learned never to interrupt the Queen during a race. It would have been the height of rudeness. For those three minutes, anything and everything could wait.

The Queen never snacks or drinks between meals. Wherever she was in the world, tea was served on the stroke of five o'clock. Whether she was in a Saudi Arabian royal palace, aboard the Royal Yacht *Britannia* or at Buckingham Palace, I ensured there was Earl Grey tea with a spot of milk, a sandwich with the crusts removed and something sweet. Hot fruit scones, baked daily by pastry chef Robert Pine, were hardly ever eaten by the royals. The Queen always broke them up and fed them, piece by piece, to the corgis. This was their treat for which they would beg, roll over or spin round on the spot.

Tea finished, the drinks tray reappeared but never before six, and the Queen enjoyed a gin and tonic. An official early-evening function, a cocktail party or dinner engagement, might complete a royal day. If a hectic diary allowed, the Queen and the Duke of Edinburgh could relax together and enjoy dinner with the corgis spread out around the room. It was always at eight fifteen – unless the Queen Mother was a guest. For the Queen Mother was always late. Always. Strict timetables overran and dinner could be at eight thirty or even nine. And she always arrived like an innocent. 'Oh, am I late? Are you waiting for me?' she would say, in her whispering voice.

Clocks stopped for her when gathering for church. Once, at Sandringham, the men had set off and the Queen was waiting, with a lady-in-waiting, as I stood by the doors as usual. They waited and waited and waited, and the service should have begun at eleven. As the clock ticked on, an exasperated Queen stretched on her black gloves, finger by finger, and said: 'Is Queen Elizabeth coming or are we waiting for nothing?'

On the stroke of eleven, a shuffling sound was heard coming down the corridor and the Queen Mother arrived with the customary large hat strewn with feathers. 'Oh, am I late? Have you been waiting long?'

Not a word was said and it was smiles all round as I walked out and opened the car door. Once the Queen was comfortable on the back seat, I had to clamber inside the car, on my knees, and place a rug over her legs. Always.

Thankfully, the Queen's routine normally went like clockwork. At Buckingham Palace, when she was alone for dinner, the television was switched on in either the dining room or the sitting room. I stood just inside the doorway – always stood – and lingered to provide a few extra moments of company as the Queen watched the start of *Morecambe and Wise*, a murder mystery or the BBC *Nine o'Clock News*.

Once, when I was standing idly in the pantry, I heard a royal commotion. A whoop of delight came from the sitting room, backed up by a chorus of barking corgis. The page, Christopher Bray, and I looked as bemused as each other.

Unannounced, we both dashed to the door, opened it and were beckoned in by the Queen. 'Come quick – come quick,' she said excitedly. She was on her feet, beaming with delight. 'How wonderful,' she said. Torvill and Dean had just won the gold medal at the Sarajevo Olympic Games with their ice-dance performance to Ravel's 'Bolero'.

After dinner before each working day was over, I had two remaining duties to fulfil. I placed two glasses on a tray with a bottle of still

Malvern water for the Queen, and a bottle of Glenfiddich whisky and a small bottle of Double Diamond beer for the Duke of Edinburgh. Then I took the corgis for their last walk. On my return, I led them to the room in which they slept on the Queen's corridor. Her Majesty sometimes joined me for this bedtime ritual. Still in full evening dress, perhaps, with a diamond necklace and earrings, she got down on her hands and knees, determined to make sure each was comfortable in its own basket or beanbag. 'Make sure the window is open for them. Goodnight, Paul.' Another day was over.

The Queen, though, had one more task to do. Before she turned out the light, she religiously filled in her personal diary – always in pencil. A record, just like the diaries of Queen Victoria, for the Royal Collection. The Queen, even at bedtime, was bound by a sense of duty.

A new girl recruit joined the household as a seamstress in May 1978. Her duties were to darn the socks of Prince Philip, make alterations to suits and shirts, patch bedsheets and wash the corgis' towels. For a time, I didn't take much notice of her. She was diligent and, my first impression, easy-going, bright and cheery. She didn't like me.

I think becoming the Queen's footman so quickly went to my head. The teenage boy from the northern pit village was now sharing chats with the monarch, trusted to make her life work. Such success broadened my horizons. I realized that anything was possible, and had a new confidence that made me walk those royal corridors as if I was ten feet tall. Even my northern accent was being chipped away and wrapped up in the grandness of palace language.

I was still the same working-class character, who could never forget his roots or values, but perhaps, to some in the royal household, I gave the wrong impression and became too big for my boots. Certainly, the new recruit thought so. The daughter of staunch Catholic parents from Liverpool, she had arrived in London from the small village of Holt in North Wales.

It seemed that my mistake had been to march into the linen room with the corgis' dirty linen and drop it at her feet with the grand announcement: 'Towels!'

She didn't need to express her disdain. The look on her face said it all. She told friends I was nothing but a 'twopence-ha'penny toff'. Her name was Maria Cosgrove. My future wife.

By 1979, Maria had been promoted to senior housemaid and was given responsibility for the Belgian Suite, a self-contained set of rooms overlooking the gardens. It was the most important suite in the palace because it always accommodated visiting heads of state.

Maria's promotion coincided with my first state carriage drive, as Queen's footman, in the spring. Dressed in full state livery, wearing the blue velvet riding cap, I perched on the back of the 1902 gilded state landau with its huge brass lanterns in procession from Victoria Station to the palace, via Whitehall and the Mall. The traditional duty of a footman is to protect all who ride in that carriage with his sword but just being so close to Her Majesty and riding out with her for the first time in front of cheering crowds brought an internal euphoria that only a proud sense of duty kept contained.

I was on the left side directly behind the Queen, who wore a pink hat. Next to her was President Nicolae Ceauşescu of Romania, who slept in the Belgian Suite – with a gun under his pillow. Riding alongside me, on one of the horses from the Blues and Royals Household Cavalry Division that flanked the landau, was someone the Queen knew well: Lieutenant Colonel Andrew Parker Bowles, married to Camilla for the previous six years.

A tiny gathering of footmen huddled around the drinks tray in the saloon drawing room at Sandringham House, the Edwardian country mansion on the twenty-thousand-acre estate in Norfolk, one of the Queen's two privately owned residences, the other being Balmoral Castle in Aberdeenshire.

Beside the grand piano and beneath the wooden balustrade of the minstrels' gallery, the footmen and housemaids had been busy: new logs were stacked beside the eight-feet-high stone fireplace, with its lion and unicorn fenders, empty crystal glasses had been collected from the vast room's side-tables, the carpets had been swept, cushions plumped and the card-table folded away after canasta and bridge. The Royal Family had retired to their rooms to change for dinner.

The footmen thought the coast was clear and decided to sneak a sly shot of gin. After all, no one would know how much had been consumed by the guests.

As one footman tilted his head to knock back that quick drink, his eyes spotted a familiar face watching from a small internal window that looked on to the room from its wooden frame adjacent to the minstrels' gallery. It was the Queen. The footman almost choked. The Queen didn't report such a serious breach of the rules. Her look said it all. Yet no one better understands how hard her household works in such an unsociable service. Such a deliberate oversight illustrated her acceptance that her staff needed a stiff drink to help them cope with arduous duty and isolation from the outside world. The tolerance of the Queen was legendary.

Once when I was with the Queen, feeding the corgis in a narrow, ground-floor passageway at Sandringham, a door leading from a flight of stairs connecting staff accommodation to the main house burst open. Out spilled a senior member of staff, clearly drunk, who staggered and bounced off the wall opposite. Weaving through a minefield of corgis, he saw the Queen – watching him with fork and spoon in hand – slurred something unintelligible and went on his way. I was convinced she would be furious and sack that long-serving individual for such behaviour.

The Queen simply raised her eyebrows, said nothing and went on feeding the corgis. The man got away with it. Unlike me. At Sandringham, I once removed a glass of gin and tonic from the Queen's sitting room, wrongly believing she had finished with it and gone to change for dinner.

Maria and the Queen's dresser, Elizabeth Andrew, were hiding in a cupboard under the stairs, out of sight as required, waiting for Her Majesty to go down for dinner so that they could tidy her room when they heard the Queen's consternation: 'The beast – the beast. He's taken my brand new drink!' and she went after me down the corridor. I took it back upstairs and apologized profusely.

The Queen never liked causing trouble in her household, even if she wielded ultimate power. One evening, she was alone for dinner at Buckingham Palace and I served her a *darne* of fish. She frowned, bounced the back of a fork off it, then looked at me forlornly. 'What am I supposed to do with that?' she said.

'I will take it back to the kitchen, Your Majesty, and have it replaced.'

'No, no, don't do that. Somebody might get into trouble,' she said, and made do with the vegetables and salad. No one ever knew.

The monarch was known to put up with drunkenness, poor food, bad manners and poor service from her favoured members of staff, understanding the pressures they were under, keen to keep a peaceful house. She has standards but has the patience of a saint. Unlike her sister Princess Margaret, who was legendary for her intolerance. Her high expectation of service and protocol came with little slack. Woe betide anyone who stepped out of line because her temper was as sharp as her wit.

A stickler for rules, the princess could not tolerate a breach. Staff were not allowed to watch the royal television set. After a barbecue at the Balmoral estate's log cabin, the Royal Family returned to the castle and drawing room. In the adjoining library, I, another footman and two pages had waited late into the night. We had turned on the television to while away the hours in the hope that no one would know.

The sound of Land Rovers on the gravel outside snapped us into action. We turned off the television and returned to our posts. But Princess Margaret suspected something. She walked up to the television, placed her hand on the back, felt the radiating warmth and announced, 'Lilibet, *someone* has been watching TV!'

There were only four possible culprits in the room and we were all mortified. Princess Margaret gave us a withering look. Thankfully, the Queen said nothing.

Princess Margaret was also independent. One afternoon I saw her under the castle stairs from behind, bent double, ferreting around in the log basket to gather more wood for the drawing-room fireplace. I thought she could do with a hand so I approached, coughed and said: 'Can I help you, Your Royal Highness?'

She rose slowly, straightened, turned and pointed out, 'I used to be a Girl Guide, you know,' and bent down again to continue. Princess Margaret had a lighter side – as my best friend at the palace, household footman Roger Gleed, discovered at Sandringham. Thinking the saloon drawing room had been vacated by senior royals, he burst in as opera music played on the record-player and loudly mocked a tenor with his arms outstretched. The rest of us, with shakes of the head and wide eyes, tried to let him know that Princess Margaret was still at the fireplace, smoking a cigarette in a long, black holder. Eventually, the penny dropped. Roger stopped abruptly and went puce. In the silence, the princess slow-handclapped him and said, 'Bravo . . . bravo. I never knew we had such talent.'

Perhaps the Queen's tolerance would not have been so great had she known the full truth of backstairs antics. Gin was the favourite of many household staff. It was also the most accessible. Footmen became expert at siphoning off gin every day from crystal decanters and pouring sneaky supplies into chrome kettles. No passing member of the household could suspect a footman walking down a corridor with a kettle. Pages were perhaps more cunning. Empty tonic-water bottles were filled with gin and concealed on the inside back of their tailcoats, which had pouched pockets sewn into the lining.

Those supplies were used to keep afloat the giddy drinking parties that were rife along the corridors of the living quarters. Household staff worked hard and played hard, and spontaneous social occasions were held almost every week at Buckingham Palace, lunchtimes and evenings. If the Queen didn't know about the secret gin stocks, she definitely knew a party-scene existed, which she no doubt tolerated because of the release it gave loyal staff.

A servant's life was insular and restrictive, tiring and unsociable. The workplace – a palace, castle or country residence – was our home too. The royal household can contain and stifle those who eat, sleep and breathe a life of duty, and live and work within its confines. It breeds a tight-knit community foreign to the world outside and the non-stop parties arose out of a sense of fun coupled with a need for escape.

It was not an environment where friends or girlfriends could be invited back to stay over. No one who was single could venture out into the capital and say, 'Come back to my place for the night.' All guests – who had first to pass a strict security procedure – had to have left by eleven thirty.

Pay was poor for many staff, with board and lodging inclusive. Those on the payroll, however, were there for the privilege and honour of serving the monarch.

Like soldiers who serve Queen and country to protect accepted freedoms, staff dedicate their lives to ensuring that the fabric of the monarchy is maintained and kept in perfect running order. Anyone who chooses that path tailors their lives to fit in with the hours, rules and regulations. Also like the Army, there was a sense of childish camaraderie. The household had its fair share of practical jokers. Junior footmen could go to their room and find every stick of furniture, including the lightbulb, had been removed. One poor maid found a dead bat, taken from the tower at Balmoral, outstretched on her pillow. We knew she had found it when we heard the screams. At Balmoral, in Pend Yard at the rear entrance, mischievous footmen decorated the washing-line with underwear as if it was bunting. Unfortunately, the prank backfired when it was discovered that a pair of bloomers belonging to a lady-in-waiting had been strung out. The lady concerned was not amused and the Palace Steward ordered the offending washing-line to be taken down because it was considered 'in bad taste'.

Pranks helped break the boredom and monotony of routine, and so did the parties. On the top floor of the palace, the dim lights that could be seen from the front gates belied the disco atmosphere everyone enjoyed. From outside my room in the Pages' Lobby, the all-male wing, to Finch's Lobby, the female equivalent, everyone mixed and mingled. The below-stairs corridors would be festooned with bunting. No one kept their door shut and every room became a different annexe, like a hotel corridor taken over by business-conference delegates. Music would fill the floors and we danced the night away to the tunes of Donna Summer, Barry White and Abba. We had to steer clear of the housekeeper, Miss Victoria Martin, who had a schoolmistress attitude to discipline. 'Boys are not allowed on the female wing!' she bellowed to me one afternoon. All I had done was take a short-cut from the nursery corridor to the Pages' Lobby via Finch's Lobby. She was fiercely protective of her girls and loathed the idea of housemaids and dressers straying on to the corridors of pages and footmen.

She patrolled those floors regularly. The housemaids dared not leave cigarette stubs in ashtrays in their own rooms. A royal standard of cleanliness was applied to servants' quarters for the women, and Miss Martin, a former naval officer, expected all ashtrays to be emptied every morning. One stub left behind would send her into a fit. Maids were often heard to mutter, 'Miss Martin has gone berserk again.' The party-scene had to be cleverly planned to coincide with the housekeeper's absence, a trip away, a vacation or when she was tucked up in bed.

The staff who travelled to Sandringham or Balmoral found more liberal housekeepers in charge. This led to daily soirées, at which everyone broke free of the straitjacket of duty and let down their hair. Perhaps it was no wonder, in the Scottish Highlands of Aberdeenshire at least, that staff labelled it 'Immoral Balmoral'.

The court moves from Buckingham Palace to Balmoral Castle every year from the beginning of August to the beginning of October for the Queen's annual summer vacation. In those days, the House of Windsor always travelled north aboard the Royal Yacht *Britannia* from Portsmouth on the week-long Western Isles Cruise, which skirted the west coast of Britain through the Irish Sea and the scattering of Scottish islets before heading east *en route* to Aberdeen.

Cabin No. 44 on the lowest deck was mine from 1979 to 1986 with its sliding metal door, one porthole, single bunk, writing bureau and stainless-steel sink. It was unnerving to know that only a sheet of metal, held together by rivets, was between me and the sea. Directly beneath were the ship's propellers which, come night-time, sent me to sleep with a rapid, pulsing, mechanical whirl as they cut through the currents. On rough passages, the view from the porthole was like a washing-machine on full spin as the waves rolled around the scuttle.

Everything forward (for'ard) of the main mast was Royal Navy accommodation, with 250 officers and 'yachties', and everything at the rear (aft) was the royal household, approximately thirty-strong and headed by the Queen.

Being at sea meant losing one crucial duty – walking the corgis. They always flew to Aberdeen aboard an Andover of the Queen's Flight. Duty focused on looking after Her Majesty on the rear veranda deck, which comprised a glass-fronted sun lounge leading on to an open deck with uninterrupted sea views as the ship's wake melted into the distance. A naval frigate always followed within sight.

Every day for breakfast at nine and tea at five I set up a card-table for the Queen and Prince Philip. They joined everyone else in the dining room on the main deck for lunch at one and dinner at eight fifteen. Crested china was used every day – the collection from the Royal Yacht *Victoria and Albert*.

Negotiating the ship's passages, while loaded with the Queen's wooden tray, was an art in itself. Instead of carrying it widthways, I had to turn it lengthways to fit the narrow gangways and steep ladder-like metal steps. On many occasions, one roll of the ship in rough seas ended with a toppled tray and smashed cups, saucers and plates. If only the trays could have been fitted with the same special finish of the dining-table: although highly polished, it had an almost magnetic field that held down the precious china, silver and crystal placed upon it.

Mealtimes in rough seas were quite an ordeal. As the ship rolled in a heavy swell, at one minute I was going uphill with two dishes of vegetables, the next downhill. I learned to stand with feet wide apart and knees bent for balance, and the Queen found it amusing not only to see members of the household turn green but also the clown-like waitering of her footman. On calmer days, in early evening *Britannia* dropped anchor in a shallow bay. Motor launches ferried the royal party ashore for barbecues on deserted beaches with meat already prepared by the chef. Naval officers manned the open fire as the royals sat on rocks and rugs. This left household staff to relax aboard and hold drinks receptions or quizzes between separate messes, with questions broadcast by the wireless operator over the Tannoy.

One highlight for the Queen, as *Britannia* sailed off the Scottish coast of Caithness, was to pass the home of her mother. The Castle of Mey was perched on the edge of a cliff. Household staff appeared on deck and we waved napkins, tablecloths or sheets as officers set off flares and sounded the deep blaring of the ship's whistle.

By way of reply, the Queen Mother's staff hung linen from the turrets and leaded windows and set off fireworks from the rooftop. It was an impressive hello and goodbye. The Queen, armed with binoculars, stood on her deck and scanned for a sight of the Queen Mother who, from land, also scanned for a sight of her daughter. When they spotted each other, they waved excitedly. The next time they met was a few days later, at Balmoral, when the Queen Mother would stay at the castle for two weeks before moving to her residence on the estate, Birkhall.

In preparation for the Balmoral vacation, and while *Britannia* was crawling up the coast, the Army had been transporting tons of luggage, in hundreds of trunks, from Buckingham Palace. The Queen packs up house and home, and deserts palace life. Huge white dust sheets are spread throughout her entire apartments, smothering her desk, sofas, chairs, dining-table and sideboards. Entire travelling wardrobes on castors, trunks of hats, china, silverware, crystal, framed photographs, boxes of books, television sets, video-recorders, radios, spirits and fine wines accompany her. Clothes for every possible occasion are carefully packed, including a single black dress and hat in case there should be a death. One leather trunk was packed with at least twenty tartan rugs and another contained a prized collection of kilts. Her Majesty wore a kilt every day at Balmoral, as did the Queen Mother, Princess Margaret and Princess Anne. The Queen wore the red Royal Stewart tartan or the green Hunting Stewart, but her favourite was the grey Balmoral tartan, which can only be worn by members of the Royal Family.

Princes Philip, Charles, Andrew and Edward wore kilts by day and kilts by night, as evening wear with a black tie, but the ladies always changed from their day kilts into evening dress. Skipping, interlinking arms and weaving across the wooden-floored ballroom, waves of dancing tartan washed and swirled together at the Gillies Ball, the highlight of the Balmoral social season when the ladies wore tartan sashes pinned with diamond brooches. It was the one party-scene of which Miss Victoria Martin approved, where the family, the household and estate staff mingled and danced together, Queen, Duke, princes, princesses, footmen, housemaids, gillies and gardeners. A contingent of the Scottish Guard, the Black Watch, with its uniform of blue and green tartan kilts, stood on the minstrels' gallery and filled the room with the strains of the bagpipes and bellowing accordions with rhythmic clapping and whoops of delight from the floor below.

It was in 1979 that I danced with the Queen – if not quite alone on a packed floor filled with 150 people. In the interchanging sea of partners, the footman came up against the monarch in 'The Dashing White Sergeant'. My linked line of three servants came face-to-face with another line of three with Her Majesty on one end. The two threesomes joined to form a circle of six and my hand linked with the Queen's. All I can remember is trying not to squeeze too hard with my sweaty palm.

The Queen's Pipe Major announced each dance and whenever there was a family dinner, he played his bagpipes around the table. But he had a more traditional duty each morning, in a custom started by Queen Victoria and continued by successive monarchs ever since. On the stroke of nine each morning, at wherever the Queen is in official residence, he plays the bagpipes and marches alone beneath her bedroom window for ten minutes, playing a selection of tunes. A morning ritual to signal the beginning of the day. It was a tradition that took on an extra charm as the sonorous sound of the bagpipes drifted down the glens around Balmoral.

It is a magical castle, built by Prince Albert in 1853 for Queen Victoria so that she could escape the pressures of public life and relax with her family in solitude. Balmoral, more than any other royal residence, still retains that feel of a warm, family home where procedures are not so tight, life is more informal and the Queen is on top form.

As it was for her great-great-grandmother Victoria, the isolation of Balmoral is the perfect haven for the Queen who, as a country-woman, loves nothing more than walking through these Scottish glens. If Buckingham Palace is her office, Windsor Castle is her favourite weekend retreat. Sandringham House is ideal for shooting parties but in an ideal world Balmoral would be her home.

Time seems to have stood still at the turreted castle, with ivy creeping round its grey stone walls. VRI – the imperial cypher of Queen Victoria – still adorns the flocked wallpaper that lines the magnificent hallways, and a green Hunting Stewart tartan carpet disappears down the gloomy corridors. Love of the country life and outdoor pursuits is seen throughout the castle in the fishing-rods, waders and landing nets that hang in the wood-panelled hallway where a grandfather clock stands on the black-and-white chequered marble floor; stags' heads stare down from almost every wall in every corridor, hunting trophies from the stalking expeditions of previous monarchs; beneath them Landseer paintings depict more stags standing in misty glens and spaniels bounding through the heather and peat.

It was a self-sufficient lifestyle. Salmon caught in the river Dee and deer shot on the hills provided the first and main course at dinner. Fruit – blueberries, raspberries and loganberries – picked fresh from the kitchen garden was served for pudding. Dinner never cost much at Balmoral, and the Queen was economical with the running costs of a private residence where she paid the bills and abhorred waste. Scraps from the dinner table fed the corgis. She walked around the castle switching off lights in unoccupied rooms to save energy. In the mornings, she switched on only one bar of the electric fire in her dressing room. Her Majesty seemed hardened to the cold and draughts. She regularly slept with the windows open to the elements. In mid-October, it was not unusual for dressers to find snow and frost, which come early to the Highlands, on the carpet beneath the window-sill. The corgis often huddled around that one bar of the fire.

My living quarters were equally chilly. So much so that a royal castle in October almost reminded me of my childhood home in Grassmoor: cold linoleum floors and ice on the inside of the windows in a sparse room without central heating.

In childhood days I scratched my name on the icy windows. In a tradition at Balmoral, honeymooning royal brides, who stayed in the Royal Visitors' Suite, scratched their names into the window-pane with the diamond of their engagement ring.

By the end of 1979, the media was speculating on the next royal bride. The search was on for a suitable Princess of Wales.

3. A Princess in Love

'Are you lost?' I asked the bewildered-looking house guest. 'Can I help you?'

'Yes. I *am* sorry. Could you please show me the way back to my room?' the young lady replied. She stood slightly ahead of me, half-way along the dim ground-floor corridor where she had wandered in Balmoral Castle on a Saturday morning in September 1980. She had interrupted my brisk walk towards the staircase to the Queen's corridor. She was scanning the typed cards inserted into brass nameplates on each guest-room door. I recognized her from the previous night when I had taken her suitcase from the front hall to her room on the first floor. Getting lost was easy. Each corridor mirrored the next, with virtually identical wooden doors, green tartan carpets, beige flock wallpaper and antlered deer's heads mounted on the walls. The castle was quiet. Prince Charles was with the Duke of Edinburgh, Princes Andrew and Edward on stag-stalking expeditions. The Queen Mother and Princess Margaret rarely surfaced before midday. The Queen was in her sitting room.

The young lady could not have been more apologetic on the short walk up the staircase. She smiled awkwardly and said, 'I *am* so sorry about this. It's difficult to find your way around a strange house the first time.'

As we approached her room, I offered reassurance. 'Don't worry. It's normal. If you need anything else, don't hesitate to ask. The staff here are a friendly bunch.'

She thanked me, stepped into her room with its single bed and closed the door. The nameplate read: 'Lady Diana Spencer'. A few feet further down the corridor was the next room: 'HRH The Prince of Wales'. On a previous visit in August, Lady Diana had stayed with her sister Jane, who was married to Sir Robert Fellowes, the Queen's assistant private secretary, at their grace-and-favour cottage, more than a mile away. It was her second visit to the Balmoral estate but her first stay at the castle, and she was being

51

entertained as a guest of Prince Charles, with a collection of his other friends.

Pauline Hillier, the housemaid assigned to the Nursery Corridor, entered the ground-floor utility room holding, at head height, a simple long black evening dress on its hanger. I was drinking a mug of coffee. 'This is my lady's dress. She's only got the one and she's here for three nights. What is she going to do?' she said, concerned for Lady Diana Spencer, the nursery-school assistant from London.

Most visiting ladies brought with them more than one evening dress, and there were anxious looks downstairs about whether she would be socially embarrassed. She was only nineteen, a mere teenager in a royal social circle full of men and ladies in their thirties and forties.

There was enough for a first-time guest to fret about without having to worry about their wardrobe. Staying at the castle could be a fraught experience for any newcomer: how to address members of the Royal Family; knowing what time to appear for drinks; the social test of dinner-table conversation and whether you would be warmly accepted into the fold. As it turned out, glorious warm evenings saved her from a fashion *faux pas*. The dress had to be worn only once to dinner because on the two other evenings barbecues were held at the log cabin, bought as a silver wedding anniversary present by the Queen for the Duke of Edinburgh.

In the eyes of the household Lady Diana was just another guest, a Sloane-type escort for the then thirty-two-year-old Prince Charles. She was quiet, and blushed easily, but there was nothing extraordinary about her. If the staff noted anything, it was that she was pretty, polite, devoid of pomposity – and her wardrobe was inadequate for a lady who was on the arm of the heir to the throne.

Ladies-in-waiting had reviewed the scant wardrobe of the woman known universally as 'Lady Di'. It was why they ordered an off-the-peg outfit from a London store: a bright blue skirt and collarless jacket with a white, high-necked blouse and matching shoes. The princess-to-be did not have anything regarded as suitable for a special occasion and something smart and businesslike was considered *de rigueur* for 24 February 1981 when the public announcement would be made at Buckingham Palace of her engagement to Prince Charles.

Downstairs was abuzz with gossip, just as the media was hysterical with speculation. Word in the footmen's room, pantries and kitchens since before Christmas was, 'Lady Di is the one.' Lady Amanda Knatchbull had been a previous favourite. She was the granddaughter of Lord Mountbatten – Prince Philip's uncle who had been murdered by an IRA bomb. But the smart money on Lady Amanda was blown away the moment Crown jeweller David Thomas visited the palace the week before the engagement. He was spotted with a small attaché case and the official word was that it contained a selection of signet rings for Prince Andrew to choose one as a gift for his twenty-first birthday. Few in the household believed this because the operation was far too cloak-and-dagger, and the gossip moved up a gear. David Thomas, who was responsible for the upkeep of the Crown Jewels in the Jewel House at the Tower of London, had in fact brought ladies' rings, with strict instructions not to include rubies or emeralds. A selection of diamonds and sapphires was set on a tray for – oddly – the Queen's perusal. Once the monarch had made her choice, the Prince of Wales gave his approval. Lady Diana was third in line to offer her opinion. The bride-to-be accepted the selection that had effectively been made for her because she did not want to appear rude and ungrateful. As she later told me: 'I would never have chosen something quite so gaudy. If I had the chance again, it would be more elegant and simple.'

On the day the secret emerged, no one downstairs had an inkling of what was to be announced. The morning had started normally when I served the Queen breakfast at nine. Then she changed the strict timetable. 'We will have tea at four o'clock,' she told me, bringing forward her schedule by an hour. 'There will be four of us – His Royal Highness [the Duke of Edinburgh], the Prince of Wales and Lady Diana Spencer.' She had to tell me this because I needed to know how many table places to set for either ladies or gentlemen. Ladies have small teacups. Gentlemen have large breakfast cups. I knew the engagement was imminent: the timetable had been changed at short notice and it was the first time Lady Diana had taken tea with the Queen.

In that regard, I was among the first in Britain to know and I was filled with excitement. After laying the table, I deliberately hung around in the Queen's corridor to catch a glimpse of the happy couple. Prince Charles and Lady Diana were smiling as they walked past me, hand in hand, and disappeared into the Queen's sitting room, then moved through to the dining room.

John Taylor, the Queen's page, went inside and put a plate of hot scones on the table. I couldn't resist peeping at the gathering through the gap at the door's hinge. Lady Diana sat, in her new blue outfit, with her prospective in-laws, bolt upright. She looked frightened to death. Afterwards, clearing the table, I noticed she hadn't touched a scone or drunk her tea. I would learn later that she only drank coffee. But it was no wonder she was a nervous wreck: tea with the Queen was followed by a loving public parade before the world's media in a carefully managed announcement. The prince and his fiancée had to walk out of the Bow Room, the central room at the rear on the ground floor, down the sweeping stone steps and out on to the lawn where a bank of TV cameras, boom microphones, reporters and photographers had congregated.

I had ten minutes to spare and had prepared to watch that moment of history from a first-floor audience room, but I hadn't reckoned on the Queen foiling my plan. 'Paul, could you take the dogs up the King's Border [a wide herbaceous border] and round the back of the lake? It will cause least bother,' she instructed me.

The corgis had probably never been leashed so quickly or walked so fast because I was determined not to miss out. With nine corgis in tow, I dashed round to the far side of the lake just in time to see the prince and Lady Diana walk down those steps.

From that vantage-point, I witnessed history in miniature: I really needed binoculars to see the two figures parading down the lawn, then standing for interviews before a constant flickering of silent flashbulbs.

'Have you seen her? She's sat down there all by herself,' said Mark Simpson late one night. He had made a discreet check on Lady Diana Spencer who had moved into Buckingham Palace post-engagement. Mark couldn't help feeling sorry for the new lady in residence. 'Let's go out and get her a McDonald's,' he suggested, a man on a mercy mission.

Lady Diana Spencer was alone in her room. Prince Charles was away on a month-long tour of Australia. His fiancée, used to living in a London flat shared with girlfriends, found herself in her own company for hours on end in the capital's grandest property. Mark was my next-door neighbour on the Pages' Lobby. He was also the household footman assigned to the Royal Nursery corridor, where Princes Andrew and Edward had kept rooms since childhood. It was also where their brother's fiancée had been allocated a suite, with bedroom, bathroom and an adjoining kitchen and utility area. She had moved to the palace for the five months prior to the wedding in July. Prince Charles's bachelor apartment was on the same floor but far from the nursery corridor. His vast suite occupied one wing and included a bedroom, bathroom, dressing room, sitting room and dining room. If Lady Diana ever wanted a friendly face in her loneliest hours, she soon learned that the likes of Mark Simpson, always a kind and thoughtful person, were available. She had friends looking out for her from the start. Downstairs at least.

Mark was tired after a full day on duty but he couldn't bear to see her so isolated. 'We could have a little picnic and brighten up her day. Come on, let's go to McDonald's,' Mark insisted. I was nervous. What if the Queen found out? What if Lady Diana told Prince Charles? What would happen if the Master of the Household saw us? It was not part of our remit to provide company and spontaneous treats for the future Princess of Wales. She was living in royal rooms and it was not our place to be there, let alone to entertain her.

I urged caution: 'I'm not sure, Mark. We must be careful. What happens if we're caught? Our heads will be on the block.'

I was not familiar with the lady he was concerned about. He knew her far better than I did because he had daily contact with her. More importantly, I was the Queen's footman and only two years into such a magnificent post.

'C'mon, Paul, she'll be grateful for the company.' Mark grabbed his coat and headed for the door.

His conviction won me over and, against my better judgement, we walked to Victoria Street and picked up three Big Mac meals. I carried my own bag. Mark clutched his, containing one meal for him, one for the lady. We returned through the side entrance, looking as if we were on takeaway errand duty for the upper floor. Staff always went out for fast-food so there was nothing out of the ordinary as we headed up to the Pages' Lobby.

I was too frightened to join Mark on his mission and anxious about how Lady Diana would respond to a face seen once in a corridor at Balmoral or, more usually, behind the Queen. 'You go, Mark,' I said, and he did. Not once did I think he would return but, having delivered his Big Macs, he came back to fetch me, after checking the coast was clear. 'C'mon, then,' he said.

Like naughty schoolchildren, we crossed the corridor. Out of uniform. A warning from training days raced through my mind: '*Never* be seen in royal corridors in your civvies.' What I was doing was virtual sacrilege and downright foolish but I was intrigued by Lady Diana, who had seemed so friendly on first meeting, and I trusted Mark. I walked directly behind him. On to the red carpet. We passed the day nursery, Prince Edward's door, Prince Andrew's door. And then we arrived at a slightly ajar door, which opened into the little kitchen area annexed to the bedroom of Lady Diana.

And there she was, already attacking her Big Mac. She giggled a lot and was so friendly and down-to-earth. She kept repeating how thoughtful Mark had been and how grateful she was to have such an unexpected interlude. If our company was unexpected then so was her relaxed, warm, familiar manner. Mark had often said how normal she seemed, but while there was a line of respect to observe, there was no barrier in communication. It was chit-chat in someone's kitchen. If I hadn't been so worried about being there perhaps I would have appreciated her charm more, but this was much worse than the prospect of being caught on the female wing in the staff living quarters. After about ten minutes we left, and I have never been so pleased to leave a royal room.

'You see? She's one of us,' he said, as we hurried back along the corridor.

I never took such a risk again at the palace, even if Mark did. He became a virtual after-hours companion and, in time, the inevitable happened. He was caught – in the bedroom of the princess, on the edge of her bed – by a staggered Prince Charles. Mark returned to the Pages' Lobby, absolutely mortified. Lady Diana had been dressed in her nightie and it didn't look good – not that there was anything in it. It was regarded as bad form but, thankfully, he didn't get into too much trouble.

Shortly afterwards, he received a copy of a press photograph of the royal bride-to-be. It was signed in black marker pen: 'To Mark, with love from Diana'. I suspect it was the first autographed picture she ever issued.

Lady Diana had a lonely time in those months leading up to the wedding. She dared not go out because of the intense media spotlight. It must have been like moving into a town hall. Buckingham Palace is a disorientating maze for a stranger, a labyrinth of connecting corridors and rooms. No one showed her around and instruction books and maps were not provided. A wrong turn down a corridor could lead to a cocktail party or an official reception. No one knew who or what was round the next corner. A closed door might have opened on to a private meeting. It is not a comfortable or easy place for any newcomer – from those marrying into the family down to punctilious staff. In staff quarters, at least there was a camaraderie, banter and a mini-community, which made life more bearable. Lady Diana did not have the same support network to depend on. She would sit up late, writing letters to her friends. Also, when the prince was away, she plucked up the courage to build up communication with the Queen. Once a week, the phone rang on the Queen's corridor. 'Will the Queen be dining alone today?' she asked, in a quiet, almost timid voice.

If there was no engagement planned, one of us would ask the Queen, 'Lady Diana was inquiring whether Your Majesty would be alone for dinner tonight?'

'Oh, do ask her to join me,' the Queen would say. 'Dinner will be at eight fifteen.' Not once did she refuse. But Lady Diana was uncomfortable that to communicate with her future mother-in-law she had to go through pages or footmen. It was a hurdle to her spontaneity and the mealtimes were formal. She made the effort once a week but preferred a quick dinner in her room, where she could curl up and relax.

She had a genuine affection for the Queen. I remember her appearing regularly on the corridor with wet hair having been for a swim. 'Is the Queen alone?' she would say. Then she tapped on the door and entered the sitting room, bright and breezy: 'Good morning, Your Majesty.' It always brought a smile to the Queen's face, because Lady Diana was so cheerful. Once married, she no longer needed to call the Queen 'Your Majesty'. She received instructions instead to call her 'Mama' and Prince Philip 'Pa' in private.

The Queen was always accommodating even if she rarely went out of her way to ensure that her prospective daughter-in-law was settled. However, adaptability and strength of character are perceived as part of duty, and the Queen herself had had to learn the harsh protocols and isolation of palace life during her childhood. It was assumed that, as Lady Diana came from the nobility and was no stranger to large households, she would cope with the transition, but where there was assumption there should have been assistance. What she didn't possess was the Queen's iron will. Essentially a people person, she did not grasp the wholly different way of palace life, which she found friendless, foreign and peculiar. It is ironic that the Queen left her to her own devices out of faith in her: she had adopted the trusting attitude that 'if she needs me, she knows where I am'. The monarch had belief in her – even if the future Princess of Wales did not share it.

The wrench of leaving behind her old life, the flat in London and the children at the kindergarten, was upsetting. When she returned one day to see the children, all the youngsters she adored kept tugging on her sleeves and asking, 'Where have you been?' and 'When are you coming back?' She found the whole experience a 'traumatic nightmare' and left close to tears.

It wasn't any easier when she returned to her old flat at No. 60 Colherne Court, where she lived with female flatmates, to remove her most precious possessions. She was alone with her thoughts in a flat full of memories as she polished and vacuumed. As she closed the door behind her, she had felt the urge to cry, she said.

But, deep down, she was excited, too, and knew she had to be strong. To tackle the boredom she kept busy. She focused on the wedding as David and Elizabeth Emmanuel, the designers charged with creating her dress, made regular visits to her room for consultations and fittings. On each occasion, the waist had to be nipped in because she was on a diet ahead of the big day.

She had ballet and tap lessons in the Throne Room, dancing in a leotard. There, on a stepped dais at one end of the room, two broad-backed thrones sat beneath a gold-tasselled dark-crimson canopy, which draped in a loose W-shape from an ornate gold pelmet. Every wall was papered in light crimson silk, which incorporated a subtle but darker diamond pattern outline.

The upholstered ceremonial chairs, with gilded arms and legs, were side by side, their crimson backs embroidered with gold thread – one marked 'EIIR', the other bearing the letter P; the Queen's throne was an inch higher than that of the Duke of Edinburgh, as tradition dictates for the monarch. The enormity of Lady Diana's privileged position could not have been lost on her.

Lady Diana was also a keen swimmer and, like Princess Margaret, used the blue-and-white-tiled swimming-pool with its springboard and diving-board most mornings. The only access to the pool was via a corridor off the Belgian Suite where each day she would cross the path of housemaid Maria Cosgrove. Polite pleasantries turned into brief conversations, which then became lengthy woman-to-woman chats about palace life. Neither woman was ever lost for words. Maria had no airs and graces and Lady Diana found in her a warm and approachable ally, just as she had in Mark Simpson.

With the staff, Lady Diana found friendship. She blended into downstairs life far better than she ever did upstairs and perhaps that had something to do with the fact that the Spencers knew the life of service as well as that of nobility. Lady Diana's grandmother, Ruth, Lady Fermoy, was a close friend of the Queen Mother, and had been a Woman of the Bedchamber to the Queen. Her father, Earl Spencer, was once an equerry to George VI. In the hive of activity downstairs, the future princess found banter and good company.

Where she had gingerly trodden along the red carpets of the upstairs corridors, wondering about every potential wrong turn, she explored the tiled floors of downstairs life freely. She often sat with Yeoman of the Silver Pantry Victor Fletcher, a no-nonsense Yorkshireman who always held one arm of his black-rimmed glasses in the corner of his mouth as if it were a pipe. He knew all about duty and devotion, and provided his insights to his fascinated listener, who afforded him respect and called him Mr Fletcher. He was always thrilled that she took an interest in his work. She visited the royal pastry kitchen and specialist chef Robert Pine, a tall, handsome man with thick black hair and moustache, whose sharp, dry wit, delivered with a Devon accent, always made her giggle. His treat was dollops of home-made ice-cream or spoonfuls of bread-and-butter pudding. She wandered into the coffee room and sat with head maid Ann Gardner, whose neat, precise dress belied a sense of fun that produced a plethora of party anecdotes, which appealed to Lady Diana as she consumed bowls of cereal.

She popped into the linen room to chat with girls toiling over the laundry, or went to the kitchen and spent time with chef Mervyn Wycherley. A stocky, muscular man keen on body-building, he was honest about everything and made her laugh. She liked his gentle nature, hidden behind a loud and larger-than-life character. He soon established himself as one of her favourites. Evelyn Dagley, a housemaid on the nursery corridor, was also a true ally. Along with Mark Simpson's, hers was one of the first friendly faces Lady Diana encountered. Evelyn – shy, diligent and as passionate about her work as she was about hockey – made sure her room was as comfortable as possible and assumed responsibility for her ever-expanding wardrobe.

Lady Diana made many friends downstairs, even with Cyril Dickman, the Palace Steward – the boss – who might have been expected to be aloof, but was easy-going and approachable. He was a natural father-figure and no one understood better than he the difficulties of the tough transitional period she was experiencing. He was the fount of all knowledge royal, and a walking instruction manual on tradition, etiquette and protocol. She never forgot his kindness and the time he gave her in those early days. In future years at Balmoral, she sought out Mr Dickman, renowned for his dancing, for a foxtrot or waltz at the Gillies Ball. So at ease was she with staff that Lady Diana began to roam alone and search upstairs corridors to find staff in the middle of their duties to share a chat or lend a sympathetic ear. It was at odds with normal protocol and some staff preferred such familiarity kept downstairs, even if they didn't say anything.

Despite having allies in the engine room of royal life, Lady Diana did not win universal approval. Among the servants, there were certain grandees and sticklers for tradition. Some long-serving members of staff frowned at the sight of this young lady 'intruding' into their world. It was a strongly held opinion in certain quarters that she should 'know her place and remain upstairs'. One woman, who had been in the household for forty years, could not believe the audacity when Lady Diana opened cupboards and helped herself to biscuits. It was the height of bad manners, said the indignant woman. One chef even confronted her when she walked into his kitchen. 'You shouldn't be down here in the kitchen,' he told her pointedly. Lady Diana, so used to friendliness downstairs, turned on her heels and ran upstairs.

The majority of staff, especially the junior members, embraced Lady Diana and turned a blind eye to the so-called breach of protocol. It was why they called her 'a breath of fresh air from upstairs'.

What few probably realized at the time was that she was also on a scouting mission, checking out and selecting a potential team to run the Prince and Princess of Wales's two new homes: the country retreat of Highgrove, Gloucestershire, and an apartment at Kensington Palace, London. Prince Charles had bought Highgrove, a three-storey Georgian country house and estate, in 1980 – the year before he became engaged. Its location in the Cotswolds was convenient for many things. It was about eight miles from Gatcombe Park and Princess Anne, close to the Beaufort Hunt and a short drive from Bolehyde Manor, the home of Lieutenant Colonel Andrew Parker Bowles and his wife, Camilla.

The Princess of Wales was grinning from ear to ear and in full flight, bounding with the grace of a ballet dancer down the red carpet, cream silk slippers in one hand, her twenty-five-foot train rolled round the other arm. She was being her free self on a wedding day suffocated by pomp and pageantry, unrestricted for one small moment by protocol. It was minutes after the world had seen her kiss her prince on the balcony of Buckingham Palace on 29 July 1981.

The rushing bride had taken me by surprise. I stood alone in scarlet livery, leaning casually against a side wall in the Queen's corridor, wondering when Her Majesty would return to her apartment – a signal that the bridal party was drifting from the Centre Room, which leads to the balcony, to the glass-ceilinged Picture Gallery at the back of the palace where everyone congregated for the wedding breakfast.

The new princess, surrounded by billowing ivory silk with a veil streaming behind her, thought she had the run of the carpet. One side of the corridor was made up of rows of floor-to-ceiling french windows overlooking the quadrangle. She danced through the broad shafts of light on the carpet and the sun glinted off the Spencer family tiara. She was full of confidence, brimming with life. She seemed so happy and radiant. I knew it was an image to be remembered for the rest of my life, but I felt conspicuous and didn't want to be caught staring at her in case I embarrassed her. I backed into the Queen's apartment and shut the door.

It had been in that sitting room that I had witnessed Lady Diana Spencer transformed into the Princess of Wales, along with 750 million other television viewers. I had sat cross-legged on the carpet in front of the monarch's television set, surrounded by her corgis. Watching the royal television was technically not allowed but, on that day at least, I knew the Queen wouldn't mind.

Like the rest of the nation, this Queen's footman was mesmerized by the images of the day: the mass crowds; Lady Diana waving with her father, Earl Spencer, in the Glass Coach *en route* to St Paul's Cathedral; her wedding train swamping the red-carpeted aisle; the Prince and Princess of Wales emerging on the steps. My duty was to stay behind for the wedding breakfast in the Ball Supper Room, next to the Picture Gallery, and the television was useful for monitoring progress, although I spent half the time looking out for the Queen's other footman, Paul Whybrew, who had been lucky enough to ride behind Her Majesty and the Duke of Edinburgh in an open landau in the state procession.

As the newly-weds swept into the quadrangle, I remained glued to the television. On the screen I watched the Prince and Princess of Wales walk out on to the balcony – and could hear outside the rapturous cheers of the mass crowd. I bolted upstairs to my top-floor room, which overlooked the Victoria Memorial and the Mall, and knelt at the long, oblong window. As thousands of people from the outside took a picture of the golden couple, I took one from inside of the people, then rushed back downstairs.

It was the same crowd that had kept me awake on the eve of the wedding, singing 'God Bless the Prince of Wales' and 'God Save the Queen', as a party atmosphere gripped the country. It had been a week-long crescendo of hype.

Two days before the wedding, a reception, dinner and ball for almost a thousand guests was held at Buckingham Palace, bringing together the crowned heads of Europe, ambassadors, high commissioners, archbishops and bishops, government ministers and prime ministers past and present, using every palace reception room. I was assigned to the Throne Room and, along with a senior page, looked after a round table of ten guests, which included the Prince of Wales, the then Lady Diana, and Princess Grace of Monaco, escorted by her son Prince Albert. I have never seen such a beauty as Princess Grace, the legendary actress the world knew as Grace Kelly, who was married to Prince Rainier of Monaco. That evening she even outshone the bride-to-be, and her tiara was every bit as magnificent as the Queen's.

Lady Diana was captivated. The two ladies struck up an immediate rapport and were locked in conversation before the dancing began. In Princess Grace, Lady Diana had found a role model and inspirational figure: an outsider like her, who had married into royalty; a film star used to the media glare; a woman in a royal marriage where love was infected by duty. She asked Princess Grace for any tips or advice. 'You will be just fine,' said the former actress. 'It gets worse, but you learn to cope.'

At the wedding breakfast, I was concerned with not stepping on the princess's dress, which seemed to spill everywhere. I served the top table, which included the bride and groom, both sets of parents, bridesmaids, pages, Princes Andrew and Edward.

Ceremony and protocol had calmed the spontaneous exuberance that had made her run down the corridor earlier. The princess was quiet, more a listener to conversation than a major contributor. She played with and nibbled at food. She would tell me, many years later: 'My stomach was in knots. I was shattered.' On that day at least, she felt a bright future lay ahead. All she ever longed for was a happy marriage with Prince Charles. The princess didn't just love him: she adored him.

In later life, the princess had one wish: that a more informed account would portray her true love for Prince Charles. She felt the public had been given a misleading impression of their relationship. Book after book and article after article have distorted history by virtually erasing the happiness and true love that existed in the early period of their marriage. It can be argued that the princess was partly responsible for some of that distortion when she collaborated with journalist Andrew Morton for the publication in June 1992 of his book, *Diana, The True Story*, which was revised after her death. In it, he claimed it was the nearest anyone would get to reading the autobiography of the princess. That could never be true. For if, one day, the princess had chosen to pen her memoirs, she would have erased the false image of eternal misery that was said to have begun on day one of her marriage. Had her true opinions been taken down in later life, with the benefit of hindsight, and not in 1992, when she made an emotional cry for help, the world would have had a different picture of the foundations of the marriage. True love, for that was what it was on both sides, survived a difficult adjustment in the early years and, far from rejecting the princess, Prince Charles did his best to understand his wife and be patient with the mood swings brought on by the eating disorder, bulimia, which she later admitted to suffering from. Indeed, the love the princess had for her husband never fully disappeared. When irreconcilable differences set in after 1985, a rift became a gulf. Bitterness led to an exchange of invective between two people who didn't understand one another's needs but there was no 'War of the Waleses': wars require hatred and there was no hatred between them. If there was a war, it was fought above their heads between their divided camps, offices and over-protective advisers.

What must be understood is that the princess, through friends, co-operated with Andrew Morton at a time when her marriage was falling apart, when she was emotionally confused, when she was grieving for her beloved father, the Earl Spencer, and when Prince Charles's friends were briefing against her and she felt under attack. As she explained in later life: 'It was as if everyone around me had six pairs of eyes instead of one, staring and judging me all the time.' She was angry, bitter, and co-operated with Morton at the most vulnerable time.

The book's publication had the desired effect. She no longer felt alone because the British people knew the truth, and why there had been no more royal children. 'Everyone understood me better. The book was a release for both Charles and I because we didn't have to pretend any more, even if he was furious with me,' she said.

But it was a classic case of acting with haste and repenting at leisure. After the book's publication, hindsight taught her that her desperation to be heard had given a misleading impression of Prince Charles, and the book had painted over the good times. In giving an angry snapshot, she had made a mistake, she later acknowledged.

For that reason, the 1992 account should not be allowed, as Morton claims in good faith, to stand as the testimony she would have given in 1997. She wanted to say more. My account, with the assistance of correspondence from a lifelong friend, gives the untold truths to balance the picture.

On their honeymoon, the Prince and Princess of Wales sailed the Mediterranean aboard the Royal Yacht *Britannia* and the princess felt blissfully happy, not – as other accounts inform us – rejected by the man she affectionately called 'hubby'. As she wrote to a close friend from the yacht:

> I couldn't be happier and would never of [sic] believed how content or wonderful I feel.
>
> The cruise on Britannia was extremely spoiling and we spent most of the time giggling and mobbing each other up. Marriage suits me enormously and I just adore having someone to look after and spoil. It's the best thing that has ever happened to me – besides being the luckiest lady in the world.

On the yacht, they watched endless reruns of the video of their wedding, the first time they had had a chance to see it. Man and wife were reduced to fits of giggles over the princess's slip-up at the altar when, in repeating her vows, she muddled the order of Prince Charles's names. So happy were they that as they sat holding each other and watching the ceremony they both cried.

As the princess wrote to that friend:

> We practically blub every time we watch a video of the wedding, and I can just imagine in ten years time, one of the minor Wales's saying 'Why did you call Daddy "Philip"?' Oh well, something to look forward to.

Unlike other brides, the princess was not going to return to her old life at a London kindergarten. A massive adjustment that few of us could comprehend was thrust upon her. With the onset of bulimia, her emotions, and consequently her moods, were up and down. It strikes me as odd that people should have been surprised, in the light of all the upheavals she faced. The truth is that had it not been for Prince Charles the princess would never have coped. She knew that. He understood the adjustment she was having to make, and for someone who was supposed to have been distant and perplexed by her moods, he did a good job at lifting her spirits. As the princess wrote: '*I overcame those depressions all due to Charles with his patience and kindness. I couldn't get over how tired and miserable I got, which was unfair to him.*'

From the yacht, the royal couple headed to Balmoral. Estate workers were so delighted to welcome them that they produced a two-seated open cart strewn with masses of purple heather. This greeted the prince and princess at the front gate and they climbed aboard, giggling at the absurdity of being pulled manually up the slight incline to the castle door by gillies, gardeners and grooms. The princess arrived with 160 mangos, a gift from President Sadat of Egypt, who had been a guest aboard the yacht.

In the romantic setting of Balmoral Castle, Prince Charles read to her and she did tapestry. They walked hand in hand into the glens and she looked forward to barbecues in the warm, summer evenings at the log cabin on the estate. She even managed to read a whole book in one day for the first time in her life. What also delighted her was a surprise visit from her former flatmate Carolyn Pride, later Bartholomew, who came to stay at the castle as a guest of Prince Andrew. The princess was overjoyed that, in both Andrew and Carolyn, she had people of her age to chat to and relax with.

It may be true that, at this time, the princess discovered that Charles was wearing a pair of cufflinks: two Cs linked together, a gift from Camilla. She confronted him, but that was not going to mar her happiness and she responded in the only way she knew how, by getting even: on Highgrove and Kensington Palace headed writing paper, the lower curve of the letter C was linked into a D beneath the logo of a crown. The princess believed that it symbolized a peaceful marriage, which would last for ever. Also, she bought an ornament of two doves entwined together.

It was tea-time at Balmoral and the princess, wearing her waterproofs, tweeds and plus fours, appeared in the hallway with blood on her face. I did a double-take as she walked past the life-size, white marble statue of Prince Albert. She had spent the day hunting with Prince Charles, a gillie and several others, and come back wearing what looked like war-paint. She had undergone a royal initiation ceremony for débutant hunters after claiming her first kill. As she stood in the glen, the stag's belly was slit open and its blood smeared on to her cheeks. She had been officially 'blooded'. The dead stag was slung across a pony and sent down to the castle with a soldier. Its head was removed, the antlers set aside and the carcass hung in the game larder – alongside rows of snipe, pheasant and grouse – to be cooked for the royal table.

The princess loved her time in the Scottish Highlands but, unlike the Windsors, didn't have a passion for blood sports. When she went hunting, she did so to please the prince. She knew and accepted that hunting – with shooting and fishing – was an integral part of life at Balmoral, and important to him. Others have suggested she sulked through the honeymoon and never made an effort, but whatever was on the agenda, she did her best to fit in.

Even two years into the marriage, she liked to be there for her husband. She wrote to a female friend in 1983: '*I believe in making an effort, so am on my way to watch polo . . . for the second day running. I would much rather be asleep but it seems to bring C a lot of happiness. I'm sure it's to show off on his part!*' In turn, the prince made concessions. He knew the princess preferred London to the countryside and made a deliberate shift in his routine. The princess had to pinch herself when, on some Sunday mornings, she woke up at Kensington Palace with her husband and not at Highgrove. There were elements of give and take on both sides.

Prince Charles was never happier than when he was hunting at Balmoral. After a hearty Scottish breakfast, including porridge, kippers and kedgeree, all-male shooting and stalking parties loaded dogs, guns and ammunition into Land Rovers and headed for the day to a pre-assigned destination in the glens. Each participant collected a waterproof satchel from the Tower Door at the side of the castle, which always contained a meat-filled bap, cold lamb chops, fruit and a greaseproof-paper parcel of plum pudding. There was also a flask of sloe gin or whisky.

Once, the prince stood in the hall and shouted for assistance: 'Can someone come and help me?' I heard him from the Pages' Vestibule and went to investigate. He was standing with two giant salmon at his feet on the marble floor. 'Could you please take them to Chef? I think we'll have them for dinner,' he said. I bent down to pick them up but their slippery scales made them awkward to handle. Prince Charles watched me juggling pathetically with them. 'Oh, come here!' he said impatiently. 'Don't mess around. Look.' He took one of my hands, and pushed two of my fingers deep into its gills. I thought I was going to pass out. 'Now take them to the kitchen,' said Prince Charles, and I carried them to Chef, holding them at arm's length.

I would never have had the heart for hunting like the royal men.

After breakfast, the Queen rode out on the estate on a horse that had travelled from Windsor. She returned to meet the rest of the ladies, who surfaced around midday, in the drawing room. The Duke of Edinburgh had already arranged with his wife a rendezvous point and the ladies, including the Queen Mother and Princess Margaret, ladies-in-waiting and other female house guests, drove out with a picnic lunch. Princess Anne was already there, having gone out with the otherwise all-male party earlier.

Stalking parties rarely returned to the castle until late afternoon. One poor man returned hungry for dinner only to be sent back out on to the moors after admitting he had wounded an animal. The Queen was appalled. As a countrywoman, she hunted but could not abide suffering and, once shot, it was imperative animals were put out of their misery. She could not bear to think of one suffering a slow death. 'You must go back out, find it and kill it,' she insisted.

The man didn't return in time for dinner.

As I stood with the Queen surveying the table plan, which needed to be hastily rearranged, she muttered: 'It's very inconvenient to be a gentleman short for dinner.' With the admonished individual still out in the cold, she added: 'We will just have to invite the officer of the guard to take his place.'

So the table plan was restored to its traditional symmetry of man, woman, man, woman. The Queen was always the perfect host, determined that every guest should have an enjoyable time. She ensured all guests never sat next to the same person twice during any one stay. It would infuriate the princess because she wanted to sit next to Prince Charles all the time but the rotation system put them further and further apart. The Queen is expert at keeping a strict mental note of who sits where and with whom, and ensures that as many different people as possible converse and mix. She also avoids having thirteen guests around one table. It is one of the unwritten royal rules. When there is no avoiding such a number, the seating arrangement is manipulated to avoid thirteen guests together. A crank-like key is turned to operate a winding mechanism that can lengthen the table top, creating gaps into which new mahogany 'leaves' are inserted. When the dreaded thirteen arises, it is lengthened but a gap is left, creating a split down the middle. There is then one table of seven, one of six.

The Queen always said that a group of thirteen was reserved for Christ and his disciples.

Her Majesty, head of the Church of England and Defender of the Faith, is deeply religious: she attends morning worship every Sunday wherever she is in the world. She spends only one Sunday a year at Buckingham Palace – Remembrance Sunday. At all other times, she worships at Windsor, Sandringham and Balmoral. Even aboard the Royal Yacht *Britannia*, the dining-room table was removed and replaced with rows of chairs. The Admiral, as captain of the ship, took the service and everyone stood to sing the 'Sea-farers' Anthem', for those in peril on the seas. The predominantly male-voice congregation sang, with all officers and ratings in uni-form, as a string quartet of the Royal Marines band, stationed aboard, played in the anteroom just outside the doors. At church on land, the Queen always placed a £5 note in the collection. Earlier, her dresser would have folded it tight, quarter-size, then pressed it flat with an iron. Then the Queen could drop it into the box with only her head visible on the front of the note. On the most holy day in the Christian calendar, Good Friday, the Queen broke from routine and received Holy Communion from the Dean of Windsor in her private chapel at Windsor Castle, a short walk away from her apartment down the green-carpeted Grand Corridor. Each Easter, a sprig of Glastonbury thorn, symbolic of the crown of thorns that Christ wore on the cross, was placed on Her Majesty's writing table at the castle, sent by the Dean of Glastonbury Cathedral. The Queen always received an Easter egg from Charbonnel et Walker in Bond Street, which travelled the world with her until every last crumb had been eaten. I have known a royal Easter egg last up to six months. The egg was packed with her favourite sweets: a box of Bendick's Bittermints and Elizabeth Shaw Peppermint Creams.

The steadfast, loyal figure of the Duke of Edinburgh stands beside the Queen through everything. The couple are happiest when alone in private after the day's duties have been performed. They have separate sitting rooms, studies and audience rooms to allow them independence, but one master bedroom connects their suites. In eleven years of serving the Queen, dipping in and out of her private world, I never once heard a raised voice between husband and wife. Prince Philip might grumble and be tactless at times in public, but he is a dutiful, caring husband. It is a strange union of the formal and informal. Most of all, it is a true partnership.

When Princess Elizabeth, then twenty-one, wed her distant Greek-born cousin, then twenty-six, on 20 November 1947, they made a vow as man and wife. Six years later, at her Coronation, the naval officer further reinforced that pledge by swearing an oath of allegiance before God to serve the monarch, his wife. He takes it extremely seriously. He knows more than anyone about being married to duty. Within four years of his marriage to the Queen, he gave up the naval profession he adored to adapt to royal life. In his own marriage, Prince Philip observes protocol, and walks one step behind the monarch in public. She leads as Queen to the Duke but, in regard to family matters, the husband leads the wife. Behind closed doors at the House of Windsor, Prince Philip is boss. From deciding whether to have picnics or barbecues – 'Ask His Royal Highness, I don't know,' the Queen would say – to keeping an eye on the privy-purse strings, he is the forthright master of the house in the eyes of staff.

Life can be lonely for the Queen, and the duty isolating, so she leans and depends on her consort as Queen Victoria relied on Prince

Albert. Prince Philip is the Queen's sounding-board, the person she trusts most, a constant source of stability. A warm affection was apparent between them. He always had breakfast at eight thirty and was often still at the table when the Queen arrived at nine. He often greeted her with a peck on the cheek and said: 'Good morning, darling.'

The other side to the Duke was not as endearing. He had a legendary temper, which reduced some valets and pages to tears. He had an awesome presence, which demanded respect, and an expectation of high standards, which was unremitting. He had a trained eye for what had *not* been done. When someone was found wanting, his volcanic temper erupted and his deep voice became a frightening bellow. Doors slammed and the entire floor seemed to reverberate to his furious parting shots: 'You are all bloody idiots,' or 'It's all a load of bollocks.' As a former naval officer, he expected his men to cope with his fire, but with his housemaids he was always kind and considerate.

The newly-wed Prince and Princess of Wales returned from their honeymoon to Buckingham Palace with the Queen and Prince Philip, as decorators and joiners prepared the marital homes of Highgrove and apartments 8 and 9 at Kensington Palace under the supervision of South African interior designer Dudley Poplak.

During the early days of her marriage at the palace, the princess focused on what she intended to be domestic bliss with her husband and was instrumental in the choice of carpets, curtains and décor for the new homes. Most weekends, she visited Highgrove to check on the progress of refurbishment. She also went into recruitment mode for household staff, tapping into the downstairs friendships cultivated at the palace. She soon encountered the prickly politics of personnel issues when, in a message passed via protection officer Graham Smith, she encouraged Maria Cosgrove to apply for the post of her dresser. In the February of 1981, Maria had been promoted as housemaid to the Duke of Edinburgh. She was keen to join the princess but Lady Susan Hussey, the Queen's lady-in-waiting, learned of the approach. Maria was given no choice. She was told she could not leave the service of Prince Philip. So the princess recruited two other allies from downstairs for Kensington

Palace – nursery-floor housemaid Evelyn Dagerly as dresser and Mervyn Wycherley as chef.

In those early days the prince and princess were known for living a quiet life. There were nights out to the opera and ballet, or social evenings with a circle of Prince Charles's friends but they were not party animals or wild entertainers. The princess did not yet have the confidence she became renowned for, or the assertiveness some staff would one day fear. She was still timid and finding her feet in a royal environment but she recognized how lucky she was to be in such a position. Until one day when a member of staff provided her with a short, sharp shock, and she realized she had not found favour with everyone.

The princess had been having a discussion with a member of the household about staff timetables and, it seems, a few choice words were exchanged about who was and was not pulling their weight. The member of staff stood opposite the princess, who was blushing as she tried to take command. He felt he knew better than the nursery-assistant-turned-princess, his new boss. He began to rant and rave. As she stood against the wall, he leaned in and put his hands at either side of the princess's head, palms on the wall. 'If you weren't so fucking boring, then we would be doing more,' he said. Within a few weeks, that member of staff had parted company with the prince and princess.

Nothing hit the Princess of Wales harder after a year of marriage than the death of Princess Grace of Monaco in a car crash on 13 September 1982. Princess Grace, with her daughter Princess Stephanie, was heading through the Alpes-Maritimes from Roc Agel, the Grimaldi family's Balmoral equivalent, to Monaco. Less than two miles into that journey, their Rover failed to negotiate a hairpin bend, flew off a mountain ridge and careered a hundred feet down the hillside. Princess Stephanie survived but her mother died in the Princess Grace Hospital. There would be much speculation about the condition of the car's brakes and handbrake.

The Princess of Wales was at Balmoral when the Royal Family received the news. She dropped everything and attended the funeral of her friend without Prince Charles. It was her first solo foreign trip as a representative of the Royal Family.

The princess never forgot the lady she referred to simply as Grace. She often talked about her elegance and style. She remembered her death as a tragic loss to the world. She had a white, off-the-shoulder, chiffon cocktail dress that she called 'my Grace Kelly dress' because it was 'so beautiful and elegant'.

4. The Queen and I

If the princess was pinching herself over the magnificently surreal world in which she found herself, then so was a certain footman. Often I sat in the seat beneath the low, oblong window of my bedroom, looking out over London from Buckingham Palace, thinking back to the cobbled streets of Chapel Road, wondering what would have happened had life kept me at the Wessex hotel.

I felt incredibly fortunate, working in the shadow of the Queen. And from that top window, the view enhanced the disbelief: looking out across the Victoria Monument and down the width of the Mall, funnelling into Admiralty Arch, the expanse of St James's Park, littered with blue and white deck-chairs in the summer, Big Ben towering on the horizon. If Mum was a huge influence in childhood, it was the Queen who influenced the man I became. Everyone's life is shaped by a multiplicity of people and places, and I was at the heart of the House of Windsor absorbing and noting the examples of the sovereign: her innate fairness, tolerance, serene calm, love of people, and that abiding, self-sacrificing sense of duty.

Where Mum spent her days putting the people of Chapel Road first, the Queen put first her duty to her country and its people. And there I was, a small cog aiding the running of her life. Many times, I wished Mum could have seen me but my job was carried out, in the main, behind closed doors. Staff rarely get credit for running a household like a non-stop performance of choreographed theatre. There are no curtain calls for the backstage crew, but a smile or a nod from Her Majesty was enough for us to feel a sense of huge job satisfaction.

Providing a glimpse of this life to my family was also a huge thrill. How many sons get the chance to ring their mum and invite them to meet the Queen and the rest of the Royal Family? Mum had had a telephone installed at Chapel Road so that we could keep in touch. 'I can't believe you're actually talking to me from inside Buckingham Palace!' She was so excited for me. She would sit in the back room of our house, clutching the phone, chain-smoking, enraptured by the routine of my day. Just telling her about serving tea to the Queen brought gasps of excitement.

In my first year as Her Majesty's personal footman, I couldn't wait for the Christmas Ball when, every other year, relatives of the staff might be invited to either the palace or Windsor Castle.

'Mum, I want you to do me the honour of attending the Christmas Ball with me – and the Queen,' I said. There was a northern shriek loud enough to bring the miners rushing out from the pit-face. But then she sighed. 'Oh, I'd love to, but I don't think I can, Paul. I'd show you up.'

'Mum, don't be daft. Everyone else's mums will be there. You'll fit in with the rest of them, and I'll be there with you,' I said.

She broke the family bank that week to buy herself a simple, long blue evening dress, with a chain belt, which she wore with a knitted shawl. She told the whole village that she was going to meet the Queen at a ball. No one knew anyone who had ever met the Queen. Certainly no one had from the Top Rank bingo hall in Chesterfield.

At the ball, Mum was in awe of her surroundings, let alone the royals. She couldn't believe she was mingling in the same social environment as the monarch, the Duke of Edinburgh, Prince Charles and Princess Anne. 'I feel like Cinderella,' she said, 'and you are my Prince Charming!' We had linked arms, and walked in together.

When the Queen introduced herself to the staff relatives, I wondered if Mum was going to hold it together. 'I could do with a fag now!' she said. I held her shaking hand tightly.

'Hello, Paul,' said Her Majesty, approaching us.

Did you hear that, Mum? I thought. She called me Paul. I desperately willed Mum to note that informality, but I think she was dazzled by the diamond necklace in front of her.

But you can always rely on Her Majesty to break the ice, and she engaged Mum in a conversation about miners and Derbyshire. Mum smiled a lot. Afterwards, she said she couldn't take her eyes off the Queen's neck. She had never seen real diamonds before, let alone so many. 'She is everything I expected a queen to be,' said Mum, and that was her introduction to my life. Over the years, she would meet my employer a couple more times at the palace, and once at Balmoral when we accidentally met the Queen walking the corgis on the hillside.

Mum's etiquette performances were slightly better than my auntie Pearl's. I had invited her to another festive ball. Dressed to the nines, she stood rigid and wide-eyed as the Queen prepared to meet and greet the relatives.

Auntie Pearl waited for the Queen to start the conversation.

'I hear the weather in Derbyshire has been dreadful lately?' enquired the Queen, well briefed as ever.

Auntie Pearl was momentarily dumbstruck. Then she said the first thing that entered her head. 'Yes, 'orrible, Your Majesty, really 'orrible,' and overdid a dramatic curtsy.

Afterwards, she was mortified that she had dropped her Hs in front of the Queen. I laughed, and reassured her that the monarch loved regional accents.

Relatives and outsiders were not the only ones struck with terror at meeting the Queen. Even people who worked at Buckingham Palace were nervous at the prospect of an introduction to her, which happened every Christmas. On the final day of residence before the court switched to Windsor Castle, as it did in those days, the Queen's last duty of the year was to meet and greet every member of the household staff, which numbered about three hundred. For two hours, she stood to receive each staff member individually, from the most junior to the most senior, to wish them a happy Christmas. It was always 'Happy Christmas', *never* 'Merry Christmas', to avoid connotations of drunkenness.

But I think drink would have made the experience more bearable for many. Coffee-room maids and washing-up ladies or under-butlers and basement porters could be reduced to quivering wrecks at the mere prospect of approaching a monarch whom they never came into contact with in their downstairs world.

The Queen insisted on this protocol to recognize the work of the staff who made her life run smoothly in every department. Once, when she was asked how many servants she had, she replied: 'Actually I have none. I have many members of staff, but no servants.'

Even the staff introduction was classically orchestrated. The household downed tools and filed into a queue that snaked up and down the backstairs corridors into the Marble Hall on the ground floor, through the breakfast room, into the 1844 Room and to the door of the Bow Room. The line-up was formed in order of seniority. There were scarlet waistcoated footmen, pages with dark blue tailcoats and their distinctive velvet collars, chefs in crisp whites and toques and maids in traditional black with white aprons. Out of fourteen footmen, Paul Whybrew went first, I second. We always thought it was peculiar because we saw the Queen every day, morning, noon and night, but had to go through a ritual of being announced and presented when, later that afternoon, we would be back upstairs helping to pack her rooms for the move to Windsor. It was second nature for us to approach the Queen, but it filled many with a dread like stage-fright.

The Queen and the Duke of Edinburgh stood at one end of the Bow Room and the staff would stand in the doorway at the opposite end until the palace steward called their name. It had the air of an investiture but, instead of a medal, staff received a small present that they had previously selected from a catalogue. Ladies who washed dishes had to swap their Marigolds for a pair of white cotton gloves because all women had to wear gloves when presented to the Queen. Interestingly, the monarch – who always wore gloves for official engagements – received her staff with bare hands.

A royal Christmas is magical and exhausting. Its yuletide spirit often came alive at Windsor Castle when children from the estate, including choristers from St George's Chapel, walked up the hill *en masse*, holding lit lanterns on rods and congregated in the quadrangle to sing carols outside. The Queen stood alone on the carpeted steps on the corner of the Sovereign's Entrance, drinking mulled wine, absorbing the atmosphere. She could relax in the knowledge that she didn't have to wrap her own presents: that was her personal footmen's task.

It was fascinating to be on the monarch's gift-production line, sharing the surprise of what the royal children and other relatives would be receiving. In early December, she selected presents when a shop came to the palace. Store owner Peter Knight brought around two thousand items – toys, games, china, gadgets, home furnishings and kitchenware – and set up a giant stall in one of the audience rooms. Each night after dinner, Her Majesty shopped alone, selected an item, wrote a loved one's name on a note and placed it outside the room to be taken away and wrapped. Paul Whybrew and I chose the wrapping-paper and ribbon, and struggled to wrap the most. There were approximately a hundred presents each year, and it was always a keenly fought contest.

One night, when I was surrounded by Sellotape, paper and ribbon, the Queen popped into the room. I was burning the midnight oil. 'It's about time you went to bed, Paul. You've done plenty.' It took about three weeks to wrap those gifts, and sometimes there didn't seem to be enough hours in the day.

The Queen did not have a tree or a single decoration in her apartments. No cards were put up until she arrived at Windsor Castle. Buckingham Palace was devoid of festive decoration apart from a solitary sixteen-foot tree, from the Windsor estate, in the centre of the Marble Hall. To this day, if you stand at the front gates and look through the archway into the quadrangle, you can catch a glimpse of its twinkling coloured lights.

Our meticulously wrapped presents were torn open after tea at five o'clock on Christmas Eve, as tradition dictated, in the first-floor Crimson Drawing Room where Sir Gerald Kelly's huge 1937 Coronation portraits of King George VI and Queen Elizabeth filled the walls on either side of the marble fireplace. Another giant Christmas tree stood in a bay window in the centre of the room, and a fifty-foot trestle-table was set up down one side. The table was sectioned off with red ribbon, allocated for an individual's stack of presents, with the Queen and the Duke of Edinburgh at one end, the ladies-in-waiting and equerries at the other. As staff, we were always outside the room but the shrieks of delight, the barking of excitable corgis, and an atmosphere of conviviality signified that the Windsors' Christmas had begun. Downstairs, in the dungeon-like cellars that insulated sound, the staff, who had worked till midnight most days, would unwind with discos and parties.

On Christmas Day around the Commonwealth, nations tune in to watch the Queen's televised broadcast. (In those days, it was prerecorded in mid-December.) Windsor Castle was no exception. By three o'clock that afternoon, all members of the Royal Family met in the panelled Oak Room and gathered around the television set. Some sat on sofas and chairs, many stood. Towards the back, the Queen stood silently. By the time the broadcast was finished, she

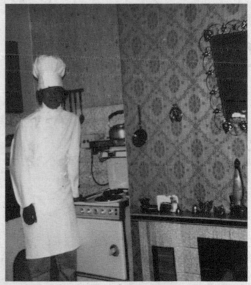

Scarborough beach, 1960

Hanging off Mum's apron strings in
the backyard of 57 Chapel Road

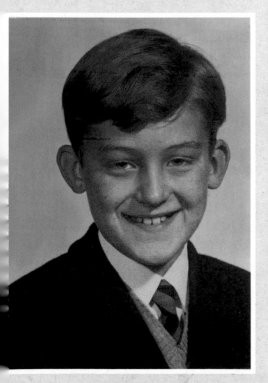

Early days as a trainee chef in
the living room at No. 47

Aged eleven

'Tall Paul' and 'Small Paul'

In the Grand Corridor, Windsor Castle

Royal Ascot

Waiting for the Queen
and Princess Margaret
at the car door

With 'my' corgis at Balmoral Castle

The log cabin where the Royal Family enjoyed their summer barbecues

The Queen and Prince Charles joining the staff party in 1977

Riding in a state procession with Prince Charles, the princess and the Queen

In full state livery

What the tabloids called 'the other royal wedding'

had disappeared into the gardens to walk the corgis. The Queen isn't one for soaking up attention.

State visits brought a special buzz, which broke up the household routine as much as Christmas. The visit of Ronald Reagan to Windsor Castle remains a fond memory; one in which the Secret Service found itself silenced by the monarch.

A week before the president's visit, a fleet of black armoured vehicles drove into the quadrangle to 'sweep' the buildings ahead of what would be the first time a US president had stayed officially at the castle. The Queen smiled as she watched the dramatic entrance of the security cavalcade. She was having none of it. Her message to them was conveyed by a member of the household. 'This is my castle, and if the security is good enough for me, then it is good enough for the president.' It was a fair point.

When President Reagan arrived by helicopter on 7 June 1982, a Page of the Presence and I were assigned to look after him and his wife Nancy in the 240 Suite, which takes up the entire first floor of Lancaster Tower, with its impressive views down the straight mile of the Long Walk.

Even then Nancy was the driving force behind the man. The president didn't need valeting because she never left his side, and his clothes arrived immaculately packed and pressed. All we had to do was be at his disposal. In the suite, we had provided boxes of chocolates decorated with red, white and blue ribbons, but it transpired that chocolate was not the American leader's favourite. Instead, he had brought jelly beans crammed into glass jars. Dozens of them. One table of his suite resembled a mini candy store, and each jar bore the presidential crest. He had a jelly-bean addiction. On the first night there was an intimate, candlelit dinner. Wearing scarlet livery, I was circulating with a tray of pre-dinner drinks in the Green Drawing Room, which was scattered with the American entourage and members of the Royal Family, including the Prince and Princess of Wales − who had moved by now into Kensington Palace and Highgrove. As I waited alongside the president and his wife, I became aware of Ronald Reagan's shyness: he hesitated in going over to speak to the Queen. 'Go on. Go over and talk with Queen Elizabeth,' Nancy Reagan urged her husband, so he did. I thought it was rather nice that even American presidents need cajoling to approach Her Majesty. Mum and Auntie Pearl were not alone.

But at least they got to meet the Queen. I had exchanged a few letters with Bette Davis, the Hollywood legend. When I first wrote a fan letter, she responded and a correspondence developed between us. She wrote to me on 3 August 1984 to bemoan the fact that she never got the chance to shake Her Majesty's hand at a dinner given in her honour at 20th Century Fox:

> We weren't even near enough to see how she looked. It was a heartbreak to one and all, especially since we went out of our way to wear white gloves. It made us all feel that Her Majesty must have thought Hollywood actors and actresses were a bunch of 'social bums' . . . but I feel very thrilled when I look at your stationery and see the words 'Buckingham Palace' – Bette Davis

State visits are the royal equivalent of bringing out your best china when a wealthier friend comes round to visit in Chapel Road. The vaults of royal residences are emptied of their treasures. It all comes out: silver-gilt candelabra, and salt and pepper cruets so large that two people must carry them. Not forgetting the gold cutlery from the King George III era. The horseshoe table in the Ballroom at Buckingham Palace can seat 160 guests, many more than at Windsor, with its single 120-foot long and 10-foot wide table. So wide was the polished table that under-butlers had to tie dusters round their feet, climb on top and walk down the middle to position the candelabra and flower displays. On these occasions, the meticulous need for precision was never more evident. Each place setting had to be measured and set with a ruler, the cutlery never more than a thumb-length away from the table's edge, and chairs were neatly set into regimental lines before the Master of the Household inspected.

Banquets were a slick operation designed to impress visiting heads of state, and choreographed to perfection with a traffic-light system operated by the Palace Steward, who sat like a lighting technician at a console with a full view of the room. Backstage, in the service areas, everyone watched the coloured bulbs light up in a vertical sequence: amber for 'Get Ready', green for 'Go'. On green, a calm procession of pages and footmen walked into the room in synchronization from different corners. It was pure theatre to witness, and its seemingly effortless execution belied the mad rush in the background, preparing for the arrival of the next course.

As a child, I was always told never to start eating a meal until everyone had been served. In royal circles, this is never observed. As soon as the Queen has been served, she starts, regardless of the fact that others are being served: it is deemed rude not to eat food while it is hot. In Queen Victoria's court, once she had finished eating, her plate was taken away – and so was everyone else's, regardless of whether they had finished. These days, plates are not removed until everyone has put down their knife and fork.

If the traffic-light system is a more modern feature of backstairs life, then the permitted spying is not: the Grille remains a feature from a bygone age. It is an ornate latticed screen that covers a back wall in the palace Ballroom. From behind the partition, staff stand and watch the spectacle of a banquet, dozens of eyes from a downstairs world spying discreetly, with permission, on the great and the good in their finest attire.

On one occasion, I wished there was a protocol procedure for the ground to open up and swallow me. When the Queen is a visiting head of state to foreign climes, the need for perfection is just as great. It was my first overseas tour with the Queen on her first visit to the Gulf States in 1979. On the morning of departure, there was a customary champagne *bon voyage* for the staff, held by the monarch's most trusted aide, dresser Margaret MacDonald. She sat bolt upright in a wing-backed chair. She was a diminutive but immaculate figure with horn-rimmed spectacles, perfectly coiffured hair, bespoke silk dresses made by the Queen's designer Sir Norman Hartnell, and three rows of pearls and a brooch, gifts from the Queen. She was every inch a royal lady, and was affectionately known *only* to the monarch and Princess Margaret as 'Bobo': she had been their childhood nursery maid. To household staff, she was 'the eyes and ears of the throne' and no one crossed her.

She double-checked every detail before departure, ensuring that every dress, hat and piece of jewellery was packed. I had to polish and buff all of Her Majesty's brown leather luggage, Brasso the engraved plates, then tie to each trunk and hatbox a yellow label – knotted and hung at the same length – which read: 'The Queen'.

Miss MacDonald also ensured that my polishing skills on the Queen's footwear were up to her high standards. Her demands were great but she never forgot her humble downstairs roots when, after arriving from Scotland, she had cried herself to sleep because she missed her family so much.

Before we departed for the Gulf, she held court with anecdotes of previous tours. Perhaps we were too enthralled, or perhaps the champagne went to our heads, but the carefully orchestrated organization on my début with Her Majesty came unstuck.

In a motorcade half-way to Heathrow, the Queen's assistant dresser Peggy Hoath turned to her colleague May Prentice and said, in complete horror: 'We've forgotten the Queen's outfit!'

I was in the front seat and have never swivelled round so fast. The women's faces were ashen. We all knew the Queen was due to embark on Concorde within thirty minutes.

On that cold February morning, she was wearing a heavy coat and woollen dress. The one still hanging in the dressers' workroom at Buckingham Palace was an Arabian-style, full length silk design, which she intended to change into before arrival in Kuwait. The chauffeur, who shared our panic, flagged down a police motorbike outrider. Another car from the palace was sent out in pursuit, carrying the dress under a second police escort.

The Queen was held up a little longer than usual in the Hounslow Suite at Heathrow, and Concorde missed its scheduled take-off slot. I had wanted everything to go smoothly on my first tour and it had been such a stupid mistake for us to make, but the Queen, as tolerant as ever, chuckled over the desperate measures taken to retrieve her dress. She was smiling when she was escorted to the aircraft steps by the Lord Chamberlain, who, by tradition, is the last person to whom the Queen says goodbye on departure, and the first she greets on arrival back home.

It was the Queen's first time on Concorde, my first flight overseas after childhood holidays in Skegness, Scarborough and Newquay. I sat next to the Duke of Edinburgh's valet, Barry Lovell, as we soared into the air and reached 'the purple corridor' – the Queen's exclusive airspace where no other aircraft is allowed to fly. Usually we flew in British Airways Tri-Stars on long-haul flights, and their first-class sections were refitted to the Queen's specifications: new carpets, a dining-table, sofas, chairs and beds. The economy section became a first-class service for the staff, who reclined across the rows of empty seats.

Having been met by the Emir of Kuwait, the Queen entertained a succession of Arab rulers aboard *Britannia* and the Royal Yacht became a treasure ship as each ruler tried to outdo the previous guest with more and more lavish gifts: Persian rugs, suites of jewellery with sapphires and diamonds, gold camels in lapis-lazuli bases and a gold water pitcher in the shape of a falcon.

In later years, staff were given generous gifts by the host in thanks for their hard work. On a tour to Jordan with the Queen, I was handed a gold Omega watch with the King's crest on its face, medals for service such as the Order of the Lion from Malawi, and a silver decoration from the King of Sweden.

In Kuwait, I boarded for the first time the floating palace of the Royal Yacht *Britannia*, with its own state apartments. It was a magnificent sight to see her fully dressed with five standards fluttering from different masts, and a string of flags strewn from for'ard to aft. No matter how many times I stepped into its interior splendour, I had to keep reminding myself it was a yacht and not a country house, such was its size and the luxury on the boat deck, upper deck and main deck. We set sail in glorious sunshine into Bahrain, having been allowed to sunbathe on the funnel deck.

The Queen was at her most relaxed when *Britannia* ruled the waves, but that regal calm slipped as she walked down the steep gangway to go ashore for dinner. It was the only time I ever saw her lose her composure. She was wearing a turquoise silk evening dress, with a diamond tiara, and her new evening shoes skidded on the red carpet and she slid the full length of the gangway. I was already on land, standing by the car, and could only look on, convinced the monarch was about to fall flat on her back. How she kept her feet, I will never know. As she slid down, she gripped the handrails for dear life, shouting, 'Help! Help!' By the time she got to the bottom, her white gloves were filthy, ruined by the polish. In the car, she replaced them with the spare pair she always carried in her handbag.

When it came to remaining on one's feet, the Queen was clearly more skilled than I. First, there had been the corgi incident at

Sandringham. Later, on a trip to Kentucky, disaster struck. It was the second time the Queen discovered me flat on my back and had to ask: 'Are you all right, Paul?'

The Queen's interest in horse-breeding had taken us to a stud farm to see her brood mares and yearlings stabled with owner and breeder Will Farrish – who became American ambassador to London – at a beautiful farm with redwood barns and white fencing, on the outskirts of Lexington. I had been having back pains ever since my fall at Sandringham, and regular treatment for a slipped disc. After the flight to Kentucky, a sharp pain returned. Over the next six days, it worsened considerably. Even bending down to pick up the Queen's shoes became excruciatingly painful, but I soldiered on, knowing that we would soon be returning home. Then disaster happened.

On the last evening, with the Queen at dinner, I was walking gingerly down the main stairs that led to the dining room. A sharp pain shot down my left leg, I lost my footing and tumbled down twelve steps. I screamed like never before, until I was silenced by the realization that I felt no sensation below the waist. The Queen and the rest of the twelve-strong dinner party had dashed into the hallway. It seemed that everyone was staring down at me, not knowing what to do. Someone dialled 911, the emergency-services number, and the Farrishes' doctor Ben Roache.

The Queen's dresser, Peggy Hoath, knelt at my side. 'Peggy, I can't feel anything below my waist,' I told her.

No one dared move me until the paramedics arrived, and I just remember a lot of concerned muttering all around. I'll never be whisked to hospital in such dramatic fashion ever again. After I had been braced and strapped to a stretcher, the ambulance took me away with a police escort.

At the Lucille Markey Parker Cancer Center in Lexington, which was also the local general hospital, they spoke about emergency surgery. It had already set aside a royal suite for an emergency in line with a procedure observed wherever the Queen visits. It was the first time a crippled royal servant had slept in the Queen's bed. My admission was afforded the same level of discretion. In the nurses' station, on the whiteboard detailing each patient, there was a margin but my name wasn't given. Instead, there was a crown, a foot and the male symbol as picture code for Queen's footman.

The diagnosis was that a disc had ruptured in my lower spine and wrapped itself round the sciatic nerve, leading to the loss of sensation below the waist.

As I lay on a trolley looking up at the lights, Lord Porchester, the Queen's racing manager, loomed over me. 'The Queen has not taken this decision lightly . . .' He went on to explain that the schedule didn't allow them to wait and fly me home: the royal party had to return without me. 'You are in the best possible hands and the Queen will take care of everything for you,' he said.

Later a doctor told me: 'The centre of a disc is like a shrimp and it has curled its way around your sciatic nerve, which is being pinched, causing the temporary paralysis. We have to release the pressure and remove the ruptured disc. If we don't act now, you may never walk again.'

At midnight, the decision was taken to operate. The first face I saw after coming round was that of Nurse Doris Gallagher. Her words sounded far better than I felt. She said the operation had been successful and the loss of feeling would be temporary. 'You will make a full recovery,' she said.

Still half drugged, surrounded by flowers and fruit sent by the dinner-party guests whose meal I had ruined, I watched a television set perched high in the corner of the room and tilted down. It showed a live broadcast of the Queen's plane taking off from Lexington airport.

Within three days, I was moving around the ward, my home for two weeks, using a walking frame. I shuffled to the next room to see who my neighbour was. 'Hi, I'm Ron Wright and this is my wife Julie,' said the cheery American who greeted me.

Julie was feeding mashed potato on a spoon to a girl propped up in bed, surrounded by tubes and machines. 'Blink once if you want some more, honey,' Julie said, to her eighteen-year-old daughter Beth.

Days earlier, Beth had had a recurrent tumour removed from her brainstem. Suddenly my pain didn't matter any more. She had been fighting her condition since she was eight. Julie finished feeding her. 'Beth has never heard an English accent before. Would you mind spending time with her?' her dad asked me.

For the next eleven afternoons, I talked to Beth. Her mum said she was listening because her eyes were rolling. When it was time for me to go home, I said goodbye to Beth. I kept in touch with Ron Wright and his brother, Claude, and Shirley, his wife who read my letters to her. Three-and-a-half years later, she died.

The Queen had kept her promise to look after me. I never saw a bill for those medical expenses and she flew me home in style in a new BAe 146 jet. It had not yet entered royal service and still needed to clock up more flying time before Her Majesty could climb aboard. I became a guinea-pig and the jet, refitted with beds in the royal compartment, was flown out to Kentucky for one convalescing footman. I was the first passenger to fly aboard the Queen's Flight BAe 146 – even before the Queen herself.

I travelled the world with the Queen – I went to China, Australia, New Zealand, the Caribbean, Europe, Algeria, Morocco – but a special trip was just a few miles away from Windsor Castle, to Royal Ascot every year. It was the Queen's favourite date in the calendar, because she could be engrossed in the Sport of Kings.

In June 1982, the household staff were more interested in having friendly bets on whether the first child of the Prince and Princess of Wales would coincide with the four-day race festival, and whether it would be a boy or a girl. A royal labour, thankfully, didn't take place, so the Queen's mind was on the racecard. She never has a flutter because she doesn't carry money (except at church) but that doesn't stand in the way of her enjoyment. She gets her excitement from trying to pick winners for fun, and seeing the finest racehorses of the flat season in action.

For me, the most amazing experience was being part of the fifteen-minute open-carriage ride from Home Park, down the country lanes, into the course via the Golden Gates and down the famous Straight Mile in a procession that has taken place since 1825. Sitting bolt upright on the back of the Queen's carriage, wearing scarlet livery and top hat, a footman must look straight ahead and remain expressionless and undistracted, but his ears prick as the distant roar of the grandstand crowds grows louder and louder by each furlong pole, and the band of the Blues and Royals strikes up.

Nor is Her Majesty distracted. No sooner have the carriage wheels trundled on to the grass than she is peeping over the side, checking what impression, if any, the wheels are making on the turf. It is all part and parcel of her horse-racing homework to see if the going is soft or firm.

It is a bobbing ride across the undulating track. It was my task to listen out for the first strains of 'God Save the Queen' and then, after a discreet nudge of my fellow footman beside me, we took off our top hats together in unison. All around ladies cheered and the gentlemen tipped their top hats. As the music died down, and the carriage slowed up in the Royal Enclosure, I had to disembark to assist the Queen. Getting off a moving carriage with aplomb takes some doing but I never fell flat on my face.

Once in position in the Royal Box, the Queen, armed with binoculars, was at her most animated, the one place where the straitjacket of duty was loosened. She urged on a horse, clapped with joy and, sometimes, let out a cheer. It was both funny and endearing to see the monarch watching the race on television inside the Royal Box, then rushing out, with some grace, to the balcony to see the horses tearing up the final two furlongs to the winning post.

Lord Porchester was always at her side advising her on form. I was there too, ensuring that Earl Grey tea was served between the third and fourth race. Princess Margaret didn't drink tea: she preferred Pimm's.

The Princess of Wales's timing for going into labour could not have been better. Royal Ascot went ahead without interruption and on the night of 21 June 1982, Prince William, or Baby Wales as she called him, was born at nine o'clock at St Mary's Hospital, Paddington. Two miles away, on the Queen's floor at Buckingham Palace, staff who were among the first to share the news cracked open a bottle of champagne in celebration.

Everyone in the household was desperate to see the baby prince and it was the main talking point downstairs, but the heir to the heir spent his initial weeks in the new nursery at Kensington Palace with nanny Barbara Barnes.

My first glimpse of Prince William came two months later in August at Balmoral. He was alone, parked outside in his large blue pram, covered with a cat-net, in front of the tower on the lawn where a stone fountain stands. Nanny was keeping a watchful eye on him from the window.

If Royal Ascot was the time to see the Queen animated, Buckingham Palace was the place to see her utterly mesmerized on the evening when the latest Madame Tussaud's waxwork of her was unveiled for her inspection in the Chinese Dining Room. 'Would you like to come and see it?' the Queen asked me.

Her Majesty, followed by a pack of scampering corgis, led the way. I walked a pace behind, encouraging the more reluctant dogs to keep up. It was exciting because it was an exclusive viewing with the Queen. The room is, of course, Oriental in style, with red, gold and green décor. The fireplace is carved with entwined dragons and serpents, the central carpet is a Chinese woven rug and there are Chinese lanterns for light fittings. It is like stepping back into the flamboyance of the Brighton Pavilion in the days of the Prince Regent.

The Queen stepped into the darkened room and immediately saw the waxwork standing alone in the centre. Before she switched on the lights, she took a noticeable step back in surprise as she saw the silhouette of a woman in evening dress. She switched on the lights and the waxwork clone was cast in bright light. It was an eerie likeness.

I knew the Queen's face so well and the sculptors had captured every line and angle, even the two wisps of grey hair above each ear. She is well practised at sitting for portraits and seeing the end likeness, but I wasn't and I just stood and gawped at the 'twin' before me.

'It's really very good, isn't it?' she said, peering a little closer at it. It was a strange and intensely personal moment for me to witness the Queen inspecting the Queen. 'How could it be so accurate?' she mused.

She stood there for ten minutes, then gave an approving nod. She turned, switched out the lights and left the room. It was the first and only time that I ever left 'The Queen' standing alone in the dark. After our sneak preview the waxwork was placed in Madame Tussaud's by royal command.

The one royal command that deeply affected the path my life would take came in 1984 when I married my wife, Maria. We had the Queen's unprecedented approval to become the first couple from the royal household to wed and remain together in service. It was a decision that undid hundreds of years of royal protocol, and one that gave us our first taste of national newspaper coverage.

5. The Other Royal Wedding

'QUEEN DELIGHTS AT PALACE WEDDING,' announced the headline in the *News of the World*. 'ROYAL LOVE MATCH FOR PALACE PAIR,' screamed the *Daily Mirror*. The Burrell–Cosgrove marriage made history at a time when weddings were meant to be private affairs in the pre-*Hello!* magazine days.

Having spent eight years in the anonymity of the background shadows of palace life, Maria and I found the media spotlight sending its full beam into St Mary's Roman Catholic Church, Wrexham, on Saturday 21 July 1984. Reporters and photographers from the Sunday newspapers had camped outside Maria's family home all morning and pursued the wedding party to the church to cover what had been dubbed as the 'latest royal wedding'; its headline-making potential was enhanced by the fact that the groom worked for the Queen and the bride for the Duke of Edinburgh.

One cunning lady reporter from the *News of the World* broke ranks and, mingling with the constant comings and goings of relatives at Maria's home, penetrated the house, went upstairs and found Maria's mum, Elizabeth, getting changed in a bedroom. She asked for her reaction. 'Get out, you cheeky beggar,' was the on-the-record reply.

Outside the church, when my best-man brother Anthony and I pulled up, we saw the press pack waiting, cameras at the ready. No royal guests were expected. We were all only downstairs nobodies: Paul Whybrew, the Queen's footman, Peggy Hoath, the Queen's dresser, and Michael Fawcett, a senior household footman. The Queen's chaplain, Canon Anthony Caesar, resplendent in his scarlet robes, helped officiate at the ceremony with blessings and prayers.

Instead of ensuring everyone got to their seats, ushers became minders on the door to keep out reporters. All I was concerned about was that our big day should not be ruined because many friends had travelled north from London. Unfortunately nine guests were missing: the corgis. Not even Chipper was there. But they sent us a Royal Court Telegram, which remains framed to this day. It read:

'*Though we corgis weren't invited, In one thing we are united, If you wish us to placate, Bring us back some wedding cake — from Chipper, Smokey, Shadow, Piper, Fable, Myth, Jolly, Sparky, Brush.*' It had an ink paw-print at the bottom.

The curious reporters never found out about that. They were far too interested in how we had met.

I have Rose Smith, a housemaid on Princess Anne's floor, to thank for playing Cupid. She, like me, was from Derbyshire and had been a fellow student at High Peak College, Buxton, but had started work at Buckingham Palace six months earlier than I. She married my best friend, footman Roger Gleed, and that union brought about her exit from the palace: in those days, it was the rule that married couples were not allowed to work together. She went to work for the Duchess of Gloucester as her dresser at Kensington Palace.

Hanging around with the Gleeds brought me into the same social circle as Rose's good friend Maria Cosgrove, who had worked in the linen room, the Belgian Suite and then in the Duke's suite; the young woman I had often walked past without so much as a double-take; the one who had called me a 'twopence ha'penny toff'. Then I noticed her. The sharp wit, the infectious laugh, the stunning brown eyes and dark hair, her 'mashed-potato dance' — a sort of front crawl in reverse with arms flailing backwards over her head. The romantic air around Balmoral played its part as we sat around camp-fires at badly made barbecues on the moors as Pipe Major McCrae entertained us under the night sky with his bagpipes, while Cyril Dickman rang his handbell and we all sang ourselves hoarse with a collection of Scottish songs. Maria became my friend, then my best friend, and then we fell in love in the spring of 1983.

On weekend visits to her parents' home in Holt on the English–Welsh border near Wrexham, I saw the same close-knit working-class values I knew so well. It felt like home. Maria's mum Elizabeth told me to call her Betty. She never stopped cooking. It was like a pie factory: fruit pies, meat pies, cottage pies, all on plates everywhere. Even royal pastry chef Robert Pine didn't make so many pies. Catholicism dominated Betty's life in the same way that the Queen dominated mine. There were as many images of the Pope as there were pies. Betty also had a little pot of holy water just inside the back door into which she dipped her fingers and blessed herself every time she left the house. 'It protects you every time you go outside. You should tell the Queen, Paul,' she used to say.

Maria's father Ron, a jovial electrician who was as sparky as his trade, sat and told me all about his 'beautiful only daughter' and fired off a round of jokes. When I next saw him, he was a different man. He sat in his lounge with a mask over his face, struggling to breathe with two oxygen cylinders propped up on either side of his easy chair. Ron was dying of lung cancer. That June, 1983, Maria desperately wanted her dad to see Trooping the Colour live from her bedroom window at the front of Buckingham Palace. The staff lift didn't reach the top floor so Roger Gleed and I carried him in his wheelchair up the last flight of stairs. Ron was excited to be inside the palace and so proud of his daughter and what she had achieved. He died four weeks later at the age of fifty-nine.

On New Year's Eve, I took Maria home to Derbyshire and proposed at the country-house hotel of Higham Farm, getting down on one knee with a solitaire diamond ring, which cost me every single penny I had. I wanted her to have the best I could afford. Marriage to Maria meant conforming to one protocol outside royal life in order to keep the prospective mother-in-law happy. I had to be confirmed into the Church of England, but pledge that our children would be brought up as Roman Catholics. The Queen's chaplain, Canon Anthony Caesar, instructed me and I was later confirmed by the Bishop of London. Betty's influence told because whenever I enter a Catholic church, I always automatically dip my fingers into the font of holy water.

With both sets of parents informed, there was only one more person to tell about this great romance. Dog-feeding chores seemed the best time to break the news to the Queen that love had blossomed between her footman and her husband's housemaid. She was delighted for us.

'It's such a shame that she will have to leave service,' I said to the Queen.

'Oh? Why is that?' she inquired. I couldn't believe she was unaware of an unwritten rule that had been upheld for hundreds of years.

'Is there nothing that can be done about that?'

'Well, with all due respect, Your Majesty, you are the Queen,' I said.

A word in the right ear obviously worked. A letter from the Master of the Household arrived to tell us that Maria would not have to leave service because the Queen had intervened and the rule was being relaxed.

In the five years of being a virtual shadow to the Queen behind closed doors, I had got to know an in-touch, approachable woman, who carried out duties of state but relaxed and joked in private, a boss who showed appreciation for the staff she knew she couldn't function without.

A week before our wedding Maria and I were summoned to meet the Queen. I was off-duty and we waited like visitors in the Pages' Vestibule. It felt strange when page John Taylor opened the sitting-room door and announced us: 'Paul and Maria, Your Majesty,' in the same way that I had announced, 'The Prime Minister, Your Majesty,' when Margaret Thatcher once went aboard the Royal Yacht *Britannia* in the Bahamas.

The Queen was in the middle of the room. It felt equally odd to be with her in civvies. 'It's going to be a very exciting weekend for you both,' she said. She handed us a small dark blue box, a gift from herself and Prince Philip. We opened it in front of her and it was a gold-metal and enamelled carriage clock, bearing their personal cyphers. Then she opened the hinged lid of an even larger box and presented us with two china candlesticks, handpainted with flowers. We were overwhelmed. They were our first wedding presents.

'Do have a wonderful time and I shall see you both at Balmoral,' said the Queen. Maria curtsied. I bowed.

We would be working in royal service as Mr and Mrs Burrell.

When the big day came, one special person was missing from church, Maria's dad, Ron. It was a day tinged with sadness for the entire family but it was also a proud moment when her brother Peter, standing in for their dad, gave his sister away.

As the stirring sound of the Trumpet Voluntary on the church organ swept my beautiful new wife and me out of church, we were confronted with a fresh media problem. We could not get from the church door to our awaiting wedding car because there were so many reporters, photographers and others outside. In stepped Canon Caesar and Michael Fawcett and, together, they kept the press at bay. We posed for photographers outside the main door and escaped.

It was a stifling hot summer's afternoon when we arrived for the reception at the Bryn Howell Hotel, Llangollen, where the best man read out cards and telegrams from friends. One was left to the end. It read: '*With congratulations and our very best wishes for your future happiness – Elizabeth R and Philip.*'

That night, Maria and I set off on a two-night honeymoon to Llandudno. We knew that later in the week we would be returning to duty at Balmoral. On the Sunday morning, the newspapers were placed outside our hotel door. We were front-page news.

Balmoral wasn't prepared for the change in protocol to receive a newly-wed couple below stairs. Maria's usual housemaid's room was more comfortable so we decided to share her single bed while corgis Chipper and Shadow slept on the floor. One person eager to find out all about our big day was the Princess of Wales, heavily pregnant with her second child. Maria went to her suite and the two women sat on the bed, chuckling and giggling like schoolgirls as Maria showed off the proofs of our wedding photographs. They had sat there for about ten minutes when they heard a voice calling: 'Diana? Diana, where are you? It's lunchtime.' It was the Queen.

'I'd better go. I'm late,' said the princess, 'but leave the photographs and I'll look at them again later.'

Through Maria, the princess got to know me better: I was the husband of a staff member she trusted. More importantly, I was the Queen's footman and had the Queen's ear. She viewed me as a good ally to have on-side but needed to do more homework first. In the three years since her engagement, she had seen me every time she went to a royal residence, not far from the Queen's side.

That August, the princess still looked for reasons to be among downstairs staff. At Balmoral, she missed London lunches with friends such as Janet Filderman, Caroline Bartholomew, Carolyn Herbert and Sarah Ferguson, who was then dating Prince Andrew. She began to seek me out more and more in the Pages' Vestibule, near to the main staircase. We exchanged pleasantries and indulged in small-talk. The princess, while giving the impression of being super-friendly, was doing what she did to anyone new she met. She was working me out. She said how much she missed London. I inquired about her health as an expectant mother, spoke about the joys of marriage, and how Maria and I longed to have children. All the time during those snatched conversations, there was a nagging doubt in my mind that it wasn't appropriate to be on such friendly terms with her.

At this time, the princess joked that the constant smiling she did in public would make her facial muscles sag. She was touched that everyone still referred to her as 'Lady Di'. 'That should put the republicans in the shade for a while,' she said. She was adamant that her 'Spencer determination' should not allow the media to catch her looking fatigued, sad or nervous. She felt she was growing in stature and confidence, daring to enter social debate about politics. In a letter she sent to a lifelong friend, she reflected on the dichotomy it was to be her: '*It is quite amazing the change that is going on inside me – the Diana bit wanting to go and hide rather than be out in the public eye and the Princess who is here to do a job to the best of her ability. The second lady is winning but at what cost to the first?*'

It drained the private woman of her energy. The glare of publicity made her even more conscious of her image. Worry over whether she was up to the job made the bulimia worse, but Prince Charles was a crutch. She wrote to a friend:

> We are moving at quite a pace . . . I have to get used to being here, there and everywhere. Charles is wonderful, so understanding when I sometimes feel a bit bemused and sad with the pressure. I never realised what a support he could be to me. I am trying to support Charles too and be a mother. Strange to know which should come first. C does actually, but what can I do when the press draws comparisons with us both, making [*sic*] C into the background?

The unsympathetic claimed the princess had no consideration for how Prince Charles might be affected by walking in the shadow of his wife during the 'Lady Di-mania' of the times, but she wrote to that same friend: '*We must also understand it's his first time with another person and crowds scream for me to come and talk to them. Putting myself in his position, it must be so difficult.*'

It was around this time when the princess first confided in me: her first test to see if anything she told me would reach the Queen. I was alone in the Pages' Vestibule, waiting for the Queen to call, when the princess appeared round the corner. Her pregnancy and health were the main topics of conversation again. Then, out of the blue, she told me: 'I'm having a boy.'

I don't know whether it was meant to shock or draw a response but it seemed such a personal thing to say to me. Did everyone know? Was it a secret? And why was she being so unguarded? With Prince William's birth, household staff had been taking bets on whether it would be a girl or boy. I think my wide-eyed surprise was clear. 'I really don't think you should be telling me that, Your Royal Highness,' I said.

The princess laughed. She liked to surprise people. I asked Maria and she didn't even know. If it *was* a test I passed, because neither of us said a word to anyone.

There was no hint of trouble in the royal marriage. The princess was still so in love. She was still writing to her friends about how wonderful her life was.

On 15 September 1984, a boy called Henry, to be known as Prince Harry, was born at St Mary's Hospital, Paddington, at four twenty p.m.

For the princess, it was a special time: 'I have to admit, I feel very chuffed with life at the moment.'

Around the same time, there was another cause for celebration: Maria was pregnant with our first child.

'Paul, you go. The poor girl has been there long enough,' said the Queen.

Maria was two weeks overdue and in Westminster Hospital. I was in constant touch with the maternity ward and on normal duties at Buckingham Palace, but Her Majesty, who was anxious about our baby's delayed arrival, insisted that my rightful place was at my wife's hospital bedside. The Queen's only instruction was for me to ring her page John Taylor as soon as there was any news.

Best-friend Roger Gleed wanted to be with me and we both ran from the palace to the hospital in a thunderstorm, arriving drenched to the skin. From three o'clock that afternoon until six forty a.m. the next day, I never left Maria's side.

On 22 May 1985, I witnessed Alexander Paul Burrell arrive in the world with a piercing scream. The most incredible thing in life is watching your child born. Nothing could ever match the magic of that moment. I went out into the corridor and Roger was still sat there waiting for me. I remembered what the Queen had said so I rang the page with the good news. The Queen, not Mum, Dad or my brothers, was the first to know.

Frances Simpson and Harold Brown, housekeeper and butler to the Prince and Princess of Wales at Kensington Palace, arrived bearing a bouquet of flowers, foam bath and a handwritten note that read: '*What a clever lady you are! With love from Diana, William and Harry*'.

The headline in the *Sunday Mirror* was less significant: 'MARIA'S ROYAL BABY', but reporter Brian Roberts labelled Alexander 'a new royal child'.

The Queen was as amused as we all were by the headlines, and she was keen to see our first child. Not many babies, aged seven days old, could have had an audience with Her Majesty in her palace sitting room. Mum, carrying son, joined an extremely proud dad and stood before a casually dressed Queen, wearing black riding boots – spit and polished by me the previous day – breeches and long-sleeved shirt. She had just returned from riding Burmese round the gardens. He was a working policeman's horse on 364 days of the year, but for one day he was the Queen's ride for her official-birthday parade, Trooping the Colour, and she had been familiarizing herself with an old friend.

Maria curtsied. I bowed. Alexander was fast asleep, oblivious to the momentous occasion. 'It's so good of you to see us, Your Majesty,' I said.

She smiled and approached the little bundle in Maria's arms. 'What tiny fingers,' said the Queen, and she placed one of hers in our son's clenched fist. 'I want you to have a little something from me,' she said, picking up a parcel from the table. She added: 'It's for Alexander.'

Maria opened the box, which contained two knitted cardigans, folded neatly in tissue. Our audience lasted five minutes, but for two parents it was a proud, overwhelming moment. As we left, that special moment was spoiled somewhat by a senior male member of staff who passed us in the corridor and was overheard to snipe: 'He could have worn a tie.'

★

We had left the staff living quarters on the top floor and moved into a two-bedroomed grace-and-favour flat in the Royal Mews at the rear of the gardens, in the south-west corner off Buckingham Palace Road. Maria had left the service of the Duke of Edinburgh to concentrate on motherhood. Our next-door neighbours were Roger and Rose Gleed, and they were happy days. The accommodation, predominantly for grooms and chauffeurs, is situated above ground-floor archways that lead to garages for a fleet of Rolls-Royces and stables for the thirty-five horses that pull the state carriages. Stored in the largest central bay was the spectacular Gold Coronation Coach. The Royal Mews, like the palace, is built round a courtyard and is under the command of the Crown Equerry, whose job is to oversee all modes of transport for the Royal Family and household.

The Royal Mews became a regular stop-off point for the Princess of Wales after her regular morning swim at the palace. A week after the birth, she brought Alexander a knitted, double-breasted matinée jacket. She enjoyed a chat and a mug of coffee with Maria and giggled as she raided our cupboards for chocolate biscuits.

The Queen knew when the princess was swimming. She heard the crunch of the gravel beneath her sitting-room window as the car rolled into the quadrangle so it was difficult for the princess not to visit her mother-in-law. Between the swim and seeing Maria, she nipped upstairs to the Queen. When she emerged she would say to me: 'Is it all right if I pop round and see Maria?' As she drove out of the front gate, round the Victoria Monument and down Buckingham Palace Road, I would ring Maria: 'Make sure everything's tidy, chuck, the princess is coming round.'

My mum and Maria's mum were both visiting when the princess arrived to take her first peek at Alexander. She never knocked, just walked in with a cheery hello. When Maria introduced both grandmas to her, they didn't know what to do with themselves. 'Ah, he's gorgeous!' cooed the princess, as she and Maria gazed at our new son in his carry-cot. When they looked up, Grandmas Burrell and Cosgrove had left the flat and were waiting outside on the balcony. Maria asked her mum why they were outside. It seemed they felt their presence in the room was a bit presumptuous when the Princess of Wales was there.

The princess herself put them at ease. 'Don't stand out there, come on in and let's all look at Alexander.'

Maria and the princess were like neighbours while their husbands were away at work. The princess always sat back in the sofa and cradled Alexander. Over the spring, summer and autumn of 1986, she had started to wonder aloud how nice it would be to have Maria and me working for her. It was five years since Maria had been forced to turn down the initial approach from the princess to be her dresser.

'I would love to work for you, but Paul will never leave the Queen. He's totally devoted to her,' Maria said. The princess noted the obstacle but was determined. Those weekly chats over coffee turned into virtual lobbying sessions. 'It would be so wonderful if you and Paul worked at Highgrove,' she hinted heavily.

Week by week, she got the message across. As a mum, the princess also knew Maria's soft spot. She emphasized the quality of life in the countryside compared to the city. There would be a cottage instead of a first-floor flat, a private garden for Alexander instead of St James's Park and its small playground. She painted an attractive picture of an idyllic lifestyle, which Maria increasingly found hard to resist.

The drip-drip-drip was luring my wife, and I didn't know it. When I was away travelling or at Windsor for the weekend, it began to dawn on Maria, who was alone with Alexander, that life at Highgrove would mean her husband being at home all the time. No more royal tours, no more weekends away, no more Christmases at Windsor, no more voyages on the royal yacht.

As 1986 progressed, Maria began to agree with the princess. Life at Highgrove would be so much better. And the princess would have real friends among her staff.

'Leave it with me. I'll work on him,' said Maria.

On 23 July 1986, Sarah Ferguson married Prince Andrew at Westminster Abbey and they became Their Royal Highnesses the Duke and Duchess of York, a week before the fifth wedding anniversary of the Prince and Princess of Wales.

Unlike at that last great royal wedding, Paul Whybrew had to stay behind at the palace with the corgis and look after the wedding breakfast while I rode out behind the Queen and Prince Philip on the magnificent 1902 gold state landau.

The last time I had ridden through such crowds had been in 1980 on a state landau carrying the Queen, Prince Philip, Prince Andrew and Prince Edward to St Paul's Cathedral for a thanksgiving service to commemorate the Queen Mother's eightieth birthday. If anything, the crowd didn't appear as large as it had for another royal bride but there was still a lot of noise down the Mall. As we rolled along in the bright sunshine, I looked straight ahead, bolt upright as always, and didn't have time to savour the atmosphere because as the Queen's hand performed the customary wave mine was tight round the brake cable as we approached Admiralty Arch for the sharp right turn into Whitehall. It was always a nervy moment being in control of the brake's winding mechanism. It was there to ensure, on any slight downward slope, that the carriage didn't run away and crash into the horses. Thankfully, my brake application record remained intact.

I had forgone a chance to be at the wedding ceremony: I had received a gilt-edged invitation as a long-serving member of staff from the Lord Chamberlain's department. I could either sit with hundreds in Westminster Abbey or take the even more privileged seat behind the Queen on the landau. For me there was no choice and it proved a wise one because, while I didn't know it then, it was my last ceremonial carriage drive through London. As I rode through the streets, Maria took her place in the abbey as a guest, wearing a hat borrowed from the Duchess of Gloucester.

Sarah Ferguson had moved into Buckingham Palace a few months before the wedding. Unlike Lady Diana Spencer who had had to have her own separate suite before marriage, she shared with Prince Andrew the second-floor rooms in which the Prince and Princess of Wales had spent the early days of their married life. The duchess did not suffer the same isolation as the princess because, such is her bubbly, vibrant personality, she surrounded herself with people. If Buckingham Palace staff viewed the princess as the loner who found friendships below stairs, the duchess was seen as the gregarious wild one who spent all her time upstairs, entertaining friends and throwing parties.

She and Prince Andrew would order five-course dinners, and the kitchen staff wondered what had hit them. Even the Queen didn't entertain so lavishly, and as a result the duchess didn't endear herself to the downstairs staff.

'At least the Queen eats at a decent hour. Those two can have meals going up there any time after ten p.m. and we're working ourselves silly to keep up with them,' moaned one chef. Since the beginning of 1982 the duchess had shared regular lunch dates with the princess and become a confidante and friend. They called themselves 'The Wicked Wives of Windsor'. Together, they discussed the dour men in the grey suits of the royal household: the enemy within, as they said. Having married into the Royal Family first, the princess could warn the duchess about the dos, the don'ts, those people she could trust, those she needed to be wary about. The list for the latter group proved rather lengthy.

The duchess, like the princess, wanted to be liked and appreciated by their mother-in-law, the Queen. It is in the sovereign's gift to bestow on a son, on the eve of his marriage, a royal dukedom, and it was significant that she conferred on Prince Andrew the title Duke of York, because it had long been associated with her father, King George VI. The poignancy was not lost on the duchess, who took it as a clear acceptance of herself.

In that regard, she misunderstood its meaning. The monarch had not bestowed a title on her: she had bestowed it on Prince Andrew and Sarah, as his wife, would take it too. The subtle difference shows how pernickety protocol can be, but the grey suits picked up on the error when the duchess wrote to the Queen thanking her profusely for the honour. The duchess had intended to be gracious but, as she soon suspected, there were, from the very beginning, people in the household who were out to mark her tiny faults, and bring her down. The warm breath of fresh air that she brought with her mixed with the cool rising air of the household and caused unrest. One aristocrat called her 'Vulgar, vulgar, vulgar', and one newspaper dubbed her the Duchess of Pork. She was discovering how hurtful life could be in royal circles.

Even among the household staff, she couldn't win. From top to bottom in the royal household of Buckingham Palace, the duchess was poorly treated. It was determined to freeze her out. In the Queen, the Prince and Princess of Wales and, of course, Prince Andrew, she had probably her only allies.

One day, as she walked through the main hall towards the front door at Balmoral, she was as bright and breezy as ever, but as her heels echoed across the marble front hall, a passing member of staff said, 'What does that fucking red-haired mare want?' so loudly that she must have heard. But she kept smiling. The duchess always kept smiling. Outwardly, at least.

Maria was another person who had given the impression of being happy with her lot when, deep down, she was nothing of the sort. Since leaving the Duke of Edinburgh, she missed working in the royal household and, as the mother of a two-year-old son, she found life miserable in the Royal Mews flat. The on-going enticement of man-and-wife employment with the Prince and Princess of Wales at Highgrove provided the prospect of an escape route.

One evening after work she broached the subject. 'Living here isn't easy and you're always away. We need to start thinking about our future, chuck.' There was nowhere for Alexander to play. If we wanted a second child, there was not enough space. She could hardly get one pushchair up the steps, let alone two. Country life was better than city life. She needed to be happy. All this she told me as a build-up to the main point. 'There's a possibility of both of us moving on and working for the Prince and Princess of Wales and having a new life. You as full-time butler and me as a housemaid,' she ventured.

'No way. There is no way I'm leaving the Queen,' I told her.

Over the next few nights, the same conversation ended in stalemate. But Maria's unhappiness played on my mind. I had a duty to the Queen. She was No. 1, and I couldn't contemplate working for No. 2. It was, I thought, a backward career move. Besides, I was a footman and had no idea about running an entire household as a butler. Also, I'd go from travelling the world to being stuck in a mansion. It made no sense.

'Maria, why would I give up the best job in the world?' I asked her.

'For your family, that's why,' she said.

That is the one problem with royal duty: its hours, and the dedication required, get in the way of duty to your loved ones.

Maria contested that life at Highgrove would be better for us all *as a family*. She told me how close she was to the princess, and how they had discussed it in great detail.

Great detail? 'How long have you two been discussing this?' I asked.

'On and off for about a year,' she said. 'Chuck, all I'm asking is that you go to Highgrove and have a look. Go and have a look. Just for me,' she added.

I surrendered. Maria informed the princess and a discreet visit was planned. One afternoon that summer, Harold Brown, the prince and princess's butler at Kensington Palace, agreed to drive me down the M4 to Gloucestershire to see the house, estate and staff cottage. It was a weekday, and the prince and princess were both out. Harold gave me the grand tour, room by room. What a beautiful house and gardens. It reminded me of another Gloucestershire residence, Gatcombe Park, home of Princess Anne and Captain Mark Phillips, where the princess's first household friend and Big Mac courier, Mark Simpson, had become butler. The large, airy rooms had stunning countryside views and the tranquillity was in complete contrast to the hectic pace of London life. I heard sheep and cattle in the fields, rather than the horns and sirens from the Mall. I imagined Alexander and a second child growing up there. The sense of freedom and quality of life on a personal level hit home.

Then Harold drove me the half-mile to Close Farm to see the potential grace-and-favour cottage. My heart sank. It was a ram-shackle, pebbledashed semi-detached house, clearly not lived in for years. It had broken windows, peeling paint, chipped walls and a jungle for a garden. It was derelict. It needed knocking down, not occupying.

'Don't worry, the prince has every intention of fixing it up for you,' Harold reassured me.

Not even my vivid imagination could visualize a satisfactory renovation. How could I leave the splendid world of Buckingham Palace and our first cosy flat for this?

Back at the flat, I conveyed my horror to Maria. But such was her unhappiness with London life that I could have told her it was a grace-and-favour tent and she would have looked on the bright side. 'We can make it a home,' she insisted.

I stood in the palace, saw the Queen and thought there was no better boss in the world. I stood in the flat and saw Maria and thought, She cannot remain so unhappy.

I imagined working for the Prince of Wales, who had a reputation among staff for being particular and demanding when the Queen was easy and laid-back. I imagined Maria working for the Princess of Wales, and knew how friendly and down-to-earth she would be. I looked at Alexander and knew he would be better growing up in the countryside than the city. Above all, I knew family must come first.

Even as I made up my mind, and decided to say yes to Maria, I was desperately unsure. I was gambling with a safe, privileged position, trading it for the unknown. People rarely leave such a senior position beside the Queen in exchange for another royal household. If anything, instinct rather than conviction guided me.

'Are you mad?' said Paul Whybrew, when I told him. He could not believe I was leaving Buckingham Palace, and he implored me to think again. But my situation was different from his: he was single and could pursue his ambitions with tunnel vision. I had a family to consider. My mind was made up. All I had to worry about now was telling the Queen.

In June 1987, at the Epsom Derby, Prince Charles was sitting in a cane chair in the corner of the Royal Box, working on his correspondence. The Queen, the Duke of Edinburgh, Princess Alexandra, Princess Michael of Kent and the rest of the royal party were having pre-luncheon drinks just a few feet away. I interrupted the prince and asked if he would like one. He asked for his usual lemon refresher. When I returned with it on a tray, he leaned forward and whispered, 'The princess tells me you will soon be coming to work for us.'

The background buzz of lively conversation meant that he went unheard. 'Please don't mention anything to the Queen, Your Royal Highness. I haven't told her yet and would like to tell her myself,' I said.

The Queen, in her green Hunting Stewart kilt and a cardigan, was standing with her back to the open log-fire in the ground-floor sitting room at Craigowan House, her small, stone-built weekend retreat overlooking the golf-course on the Balmoral estate where she stays when the court is not in residence at the castle. She had returned from a walk and the corgis were littered around the tartan carpet. It was two weeks since the Epsom Derby.

'May I have a few minutes of your time, Your Majesty?' I asked. The Queen smiled.

'I don't really know how to begin to tell you this,' I went on, and proceeded to get my next words all mixed up.

As I looked at her, a huge part of me wanted to turn round and tell Maria I had changed my mind.

'What is it, Paul?' the Queen asked.

'This is so difficult for me.' I dithered once more, deterred by the Queen's expectant stare. I had been by her side for ten years and had never found it difficult to talk to her until now.

'I have been thinking long and hard about my future for the sake of Maria and Alexander . . .' The Queen was still smiling. '. . . and it is the hardest decision I have ever taken . . .' She could have taken the corgis for a walk twice in the time I took to get to the point. I cannot have impressed her with my decisiveness and confidence for the future. Then I said it. '. . . but I have had a discussion with the Prince and Princess of Wales about going to work for them.'

'Paul,' the Queen said, 'you do not have to tell me. Charles has already told me.' She sensed how torn I was, and broke my unease with a few words of reassurance. 'Look at it this way. You are not actually leaving me. You are simply moving to one side for now. Charles and Diana need people like you. One day, when I'm gone and they are king and queen, you will be back here again,' she said.

As I turned to leave, she added, 'Anyway, Paul, you are leaving for the best possible reason, for your family, and I understand that.'

It was my cue to depart. 'Thank you for being so understanding, Your Majesty.'

From the end of June to the start of August, I carried on with my duties as normal. Not another word was said by the Queen about my departure. For those two months, a household footman worked in my shadow, training as my replacement to work alongside Paul Whybrew.

One afternoon while I was on duty, Lady Susan Hussey, the Queen's lady-in-waiting, asked to see me in the second-floor ladies-in-waiting sitting room. I had always liked Lady Susan, wife of the then BBC chairman Marmaduke Hussey, and the Queen was fond of her. Lady Susan was an honest, forthright woman whose opinion was respected. Unlike many in the household, she was easy to get on with and not at all stuffy or grand.

She was at her desk, signing letters, when I walked in. She asked me to close the door. She started to say that she had heard I was leaving the Queen and then asked: 'Do you think it was the right decision to make? I don't know if you are aware, but everything isn't quite what it seems in the household where you are moving.'

Lady Susan was at her discreet best, but the downstairs gossip was already awash with talk of 'difficulties' within the Waleses' marriage. Gossip must be taken with a pinch of salt among staff but the Queen's lady-in-waiting was issuing a friendly warning and effectively providing confirmation. Lady Susan was well informed about the state of the royal marriage: she had long been a trusted confidante of the Prince of Wales and her 'intelligence' was the best there could have been. All I could do was reiterate the family reasons for moving out to the countryside. I told Lady Susan how difficult a decision it had been but that there could be no going back. She had spoken up out of genuine concern, reminded me how fond the Queen was of me, but wished me all the best for the future.

At the start of August 1987 the Queen's imminent departure for the Royal Yacht *Britannia* and the Western Isles Cruise signalled my last duty day. Everything I did was for the last time: my last breakfast, my last walk with the corgis, my last walk down the Queen's corridor at Buckingham Palace, my last occasion to say, 'Will there be anything else, Your Majesty?' With each duty, all I could think was, How will she say goodbye to me?

She rang her bell in the sitting room and asked if I could take the corgis for a walk. She said it as if it was any other normal afternoon. By the time I returned, the Rolls-Royce was waiting to take her to Portsmouth where she would board *Britannia*. My last duty was to see the Queen to the car, so I stood at the Garden Entrance at the side of the palace and waited. She climbed in with Lady Susan Hussey, and I offered them both a rug for their knees. I closed the car door and stood there. I looked at the Queen in the hope I would get her attention. She hadn't said anything about my last day, so maybe there would be a wave or a smile. But there was nothing. The Queen looked down, then straight ahead, and the car pulled away.

Some time later, I saw Lady Susan Hussey again. 'Do you know why the Queen wouldn't say goodbye to me?'

'Paul, she couldn't,' she replied. 'She just couldn't look at you. It wasn't easy for the Queen either.' The Queen's stiff upper lip could never quiver.

6. Deceit at Highgrove

Highgrove sprang on to red alert. Armed police, guns cocked, stood in the fading evening light on the doorstep and counted down to the moment of storming the house, all set to flush out the intruder whose shadowy figure had been spotted moving near a window in an upstairs room. The beads of sweat that broke out on my forehead symbolized the fear that took hold of me, and a bullet-proof vest was strapped round my chest, an addition to my butler's uniform, but it did nothing to reassure me. The Prince and Princess of Wales were away. I was the first to approach the back door and my hand steadied to turn the key in the lock before I stepped aside. Surrounding me was an armed unit from the Gloucestershire Constabulary, dog handlers with Alsatians, and around six police who patrolled the estate. It was their unit which had raised the alarm by telephoning our home in the middle of that evening.

Maria had taken the call. 'Hello, Maria, is Paul still up at the house?' asked one of the officers.

'No, he's been home about ten minutes. I'll put him on.'

I took the receiver.

'Paul, is anyone else in the house?'

'No. I've just locked up.'

Then the policeman knew something was wrong. 'Well, a light has just gone on on the landing. One of the guys in the backyard noticed a figure in the window, and he thought it was you. You'd better come up.'

As I made my way to the police post near the house, an urgent call for assistance was put out for the attendance of the dog-handlers and an armed-response unit. When the entire collection of police came together, bulletproof vests were handed out.

'Right. Keep at the back of us,' whispered an officer, as the back door was pushed open. The police went off in different directions. They were armed with guns. I was armed with the layout of the house for what would be a perfectly executed search. The officers swept through each floor, starting at the basement and walking stealthily, landing by landing, room by room. The nature of the *Starsky and Hutch*-style flush-'em-out operation was funny, looking back, but at the time the police could not have been more deadly serious. My heart was in my mouth.

As we crept on to the top floor, I pointed out William and Harry's bedroom, the nanny's room and the day nursery. Suddenly the two dogs began to snarl. 'They're getting something,' said one handler.

Everyone was convinced that someone was in the house. Each top-floor room was checked, but there was nothing.

Then the armed officers peeled off and climbed into the loft-space. Nothing.

On to the roof. Nothing.

The officer who had spotted the movement in the house was bewildered. He was convinced it had been me. Only a check-call to the house told him otherwise. He couldn't understand or explain it. Both the prince and princess were informed of the incident but it was put down to a mistaken report. It remains a rather spooky mystery.

As soon as I arrived at Highgrove, only one thing reminded me of 'home': the wooden box fixed to the wall in the butler's pantry. Like the Queen, Prince Charles called staff by pressing a bell and a little red circular disc dropped, like a miniature car-park barrier, into a small round window. At Highgrove, that red disc might as well have been a warning flag heralded by an urgent klaxon rather than a bell because Prince Charles never liked to be kept waiting. You should have been there fifteen seconds ago. From the ground-floor pantry, it was a stop-watch dash across the carpeted corridor and into his rooms.

Whenever the princess saw me hurrying to him, it tickled her. 'Go on, run along! Run!' She laughed. 'You don't run that fast for me!'

I didn't *need* to run that fast for the princess. Or for the monarch. But everyone in the household staff knew how exacting Prince Charles could be. Even the princess knew how demanding her husband was, and how high his standards were. That was why she enjoyed making fun of me rushing at his beck and call, and especially when I had to go out on the rooftop in all weathers to raise his standard. His flag had to fly when he was in residence. The Queen had a flag sergeant for this job, but at Highgrove it was my task. I had a million and one other duties, but the prince insisted. When word was telephoned through that he was five minutes away, the rooftop circus routine began. I climbed into the dark attic via a ceiling hatch on the nursery landing then squeezed, on my knees, through another hatch that led out to the grey-tiled, sloping roof. A wooden gantry, with a handrail to one side, ran along the curved ridge for me to walk on. For 'gantry', read 'plank'. For 'walk', read 'dice with death'. In gale-force winds and driving rain, that white flagpole became my stabilizer. I waited and waited, and hung on, for the car or helicopter to come into view before I had the flag up and fluttering. Thankfully, the standard of the Princess of Wales did not have to fly when she was alone in residence. Of that, she always reminded me.

When the red disc dropped into the box window, I had to drop everything and make my way to the library, whose window, behind Balmoral tartan curtains and limed wood shutters, looked out on to the immaculate gardens and terrace at the back of the house. The prince was invariably sitting at a round table in the middle of the room in a basket-weave chair. The room was suffused with the scent of white Longi lilies in the table's centre, sprouting from a vase hidden by piles of books, with just enough space clear for him to write letters. He stood up and told me a 'very special visitor' was coming to Highgrove that summer's day. 'Queen Elizabeth will be arriving this afternoon,' he said. The Queen Mother was always referred to as 'Queen Elizabeth' by the family when addressing staff. It was her first visit to Highgrove, in July 1988. I knew how important the occasion was for the prince, who famously adored his granny. A special five o'clock tea – which, unlike his mother, the prince never had – was planned. I set a table on the terrace and put up a parasol to shield the Queen Mother from the hot sun. I wanted it to be perfect.

As the Daimler crawled up the sweeping gravel driveway, I stood with him on the two stone steps at the central stone porch where white double doors led into the three-storey, eighteenth-century home. I opened the car door and the Queen Mother, wearing a large hat with silk roses in its deep brim, climbed out. Her grandson bowed, took her hand, and kissed it. 'Welcome, darling Granny,' he said, and they went inside before enjoying a slow walk around the prized maze of gardens he had designed and created.

In the kitchen, chef Chris Barber and I busied ourselves with the production of smoked-salmon, chicken, ham and cucumber sandwiches, cut into squares with crusts removed, together with the tiny circular jam sandwiches, known as 'jam pennies', a favourite in the royal nursery.

I walked through the french windows and out on to the back terrace where the fanned branches of an ancient cedar tree cast a shadow over the stone flags, with two pepperpot-shaped Gothic pavilions in each corner, at forty-five degrees to the octagonal pond in the middle.

At the table, set in the centre of the terrace, I offered the Queen Mother a smoked-salmon sandwich. She hesitated. 'No, thank you, Paul. Do you know, they are my *least* favourite,' she said, tilting her head to one side as she often did when she spoke.

The prince looked mortified. 'Would you like something else, Granny?' he said.

'No, tea is fine,' she said, hand raised, palm forward. She didn't eat one sandwich that day.

A couple of hours later, the Queen Mother got back to her Daimler, took out a cream chiffon headscarf and draped it out of the partially opened rear window. It signalled the start of the farewell ritual between grandmother and grandson. As he saw the headscarf drop from the window, the prince took the handkerchief from the breast pocket of his blazer, held it by one corner between his thumb and forefinger and waved it in response. He was visibly moved. 'I don't know what I would do without her,' he said, as the car disappeared down the drive, its wheels kicking up dust. He stood there waving his handkerchief until she had disappeared out of view and then we turned and went back inside.

Then the mood changed. From reflection to reproof. I had turned into the hallway after closing the front doors behind me. 'Such a pity that tea was ruined,' said the prince.

It seemed that the Queen Mother's staff at Clarence House – William Tallon, the Palace Steward, and Reginald Wilcox, the page – *should* have been consulted. 'Next time, would you please ring

William or Reg and find out what Queen Elizabeth likes instead of guessing,' he added.

'I'm terribly sorry, Your Royal Highness. Smoked salmon is always served at royal teas.'

It was a futile protest. In his eyes it had been a failure, and his cutting remarks had the desired effect. They made me feel lousy. One smoked-salmon sandwich and a visit from the Queen Mother made me realize the stark difference between life at Highgrove and life at Buckingham Palace. Serving the heir to the throne was going to be more challenging than serving the monarch.

It's hard to say what the prince did more of: write memos or shake people's hands. For a man so concerned about environmental issues, a small forest could have been chopped down to supply Highgrove with memorandum pads. The Queen never left me memos with instructions. She preferred to tell me. Prince Charles wrote everything down. Memos rained like confetti at Highgrove.

Did someone pick up the seeds for the garden?

Is there a bottle bank in Tetbury?

Can you get someone to look at my telephone?

Could the china dish be mended, please?

Nor, it seemed, was he inclined to do much for himself. He wrote once: '*A letter from the Queen must have fallen by accident into the wastepaper basket beside the table in the library. Please look for it.*' Then, after the Andrew Morton book was serialized in the *Sunday Times*, he left a memo stating: '*I never want to see that paper in this house again! As for the tabloids, I don't want to see any of them either. If anyone wants them, they will have to find them themselves – and that includes Her Royal Highness!*'

My duty began at Highgrove, a mile from the town of Tetbury in Gloucestershire, on 1 September 1987. The Prince and Princess of Wales were in Spain as guests of King Juan Carlos before heading to Balmoral. It would not be until the second week of October that I saw my new employers. I had five weeks to familiarize myself with the strange house and a different way of life. Without Wendy Berry, the housekeeper, I don't know what I would have done. I knew her son, James, a footman at Buckingham Palace. She had got the job at Highgrove when he moved as an under-butler to Kensington Palace and recommended his mother for the post of housekeeper. Working alongside her was like being on probation again, training in her shadow. I had transferred from the capital without Maria and Alex at first so I moved in with Wendy at her grace-and-favour single-storey, stone-built gate lodge, at the bottom of the driveway.

We held the fort at Highgrove but, with its master and mistress away, the house was closed down. The furniture was covered with dust sheets. Wooden shutters were latched down for security reasons at the great windows on the ground floor. It was like living in a deserted house. It was strange going from the constant occupation of Buckingham Palace, with its background noise and downstairs life teeming with staff, to the emptiness and silence of an unoccupied Highgrove in the middle of arable countryside. We rattled around the building like lost souls. Instead of wild after-duty parties, I shared a bottle of wine and a quiet chat in Wendy's company. Among the outdoor staff, there were other friendly faces, especially the estate's groom, Paddy Whiteland, as old as some of the rosewood furniture. In fact, he had come with the furniture, having worked at the house for more than forty years. Or, as Prince Charles put it: 'We're going to have you stuffed and mounted when you die, Paddy, and put you in the front hall!'

Paddy's knowledge of Highgrove was encyclopedic and his brief was varied. If the prince wanted a tree felling, he told Paddy. If he wanted a fence erecting, he told Paddy. If a flower-bed was messy, he told Paddy. If he wanted to hear gossip, well-informed Paddy told him. The prince trusted his word as much as he trusted anyone. Paddy was a wily old soul and everyone, especially the prince, loved him.

Then there were the gardeners. Dennis Brown nurtured his plants and vegetables as if they were children. With a flat cap on his head and shirt-sleeves rolled up, he was always found with a spade or trowel in the walled Victorian kitchen garden, which supplied organic vegetables and fruit for the house. His colleagues David and James tended the remainder of the gardens, which, on each side of the house, provided a different colourful vista: an avenue of golden yews stood like giant, balled hedgehogs; boundaries of lush green topiarized hedges; the multicolours of wildflower meadows; the carpet of yellow of the buttercup fields; the belts of trees. It was, by far, one of the finest gardens in England.

In September, Maria and Alex joined me. We were now expecting our second child: Maria had discovered she was pregnant two weeks after I left the Queen. Our new home, the ramshackle cottage at Close Farm, was far removed from the estate, but the builders had spent the previous month renovating the interior and the smell of fresh paint hung in every room. But a lick of paint and a new green carpet couldn't paper over the cracks. The garden was still grossly overgrown, the guttering loose and there were broken panes in the downstairs windows.

My first domestic duty was to patch up the windows with polythene to keep out the rain. It was a bleak home, even with Maria's choice of pink and white Laura Ashley wallpaper. Although she had been the prime mover behind our relocation, she missed the Royal Mews and was having second thoughts.

Living in that house, working in a residence smothered by dust sheets, being 110 miles away from the friendships and banter of the palace and with a homesick wife, I thought: *What have I done?* It had been a career gamble and first impressions were not encouraging. It was an unsettling time but there was no turning back. We had to make the best of a bad job.

Wax-jacketed Paddy, who brought the smell of stables and horses into our home, was always there to make us smile. 'If you'll be having a new baby, you'll be needing fresh eggs,' he said. He arrived that afternoon on his tractor, pulling a trailer with a flat-pack shed, which he constructed there and then in our back garden, and six Rhode Island Red chickens. 'Fresh eggs on tap every morning,' he announced. Maria said it was a good job he didn't see the importance of using fresh milk.

When he saw our new green carpet, he said it was grand. 'It's God's colour, so it is. God always paints in green – trees, grass . . . carpets!' He laughed.

If the living conditions seemed tough, the job was tougher. When the prince and princess returned in October, the real test began. The support network of three hundred staff at Buckingham Palace had gone. No longer was I one of two footmen where the duties were shared and two pages provided back-up. I was a butler in isolation, responsible for the running of an entire royal residence, not one corridor and one suite of rooms. Burrell and Berry were the only full-time indoor household staff when there was really enough duties to keep five on their toes.

Staff always knew that the prince was the man who paid the wages. Good wages. The Waleses' staff were the best paid in royal service. The switch from the monarch to heir to the throne brought a £10,000 increase, taking my annual salary from around £8000 a year to £18,000. For that hike, the treadmill went faster. I was thrown in at the deep end. There was no wine butler to decant the bottles of port and claret, no under-butlers to clean the silver or wash the dishes, no footmen to greet guests, take their coats or fetch logs for the fire, no florist to arrange flowers for the table, no one to run on to the roof to raise the standard, no one to do the shopping. All of a sudden, it was down to one butler. No longer with state livery uniforms hung in the wardrobe. Just a simple double-breasted gold-buttoned dark blue blazer, with lapel badges carrying the Prince of Wales's three feathers encircled by the garter, dark blue trousers, white shirt and dark blue tie.

There was one blessing in disguise, I suppose. I went from nine corgis to the prince's two Jack Russells, Tigger and Roo, and the chore of walking them was not, thank heavens, my responsibility. Prince Charles did that. There was no manned switchboard. Even answering the telephone became my job. One day, I picked up the receiver in the pantry. 'Hello, Tetbury [and the number]?'

'Hello Paul.'

I immediately recognized the voice. It was the Queen. 'Good morning, Your Majesty.' I was thrilled to hear her. It was the first time we had spoken since my departure. I couldn't help but ask how she was. And how was my favourite corgi Chipper. And how was—

'Is His Royal Highness there?'

She interrupted me in full flow. I had obviously talked too long, and I put the call through to Prince Charles. 'It's the Queen, Your Royal Highness.'

★

On moving west along the M4, I was told that the prince was 'not intending to use Highgrove a great deal'. It was like Windsor Castle for the Queen and Royal Lodge for the Queen Mother, a weekend retreat. The prince and princess were meant to spend from Monday to Friday together at Kensington Palace, where Harold Brown was full-time butler. At least, that was the official line. But from that first autumn Prince Charles began to spend weekdays at Highgrove by himself. The prince, who brought with him a valet, travelling chef and protection officer, stayed at least three days a week. I got used to the sight of the red Wessex helicopter of the Queen's Flight hovering into its landing position in the paddock a few hundred yards from the front door. A weekend post became a weekday job, too. When the prince was alone, life at Highgrove had the atmosphere of a doctor's-surgery waiting room, formal, quiet, timetabled. He filled his days with engagements and appointments. His lunch guests included friends such as Vernon Russell-Smith, Camilla Parker Bowles, Candida Lycett Green, the Duchess of Devonshire, Charles and Patti Palmer-Tomkinson, and Nicholas Soames MP.

When alone, he could spend hours on end in the garden. I remember him digging out the earth and laying a carpet of thyme from the back terrace down to a pond. He called it his 'thyme walk' and said he'd almost broken his back making it. Otherwise he stayed in the library listening to classical music, which drifted through the corridors, so loud that a knock on his door could go unnoticed. I often walked around the house in step to Verdi's *Aida*. The princess was never a weekday visitor. She stayed in London with the children and lunched at the palace with friends, such as fashion designer Jasper Conran, Laura Lonsdale or Carolyn Bartholomew, or dined at Harry's Bar, Mayfair, with ex-King Constantine (whom she called Tino) and Queen Anne-Marie of Greece. Or she went to San Lorenzo's, Knightsbridge, with Lady Carina Frost, wife of television presenter David Frost. In the week, she had riding lessons on two mornings, at seven thirty a.m., with Major James Hewitt at Knightsbridge Barracks, Hyde Park. At that time of her life she was keen to learn new skills. On other mornings she had what she called 'deaf lessons', learning sign language, or dance tuition in the drawing room.

On Friday afternoons, husband and wife came together when the princess drove to Highgrove with William and Harry, then five and two. They headed back to London every Sunday after lunch, travelling with a nanny, a dresser and a protection officer. The princess viewed London as her social scene and Kensington Palace as home. Conversely, the prince preferred dining with the 'Highgrove set' and used the house more and more as his base, staying the odd night in the capital with his wife.

In royal life, it was not unusual for a couple to lead separate lives. It didn't seem odd that the prince pursued different interests from his wife, which kept him in the countryside. The Queen and Duke of Edinburgh's lives had, after all, run along separate paths and met at regular intersections during their lasting marriage. In my early days at Highgrove, the prince and princess always shared each other's company at weekends. Contrary to popular myth that clings to the late 1980s, I never had to take a dinner tray to the princess in her room. A card-table was set up every evening in front of the television in the sitting room and they ate together. They chatted like any ordinary man and wife coming together after time spent working apart. I read somewhere once that the prince never asked about the princess's week or how she was. Utter nonsense. The prince, civil and talkative, was normally first to start the conversation and took great interest in his wife's work or what she had done that week. If she wanted to talk to him at other times, she always knew where to find him – the library. He sat up late, listening to music, working on stacks of paperwork. The princess retired to bed where she had her own stereo and more contemporary music. As Verdi and Haydn played downstairs, Whitney Houston played upstairs. Over and over again, one of her hit songs was played – 'I Will Always Love You'. (It was not until later years that the princess developed a love of classical music.)

Each night, one of my duties was to attend to the drinks tray in the drawing room, and fill a silver flask with freshly squeezed orange juice for the prince but, to his mild irritation, the princess liked it and often got there first, as Prince Charles reminded me in an official memo: '*Please, in future, could you check the flask of orange juice at the end of dinner because Her Royal Highness tends to drink it all and there's none left for me! C.*' One more memo.

In the drawing room, one of four main rooms off the central

hallway, I had another duty: to set up a small altar each Sunday morning so the prince could take Holy Communion from Bishop Woods, dressed in his robes. I draped a white cloth over a folded card-table and placed two silver candlesticks, with lighted candles, on each side, then placed a small silver salver, silver chalice and crystal jugs of water and red wine between them. It was a ceremony the prince took extremely seriously but the princess never joined him. In the early days, they had attended the local church in Tetbury. She thought it a lazy and pointless exercise if it was not carried out in God's house.

When the princess came with the children, Highgrove burst into life. It was the only time I saw the princess, and the house was filled with laughter, the joyful shrieks of the two boys, running across the wooden floors, the princess chasing them around the hallway playing hide-and-seek, the prince growling like the Big Bad Wolf. By day, as her boys stood at her side, the princess played the piano that stood upright against the plain peach wall of the hallway, next to the door into the drawing room.

In a family atmosphere, whatever the warnings of Lady Susan Hussey about all not appearing what it seemed, I couldn't see huge problems on the surface. As parents, the prince and princess appeared blissfully at ease and no one worked harder than they to provide a warm, happy home for their children. They were an unbeatable team. There was no 'War of the Waleses' to witness. If there was anything, it was an amicable truce.

A lively atmosphere returned to the staff dining room too. It was no longer just two people: there were the nannies, Barbara Barnes or Ruth Wallace, dressers Evelyn Dagley or Fay Marshalsea, and protection officers Graham Smith or Dave Sharp. As staff of the princess, they had a shared sense of humour. The only person who went into a slight flap with the princess's arrival was Paddy. He knew she liked to take a morning swim in the outdoor heated pool, which, in winter, was covered with a giant inflatable bubble. He worried endlessly about getting the temperature right and never quite knew how much chlorine to use. He often guessed, then panicked when the princess emerged from an early-morning dip with reddened eyes, but she always saw the funny side.

The princess was close to her staff and cared deeply about them, some more than others but none more so than protection officer Graham Smith, who was unique in being universally liked. He was easy-going and had no airs and graces, and in later years, the princess always said he was her genuine favourite. Graham was the initial conduit between the princess and Maria when she was first offered the post of dresser and he was delighted to see us both at Highgrove. He developed a cough and a sore throat, then cancer of the throat. Whenever she could, the princess took time out of her morning schedules to accompany him on hospital visits for chemotherapy sessions. His illness ultimately forced him to retire from duty and, some years later, he died. His shoes were never truly filled again in the same way.

Maria was another favourite of the princess. On her first weekend in October, the princess visited our new home and brought us a welcome-to-your-new-home gift: quilted cushions to match the Laura Ashley wallpaper. The princess liked to see a sofa scattered with cushions. 'You're a bit too far away for my liking. I must work on that,' she said.

Unknown to me at the time, she also had to work on me. I was still Maria's husband, Paul, the Queen's former footman, now butler at Highgrove, which was, effectively, regarded as Prince Charles's territory. I was, in those early days, marked as the prince's man, regardless of Maria's friendship with the princess. When the prince was alone at Highgrove, it was my duty to serve him and protect his world. But not for long, if the princess had anything to do with it.

Cushions were a regular gift to friends from the princess. She had a good eye for home interiors. She had overseen the decoration of both her royal residences without requiring any of the baroque splendour of Buckingham Palace. At neo-classical Highgrove, there was a simple décor behind the washy façade of ochre and stone with its Venetian window above the front door. Inside, there were light yellow walls, lime-green upholstery, cane furniture in the library, wooden floors and green carpets. It could have been any large, chintzy house in Chelsea. On tables and walls, there were photographs of William and Harry, and Herend pillboxes. Prince Charles's touch was apparent too: his own watercolour paintings were framed on walls, his favourite Wemyss-ware pottery massed in groups on mantelpieces and tables, plants and flowers scattered everywhere. On a round table in the middle of the hallway, a spectacular dried-flower arrangement was the first thing that came into view. At either side of the entrance large pots contained miniature trees or fuchsia bushes.

It was in the outside appearance of Highgrove that the prince really made his influence tell, showing off his love and knowledge of architecture and gardening. The house didn't look grand enough when he purchased it in 1980 so he added Ionic flat-faced stone columns to the front beneath a new pediment with a round glazed window at its centre. All around the rooftop, he created a stone balustrade surmounted by four stone urns on each side. The house was his sanctuary, even though it is only a few hundreds yards from the main Tetbury–Chipping Sodbury road, reached by a curving driveway that cuts through a red and yellow meadow of poppies and corn marigolds.

The intricately designed gardens were the prince's escape; his exclusive world where he spent hours digging, weeding, planting and clipping. Aside from his other passion, watercolour painting, a once bare garden became the canvas for his true, natural masterpiece. Windows and arches were cut into high hedgerows, climbing roses were teased and trained to grow over a pergola to form a rose tunnel, a grass path cut a swathe through a wildflower meadow. He restored the Victorian kitchen garden, reached by a pink gate in a brick-wall surround, to its former glory. Flowers, fruit and vegetables filled it but the centrepiece was a pond and fountain surrounded by a little white picket fence. There was the woodland garden: a mass of roots, tree stumps carved into chairs, willow screens and bark flooring. At its centre was a giant, rust-coloured Amazonian nude lady. The prince handed me a pot of wax and I had to buff and polish her twice a month. Perched above the figure, lodged twenty feet up a holly tree, there was William and Harry's thatched tree-house, painted red and green, with its hand-made cupboards and chairs. It would become a hide-out and a place of many happy hours for the two young princes and two other boys: Alex and my second son, Nicholas, who was born at sixteen minutes past midnight on 19 April 1988 at Princess Margaret Hospital, Swindon. With the prince's permission, I planted a flowering cherry tree in the garden of our house at Close Farm to commemorate the arrival of our second son.

The prince even had his own environmentally friendly sewerage system installed: a system of tanks and reed beds treated and filtered waste. Even this part of the natural garden failed to escape the prince's attention as yet another memo made clear: *'Would you please inform guests staying at Highgrove NOT to dispose of tampons or condoms down the toilet as they strangle the reed beds.'* All I could think was, How am I possibly going to find the words to tell guests of such a royal command? I have to admit that, when it came to it, I was too embarrassed to relay that particular order. I merely asked guests to refrain from placing foreign objects down the toilet. I didn't have to be as precise as the prince. The prince recycled whatever he could. He asked that all carcasses from the kitchen and any leftovers from the dinner table, including eggshells, be thrown on to the compost heap.

The princess, of all people, knew how important the development of the estate and its gardens was to her husband. From the very beginning, she took a photographic record – stage by stage, season by season. Carefully, and for the sole purpose of pleasing him, she plotted progress and pasted hundreds of colour photographs into leatherbound albums. For those who wrongly believed that she turned up her nose at her husband's love of gardening, those albums are a vivid testimony to the opposite being true. She did it for him. She did it to take an interest in one of his passions even at a time when, as history has informed us, third parties were involved on both sides of the royal marriage.

An A4-sized desk diary was kept in the butler's pantry so that Wendy and I could keep track of the prince's peripatetic lifestyle. It was our arrivals-and-departures logbook. When a corner of the page-a-day diary was filled in with red felt tip, Prince Charles was at Highgrove alone. A thick green stripe told us that the princess was in residence alone and a capital N, for nursery, meant William and Harry were staying. When red, green and N appeared together, mainly at weekends, the Waleses were there as a family. Through diligence and duty, we religiously wrote down the names of the guests who were expected and at what time so that we could keep on top of a hectic schedule in an ever-changing, timetabled world. Names were recorded without so much as an afterthought. I never thought our well-organized system would cause trouble.

This diary for staff use was left in the butler's pantry. It was not hidden because, for its intended purpose of the efficient running of the house, I never considered it to be a secret.

In the spring of 1988, with a red coloured-in corner denoting the prince was alone, the guests for lunch were recorded without the need for disguise: '4 for lunch – HRH, Mrs Parker Bowles, Mr Neil Foster and Mr Vernon Russell-Smith', alongside a reminder that the electrician was coming to fix lights in the library. Nothing extraordinary. Just another run-of-the-mill lunch appointment. In the same way I wrote down 'Emma Thompson and Kenneth Branagh for lunch', 'Michael Portillo for lunch', 'Jimmy Savile for lunch', the only person allowed to smoke inside Highgrove, 'Selina Scott', the television presenter, or 'Mr and Mrs Hector Barrantes for lunch' – the Duchess of York's mother and stepfather. And I continued to note down: 'Mr and Mrs Oliver Hoare and Mrs Parker Bowles for lunch', 'Mrs Candida Lycett Green and Mrs Parker Bowles for lunch'. Or 'Mr and Mrs Parker Bowles with their children'.

Out of the blue one day in August 1988 – three months before Prince Charles's fortieth birthday party, the red disc dropped into the box under the label library and I went to see what he wanted. 'Paul, can you tell me how the princess knows who exactly has visited Highgrove this week?'

It made no sense to me. I had not mentioned a word to the princess. I was confused. 'I am sorry, Your Royal Highness, I don't understand,' and, at that moment, I truly didn't. I didn't think of the times the princess had joined me in the butler's pantry for a sly read of a newspaper, a snatched gossip over a mug of coffee or at the kitchen sink where I washed, she dried. It hadn't dawned on me when I came in from the main house and found her waiting for me in the pantry. The princess's had been a familiar face in staff areas since her days at Buckingham Palace. I didn't know how cunning she could be. Not then.

As the prince grilled me, suspected me and asked me to think, the penny dropped like a lead weight on my foot. 'Well, I do keep a record of the lunch guests, Your Royal Highness,' I said meekly.

'Why?' We both knew what had happened then. 'Why do you write names down in your diary?' he demanded.

It was so that I could tell the police who to expect at the front gate, so that Wendy and I kept up to date and –

'Well, don't. Do not write any more names in that diary,' he interrupted.

From then on I abandoned the efficiency for which I had been scolded. The colour-coded page system was stopped and the page-a-day entries became: '4 for lunch'. No names required.

After the annual family vacation to Balmoral, something else changed. The Prince and Princess of Wales no longer came together regularly at Highgrove for weekends. Only on odd occasions did that happen, and only when other guests were present. Throughout the autumn and winter of 1988 and into 1989, the princess was alone with the children from Friday to Sunday or did not come on some weekends when the prince was at the house.

A distinction grew between what we called the princess's house when she was in residence and the prince's house when he was alone. When the princess arrived with the boys and her staff from London, the atmosphere was lighter, more relaxed. Self-service meals were taken in the dining room, and the long mahogany table had a laminated cloth. When the prince returned, he was waited on at mealtimes and a white, linen tablecloth was used.

When the princess was there, she came to speak to me in the pantry, nibbling bars of white chocolate, which I kept for her in the wine fridge. As she walked in she closed the connecting door into the kitchen. It was a signal to the rest of the staff, a sort of 'Do Not Disturb' sign. The other door, into the corridor, was left slightly ajar and it was not unknown for Prince Charles to walk past and spot his wife leaning with her back against the kitchen top, chatting or, as he viewed it, gossiping. He told the princess not to listen to staff gossip or tittle-tattle, and it worried me that these idle chats might reflect badly on me and affect my relationship with him. At one staff Christmas Ball, held at Buckingham Palace by the Queen, the princess spent half an hour chatting to Maria and me as we stood at the far end of the Picture Gallery. That night, she was wearing a Zandra Rhodes cocktail dress with a ragged hem. I remember thinking that we were monopolizing her company. 'Your Royal Highness, you'd better move on,' I said. People were staring at us, noting that an acceptable five- or ten-minute chat was turning into a drawn-out conversation and the princess and Maria were giggling like old friends. I found it extremely embarrassing on the outside but I would be lying if I said I was not flattered that the princess spent so much time with us. She didn't share my concerns.

In the pantry, she dropped by for no longer than fifteen or twenty minutes. She laughed and joked. She spoke about William and Harry and their progress. One day she was excited because William had lost his first tooth. It was at those times that the lonely princess I had first observed over a Big Mac meal with Mark Simpson reappeared, but this time it was in her own home. She said how lonely she had been feeling, how strong she needed to be, how unappreciated she felt. It was all generally said and rather vague; she gave no details. It was as if she was floating her concerns by me, perhaps fishing for a response or reaction, but none was ever given. I listened. I felt sorry for her, but I just listened. And she ate her white chocolate. She told me she had a 'special friend' no one knew about. Again, I said nothing. It would have been rude to ask.

In that room, when we were alone, she seemed vulnerable, insecure, but when she walked out of the pantry door, she snapped back into a princess, and the staff, especially Wendy, were curious. What had she said? What was going on? Family stuff, I said.

What was the prince like with me when he was at home alone? Well, he left me memos.

Wendy knew long before I did what was happening. I had to find out for myself. Like a jigsaw puzzle without the front of a box for reference, a picture came together piece by piece. My desk diary might have been devoid of names and colour-codes but I still wrote the word 'Private' on countless days in the spring of 1989: a reminder to butler and housekeeper that Prince Charles was staying elsewhere in a private residence. Only his then assistant private secretary Richard Aylard, his personal protection officer Colin Trimming, and his valet, either Michael Fawcett or Ken Stronach, knew exactly where he was.

By late 1989 and early 1990, the truce was at straining point. Staff might have been left in the dark but we were not deaf. On the increasingly rare occasions when prince and princess came together, and when the boys were fast asleep, raised voices were heard in the downstairs rooms, doors slammed, heavy footsteps marched up the stairs and across the landing and there was a deadly silence in an echoey house.

Nor were we blind. I walked into the sitting room one Saturday evening and the card-table I had carefully set for dinner for two was in chaos. Glasses were overturned and broken, herb salt in a dish had been scattered and the white linen tablecloth was soaked with spilled water. The prince, in his silk dressing-gown with his feathers emblem on the breast pocket, was on his hands and knees picking up cutlery from the floor. 'Oh dear,' he said. 'I think I must have caught my dressing-gown on the table and caused this dreadful mess.' The princess was nowhere to be seen.

When the prince was alone midweek, and very often on a Sunday night, the usual dinner time of eight thirty was brought forward. 'I think I'll have dinner early tonight, Paul, and then retire,' said the prince. The card-table was set for one. As instructed, I also laid out the television page of *The Times* for that evening's programme schedule on an upholstered stool in front of the sofa with a remote control to one side, the television on standby. New logs were piled high in a basket beside the open, black-leaded fireplace. A sitting room laid out to give the impression that the prince was having a quiet night in. Until, one evening, Wendy said: 'He'll light it for two minutes and then go out. What a waste.' The prince enjoyed leisurely dinners but, at these times, they were rushed. When the red disc dropped into the sitting-room box, it was time to clear the card-table. No sooner had I returned with the tray to the pantry, than I heard car wheels slowly crunching across the gravel of the driveway and disappearing into the distance. 'That's him gone until the early hours,' Wendy noted.

Prince Charles had a green Aston Martin car for his personal use, which was kept in an outside triple-garage, a converted stable to the rear of the house. It lined up alongside a classic Bentley, with a cream interior, and a vintage Aston Martin, with a silver dragon statuette on the bonnet, which the Queen had given him as a present for his twenty-first birthday. But he drove out by himself with Colin Trimming in the passenger seat. It was those wheels we had heard crunching across the gravel.

I never thought anything more of these mid-evening drives until one day I visited the police lodge, close to the house, where a team of officers from the Gloucestershire Constabulary were stationed on permanent patrol. I had gone there with leftovers from the kitchen as a treat. The comings and goings of the prince were raised in light-hearted banter, and a well-kept secret within police circles spilled out. I think they assumed I already knew it. It was said that Prince Charles, on his mystery drives, consistently performed a twenty-two-mile return journey, eleven miles there, eleven miles back. And Middlewich House was exactly eleven miles away. Home of Mrs Camilla Parker Bowles.

'Oh, come on, Paul, you must have known,' said Wendy, when I returned to the main house with the gossip. I thought back to the princess telling me how lonely she was. The warning of Lady Susan Hussey about all not being as it seemed. The changed routine of more weekends spent apart. The diary. The names. And the princess had seen this. She had known. And all those realizations combined to leave me with a heavy heart.

On her next weekend visit to Highgrove the princess, then twenty-eight, breezed into my pantry and asked if there was anything to eat in the fridge. Living in two separate worlds – one with the prince, one with the princess – meant that the world of household staff was torn by divided loyalties. It meant abandoning the baggage of knowledge from one camp and picking up where you had left off the last time with the other. Switching effortlessly between modes became a robotic function where emotion and morals could play no part. To be butler at Highgrove was to know your place, to observe every detail and not pass comment. Turning a blind eye is a prerequisite for the job. I had intended to remain impartial. Until the day the princess decided to involve me. It was going to be my first test of trust. In that summer of 1989, I learned a secret – until she spoke publicly about it – that fostered a bond for ever.

It was a Friday, a hot, summer's afternoon. After lunch William and Harry had returned to the second-floor nursery with nanny Olga Powell. The princess came into the pantry and got straight to the point. 'I want to ask you something, Paul. I would like you to run an errand for me. I don't want anyone, and I mean *anyone*, else to know about it.' She explained the mission. 'Will you go to Kemble railway station tomorrow afternoon and pick up someone for me?' she asked.

'Of course, Your Royal Highness,' I replied.

'You will be picking up my special friend Major James Hewitt.'

Whatever the prince or princess asked me to do, I did to the best of my ability, no questions asked. But in asking me to carry out such a clandestine pick-up, she took a giant leap of faith. It was a risk, however calculated, to ask me, the former Queen's man and the butler who spent most of his time with Prince Charles. She gambled that her close friendship with Maria would pay off. What she couldn't have known was that I was determined not to let her down. I had known her misery, and sensed her loneliness. This 'friend' brought her excitement and happiness. That much was noticeable.

After lunch, I set off in my silver Vauxhall Astra on the seven-mile journey to Kemble, turning left out of the driveway and on to the A433, which skirted Tetbury, before turning right into a narrow back road that led to the tiny village where the guest was waiting in the deserted car park. I saw him before he saw me: a man leaning back against an open-top sports car, dressed in a tweed jacket with a white, open-necked shirt, and sunglasses. 'Hello, Paul, how are you?' he said, with an outstretched hand. He had been expecting me. He got into the passenger seat and I began the journey back, sensing his slight discomfort.

'I can trust you, can't I, Paul?' he asked. I told him that he could trust me because the princess could.

Privately, the mission excited me. In coming years, arranging secret rendezvous and facilitating male guests became the norm. Those times, those names, those circumstances are irrelevant. But this was my first-ever mission of making a meeting happen, and no one would find out about it. Not even Wendy could know.

I drove into the backyard, then took Major Hewitt through a side gate beside the swimming-pool, through the garden, on to the terrace and into the house via the french windows, which opened out from the hallway that ran through the house from front to back. The princess was waiting for us. She embraced her 'special friend', who was leaving for a military posting to Germany that autumn. She was glowing. 'Thank you, Paul,' she said.

'Just call me when you need me again, Your Royal Highness,' and I went back to do the lunchtime dishes left in the sink.

It needs to be stressed here that Major James Hewitt was a visitor to Highgrove long after Camilla Parker Bowles. Prince Charles had struck the first blow in that regard. The princess merely rose to equal her husband's level of deceit. Of course, the prince would never know about the visitor. It was something I would never tell him. I was the butler at Highgrove but, on that particular weekend, it was the princess's house. Far from wrestle with my conscience, I felt happy to have been of service. Colin Trimming, Richard Aylard and Michael Fawcett had helped organize the prince's private life. I was helping to facilitate the life of the princess. More importantly, I was helping engineer her happiness.

On Thursday 28 June 1990 – seven days after William's eighth birthday – there was a freak accident, which proved to be a watershed in the royal marriage for the princess. That event made her feel more unwanted than she had ever felt before.

The princess was at Kensington Palace, preparing to go to her sons' school play. Meanwhile, it was a mad day at Highgrove where the prince had been alone all week. I served lunch for ten and then had to rush around preparing an evening reception in the drawing room and hallway for the Wildfowl and Wetlands Trust at which Michael Caine was to be guest of honour. Prince Charles squeezed in a mid-afternoon game of polo at Cirencester.

Suddenly a phone rang, and all hell broke loose in the world of the prince's valet, Ken Stronach, who was having serious palpitations over something. He screeched away in his car to dash to the prince's side. Prince Charles had fallen off his polo pony and broken his right arm. In excruciating pain, he had been admitted to hospital. As around fifty guests began arriving for the reception, the show had to go on. As I greeted Michael Caine at the front door, it fell to me to inform him that he had now to step into the shoes of an absent prince. Hosting a reception on behalf of HRH the Prince of Wales was a new role, which, as an actor well used to taking centre stage, he carried off with aplomb.

My usual role took me into new surroundings: from a grand country-house to a basic room off an NHS ward in Cirencester eleven miles away. I became a royal meals-on-wheels, ferrying the prince's food from the Highgrove kitchen and delivering home comforts, replacing the stainless-steel cutlery with silverware; swapping a plain glass with engraved crystal; substituting ordinary white plates with crested bone china; even taking his favourite framed painting of his two Jack Russells – Tigger and Roo – and placing it on an easel in the corner of his room; a little bit of Highgrove to ease his pain, along with a strong painkiller.

That weekend, the princess celebrated her twenty-ninth birthday by driving to the hospital in her gleaming new Mercedes to pick up her husband, his arm still in a sling, and take him back to Highgrove. For her, it was a chance to nurse and care for him, to mother him. Or, as she put it, do what she did best – look after people. But as she fussed, bothered and tried to take control, Prince Charles didn't want to know. Irritated by his pain, he rebuffed her and said he wanted to be alone. She felt utterly rejected and unwanted in her own home. She stayed for less than half an hour and fled back to London in tears. That rejection was, without doubt, the final straw that broke the camel's back as far as their marriage was concerned. No sooner had she made her departure than Camilla Parker Bowles arrived. And Prince Charles was pleased to see her. She didn't stay over. In fact, I don't recall her ever staying over.

Camilla Parker Bowles was seen more at Highgrove than ever before but, contrary to established myth, she did not effectively move in or host dinner parties. From being a regular lunch guest, she became a regular dinner guest or day visitor, with her Jack Russell, Fred, but over that summer she visited on no more than twenty occasions.

If she had been the only visitor life would have been easier, but she wasn't. She was one of many friends who came to lift the prince's spirits or official guests who arrived to keep him busy. Prince Charles was an irascible patient who could no longer write letters, let alone indulge his passions for polo, watercolour painting or gardening. The accident sentenced him to a tedious spell of rest and recuperation at Highgrove for July and August. He spent his days in his library or reclining on his *chaise-longue* in the sun on the back terrace. He was restless and determined that his private audiences should continue, lunch and dinner parties go ahead, and friends visit him. Some, like Nicholas Soames MP or Lord and Lady Romsey, stayed the night, which meant there was another room to attend. The prince was hardly the most independent of people at the best of times but the loss of use of his right arm meant that his valets and I became even more of a household crutch for him to lean on. His irritability grew worse when he tried to learn to write left-handed, penning short letters and notes in the spidery scrawl of a four-year-old. 'I feel so bloody useless!' he moaned one day.

I had never felt so exhausted. It had all combined to create an intense workload. And put me, ultimately, in hospital. My hours, duties and endurance were stretched to the limit due to the round-the-clock attention the prince needed. Before, he had spent perhaps three days at the house and gone away for a day or two, providing me with a natural break. After the accident he was there constantly, and a royal duty became akin to looking after an infirm relative. I worked from seven a.m. to eleven p.m. for almost two months solid.

I had finished at midnight one day and got home with every intention of flaking into bed. Maria found me collapsed on the bathroom floor, doubled up in pain. Local GP Dr Walsh was called and he sent me to Princess Margaret Hospital, Swindon. The consultant said I was totally exhausted and, as a result, had contracted a viral infection. Butler, like prince, was ordered to rest and I spent the next week in hospital in a private room on an NHS ward.

Lying there, all I could think about was getting back to Highgrove. No one is indispensable but, in my mind, no one could run the house better. It is either a strength or a fault but I remain a hands-on person who strives for perfection and needs to do everything himself whenever possible. On the second day, I dwelled on it all, until three familiar faces appeared at the door: the princess and the boys. William and Harry came in, each holding a helium-filled 'Get Well' balloon, and their mother sat on the end of my bed. The princess struggled to contain an infectious giggle. Out of uniform and in a white T-shirt, looking forlorn and not chirpy, the sight of her butler laid up was hilarious. 'I've never seen you so still,' she said, and with another giggle, added: 'You look so pathetic!' Then she did what she always did in a hospital: wandered off on her rounds. 'Let's see if there's anyone else interesting in here,' she said, and went off down the corridor on to the ward with William. I could only imagine patients' reactions, coming round from an anaesthetic to find the Princess of Wales beside their beds. Mother and son met a woman recovering from an operation on her birthday. The princess came back in buoyant mood to 'check on my patient'. She was thrilled with William because he had bought some flowers from a kiosk for the woman they had just met. She talked about the imminent Balmoral vacation, Maria, our children, and life at our new home – which the princess had secured us before I was taken ill. It was a gorgeous cottage on the Highgrove estate that she had 'officially opened' on 10 August 1990.

The Princess of Wales, wearing yellow shorts and a turquoise sweat-shirt, stood in the doorway at the back door of the eighteenth-century stone cottage with Cotswold slate on the roof. As she held open a pair of kitchen scissors above a taut section of red ribbon, Harry rode his bicycle on the grass and William ran around laughing with Alexander and Nick. The momentous ceremony seemed lost on them.

The princess wasn't taking it very seriously either. She stood outside the back door, facing into the kitchen: 'I declare this house open,' she tried to say formally, but giggled half-way through.

It was a Friday evening and I had nipped down from the main house before preparing dinner for the prince and princess, who were due to leave for Mallorca that weekend. I left Prince Charles in his library but he had given us a moving-in present: a collection of his watercolours – one depicting tiled rooftops in Florence, a land-scape of the Italian countryside, a scene from a polo match and an aged-drawing of the HMS *Sirius* sailing ship.

The princess's long-held plan to move the Burrell family closer to Highgrove had paid off. From the basic bleakness of Close Farm, we moved to No. 3 The Cottages. It was a property that can only normally be found on chocolate-box lids. The three-bedroomed house had low-beamed ceilings and roses climbing up the front wall. A white gate broke up the Cotswold stone wall that surrounded it. It was the home Maria had dreamed of and it was perfect. Prince Charles had even had a derelict storeroom converted into a playroom for our boys. The princess had ensured Dudley Poplak brought class to it: ropes for the staircase, borders for all the rooms and new materials for the curtains and cushions, all for free. The property, formerly occupied by the prince's valet Ken Stronach before he moved to

London, was a short stroll from the main house. There cannot have been a more beautiful walk to work for any employee in England. From the west side of Highgrove, the scenic route led under a hedged archway, down the grass path through the wildflower meadow, past the woodland garden, then through the kitchen garden.

I don't think either the prince or I will ever forget the visit of eccentric comedian Spike Milligan who stayed over at Highgrove one Saturday night. He didn't want to be valeted and alarm bells rang when he didn't show for breakfast. We later discovered that he hadn't slept a wink in his four-poster bed because, for some inexplicable reason, he had spent the night stretched out on the hard bathroom floor of the 'Blue Room'. Some weeks later, he sent a specially made china plaque through the post with written instructions that it be screwed to the bathroom floor. The plaque read: 'Spike Milligan slept here.' Prince Charles found it hilarious.

The bell rang and that red disc fell into the box. The prince was standing in the centre of the room. With Camilla Parker Bowles. Both of them were looking at framed pictures leaning in a stack against the wall.

'Paul, where are those pictures that were over there the other day?' he asked, pointing to the fireplace.

His guest smiled at me. I knew exactly which ones he was referring to. How embarrassing, I thought. 'Do you mean your watercolours, Your Royal Highness?'

'Yes – the ones of the tiled rooftops and landscapes of Florence.'

'You gave them to me when we moved into the cottage,' I replied.

He thought for a minute. 'Oh, so I did.' Then he turned to Mrs Parker Bowles. 'Well, we'll just have to find something else for you.'

It transpired that the prince and his guest were looking for pictures to hang on the walls of her home. She had received many gifts from the prince over the years. Even today she can be seen wearing a diamond brooch in the shape of the Prince of Wales feathers. Thinking back, I was helping the prince to select gifts for his mistress behind the princess's back, but I was only doing my duty. Blind eye, no opinion. As taught.

An assortment of jewellery arrived in regular dispatches along with a trusted party heading west down the M4, sent by Genevieve Holmes, the prince's personal assistant at St James's Palace. These boxed assortments, wrapped in crisp white tissue paper, were from Kenneth Snowman, of the London-based Wartski jewellers. He had often visited the Queen with pieces of Fabergé. Now it was my task to unwrap and set out the selection on a wooden tray that I placed on a stand in the corner of the library, covered with a white linen cloth. With me out of the room, Prince Charles selected an item for Camilla Parker Bowles and the rest was packed away and returned.

Yet the prince never forgot the princess. For their tenth wedding anniversary in 1991 – when the media had us believe that deep loathing existed between man and wife – he sent her a keepsake charm to add to her gold-link bracelet, itself a gift from him to her. When she unwrapped the paper, she found a two-centimetre X in gold, not a giant kiss but the Roman numeral symbolizing the figure ten, to accompany the gold W and H he had sent in 1982 and 1984 to mark the births of their sons. Each year, he had sent her a new charm, always gold: a pair of ballet shoes for her love of dance; a tennis racquet for the lessons she enjoyed; a bear because she always had teddy bears; a polo cap; an apple and, poignantly, a gold miniature of St Paul's Cathedral, where they had got married.

The princess treasured the bracelet and kept it in her safe. The marriage might have been in trouble but the bracelet was a special reminder of all the good times, she said.

She continued to send her husband an anniversary card and a Valentine card, even after they separated in 1992 until the divorce four years later. The last gift the prince ever sent the princess was a straw hat trimmed with sea shells. She wasn't sure whether it was a joke or just his bad taste. 'What am I supposed to do with that?' She giggled.

I had thought royal overseas tours for me were a thing of the past: only Kensington Palace butler Harold Brown accompanied the Prince and Princess of Wales abroad. Then one day the princess came into the pantry, told me about a five-day trip to Japan to mark the Emperor's Coronation and asked me to join them in November 1990. 'I don't see why Harold should be the one who always gets to go away,' she said.

It was the beginning of the end for Harold and the princess, but it was the beginning of a much closer relationship with her for me even if I didn't know it at the time. Japan was not easy for anyone on the royal tour. The divisions between husband and wife were sharply evident even before they arrived at the British Embassy and were allocated separate master suites on the first floor. They were business partners with nothing else in common, together because of the nature of their work. Frostbite had set in on the relationship, and there was no hint of togetherness in anything they did or said. I saw a different princess from the one I had known at Highgrove. There was an unsettled edge to her personality; tetchiness and frustration. She was highly strung in the prince's presence and snapped at me and her dresser Helena Roache over the smallest things: more towels were needed, the hairdryer wasn't working properly, there was a watermark on a dress. The carpet between the prince and princess's rooms might as well have been made of eggshells, and that surprised me because I had never felt uneasy before in her company. I didn't recognize the drained, flat and weary princess. She had muttered that she did not feel valued or considered, yet the Japanese people adored her. But the princess wanted adulation in her private life. She also felt stifled by the strict protocol of a joint trip and the stuffy attitudes of the prince's household.

'I want to travel the world and do things I want to do and not do what everyone else wants me to do. I want to do things my way,' she said in her room. Joint tours, with their timetable and protocols, placed a free, spontaneous spirit in a strait-jacket. The princess was at her best and happiest when she was away from the prince. She desperately wanted to break free and do solo tours.

I saw the confidence-crushing effect Prince Charles had on her in Japan when she tried to win his approval. Prince Charles and his staff were checking their watches as they milled in the grand hallway ahead of an official function when the princess, looking radiant, came downstairs wearing a Catherine Walker red tartan coat-dress with red velvet collar and cuffs. It was loud but elegant and she was smiling. I was waiting at the bottom of the stairs when she walked to the prince's side and said, 'So, do you like my outfit, Charles?'

His reply was soft and devoid of bitterness, but its effect was brutal. 'Yes. You look like a British Caledonian air stewardess.' With that, he turned and walked out of the front door to an awaiting car. The smile vanished from the princess's face and she looked down. Then she did what she became expert at: she mustered confidence from somewhere and followed him out of the door.

It was not the only time he crushed her confidence, intentionally or otherwise. Six months later, in May 1991, on a joint tour to Czechoslovakia, the royal party stayed at President Havel's palace in Prague where husband and wife not only had separate rooms but stayed on different floors. The princess had changed for an afternoon engagement and, again, came down the stairs to where the prince was waiting. She wore an off-white jacket and skirt, with black buttons and black handkerchief in breast pocket, with black and white shoes. She didn't ask how she looked this time but Prince Charles poked fun at her appearance. 'You look like you've just joined the Mafia.' He smiled. Perhaps it was meant to be a joke but no one laughed. The sad thing was that she always looked stunning, but it was other people who told her so.

Only when she snatched the odd few minutes away from the protocol did she revert to the fun, warm princess I knew. Like the time when she led Helena Roache and me out through the french windows into the embassy garden before she left for the Emperor of Japan's garden party. 'Come on, you two, let's have a happy snap,' said the princess. In all my years with the Queen, I had never been photographed with her informally, yet there I was, side by side with the future Queen of England. As Helena said, 'Cheeeese,' I was momentarily uneasy about protocol. 'I'm not sure this is the done thing. Hope His Royal Highness doesn't see us,' I said.

'Oh, don't worry about things like that. Now, smile for the happy snap,' said the princess, and the camera clicked.

That picture remains a cherished memory. I look at it now and see myself rigid, standing to attention, wearing the Hermès tie the princess had bought me the previous June. (The princess *never* forgot anyone's birthday.) I see her in her three-quarter-length jacket worn over a simple shift dress in the colours of the Japanese national flag with a red disc on her hat to depict the rising sun.

I took the camera and captured Helena and the princess in a similar image, and we did the same on a balcony in Czechoslovakia.

Happy snaps, taken at a time when the princess was anything but happy. I couldn't wait to get those films from Japan and Czechoslo-vakia developed and they went on proud display on the mantelpiece above the fireplace in our cottage alongside another memory, a portrait of the princess taken in July 1990. She had beckoned me to join her in the dining room where, on the table, she had spread out a collection of black and white prints from her first *Vogue* magazine shoot with photographer Patrick Demarchelier. She looked stunning with tousled hair and a high-necked black jumper. 'Would you like one?' she asked, and gave me the pick of the collection. When my choice was made, she took the photograph, leaned on the sideboard and signed it: 'To Paul and Maria, with much love from Diana'. One more smile to hide a thousand inner turmoils.

Her generosity matched that of Prince Charles. That same year, for my thirty-second birthday, he presented me with the first litho-graphic print of his watercolour paintings of Wensleydale. He signed it in pencil 'Charles 1990'; every other print thereafter was signed 'C'. We hung it on the wall above the fireplace where his wife's portrait stood in its frame.

My passport had rid itself of the cobwebs after a small upsurge in foreign stamp marks from Japan, Czechoslovakia and then, in September 1991, to Pakistan, the princess's first royal solo tour. Her wish to travel and do her own thing had been granted and she was free of the binding, merciless protocol of joint visits, away from her husband's strictures on her dresses and outfits. She was on the world stage by herself and determined to shine as an independent royal figure, representing her nation, without Prince Charles by her side. Buckingham Palace and the Foreign Office would be watching.

The princess was in a buoyant mood because the tour had been given the go-ahead by the Queen, who had sanctioned one of her BAe 146 jets to fly to the Himalayas. The princess knew that her reputation as an able ambassador for Britain was at stake so the significance and importance of that tour was not lost on her. Like an athlete preparing for the biggest test, she trained mentally for her duty and focused on nothing other than triumph. Over and over again, she dotted every I and crossed every T of the itinerary and carefully organized her wardrobe to suit different engagements with something simple, yet elegant for each day. She approached me in the pantry at Highgrove. 'This tour is so important to me, Paul, and I want the A-team with me,' she said.

I joined that team, headed by her assiduous private secretary Patrick Jephson, and including dresser Helena, hairdresser Sam McKnight, and a protection officer. Erstwhile radio journalist Dickie Arbiter was also on hand to handle and cajole the media. He was a huge supporter of the princess, who held him in such high regard that she placed him on her birthday-card list.

It was a privilege to be on such an historic solo tour with the princess, especially when its ultimate success and smooth running exceeded expectations everywhere we went: the mountain village of Chitral, the Khyber Pass, Lahore, Rawalpindi and Islamabad. As always, she was the consummate professional, loved the people and made a terrific impact everywhere she went, no more so than in Chitral, in the clouds of the Himalayas, where the entire 500-strong village turned out to see her. The laudatory newspaper and television coverage that greeted the trip gave her such a thrill and sense of achievement. At a time when wicked off-the-record briefings described her to royal reporters as mentally unbalanced, she strode out and silenced them all. As a wife, she might have been vulnerable and needy, but only among 'old guard' could such understandable emotions have been dismissed as a sign of instability. As a royal figure and ambassador for Britain, she was simply untouchable. From that moment on, she went from strength to strength and grew in stature, with her reliable 'A-team' alongside her every step of the way.

Upon our return from the tour, she presented me with an illustrated book about Pakistan. Inside, she had written a special message to remind me of the depth and humbleness of the people we had met, especially at a centre for the deaf. It read: *'For Paul. "There are many who love God . . . they roam the jungles in their search . . . but I will love that person who loves all of God's humanity" – Iqbal. With love from Diana, Pakistan 1991.'* That verse, from the Pakistani national poet Sir Muhammad Iqbal, had been her inspiration and guide on her first solo tour, and it encapsulated the emphasis she placed on the benevolence she took with her everywhere she went.

The memories of that tour were great: the snake-charmer, who reduced her to a fit of giggles as he popped a cobra's head into his mouth; her 'crowning' with a turban as an honorary scout in Chitral.

I will never forget the first day as I stood among the bleached white headstones of the Commonwealth War Cemetery in Rawalpindi where the princess paid her respects to fallen heroes. As she laid a wreath on behalf of the Queen, it struck me how odd it was, as her butler, to be witnessing the event. I was not a private secretary or equerry, whose presence was essential. My proper place was back at the residence preparing lunch or tea but, more and more, the princess had encouraged me to be part of her entourage. I wore suits, not a uniform, like everyone else. Increasingly, in 1991, I found myself getting to know the princess better, getting closer.

In Pakistan, I began to understand more about what made her tick. She told me about a long-term friend called Adrian Ward-Jackson, introduced to her by Princess Margaret. He was HIV positive. She confided her troubles to him. He spoke openly about his illness to her. It was from this friendship that her positive campaigning for AIDS began and her awareness of the disease was awakened. She first noticed the impact of the disease, in what she called 'a major way', when she visited an AIDS unit and opened a wing at Middlesex Hospital. I will never forget what she said: 'Not since TB has there been a disease killing people *before* their parents, and no other member of this family [the Windsors] has taken it up.' She felt that too many people took only a temporary interest when an awareness campaign needed to be constant and relentless. She received hate-letters, asking, 'Why are you so supportive of the gay community?' and felt they were indicative of the confusion she hoped that education and awareness would end.

Cynics have often cruelly suggested that the princess's charitable work was all for PR purposes and she would do anything for a caring photo opportunity. What they never understood was her compassion, her genuine desire to help others, the huge importance she attached to humanitarian work. And when it came to true friends in need, there was no better friend to have on your side than the princess. Adrian Ward-Jackson died knowing that.

He had asked her to be with him at the end, and she considered it a privilege. In mid-August, when their friend Angela Serota rang to say he was gravely ill, distance and duty did not get in the way of her promise. She was at Balmoral but, after failing to get a flight, embarked on a seven-hour drive through the night to London, accompanied by protection officer Dave Sharp, so that she could be by Adrian's side with Angela.

The princess sat with Adrian for four days. In his final moments, as she asked him a question, he moved his thumb in response. It was one of the most humbling and poignant moments of her life, she said, and she was mesmerized by his peace in suffering. Angela lay on the bed beside him as she and the princess said the Lord's Prayer. To understand what this moment meant to her is to understand the princess. It was then she discovered her inner self, the meaning of commitment, how people faced death, the journey of a soul, she said. If her sense of spirituality came from anywhere, it came from that hospital room when Adrian passed away shortly after midnight on 23 August 1991. Then, as she always did in hospitals, the princess went on a private walkabout and visited the baby unit on another wing while Angela stayed with Adrian's body. The princess had seen a life end; she wanted to witness a new one beginning. After that night she often spoke about death and the courage of Adrian Ward-Jackson. She bought a book called *Facing Death and Finding Hope*, billed as 'a guide to the emotional and spiritual care of the dying'.

In the months following the Pakistan tour, I found myself seconded from Highgrove to Kensington Palace as cover for Harold Brown on his days off. For several weeks during the year, I was back in London in a small room on the top floor of apartments 8 and 9, down the corridor from the royal nursery. Meals were generally for one, set on a trolley and wheeled into the sitting room. The princess was curled up on the sofa in her white towelling robe watching *Brookside* or *Coronation Street*. Rather than dismissing me, she allowed me to remain and we chatted. She ate. I stood. When she had finished her meal, invariably salad or fish, I pushed the trolley out of the sitting room, through the drawing room and into the first-floor pantry. She followed me and the chats continued as I washed, she dried. Like at Highgrove. But I was seeing more of her world and a comfortable rapport was developing. She let me in, while Prince Charles kept me at arm's length. When we stood together in the pantry at either residence, I was chatting idly with Maria's friend, not the Princess of Wales, even though I insisted on calling her 'Your

Royal Highness'. In spite of that, all the barriers were down and the public princess was gone. In her robe, she was scrubbed clean of makeup. At those times, she was so ordinary, so normal. I was serving two different people, the fantasy figure everyone saw on the outside and the lost girl no one knew on the inside. I knew where the fantasy began and, within KP, where the reality took over.

I had heard much in staff circles about how difficult she could be, how her moods were unpredictable but, one-to-one, there was no one easier to talk with or listen to. All I could think was that Harold Brown had a fantastic job and boss. I found myself looking forward to his days off.

Family life in the countryside with Maria and the boys could not have been happier. Alexander and Nick were settled and, at weekends, loved nothing more than being with their best friends, who happened to be Princes William and Harry, the royal brothers whom their mother called 'my boys' or, when recounting an affectionate anecdote, 'the little chaps' or, when William was a toddler, 'my little man'. In private and in correspondence, both the Prince and Princess of Wales called William by his pet-name 'Wombat'. Harry was simply 'Harry'.

William and Harry, Alexander and Nick grew up together. Two sets of boys from starkly different backgrounds who ran around at Highgrove and, in later years, Kensington Palace. The princess gave us the princes' cast-off clothes and shoes. At weekends, they all lived in each other's pockets.

Childhood memories for each of the boys will revolve around those happy days and years; the same memories captured in our family photograph albums. From the moment we moved on to the estate, the young princes were under our feet, visiting for fizzy drinks and chocolate biscuits, playing in our back garden, riding through the grounds on their bikes, screaming and laughing in the playroom, digging in our sandpit, making snowmen in the winter, splashing about in the swimming-pool in summer. They made us smile as much as our own boys.

William's face was a familiar sight in our kitchen. He would pop his head round the back door, throw a cute smile and say: 'Have you got any chocolate biscuits or sweets, Maria?' He knew we kept a tin of KitKats, Twix and Penguin biscuits, and he raided it as often as his mother did. Alexander's first memory is of his third birthday in May 1988 when we threw a small party at Close Farm and William, then five, and Harry, three, were among the six children who tucked into blue tractor cake made by their parents' chef, Mervyn Wycherley. As Prince Charles played polo in Windsor, the princess stood with us marvelling over the messy feast taking place on a Thomas the Tank Engine paper tablecloth, and took it in turns with Maria and Wendy to cradle our newborn son Nick, then only a month old. The princess gave Alexander a green soldier's jumper with patches on the elbows and shoulders with a plastic toy rifle and burgundy beret from the Parachute Regiment. She knew that, like Harry, he was mad about playing soldiers.

Very often over the years, the young princes were alone in the countryside with no other children to play with and the princess invited Alexander and Nick to the nursery, which occupied the entire top floor at Highgrove, with William's bedroom, Harry's bedroom, the nanny's room, a kitchen and day nursery with an alphabet border running round the middle of the lemon and blue walls. When I went upstairs, carrying plates of fish fingers and chips for two princes and my sons, I stood there and watched Alexander and Nick munching away with the future King of England.

If the princess and nanny Ruth Wallace took the princes out for a day, Alexander and Nick often went along. In September 1989, after the princess had returned from Balmoral, leaving Prince Charles in Scotland, all the boys went to Bristol Zoo. The surprise for me was that I was invited to take an impromptu day off and go on the first of many family days out with the princess. It felt unusual to relax out of uniform as the princess melted into the crowd like any other mother, wearing a blue 492 baseball cap. The princess, Maria and Ruth, with Nick in his pushchair, strolled together as protection officer Dave Sharp and I kept watch on the three other boys. Ever since the days when the princess and Maria first met at Buckingham Palace, marriage and motherhood had always been the common link that bound them, and shared experiences over the years, with boys who were constant playmates, ensured a lasting friendship. When we moved into the cottage in 1990, Maria and the princess were like neighbours. The princess was both employer and family friend.

Alexander and Nick always said, 'Hello, Princess,' and I thought it odd, in a nice way, to hear them be so informal while their mum and dad insisted on calling her 'Your Royal Highness'. I'm convinced that our boys grew up thinking that 'Princess' was her Christian name.

It helped create an affectionate blend of the formal and informal. When the princess came into our kitchen, Maria flicked the switch on the kettle and asked, as routine, 'A cup of coffee, Your Royal Highness?' and then Nick jumped on to her lap, gave her a hug and asked: 'Where yer been, Princess?'

It led to some classic moments, the best of which was when three-year-old Nick, in his shorts and T-shirt, wandered from the cottage and up through the meadows to the main house. I was on the front doorstep waiting for the prince to depart as his Bentley waited on the driveway. Then Nick came up the path, ignored me and skipped on to the step just as the prince appeared in black tie for an engagement in London.

Nick looked him up and down, then piped up: 'You look smart, Prince Charles. Where you going?'

It was one of those moments when, as a parent, you cannot believe what your child has said and a gap in the earth could not open quick enough. Not that Nick sensed his father's horror. Having delivered such childlike audacity in the face of protocol, he didn't hang around. As he asked the question he was squeezing past the prince to go inside and find William and Harry. Prince Charles couldn't help but smile.

Highgrove, the great house and its acres of land, was a playground for the four boys. I built a ballpool in one of the outside sheds and it was an often raised debate as to who enjoyed the facility more: the boys or the princess. She would sneak up behind William, Harry, Alexander and Nick and push them into its multicoloured depths then join them. The Princess of Wales slipped on to her back to 'drown' quite regularly under these balls and the boys jumped on top and tickled her.

When the princess was not around, one of my more casual duties was to keep the children occupied and we devised a game called: 'Find as many eggs as you can', an alternative version of the Easter Egg Hunt that the Queen organized in Frogmore Gardens in the grounds of Windsor Castle for the royal children. She took a basket of chocolate eggs down to the gardens and hid them in various nooks and crannies of walls and trees or among the daffodils and primulas. It became a race between the corgis and the children as to who would find them first. The butler's version at Highgrove led to hours of fun. I hid clutches of fresh hens' eggs between bales of hay and straw in the barn opposite the stables. Admittedly, it was not half as much fun as finding chocolate ones but the excitement still propelled the winner, often William, into finding the most eggs.

William had a guinea pig and Harry had a grey, floppy-eared rabbit, which lived in a hutch in a corner of the stableyard where Paddy Whiteland kept two ponies, Smokey and Trigger, for the princes. They were taught to ride by a girl groom called Marion Cox. There were also their father's two Jack Russells, the black Aberdeen Angus cows, Prince Charles's polo ponies and the tawny owls in the barn. Carp swam in a pond in the garden, and William and Harry's tropical fish tank stood in a corner of the kitchen. Then there was the hamster, which travelled with the young princes from Kensington Palace to Highgrove. William and Harry came into the kitchen to help chop up apples, carrots and lettuce for guinea pig, rabbit and hamster and they always cleaned out the hutches themselves.

The best part for my sons about having two princes as playmates was the electrically powered miniature Aston Martin soft-top, a toy version of their father's car and a gift from the manufacturers. The British racing-green two-seater was, as my boys often told me, the best toy ever, with its cream leather interior, rosewood dashboard, working headlights, cassette player and leather steering-wheel. Most young boys run round to a friend's house to see if he or she is playing out. William drove, and we got used to seeing him in the driver's seat with Harry beside him when they appeared outside the cottage to take Alexander and Nick for a spin on the estate. William always argued with Harry about who was driving and, as the eldest, he always got his way. He loved cars and motor-racing, and considered himself, aged ten, an expert driver! Until, that is, he tried at snail's pace to squeeze his pride and joy through a narrow gateway that led past a greenhouse to our back door and scraped one entire side of his gleaming car against a stone pillar. Maria was in the kitchen when a panic-stricken William raced in. 'Maria, Maria – there's been a terrible accident!' She wondered what on earth had happened, especially when he added: 'Papa is going to go mad. I need a tin of green paint.'

Maria went outside for a vehicle inspection and had to tell William that a lick of paint was not going to solve his problem. The stone had grated into the metal, leaving a deep groove down one side. William was horrified. He thought about parking the car in the garage with the crumpled side against the wall so that Prince Charles would not find out but Paddy and I ensured he came clean. Prince Charles was not amused that his son had 'been so silly' but the car was sent for repair with Aston Martin and returned as new. William had to settle for driving with Paddy on the grass-cutters until he was back in the driving seat of his Aston Martin. His parents allowed him to continue driving the car because they knew he was safe at Highgrove. Besides, William and Harry, Alexander and Nick had sampled much faster thrills when they went go-karting in London with the princess, tearing round an indoor circuit at up to 40 m.p.h. They enjoyed it so much that, in a far-flung corner of Highgrove, a makeshift go-karting track was built and karts hired for summertime fun.

William and Harry were confident, expressive boys, who were not shy when it came to approaching or talking with the adults around them. Only individual bedrooms separated their lives. They went everywhere and did everything together, even if William was the natural leader by age. They both attended Wetherby's private school in Notting Hill, London, and each arrived home desperate to show their mother the day's artwork. At both Highgrove and Kensington Palace, the princess, who was keen to show she was proud of both boys' work, covered the walls of her combined dressing room and bathroom with untidy pictures of butterflies and flowers made out of egg-cartons, crêpe paper and eggshells.

Harry's passion for soldiers came through in his artwork: he was forever depicting pitched battles around castles with fighter planes dropping bombs from the sky, splashing the page with red to complete the bloody scene. He clearly believed that water balloons were bombs, too, and that his father's prized south-facing garden was the battlefield when a summer barbecue was held. Harry and William joined forces with my brother Graham, visiting with his family for the weekend, and the mischievous trio engaged in a water-balloon bombardment of the princess, who was chased around the garden, failing to escape her sons' sure-fire accuracy. Staff barbecues were a regular treat staged by the princess. They were often held when the prince was not in residence so that everyone, princess included, could let down their hair. Mervyn Wycherley would produce mountains of food for the dressers, protection officers, nannies, housekeeper and butler. It was our night off, said the princess. When it came to dessert she went into the kitchen and came out on to the terrace carrying a silver platter of Magnum lollies and Cornettos. Afterwards she helped clear and stack the dirty plates.

Then came her greatest thrill: pushing everyone into the pool. The shrieks of delight and splashing about signalled the start of a caper that I labelled 'People Soup'. As with the water balloons earlier in the evening, the princess didn't mind getting wet and couldn't resist jumping into the pool to join in.

The princess never tired of indulging in such frivolity. For her, it represented her rebellious streak, defying the impeccable behaviour that would ordinarily be expected of a future Queen of England. Splashing about in the pool in her clothes, she was on the same level as her staff. She loved seeing the look on people's shocked faces as she leaped in in her jeans or shorts, sweatshirt or T-shirt.

But nothing could have matched the horror on the face of the British ambassador in Cairo when I joined her second solo visit overseas in May 1992.

We were on the deck of a riverboat heading for the Phillae Temple on a small island near the Aswan Dam when the princess, on my right looking out across the Nile, turned to me and said: 'Time for a happy snap, Paul.' She pushed her sunglasses up into her hair. 'Now, don't lean in too close,' she said, from the corner of her mouth, as Helena lined up the pose. 'It's been a hot day!' Even with a stiff breeze, she was conscious that she had been sweating beneath her taupe coat-dress, but it was a mischievous comment, aimed to startle, designed for a laugh, a moment captured on camera.

Seconds later she startled me again. 'Now, can you make some-body else happy? I want you to organize a birthday party tonight back at the embassy for Sam.'

Floating down the Nile was not the best time to become spon-taneous party-planner for hairdresser Sam McKnight, but I had learned that nothing was impossible when the princess asked for something. As the royal party disembarked for a short stop-over at a hotel on the banks of the Nile, I sloped off, commandeered a telephone and plotted a poolside surprise.

That night, in the lush garden of the embassy in Cairo, Sam walked down the terrace steps into a chorus of 'Happy Birthday To You' belted out by eleven members of staff, led by the princess, clutching a bottle of champagne in one hand. Even the dour ex-naval officer Patrick Jephson let his hair down for once, acting the fool in a Tommy Cooper-style fez, similar to the ones I had bought for William and Harry as souvenirs, with ornamental Pyramids, that the princess had sent me out to find. Then, as sure as camels are born with humps, high spirits led to high jinks and we all ended up in the pool, fully clothed. The princess was bobbing up and down, letting out drowning yelps, before her blonde hair dipped beneath the surface. Patrick Jephson's eyebrows arched: as the man in charge of her public diary, he was not accustomed to such scenes. Neither was the British ambassador who frowned, when he learned of the mass dip. I think he felt such antics were inappropriate and reckless, especially because two days earlier the paparazzi had sneaked on to a neighbouring rooftop and photographed the princess in her black swimsuit. Fortunately, the lenses were not trained on the late-night 'People Soup' and the headlines focused on another triumphant tour, showing the princess wandering among the giant columns of the Temple of Karnak in Luxor and through the Valley of the Kings, then marvelling at the Pyramids and the Sphinx.

The headlines in Britain confirmed that the princess was an ace card on the diplomatic front. Whatever her personal battles at the time, she was becoming virtually infallible as the roving ambassador she had always intended to be. No amount of whispering campaigns from the men in grey suits could dislodge her confidence or the global esteem in which she was held.

Egypt was a defining moment in my relationship with the princess. She had brought me on the tours, used me more at Kensington Palace and shared the secret about her 'special friend'. Now, in the year that the Queen famously described as her *annus horribilis*, she was drawing me further across the invisible line separating her professional from her personal life. Because she had been a familiar face at our flat in the Royal Mews and then at the cottage at Highgrove, because she was a friend of my wife, because she was a virtual auntie to my sons, crossing that line did not seem as problematic as perhaps it should have done.

The princess was sitting in her embassy bedroom in front of a large mirror on the dressing-table, fiddling with her hair. I had come from the kitchen with a glass of carrot juice. 'How did you manage that in the middle of Cairo?'

'Mervyn Wycherley,' I answered.

She loved carrot juice, or carrot and celery juice. I turned to leave but she swivelled round on the upholstered stool and said: 'Sit down, sit down.' As she turned back to the mirror, I sat on the edge of the neatly made bed. 'Next time you come to London, there is somebody I want you to meet. Lucia is one of the most beautiful and elegant women I have ever met,' she said.

Lucia Flecha de Lima was the wife of the then Brazilian ambassador to the Court of St James and she was, first and foremost, a mother-figure to the princess. Her ambassador husband Paulo Tarso, who went on to become the ambassador in Washington and then Rome, was a father-figure. The princess regularly used their embassy in Mount Street, London, to meet someone. *Not* James Hewitt. In that room in Cairo, the princess told me all about this someone and the meetings they had been having.

She had confided in me again, and more than that, she wanted me to meet Lucia, a key member of the surrogate family the princess had hand-picked to be around her. Anyone could work for the princess. Anyone could feel that they knew her well because her skill was to make people feel that way. But she knew where the professional line was and, in some notable cases, when to dispose of someone's services. Access to her inner circle was by invitation only. Not even Maria, a friend of old, was included. Meeting Lucia and a handful of the princess's closest friends would happen later, but my invitation into that circle came that morning in Cairo.

Before setting off to the Middle East, the princess had been excited by the Catherine Walker dresses designed for the trip. At the embassy, Mervyn Wycherley, Helena Roache and I became the fashion sounding-board. When she emerged from her bedroom, she would ask, 'How do I look?' or 'What do you think?'

We could all have stood there, gawped and told her she would look good in a bin-liner but, instead, we gave a more subdued favourable opinion. She walked away knowing she looked divine, knowing that on solo tours there was no Prince Charles with his acerbic tongue to knock her off her perch. On that trip, she was more friendly and open than she had ever been, but there was sadness behind the confident façade.

The bedroom door she normally left ajar was locked. She emerged with reddened eyes. She said she needed time alone to open an emotional valve. With the Queen or anyone else, I would never have dared ask. With the princess, I couldn't help it. 'Are you all right, Your Royal Highness? Is there anything I can do?'

She smiled. 'Everyone needs to cry now and again, Paul,' she said, and then, with a straightening of her shirt, she pulled herself together, took a deep breath and strode out as the indefatigable Princess of Wales.

Her stoicism and bravery were remarkable, considering what she was going through. The princess was under immense pressure. The father she adored, Earl Spencer, had died in hospital while she was skiing in Austria in March. That same month, the separation of the Duke and Duchess of York was announced. Then Princess Anne started divorce proceedings against Mark Phillips. All eyes were on the publicly strained Prince and Princess of Wales after a disastrous joint tour of India, which was remembered for one image: the princess, alone and isolated, in front of the Taj Mahal.

Also playing on the princess's mind was her collaboration with journalist Andrew Morton and the book he was about to publish: *Diana, Her True Story*. With hindsight in later years she regretted it, and in Egypt, as the media speculated about her involvement with the project, she might have been having second thoughts.

When I returned to Highgrove, I told Maria how concerned I was for the princess, how she was opening up, how she wanted me to be introduced to her friend Lucia. Maria could see I was becoming absorbed with wanting to ensure the princess was all right. I knew Prince Charles was all right. I could see that. But I could not know the princess's state of happiness or otherwise at Kensington Palace.

'Chuck,' Maria said in bed that night, 'you are the butler *here*, not there. You can't afford to get too close.'

7. Caught in the Crossfire

In 1992 change swept through Highgrove as the gardens blossomed with the onset of summer. The polite formalities of everyday life couldn't calm a disturbing undercurrent that ran through the house. Outside, an hysterical media anticipated catastrophic failure within the Waleses' marriage. Inside, there was an unnerving sense of anticipation and we didn't share the same hunger as the press. That something was wrong was evident. It was the suspense of what the consequences might be that hung in the air beneath the high ceilings.

There was a change in Prince Charles. He was locked into a period of melancholy and seemed, all of a sudden, rather vulnerable. One night, I had set the card-table for dinner for one. As he sat down, facing the television in the sitting room, I stood behind him, unloading my butler's tray. The television wasn't on. All that could be heard was cutlery against the plate and the sounds of the countryside coming through the wide-open windows.

Then the prince said, turning to face me: 'Paul, are you happy here?'

'Yes, very much so, Your Royal Highness,' I replied, transferring the main course from the tray to the plate on his table.

'Is Maria happy here too?' he asked.

I was somewhat perplexed as to where his doubt had sprung from. 'Yes. We're both very happy here, Your Royal Highness.'

'Good. I'm glad to hear it,' he said, and that was that. He started his main course.

I returned to the pantry wondering why he had seemed so concerned. Maria said it was probably because of our ever-increasing closeness to the princess. 'Look at it through the prince's eyes,' she said. 'His wife chatting in the butler's pantry. You covering for Harold at Kensington Palace more and more, requiring an under-butler to replace you at Highgrove. You going on her solo tours. Days out with the princess with our sons and the young princes. And, from the moment we moved into the cottage in 1990, the princess being a constant visitor to our home.' Duty had placed me in the most undesirable position, and the prince had been querying which camp I was in and whether I was sufficiently happy to remain.

Of course he had noticed the amount of time the princess was spending at our cottage. 'I suppose she's down at your house again, Paul, is she?' he asked, when he couldn't find his wife in the main house.

The princess would go for a walk in the gardens, pick a bunch of flowers, sweet peas or lily-of-the-valley, and arrive at the back door of the cottage. 'Maria, are you in?' she shouted, but walked in nevertheless. She flicked the switch of the kettle, reached up to take two mugs from an overhead cupboard and began making coffee. Both women drank black coffee, no sugar. William and Harry, Alexander and Nick were out playing somewhere on the estate. The princess hitched herself up on to the tiled kitchen top and kicked off her shoes, legs swinging. She poured out her heart to Maria time and again, talking about life with her husband and how unhappy she was. It seemed not as awkward for Maria to get close because she wasn't in a professional predicament. She was the wife of the butler, friend to the princess, and loved life at Highgrove. She said she only listened to the princess and didn't interfere with opinions.

'You don't know how lucky you are, Maria,' said the princess one day. 'This is all I've ever wanted, a happy home and a loving family,' and her eyes welled.

She had got to know our family well. Mum and Dad and Maria's mum had known her from the days at the Royal Mews. My brother Graham and his wife Jayne, Maria's brother Peter and his wife Sue were constant visitors to the cottage too, and the princess eased herself into our family. There were no airs and graces when she was around, and whether we were sitting round a wooden table in the garden or chatting in the kitchen, the princess was one of us. When she knew one of the family was visiting, they would be invited to one of the summer barbecues. I'll never forget the first time Graham met the princess at Highgrove. He shaved four times that day, he was so nervous. Then he met her and realized how breathtakingly normal she was.

Maria's mum, Betty, had a special place in the princess's heart. She adored her. Once, at a Christmas cocktail party for staff and tradesmen in the state apartments at Kensington Palace, she invited her to join them. The Wales family stood by the door, receiving the guests, who shook hands with William, Harry, and then the prince and princess. When the overawed lady with the white hair and rather large glasses approached the princess, she broke from protocol, grinned widely, embraced her and kissed her cheek.

The prince looked taken aback. After the elderly lady had shaken his hand, he turned to his wife and said: 'Who was that?'

'Oh, that was Betty.' The prince was none the wiser. 'Maria's mother,' added the princess.

On another occasion, she telephoned Betty, knowing she lived alone in North Wales. 'Hello, Betty, it's Diana. What are you doing?'

'I'm sat on the bed talking to you,' said Betty simply. She always managed to make the princess laugh.

The princess had rung because Betty was having central heating fitted in her old people's bungalow, and she wanted to check that everything was in working order.

One day in 1992, the princess made a dream come true for her, a devout Catholic. She rang her at home and said, 'Betty, I would like you to come and join me and meet Mother Teresa.'

Betty nearly fell off her chair. 'I can't come out to India!'

She had the princess laughing again. 'No, Betty, you won't need to because Mother Teresa is going to be in London for twenty-four hours. If no one can bring you down, I'll send a car for you,' she said. As it happened, a relative drove her to Highgrove where she met the princess and the two drove to Kilburn, in London, and on to a mission that housed twenty-two nuns.

Mother Teresa was outside to greet the princess. The princess turned to Betty and said: 'And can I introduce you to my friend, Betty?' The press reported that Betty was a lady-in-waiting.

Mother Teresa kissed her and the three went into a room alone and sat round a small wooden table. They spoke about the homeless and poor in Britain, the sick and dying of Somalia, the need to say the rosary as often as possible. Mother Teresa was holding something in her hand. As she opened her palm, she revealed two medals of Our Lady and a set of rosary beads. 'What would you like?' she asked Betty.

Betty took the medals. The princess took the rosary beads. She did not know how to say the rosary but Betty assured her that she would teach her. In fact, the princess followed Betty's lead that day: as they walked into the chapel where the novice nuns were waiting, Betty turned to her and said, 'Do what I do.'

Following her example, the princess dipped a finger into a font of holy water and blessed herself, then removed her shoes. The three knelt with the nuns and prayed. Betty said she was on a spiritual high for weeks afterwards and woke up every morning thinking it had been a dream.

In February 1992, after her tour of India with the Prince of Wales, the princess gave Betty a special present: the garland Mother Teresa had placed round her neck in front of the world's media. Betty treasures it to this day. It takes pride of place alongside a photograph of her, the princess and Sister Teresa, a nun from a convent in Galway who visited Highgrove with Betty one weekend. Sister Teresa said that the princess was 'a lonely, lonely woman', but that day she still managed to pose for a happy snap.

Prince Charles was living full-time at Highgrove and had effectively abandoned Kensington Palace, although the princess still came down at odd weekends. The prince had started to change the Dudley Poplak-inspired décor. He hired Robert Kime, interior designer and friend of Camilla Parker Bowles, and the house switched from light pastel greens and yellows to richer reds and browns. It was dark, sombre. Large pieces of rosewood and mahogany furniture arrived: a grandfather clock for the hallway; a new brass fender with up-holstered seat to surround a slate hearth for the fireplace in the drawing room where a gilt overmantel mirror was placed on the wall, rush matting replaced the green carpet and new curtains hung in the windows. In the hallway, a huge William Morris tapestry was draped from a brass rail. In the sitting room, the portrait of Lord Byron that had hung over the fireplace was sent away on exhibition and replaced with an oil painting of Windsor Castle. Bit by bit, month by month, the prince was making the interior his own.

When the princess visited one weekend, she spotted a dark wood sideboard in the dining room, and winced. I told her that two marble statues were being considered for the alcoves beside the fireplace. She grimaced. The prince even instructed his valet Michael Fawcett to remove pictures dating back to 1870 of HRH Albert Edward,

Prince of Wales, from his dressing room at Kensington Palace to Sandringham House.

The princess was making her own decisions about the interior of Kensington Palace. She removed the Victorian mahogany half-tester marital bed from the master bedroom and consigned it to the Royal Collection at Windsor.

On my thirty-fourth birthday, 6 June 1992, the Queen's private secretary, Sir Robert Fellowes, telephoned the *Sunday Times* news-paper demanding to know the contents of its serialization of the Morton book, but the real storm had brewed at Highgrove on the previous day when Prince Charles and his private secretary Richard Aylard set out on their own fact-finding mission.

That morning, the princess was at Kensington Palace, first with her personal trainer, Carolan Brown, and then with her beauty therapist and friend, Eileen Malone, for her usual ten a.m. facial.

Unknown to the princess, as she relaxed into the cleansing, toning and massage ritual, Prince Charles's camp was working up a sweat over a fax sent from Broadlands, the home of Lord and Lady Romsey. Two sheets of paper had spewed out of the machine under my desk in the pantry. I saw the words 'Broadlands' first. Thought, Romseys. Thought, trouble. It was a transcript from a broadcast interview with Andrew Neil, then editor of the *Sunday Times*: he had said, on tape, that the princess had given her tacit approval for the book and Prince Charles had every right to feel betrayed. From Broadlands to Highgrove, from Richard Aylard to the Prince of Wales, the knives were out for the princess even as she made herself look beautiful at the palace. More than ever my loyalties were split: serving the prince at Highgrove and thinking about the princess at Kensington Palace. But one event would end the dilemma once and for all.

It was the end of a particularly exhausting, warm day. Lunch had been taken outside on the terrace in the sunshine. In the evening, Prince Charles had his dinner for one on the card-table in the sit-ting room, early again, so that he could disappear on another of his twenty-two-mile drives to Middlewich House and Mrs Parker Bowles. The phone had been ringing all day. As the sun set Gerald Ward, a local landowner, had left a message for the absent prince, as had many others, including his press secretary, Dickie Arbiter. With the washing-up still to be done in the pantry, the phone rang again.

'Hello, Paul, how are you?' said the princess. She laughed when I told her I had been run off my feet all day. 'I don't suppose the hubby's around, is he?' she said. She never referred to him as His Royal Highness, as protocol dictated, when talking to members of staff.

I wished she hadn't asked that question. It was the first time she had rung Highgrove when he was away 'privately'. Now what did I say? Should I lie? I couldn't lie to the princess.

She asked again: 'Well, is he?' This time she sounded impatient.

Thinking on my feet, I was honest if inexact. 'I'm sorry, Your Royal Highness, he's not. He's gone out.'

Out. It was past eight o'clock in the evening. Damn. Shouldn't have said that.

'Well, where's he gone?' she insisted.

'I don't know, Your Royal Highness.'

'*Of course* you do, Paul.' And she had me. 'You know everything that happens down there. Now, where has he gone?'

If the princess knew anything about me, she knew honesty was my strength as well as my weak spot. Trapped between duty and loyalty to both parties, my instinct was to come out with a plea, for her sake as well as mine. 'Please don't ask me, Your Royal Highness. The best person to ask would be His Royal Highness, not me,' I said. I felt awful. I didn't want to land the prince in trouble or lie to the princess. She had been too good to me.

She changed the subject, but only to another form of questioning. 'Has anyone else phoned this evening?' she asked.

I failed to see the danger in telling her that Dickie Arbiter and Gerald Ward had left messages. It seemed harmless on the face of it, but not when the princess could use such information as proof that she knew *exactly* who was calling the house, creating the impression with Prince Charles that she was not missing a trick. I had given her ammunition and knew it.

'Please don't say anything, Your Royal Highness. I could get into terrible trouble, you know that,' I said.

She told me not to worry, but the way she hurried off the phone told me it had all been logged. Nor, in the midst of a marital rift, was it going to be forgotten. The princess was too angry for that. That night I went to bed worried sick.

Maria was unsympathetic. She scolded me for opening my mouth. 'You should have thought, chuck, you should have thought,' she said.

The next morning I walked to the main house accompanied by dread. An ordinary morning passed and provided false belief that, perhaps, the princess had not said anything. That was until the prince's valet Michael Fawcett came into the pantry as I prepared the china and silverware for lunch. He had a face like thunder. 'He wants to see you and he *isn't* happy,' he said.

For once, the red disc hadn't dropped into the box. A messenger had been sent. It was a summons, not a duty call. From my pantry, I heard the thuds of the prince's footsteps coming down the staircase, across the polished boards of the hallway. I heard the library door open and slam shut. I waited a few seconds, my heart racing. I walked out of the door, turned left, through the doors and right, and knocked on the door of the library with a deep sense of foreboding. If the princess had dropped me in it, I'd lose my job. That was all I thought.

Prince Charles was standing near his round table. 'Close the door behind you,' he said, in a clipped voice.

The door clicked shut. 'Your Royal Highness?' I inquired.

He was indignant. 'Can you tell me why – *why* – Her Royal Highness is constantly aware of whomever visits or telephones Highgrove when she isn't here?'

'I don't know what you're talking about, Your Royal Highness.'

'Have you spoken to Her Royal Highness recently, Paul?' His voice was quivering with anger.

I told him that the last time I had spoken to her was the previous evening. 'When you were out,' I said.

'And *what* exactly did you say to her?' He was on the edge now. His notorious short fuse was burning out. I could almost hear it fizzing to its end.

'That you were out, Your Royal Highness.' Even I noted the tone of resignation on an issue I wasn't going to win.

His face was puce red. 'WHY?' he bellowed.

'Because you *were* out, Your Royal Highness.'

Puce now turned to virtual purple. 'And did you tell her who rang the house last night?'

'Well, I said Mr Ward had rung but that you were out because, that way, it confirmed I was telling the truth,' I said.

The prince was incredulous. My stupidity was now mutually recognized. He could not believe what he was hearing. 'Why on earth couldn't you simply have said that you just couldn't find me?'

Something told me to stand up for myself. I was not Michael Fawcett. Or Richard Aylard. Or in the camp that willingly covered his tracks. 'Are you asking me to lie, Your Royal Highness?'

And then, with the temerity of that question from a servant, he exploded: 'Yes! YES! I am!' His bellow bounced off the walls and watercolours. In a flash, he picked up a book from the tower on his table and hurled it in my direction. I can still see its fluttering pages whirring through the air. It missed me but I don't think it was intended to hit me. It was a randomly thrown missile. Prince Charles was a renowned object-thrower when he lost his temper. As the book landed on the floor, he was still ranting: 'Yes, I am! I am the Prince of Wales,' he screamed, and stamped a foot to emphasize his authority, 'and I will be king! So Yes. YES!'

I didn't dare ask if there would be anything else. I made a sharp exit. I was stunned. His temper was legendary but until then I had never had the misfortune to witness it. I pulled out a chair in the pantry and sat down with my head in my hands, cursing myself for my own stupidity.

Minutes passed and then the bell rang. The red disc dropped into the box under LIBRARY. Scene two.

I opened the library door and entered awkwardly. Before me was a starkly different picture. The anger had abated and the prince was sitting at his table. I should have been the one who was embarrassed but it seemed that he was the one who didn't know where to look. He could not have been more contrite. 'Paul, I'm terribly sorry. I really didn't mean to do that. I do apologize.'

On the floor, the literary missile he had thrown in my direction was splayed out, pages down. As I bent down, picked it up and returned it to the pile, I told him: 'If you can't vent your feelings on me, Your Royal Highness, who can you vent them on?'

He sat back in his chair, forlorn, as if his anger had sucked all the energy out of him. He nodded, and that was my signal to leave again. I had tried to pretend to the prince that everything was all right but I knew it was far from that. Both of us had been wrong but, from that moment on, things could never be the same again.

No longer was the sense of divided loyalties merely a psychological dilemma. I had been caught in the crossfire and, with both the prince and princess demanding 100 per cent loyalty from their staff, duty to one had to give. In my own mind, I already knew where allegiance and instinct would take me. I just couldn't tell Maria. She loved life at the cottage in the countryside.

The book *Diana, Her True Story* was published on 16 June 1992. The princess went to Royal Ascot and she strode in appearing ultra-confident. She knew all eyes would be on her but such an experienced public performer gave no reaction. Behind the façade, though, she was crumbling when she walked into the Royal Box. It was there that she was struck by the enormity of the damage that the book had caused. She felt the rest of the royal party ostracizing her, she said, and conversations were stilted, awkward and cold. As she stood looking around the room, doing her public best, she saw that Andrew and Camilla Parker Bowles were guests, laughing and being jolly, performing another charade of marital happiness. Then she witnessed Princess Anne posing for a photograph with her old friend Andrew Parker Bowles. She found it offensive to see her sister-in-law cosying up to the husband of her brother's mistress; approval of the situation that was at the root of the princess's unhappiness.

Later that year, Princess Anne assuaged the princess's hurt. Indeed, she took the princess aside and offered words of comfort.

In 1992, Princess Anne was in love with Commander Tim Lawrence following her divorce from Captain Mark Phillips, and a new royal marriage was nigh. It was wrongly reported at the time that the princess had 'snubbed' Princess Anne by not attending her wedding, but nothing could have been further from the truth. Princess Anne herself offered an escape clause out of her invitation. She felt guilty that she was in love at a time when the Prince and Princess of Wales were finding life so difficult. The princess was reassured when her sister-in-law told her, 'A lot of us in this family are praying for you.' Princess Anne understood that her sister-in-law might not want to attend the ceremony because it would be too painful, and her compassion was appreciated by the princess. The only reason she did not attend was because she had the Princess Royal's prior consent.

After the Ascot meeting, there was a hastily arranged summit at Windsor Castle where the Queen and the Duke of Edinburgh sat down with the Prince and Princess of Wales. The atmosphere was tense, but the views exchanged were frank and honest. The princess told me: 'Mama despaired as she listened to me. I think she aged at that time because all I seemed to be doing was relaying to her my anguish.'

At Windsor, Prince Philip made it clear that everyone was upset by the biased account in the Morton book. He told the princess that everyone was suspicious of her involvement. The princess, by then in denial, insisted that she had not assisted the author. I honestly believe that she was taken aback by the scale of what she had unleashed.

'The publication of that book was an unbearable time. Only my friends guided me through,' she said. But, deep down, she knew that devastated and angry as she was at the state of her marriage and still grieving for her father, she had been rash, impulsive and confused in co-operating with Morton. Her friends had been given permission to get across her case that she was a victim and isolated. In doing so, she had wrecked any chance of a reconciliation and the small prospect that Prince Charles might change his ways.

The self-imposed damage was something she struggled to accept in later years yet, bizarrely, fresh bitterness propelled her into another disastrous move with the filming of the BBC *Panorama* interview three years later. On both occasions, she had wanted the truth to be known but, essentially, she was making cries for help, hoping to win sympathy and be rescued. But no one, especially the one man she wanted to rescue her, Prince Charles, was going to help. But she still loved him. In her eyes, which had a tendency not to see the other side of many stories, she had been abandoned in favour of Camilla Parker Bowles.

Even when she knew she was wrong, the princess marched on with purpose, and there was no abatement in her anger and sense of injustice. She told the Queen and Prince Philip that she had tried to be civil to her husband but she had come up against a stone wall and, regrettably, she felt separation was the only answer. A trial separation. Not a divorce. She wanted freedom. Not a severance of ties.

The Queen and Prince Philip did not countenance the suggestion of a split. Both the prince and princess were told that they must learn to compromise, be less selfish and try to work through their difficulties, for the sake of the monarchy, their children, the country and its people. At the Windsor meeting, as Prince Charles listened, the princess made her loathing for Camilla Parker Bowles quite clear. She said that being able to express her anger openly to her in-laws was a huge relief: 'Everything was out in the open then. In the book and within the family.'

Indeed, there was one positive aspect about the book: it stopped, for a time at least, the princess's bulimia. 'I think that whole episode represented the biggest challenge of my life,' she said.

The Queen felt the candid discussion had gone well and suggested a follow-up meeting the next day. But the princess failed to take up the invitation. In fact, she refused to stay at Windsor that week, breaking with tradition, and attended the Ascot meeting on only two out of the four scheduled days.

The Duke of Edinburgh fired off a letter, making clear his disappointment that the princess had not turned up for their second meeting when he and the Queen were taking the time and making the effort to listen to the couple's marital problems.

But the princess, upset by the presence of Camilla Parker Bowles at Ascot, had retreated to Kensington Palace, wounded and angry.

And it was her refusal to accept an invitation to stay at the castle in Ascot week that lay behind a stream of correspondence between her and the Duke of Edinburgh.

Never let it be said that either the Queen or Prince Philip did not have the best intentions to save the royal marriage, however their involvement was interpreted. From that moment, they did everything they could to avoid a public separation. They had decided that a delicate, volatile situation required a wise head. Oddly, that wise head was deemed to be that of Prince Philip, whose reputation for tact did not augur well. Nevertheless, he stepped in as mediator. The significance of the counselling role that he and the Queen adopted cannot be overstated: until then, as a mother and father, they had never interfered in any of their children's marriages, believing that wisdom is only learned through life experience. But they clearly decided that on this occasion they could not stand by and watch the Prince and Princess of Wales allow their marriage to disintegrate. Like Her Majesty, Prince Philip tried hard to remain impartial and understanding of the princess's plight but, as with all mediators, his role required him to be candid and impart some harsh truths. In doing so, the princess struggled to accept that he had adopted a neutral role. 'How many other wives would have to discuss their marital problems with their father-in-law instead of their husband?' she said, in her frustration.

It was another indication to her of the Royal Family behaving abnormally when it came down to handling personal relationships, of Prince Charles putting his head in the sand. Moreover, it was a clear sign that neither intractable side was going to see eye to eye within a maelstrom of conflicting emotions.

To be fair, Prince Philip was doing more to save the marriage than Prince Charles and, whether his motivation was to protect the institution or the individuals, he acted with good faith. No one was better qualified than he to understand what it was like to marry into the Royal Family and abandon a previous way of life in the name of duty. The inherent problem of using Prince Philip as mediator was that he rarely pulled any punches, and as someone who didn't understand the princess, he could hardly be expected to know how to handle her personality and fragile temperament. As impartial as he attempted to be, he wore steelworker's gloves for a situation that required handling with kid mittens. In a bombardment of correspondence, he upset and infuriated the princess with comments she described as brutal. She never shredded the letters. Instead, she tied them into a bundle and kept them, a deliberate preservation of the truth, and to back it up she made several photocopies that she dispatched to friends she trusted. Others, like television interviewer Martin Bashir and me, were shown the originals.

I saw them in 1993, Bashir in 1995. I was sitting on the stairs with the princess at Kensington Palace. Even then, a year after she received them, she still shook her head over their contents. A lot of nonsense and plain lies have been written about them. Much later, newspaper reports, aided by wild exaggeration from dramatic sources, claimed that they were 'the nastiest letters Diana had ever received', and that they were short, curt and written on A5 paper. Such gross inaccuracies cannot be allowed to linger. The letters offered some harsh truths but they were never poisonous. Indeed, in time they became understanding and sympathetic. Nor were they curt and rude. They were long and rambling, and some were four pages long. All were written on A4 paper.

What I can also say, contrary to those same newspaper reports, is that I never recalled Prince Philip ever using the words 'harlot' or 'trollop' in any of the correspondence. Nor, in what I witnessed, did he ever accuse the princess of damaging the monarchy.

When he sat down to write them, Prince Philip was clearly bristling from the revelations of the Morton book, which he had digested, page by page, in full. He, too, was suffering from wounded pride on behalf of his son and family. That placed him on the defensive and, I believe, hampered his objectivity. However much he tried to be even-handed, an accusing finger tended to leap out of the pages.

His intention was clearly to put his thoughts on paper and demand that the princess did some soul-searching. He wanted to jolt her into thinking more about her marriage, her behaviour, her motives. On reading them, one conclusion could be drawn: in his eyes, he was being cruel to be kind. On one hand, he praised the princess for her solo tours and charity work, then said that being the wife of Prince Charles 'involved much more than simply being a hero with the British people'. The remarks kept punching away at the princess's ego and spirit, delivered by the man she had held in great respect ever since she married into the family, and that was what bothered her most.

It got worse before it got better. Prince Philip said that jealousy had been the cancer within the marriage. The princess took that as an attack on herself. He also said that, following the birth of William, her irrational post-natal behaviour had not helped matters. My role as an interfering butler had not been forgotten. I winced again as the duke recounted one of many examples, the time she had quizzed me over the telephone about where Prince Charles was after he had left Highgrove in the middle of the evening. He said there was a deep-seated suspicion with his son that the princess was a jealous spy: listening at doorways and questioning the butler about his whereabouts. 'If Charles had been honest with me from the start, I wouldn't need to be suspicious of him,' she told me.

It is hard not to sympathize with the view that when a husband continues to see an old flame it is hard for any woman not to attempt to reassure herself.

As the actions of the princess had made Prince Charles suspicious, his sneaky private life made her doubt him. The irony of the vicious circle seemed lost on both Prince Charles and the Duke of Edinburgh. Blow by blow, the parental-like advice came wrapped in barbed wire: she had not been a caring wife; while she was a good mother, she was too possessive with William and Harry. I had seen her with her boys, and all she had ever done was smother them with love and affection; she wanted to be there for them twenty-four hours a day, seven days a week. At weekends, she had ensured that they went to Highgrove to see their father. Only in a royal world, where the nanny's hand rocks the cradle, could the attention and love she gave those boys ever be misconstrued as overly possessive.

But what stunned the princess was when Prince Philip raised the thorny issue of her husband's mistress. He wrote that she should have been grateful that her husband had, initially, cut himself off from Camilla Parker Bowles. Prince Charles felt he had made 'a considerable sacrifice' in cutting ties with her and that the princess had 'not appreciated what he had done'. Then came the knock-out blow that had left the princess sobbing. Prince Philip had written: '*Can you honestly look into your heart and say that Charles' relationship with Camilla had nothing to do with your behaviour towards him in your marriage?*'

The princess was being accused of driving Prince Charles into the arms of the one woman she had tried to keep him away from. Even a year on, the idea made her blood boil. 'They are all the bloody same – looking after one another!' she said.

On the one hand, Prince Philip was telling her that he was not apportioning blame but on the other he was laying responsibility at her door.

That summer of 1992 Highgrove was not a place where I saw much of the princess. The marriage had irretrievably broken down. But communication was maintained into that autumn with the Duke of

Edinburgh. Where one letter had made the princess despair, a new one arrived and lifted her hopes. The princess always wrote back, firing off an angry response to the first few letters. One letter from the duke famously started: '*Phew!!! I thought I might have gone a bit too far with the last letter . . .*' Eventually, he accepted that Prince Charles shared equal blame for the marriage breakdown and had been equally stubborn.

As his attitude changed, so did that of the princess. However hard she found her father-in-law's opinions and observations, she learned to respect his honesty. After she had challenged some of his comments, his letters became warmer, kinder and more considerate. More importantly, for the first time since her troubles had begun in the mid-eighties, she felt someone from the House of Windsor was taking the trouble to listen to her without dismissing her as unhinged or emotionally hysterical. In meeting each other head-on, the princess and the Duke of Edinburgh had broken down barriers and brought many unspoken issues into the open. The princess saw the effort her father-in-law was making, noted the length of his letters, and admired him for it. It was a marked shift from the rash assumption of others in the Royal Family, who were too quick to dismiss her concerns as the rantings of a mad woman. Had anyone stopped to think, her mood swings, bulimia and screaming fits were born of a maddening frustration at simply not being heard. A wave of relief, almost of vindication, swept over her when he made it clear that he didn't subscribe to the belief, peddled by the warped ignorance of some in Prince Charles's camp, that she was 'mentally unbalanced' or 'unstable'.

The princess's memory was sullied later *after* her death, when she was unable to defend herself, with the appalling suggestion that she had suffered from borderline personality disorder. Royal author Penny Junor researched the illness for her 1998 book *Charles: Victim or Villain?* and 'discovered it was spot on for the behaviour Diana exhibited'. It is worth remembering that, in reaching such a speculative conclusion, she was aided by the unused research of Jonathan Dimbleby for his 1994 book *The Prince of Wales*.

The princess juggled a hectic life in the full glare of the world's media. If she had suffered from BPD, she would never have coped with such a burden of duty in such a demanding environment. Take it from someone who lived with her, who witnessed an ordinary human being battling with an extraordinary life, she suffered, quite simply, from an eating disorder.

Thankfully, the Duke of Edinburgh acknowledged that simple fact. In one letter, he recognized that bulimia could affect a sufferer's behaviour, and he said she could not be blamed for the 'behavioural patterns' the disease had caused. That admission was of huge significance to the princess. At a stroke, Prince Philip had disassociated himself from the venomous off-the-record briefings that had left her feeling for so many years that no one cared or understood. For the sake of her memory today, the world should rely on the conclusions of the duke, stated when the princess was alive, rather than those of a royal author, put forward when the princess was dead.

What provided her with even greater hope was that both the Queen and Prince Philip still shared the belief that the marriage could work if compromises were made on both sides. The duke even made a numbered list of common interests and activities, which might bring the couple together again. This bolstered the optimism that the princess still felt. Beneath all her bitterness and anger, the princess still loved Prince Charles and believed, naïvely or otherwise, that one day they could try again. In 1992 she recognized that separation was inevitable and might even be healthy. She did not, as some royal autobiographies have suggested, believe the marriage was dead but that it could be revived from its coma.

Just as the duke had made the princess cry with some of his words, he also made her laugh. Indeed, she had leaped around her room with unbridled joy when he expressed his private thoughts about Camilla Parker Bowles. Both he and the Queen had long been deeply worried about their son's friendship with a married woman and they had strongly disapproved, he said. Then he wrote: '*We do not approve of either of you having lovers. Charles was silly to risk everything with Camilla for a man in his position. We never dreamed he might feel like leaving you for her. I cannot imagine anyone in their right mind leaving you for Camilla. Such a prospect never even entered our heads.*'

That confirmed everything the princess needed to know. Nor did it escape her notice that the Duke of Edinburgh had begun signing off his letters 'With fondest love – Pa'.

The correspondence became a rollercoaster ride through despair, hope, tears, then laughter, defiance and concessions. In sharing with me what she was going through, it was almost as if the princess was looking for an independent witness to prove that her view of the royals – the family, the marriage, the household, the way she was treated, her perceived injustices – was not an insane misinterpretation that suited her own agenda. Perhaps she also wanted to share the vindication the letters gave her, as if proof were needed of what the Duke of Edinburgh had written. She was also aware, of course, that I knew the Queen and her husband.

It was true that the princess did not take criticism well but, on balance across the months, she felt she had made progress and got her points across. When she died, she was a great admirer of the Duke of Edinburgh. Despite the hurt his initial missive had caused her, she said she would never forget the role he had played as a counsellor.

Eventually the well-intentioned intervention of the Duke of Edinburgh reached an impasse. More scandal appeared in the newspapers, and the princess did her best to quell the media's thirst for tabloid headlines. She released a statement following speculation about Prince Philip's letters. It read: 'The suggestion that Her Majesty The Queen and HRH The Duke of Edinburgh have been anything other than sympathetic and supportive is untrue.' The princess was again putting on a brave public face at a time when all sides recognized that the marriage was at the point of no return. Nevertheless, the Duke of Edinburgh continued to plug away, determined to ensure that the business relationship between the Prince and Princess of Wales trundled on, wearing its mask of togetherness, for the sake of the monarchy and the country. Indeed, it was Prince Philip who, during a private conversation at Balmoral, gently persuaded the princess to accompany Prince Charles on the tour to Korea when she had said she would prefer not to go. It was a disastrous trip, in terms of PR for the marriage.

On 27 November I penned a letter to my Kentucky friends Shirley and Claude Wright: '*It will take a major scandal or a public statement to change this situation, none of that is likely to happen this year unless there are dramatic weeks ahead. I will always be at Highgrove to look after whoever lives here. I'm sure 1993 will be an eventful year but my job is quite safe and I very much doubt our lifestyles will change.*'

Little did I know that, earlier in the month, the offices of the prince and princess had been arranging a separation. At Highgrove, we were all in the dark, and the princess had had good reason for not informing me because she knew the impact it would have on all our lives.

I had ordered the Christmas tree for Highgrove. Prince Charles was staying away 'privately', and the princess was in Tyne and Wear with her friend and secretary Maureen Stevens. Wednesday 9 December dawned as any other. Then news came through that, at three o'clock, we should expect the arrival of Jane, Countess of Strathclyde, palace personnel officer. We knew she was the bearer of bad news as soon as we saw her face – it seemed unfair that someone of whom we had become fond should have to carry out such a task. She looked flustered and, instead of exchanging small-talk and pleasantries, she had been instructed to ring the prince's private secretary Richard Aylard as soon as she arrived. As she made the call, she told me to gather all the staff – Wendy, Paddy, Lita and Barbara (the daily ladies) and Maria – in the kitchen.

Jane had timed her arrival to coincide with the announcement by Prime Minister John Major that the Prince and Princess of Wales had, regrettably, decided to separate.

Behind the scenes, at Buckingham Palace, Kensington Palace and Highgrove, the private determination shared by all parties was to ensure that, while the prince and princess lived separate lives, there was going to be no divorce. The British constitution would be intact if everything else lay in tatters around it.

As John Major delivered his statement to the House of Commons, Jane emerged from the dining room, with a look of sorrow on her face, already regretting the upheaval she was about to cause.

'Can I see Paul and Maria first?' she said, and we followed her into the staff dining room. 'Please, close the door behind you.'

I sat there, holding Maria's hand tight. Then Jane, in a sombre voice, started: 'I have only this minute learned myself. I had driven to Highgrove not knowing why I was coming here. But it has just been announced that Their Royal Highnesses The Prince and Princess of Wales are intending to live apart . . .'

It had been inevitable but the sadness of hearing it made our hearts sink. But Jane hadn't finished.

'. . . and Her Royal Highness The Princess of Wales wants you both to go to London and look after her.'

She wanted me in her team, to work alongside the existing butler at Kensington Palace, Harold Brown.

Maria burst into tears and wailed: 'I don't believe it. I don't believe it.'

Jane and I sat in silence as Maria wept. 'What are we going to tell the boys? Their friends are here, their school, our cottage. No. No!'

Jane crouched down and put her arms round Maria. 'I don't know what to say to you,' she said.

My thoughts raced, too, but for different reasons. The inevitability of the announcement was matched, in my mind, by the inevitability that our future lay with the princess. I felt strong, convinced that things were happening for a reason. If anything, I was puzzled about why the princess had not informed us earlier. That was all I couldn't understand.

As we walked out of that room and into the kitchen, with Maria in pieces, Wendy saw us first. 'What on earth . . .' she said, racing over to Maria.

'Can I see you now, Wendy?' said Jane. Ten minutes later Wendy emerged. She had been made redundant. It is a tribute to her that she remained philosophical – 'I'm nearing retirement anyway' – and was more concerned about us.

We sat around the kitchen table for most of that afternoon, long after Jane had gone, all of us contemplating change over many glasses of gin and tonic. Paddy's role was unaltered, and he returned to the stableyard; the two daily ladies had gone home in a state of shock.

Wendy offered Maria a cigarette. 'We're not supposed to smoke in the kitchen but I can't see that it matters now,' she said, and they chain-smoked a packet of twenty. Back to London. Another duty. Another royal residence. We would never see the princess or William and Harry again at Highgrove.

That night, after she had returned to Kensington Palace from the North East, the princess telephoned the cottage. She, of all people, knew how upset Maria would be at the prospect of leaving the countryside, and the life she had always dreamed of, for London. 'Don't worry, Maria,' the princess reassured her, as she wept again. 'You and Paul will be better off here with me. I know you don't want to come back to London but I will take care of you all.'

Maria put down the phone feeling so sorry for the princess. She knew how lonely her life was at Kensington Palace, and that all she was doing was ensuring that the family she had grown close to went to work for her, not her husband. In the separation of the royal marriage, the princess had included the Burrells among the possessions she wanted to keep.

Meanwhile, the princess was dealing with her own domestic bombshell, delivered in another envelope from Buckingham Palace and primed by the hand of the Duke of Edinburgh. As the lawyers and advisers from both camps held summits to negotiate the terms of the separation, Prince Philip came out with his own suggestion: that the princess move out of Kensington Palace apartments 8 and 9, her main home for the previous ten years, so that Prince Charles could keep the residence as his London base.

As alternative accommodation, more appropriate for a mother with sons at boarding-school, the duke suggested she move next door into apartment 7: empty, derelict and previously occupied by the Claytons, distant relations of the Royal Family. The princess said it was a shoebox and not a fitting home for two royal princes. Apartment 7 had more significance to the Duke of Edinburgh. It had been the apartment where he had stayed on the eve of his wedding to the Queen on 20 November 1947.

The duke called it a 'semi-detached' arrangement. But the woman whom I was about to start calling 'The Boss' dug in her heels and refused to move an inch. The benefit of frank communication with her father-in-law allowed her to tell him exactly how she felt without fear of causing upset. She told him there were no circumstances in which she was going to make way for Prince Charles. He remained at Highgrove and settled for a new apartment in St James's Palace. The princess remained in 8 and 9, where my sole employment with her would begin and Maria joined her, on a part-time basis, as a housemaid.

8. KP

'Would you like to watch a film?' asked the princess.

It was a Saturday afternoon at Kensington Palace and we had returned from shopping in the nearby high street. The chef had been sent home for the day, having left a salad in the refrigerator for dinner, and the 'house' was quiet. It was a free afternoon with nothing scheduled, and the princess had a couple of hours to spare.

She was standing in the doorway of the ground-floor pantry as I made two cups of instant coffee. 'You choose the film. Give me five minutes,' she said, and went up the angular staircase that hugged the half-white, half-yellow walls.

Both of us could talk endlessly about movies and, as I stirred the coffee in the blue and white mugs she preferred to fine china, I knew exactly which to select.

Her collection was not a patch on the vast hoard of films William and Harry had amassed, but she had a number of fine classic movies, most with a heart-tugging romantic theme. 'Weepies', she called them.

In the sitting room, I crouched down and scanned the spines of the VHS video cases that filled two shelves of a white cabinet that formed the base of an almost ceiling-high bookcase: *Gone With the Wind, Silk Stockings, My Fair Lady, Top Hat, Carousel, South Pacific, Ghost, The English Patient.* My eyes stopped on *Brief Encounter.* A guaranteed weepy, which she had watched more times than I had made her black coffee or carrot juice. 'I think this one,' I said, as she came into the room, and pushed the tape into the recorder.

Princess and butler sat down at either end of a pink-and-cream striped three-seater sofa, which backed on to her mahogany desk, facing the grey marble fireplace at the opposite side of the room. Daylight flooded in from behind us through the white-framed sash windows. A box of Kleenex lay on the cushion between us. 'I always blub at this!' she said, snatching a tissue, and the movie began.

She shifted into a more comfortable position, and sniffled her way through a chance meeting turning into a love affair.

Ask anyone who ever sat with the princess through a concert or joined her to watch *Brief Encounter* – the strains of Rachmaninov's Piano Concerto No. 2 reduced her to tears every time. As the steam train pulled away in the climactic scene, and that stirring music filled the sitting room, sobs broke out beside me. The princess half turned to me and tears were streaming down her cheeks. She rocked backwards with laughter when she noticed that I, too, had a tissue in my hand. 'We're both so silly!' We laughed – God, how we laughed. To this day the strains of Rachmaninov make me smile. That night, and on countless other occasions, she played the concerto endlessly on her portable CD-player, which she carried from room to room. Or she would sit at the grand piano, next to the drawing-room window, looking out on to the rear of the palace gardens, and play the *Brief Encounter* theme. I would creep upstairs and stand at the door unnoticed to watch her play the dark-wood piano, lost in thought, eyes closed. Forget about possessions or items. That sound was the most important thing that I took away from Kensington Palace.

But before either she or I could feel comfortable enough together to share such tear-jerking movie moments, I had had to earn my stripes. Trust came with time. After leaving Highgrove, duty, shared initially with fellow butler Harold Brown, came first.

The furniture van stacked with all my worldly goods pulled up outside the Old Barracks where first-floor flat No. 2, with two bedrooms, bathroom, sitting room and kitchen, became our new home. Its broad back stood on the periphery of the capital's hustle and bustle, insulating us from the congestion of Kensington High Street, and it looked out over a wide expanse of lawn. The three-storey red-brick rectangular frontage of Kensington Palace, or 'KP' as it was known to staff, stretched out in the south-west corner of Kensington Palace Gardens, set back from the western edge of Hyde Park. It was a planet away from the Gloucestershire countryside. We had arrived on a warm, spring day in April 1993, and found ourselves in a London oasis, surrounded by green spaces.

A familiar face was waiting to greet us: The Princess of Wales was smiling and holding a bunch of flowers for Maria. What other boss would take the time and trouble to do that?

As Maria opened the car door, the princess bounded over with excitement. 'Welcome! Welcome! Welcome! You're here at last,' she said, hugging Maria, as Alexander and Nicholas ran up to her and clung to her legs.

As the removal van was emptied, the princess stood outside in the sunshine, intrigued by our household goods. 'I love a good nosy,' she said. 'Oh, that's nice, Maria, I didn't know you had that.' Then she clapped her hands together, 'I'm off now to leave you to settle in,' and walked off, across the grass, back to the palace before she headed off for Easter to stay with her sister, Lady Sarah Mc-Corquodale, in Lincolnshire. She had Easter eggs to pack for her nieces and nephews.

We inspected the flat. There were new carpets, and a new tiled floor in the kitchen. The Old Barracks is a converted stable block that once housed the grooms and soldiers who guarded the palace, which was bought by King William III and Queen Mary II in the late seventeenth century. In modern times, it had been divided into grace-and-favour accommodation for the royal household and staff. Our neighbours were the princess's sister, Jane, and her husband Sir Robert Fellowes, the Queen's private secretary; Brigadier Miles Hunt-Davies, the Duke of Edinburgh's now knighted private secretary; Jimmy Jewell, the duke's accountant; and Mr Ronald Allison, the Queen's press secretary. Fellow butler Harold Brown didn't have staff quarters. Somehow, through well-connected friends in high places, the one-time under-butler at Buckingham Palace had secured himself a royal apartment within Kensington Palace. He was known as the servant who lived like a royal and apartment 6 was his grand home. We worked separately, splitting the day into two shifts to attend to the princess's every household need.

But my first day at KP had been four months earlier. As I walked through the palace doors on that day, the princess shook my hand and said: 'You're now part of my team. Welcome to the A-team!'

I settled into a routine of working in the city during the week and going back to see Maria and the boys at our cottage at Highgrove at the weekends while the flat was made ready for us. It was a tiresome journey but no more than the princess had done for the previous two years. It was awkward for Maria to be living on the Highgrove estate. She and the boys were told they were not allowed to go up to the main house any more. Anyone would have thought that our cottage housed the plague because we were treated like outcasts. In the eyes of the household we no longer belonged. I cannot say that we were not warned: Prince Charles's valet, Michael Fawcett, had said before the separation, 'Be sure which side you back. Remember, the prince will be king one day.'

He was devoted to the prince, but I had been chosen by the princess. She didn't inherit me, and nor was I an appointee, like an equerry sent for service or a protection officer sent by the police. She had requested me, and I wasn't going to let her down.

But Maria, still living in Gloucestershire, suffered. In the first weeks of 1993, Lita Davies, a daily lady at Highgrove, was approached by someone from Prince Charles's camp who wanted to speak to her about why she was maintaining her friendship with Maria: it was 'probably for the best' that she stopped having contact with her. Lita was adamant that she would not be told which friends she could keep.

Then she faced another, stiffer warning. She was told not to discuss anything that went on at Highgrove with Maria.

Lita handed in her resignation the following day.

There was clearly deep concern in the prince's camp that the princess still had eyes at Highgrove. It was a sign of how difficult the situation had become. It convinced Maria that we had made the right move.

In our first week as a family at KP, the princess was extra hospitable and generous, as if she wanted to erase any doubts we might have had about leaving the countryside. The day after she returned from visiting her sister at Easter, she treated William and Harry, Alexander and Nick to a day out at Thorpe Park in Berkshire. The princess, dressed in black leather jacket and black jeans, gave them all a memorable day of fun, buying all four boys water-pistols and joining them on the rides. Little Nick was only five and didn't let go of the princess's hand for most of the day. She called him her 'little sexpot' and, that day, as press photographers followed them everywhere, she gave him piggy-back rides and carried him on her shoulders.

The following day, the *Sun* dedicated a whole page to the trip with the headline: 'WILLS AND HARRY LEARN COMMONER SENSE WITH BUTLER'S SONS AS PALS'. The article quoted royal photographer Jim Bennett, who had said what we already knew: 'The princess treats the butler's boys like her own. If you were a casual observer and you didn't know she was the Princess of Wales, you would imagine it was a young mum out with her four kids.'

That same week, I joined the princess at the Royal Opera House, Covent Garden, to see the ballet *Don Quixote*; I served dinner in the back of the Royal Box for the princess and a party of friends. From the shadows, I witnessed my first ever ballet performance and the costumes and music were spectacular.

Back at KP, I was busy in the pantry washing up when the princess popped her head round the door. 'What did you think?' she asked.

This was my chance to impress my more worldly-wise boss with my basic review and prove that her new recruit was no Philistine. I told her I thought it was amazing. Then I asked her what she thought. 'Rubbish,' she said, and burst out laughing when she saw the surprise on my face.

In the four months before we moved into the Old Barracks, I slept in a simple single room in the top-floor nursery: apartments 8 and 9 occupied three floors at the heart of KP in an L-shaped layout, overlooking the back of the palace. In total, KP housed a hundred people and four royal households, all living their own independent lives with their respective private secretaries, equerries, ladies-in-waiting, butlers, chauffeurs, maids, dressers, chefs and police protection officers. The princess's apartments were tucked behind the palace front, out of sight, on the north side. They were accessed via the long drive that passed the Old Barracks and continued straight ahead, passing a row of cottages for other household staff, before a sharp right turn brought visitors to the rear of the palace and the front door of No. 8, which faced on to a small green. Its Georgian windows had a view, to the right, of the princess's private walled garden, where she retreated in the summer months. It was her sanctuary in the centre of the capital. Every day, when the sun was out, I would set out a sun-lounger, spread a towel, and place a cooled bottle of Volvic water underneath it in the shade. 'It is so peaceful in there – there is a tranquillity which is hard to explain,' she said.

She could spend hours topping up her tan, reading or listening to her CD Walkman.

Her privacy, and that of visitors she didn't want to be spotted, was also protected by a secret passage into her apartments, accessed through an archway, topped with a white-painted tower and black-faced clock, into the cobbled square of Clock Court. It was the one area of the palace not covered by CCTV cameras, on the insistence of Princess Margaret, who guarded her privacy vehemently, too. That way, visitors were kept away from the monitoring eyes of the police. It became a well-trodden route of mine in my duty to meet certain guests and bring them in through the back door.

KP was not the cosy home the princess had often dreamed about, but it was a fortress she regarded as ultra-safe for herself, William and Harry. After 1992, when it became solely her home, she ensured her decorative stamp was in every room. She got rid of carpets that bore the Prince of Wales feathers. But she did not, as the misinformed have suggested, match Prince Charles in expunging all memories of her estranged partner. She respected that it was also her sons' home, so it was only right to have photographs of 'Papa' in many rooms.

But when it came to photographs, images of William and Harry had the monopoly. On the peach-painted walls of the dressing room, which she walked through to get from bedroom to bathroom, there were around twenty 35 × 25mm official portrait photos of the princess with William and Harry, taken over the years by Patrick Demarchelier: black-and-white images of unguarded moments in a photo studio, both boys' arms slung round their mother in almost every shot. There were also framed montages of their school artwork.

Wherever you looked around the apartments, images of William and Harry, at all ages, stared back from virtually every flat surface: on the piano in the drawing room; on the princess's desk in the sitting room and on a table in the corner; on the walls of the corridors. The boys were, quite simply, her life.

She turned Prince Charles's study into William and Harry's own sitting room, just a few yards down from hers. In this room, there were hours of fun. My sons joined the princes there to take each other on in combat games on the PlayStation. All the boys sat on a green sofa facing the television, entranced for hours. In her own

From Buckingham Palace to Highgrove,
and our new home!

A family day out at Bristol Zoo

Playtime at Highgrove

Boys and their toys

Maria's birthday party

Travelling the world with
the princess

sitting room, the princess loved nothing more than to hear the excited shrieks of the children. In the evenings, she and her sons would sometimes eat together in the boys' room. William loved watching the BBC hospital drama *Casualty* because of all the blood and gore, while his mother and Harry writhed on the sofa in mock horror. Or they would watch *Blind Date* on ITV and try to match unfortunate couples. 'Pick number one!' the princess would scream, while the boys would deliberately choose a different one. 'No, number two, number two!' they yelled.

I think there was a natural low whenever the boys left to visit their father or go to boarding-school. As the princess stood waving them off from the doorstep, she said, almost without fail, 'I'll miss ma boys!'

When the young princes were away, the princess wrote to them endlessly. Almost every day, sometimes two or three times a day. A letter. A postcard. Every letter expressed her excitement at seeing them again so that she could shower them with hugs and kisses.

The princess embraced the start of 1993 as if it was going to be the best year of her life. She was a new woman, no longer having to keep up appearances. She embarked on successful solo tours to Zimbabwe and Nepal, where Baroness Chalker went along in her capacity as minister for overseas development. Prime Minister John Major and the Foreign Office supported her missions. She might have been separated from the heir to the throne but she had the full weight of the government behind her. She was a roving ambassador and a prized asset for Britain. So much for the jealous snipers of the old guard, with their futile attempts to brand her a 'loose cannon'. She had left them behind in a different age.

The princess was working more and more with the International Red Cross and pricking consciences about the AIDS epidemic and the poverty-stricken. She was having speech-training so that she could become a better orator when she took the stand that year to talk about the homeless, HIV, mental-health issues and the plight of those who suffer, as she had, from eating disorders. She juggled public duty with private joys: an Elton John concert, the ballet of *Romeo and Juliet*, the movie *Jungle Book*, and the theatre production of *Grease*.

Her high spirits were infectious, and where there had been gloom at Highgrove, sunshine radiated through KP. Life was flexible and unstuffy. At the end of the month, to boost staff morale, she threw what she labelled in a staff memo as a 'celebration lunch party for the A-team'. She played the piano. We drank. We sang. We danced.

As if to emphasize her new-found freedom, 1993 was the year she parted company with police protection officers, shedding the final remnants of the establishment she had left behind. She felt that they were duty-bound to report to their superior about their where-abouts. That superior officer was none other than Inspector Colin Trimming, the Prince of Wales's senior protection officer. So, in her independence, she sat at her desk and made a decision. That weekend, as I brought her coffee, she made an instant note to herself. 'Self-esteem', she scrawled. Ticked it. 'Confidence'. Ticked it. 'Happiness'. Ticked it. Then she wrote 'Police' – and put a cross beside it.

I became accustomed to the princess's high voice, a chirpy sound that travelled down the wide staircase with its white balustrade and polished wooden banister. 'Are you down there, Paul?' she would shout. That staircase became her calling point for me; the 'catwalk stairs' where she would stand and twirl in a new outfit she wanted to show off; or the place where we would sit together – the princess always sat one step above me – talking or going through the correspondence she had received, or a letter she wanted help in composing.

I often waited there for her to arrive. She would burst in through the black front doors, walk along a narrow entrance corridor, turn left through an arch into the inner hallway, then pass through another arch and on to the stairs, which took her to the first-floor landing and her private rooms. Often, her voice beckoned me from the landing, as she leaned over the banister. 'You coming shopping, Paul? Give me five minutes.'

I grabbed my coat and walked with her down the drive, across Kensington Church Street, down Church Walk and out on to the high street opposite Marks & Spencer. 'Let's go to WH Smith's. We'll get some CDs for the boys,' she said, referring to both her and my sons. *En route* to the album chart, she stopped beside the large racks of humorous cards, read the punch-lines and laughed. I can hear her now. 'Look at this one! Have you seen the picture on this?' Sometimes she was doubled up with laughter.

Wherever we went, we attracted a following. There was no missing that mental registration among the public as the princess laughed at the cards. Tall. Blonde. Beautiful. Unmistakable. In Kensington. I could almost hear jaws hitting the floor. Then, as we nipped into the chemist or Marks & Spencer, she became the Pied Piper as a small entourage scurried behind her, pretending to shop.

Some people simply didn't believe it.

Two ladies stood beside us one day in WH Smith, whispering with the clear intention of being heard.

'It is, you know – it's her,' said the first lady.

'Of course it's not – it's a lookalike,' said her friend, and carried on shopping regardless. The princess? In WH Smith? Like the rest of us? Never.

Each time we shopped, and we *always* went into WH Smith, we returned to the palace with a few magazines – *Vogue, Tatler* – for her light reading, and then she wrote the cards she had bought and sent them to William and Harry at their boarding-school, Ludgrove, with a few CDs and videos. One particular day, she yelled the usual shopping invitation and we trotted off to WH Smith's. Unknown to me, it was a visit with a purpose – to introduce me to a trusted ally, Richard Kay of the *Daily Mail*. We had bought more CDs and cards, and were leaving when who should be entering but 'Ricardo', as she called him. The princess went through the 'Oh-fancy-meeting-you-here' charade, blushed and giggled. In my job, I had long been wary of reporters but this one was different. Good eggs do exist in Fleet Street.

'Oh, I'm sorry,' said the reporter, whose supportive pieces I had read over the years, and he held open the door for us.

'I trust him,' said the princess, as we walked away. Message received.

Being at KP meant becoming accustomed to another royal figure's routine. Every morning, between seven and seven thirty, a dresser went into the princess's bedroom to 'call' her but she was invariably up and about.

I stood in the corridor between the dining room and the kitchen, where Mervyn Wycherley or Darren McGrady would prepare break-fast. The barefoot princess appeared at the far end of the corridor, in a white towelling robe, devoid of makeup and with unkempt hair. As soon as I saw her, I moved into the kitchen to make a pot of black coffee.

By the time I had carried the hand-painted Herend coffee-pot to the dining room, she was settled into one of the four bamboo latticed chairs around the table, which was covered with a white linen cloth. She was tucking into half a fresh grapefruit and flicking through the daily newspapers, which I had spread flat in the same order as I had for the Queen. From the bottom: *The Times*, the *Daily Telegraph*, the *Daily Express*, the *Daily Mail* and the *Daily Mirror*. But no *Sporting Life* on top. I would enter the room, whose magenta walls provided an early-morning warmth, and stand in the half-open doorway until I saw the princess raise her eyes from the paper.

That was my signal. I gave a short, sharp bow from the neck down. 'Good morning, Your Royal Highness.' As time went on, my insistence on tradition and using YRH clearly irked her: 'Paul, please don't do that. There's only the two of us in this room. There really is no need,' she said.

But I insisted on keeping to protocol. It was the only time when I didn't listen to the Boss. If she wanted to invite me across the professional line to share her world, that was fine. But, by addressing her as Your Royal Highness, I showed respect and defined my role. I *needed* to show her that respect even when, at her down-to-earth best, she did not require me to do so. Each morning, from 1993 until the day she died, I called her 'Your Royal Highness'.

I walked across to the sideboard and popped a slice of granary bread into the toaster. Then we chatted about the previous night and what lay ahead that day. Often I turned round to find she was twirling a spoon, with a silver beehive on the top of its handle, into a jar of white honey then popping it into her mouth. Sometimes she asked if I had seen the newspapers. It was not always easy to answer, especially if I had spotted a negative article. If a particular paper was missing, she knew I was protecting her from a bad press. 'Oh, you don't want to see that,' I would tell her, knowing full well that I had ignited her curiosity and she would go looking for it. One paper she never looked at over breakfast was the *Sun*. But that did not stop her taking a sneaky look at chef Mervyn's copy in the kitchen, when it was left in his dispatch tray above the telephone.

Mondays, Wednesdays and Fridays were exercise days, sometimes at Chelsea Harbour Club, sometimes in the drawing room where Harold or I had pushed back the furniture to make room for the princess and fitness instructor Carolan Brown or Jenny Rivet. Later, I had to drive the princess in one of her cars to a gym in Earls Court. The fitness classes sometimes took place before breakfast. Following the separation, the KP timetable had to be flexible because it was dependent on whether William and Harry were back from Ludgrove and with their mother or at Highgrove with their father. Prince Charles ensured that the visiting arrangements were set in stone, writing to the princess every two or three weeks with lists of his available dates, for months in advance. It was in 1993 that he appointed Tiggy Legge-Bourke to help him look after William and Harry. She was more nursery assistant than nanny but the princess was infuriated when the media began describing her as a 'surrogate mother'. In countless newspaper images Tiggy – a good-natured young woman who lived the quiet life in a terraced property in Battersea – was seen larking about with William and Harry. In time, she became a confidante and personal friend of Prince Charles, and the princess began to view her as a threat.

As part of her daily routine, the princess said that her one true extravagance was having her hair washed and blow-dried every weekday morning, first by hairdresser Richard Dalton and then by Sam McKnight, and both men became trusted confidants. All women gossip to their hairdresser and the princess was no different. There were many light-hearted moments between princess, hairdresser and butler and she always SPOKE LOUDER SO HER VOICE COULD BE HEARD OVER THE HAIRDRYER!

When she saw my reflection behind her in the oval mirror on the dressing-table, she would shout, 'LOOK AT THIS!' It might be kind correspondence – or otherwise – a magazine photograph or a comment by a newspaper columnist. Nobody but dresser, butler, hairdresser and housemaid was ever invited into this inner sanctum. At these times, she was at her most natural, most relaxed, most easy-going: the princess the world never got to see. To me, at home, she was a fresh-faced girl stripped of the mask of royalty, as vulnerable as the next person. As soon as she was outside the front door, immaculate in one of her many stunning outfits, she drew on her inner reservoir of strength and strode out with majestic confidence. From white towelling robe to Catherine Walker dress or Chanel suit, I witnessed that remarkable transformation each morning and it never ceased to amaze me.

An L-shaped room the size of a small bedroom was needed to accommodate the hundreds of day dresses, blouses, suits, jackets, trousers and cocktail dresses that constituted her wardrobe; a multi-coloured assortment, all hanging from rails above the racks of her hundreds of pairs of shoes, hidden behind floor-to-ceiling curtains. Even the wardrobe layout was immaculate. A blue and white fleck Chanel suit hung directly above matching blue suede shoes; a pink Versace suit above matching pink leather shoes; a scarlet Catherine Walker coat-dress above a pair of red satin shoes.

The princess's week could be filled with 'away days', when she had engagements in the counties or was busy at charity meetings in the capital. When her diary allowed, lunch was taken either at the palace or a stone's throw away at Launceston Place or San Lorenzo, in Knightsbridge. Lunch was a social occasion for the princess and she preferred to dine one-to-one, with guests from her close-knit circle of friends: Lucia Flecha de Lima, Rosa Monckton, Susie Kassem, Lady Annabel Goldsmith, Julia Samuel, Laura Lonsdale, astrologer Debbie Franks and, her closest royal ally, Sarah, Duchess of York. The princess surrounded herself with her kind of people. On many Sundays, she went to the duchess's home at Virginia Water, near Windsor, or to Lady Annabel Goldsmith's in Richmond. Both homes had ample security and swimming-pools to keep William and Harry safe and occupied.

If the princess had lunch by herself at the palace, she often sat on a high stool at the open breakfast bar, looking into the kitchen, sharing jokes with chef and myself. It was a one-course meal that always incorporated a salad, washed down with iced Volvic water. If there is one image I remember from those rushed lunchtimes, it is of the princess with her mobile telephone balanced between shoulder and neck, speaking from the corner of her mouth as she used her knife and fork.

Whenever she left KP, I followed her out to the car. Whether she was a passenger or the driver, I waited until she was seated, then leaned in, grabbed the seatbelt and pulled it across her.

If she had been out, she would invariably have returned by seven thirty, and I would make her a cup of her favourite ginger-root tea. Dinner would be grilled trout or a pasta dish; or a plain jacket potato with a scoop of caviar, served with a vinaigrette dressing. It was often a solitary meal, served on a wheeled wooden trolley that I pushed into the sitting room before the striped sofa where the princess sat in her white towelling robe. I had already pulled the television out of its cabinet at the bottom of the bookcase and into position. Evenings were the loneliest, quietest times for the princess. The chef had gone. Her dresser had gone. And her private secretary, Patrick Jephson, never penetrated her private world at these times. His office was at St James's Palace where he worked from nine to five. At the day's end, as the princess wound down from an energetic, engagements-filled morning and afternoon, I got to know her better on a personal level. She was relaxed, not fraught, and talkative. It became clear, as I wheeled in her two-course evening meal, that with William and Harry at boarding-school she preferred not to be left alone. 'Stay a while,' she said, more times than I can remember.

I stood, leaning against an upholstered chair and we talked about her day, my day, the week ahead, what he had said, what she had said. Or the plot lines in *Coronation Street* or *Brookside*. These night-time chats might be brief or extend into a chat that lost all track of time. Sometimes the ITN news at ten o'clock was the signal for bed. As I wheeled away the trolley, she got up from the sofa and followed me into the anteroom that acted as a first-floor pantry. There, I washed up and the princess dried.

'What do you think tomorrow's going to bring?' she asked. She felt every day had the capacity to bring a new drama, a fresh problem or a particularly difficult incident.

'Whatever happens, we'll tackle it,' I told her.

When bedtime came, she disappeared down the corridor, with a girlish skip and hop, as if she was suddenly full of energy again, looking forward to the next day. I followed a few paces behind, switching out the lights along the way, except one: the light in the corridor outside her bedroom. She had been scared of the dark as a child and, throughout adulthood, preferred to sleep in half light.

As she disappeared into the bedroom, her final words each night were exactly the same: 'Night, Paul.'

'Goodnight, Your Royal Highness,' I said.

Some time before eleven, I would leave the palace, walk through the darkness of the grounds and into No. 2 the Old Barracks, where my wife and two boys were already asleep.

Having lost Highgrove to Prince Charles, the princess had no week-end retreat, which she missed. There was no question of her leaving Kensington Palace but from the start of 1993 she had been on the lookout for a private bolt-hole where she and the boys could spend long weekends. She would go, of course, to the Duchess of York and Lady Annabel Goldsmith, but 'It is such an imposition relying on them all the time,' she said. 'I want my own country retreat away from London.'

Suddenly an escape route was provided from the unlikeliest source – her brother, Earl Spencer. It seemed strange that he was coming to his sister's rescue because they were not close. Since her marriage in 1981, brother and sister had seen each other fewer than fifty times. A distance had crept between siblings who had been close in childhood. However, following a request from the princess, the earl offered her the use of the Garden House in a corner of the Althorp estate at a rent of £12,000 a year. 'The dream solution,' said the princess. It guaranteed privacy and there was also a swimming-pool near the main house; her brother promised a cleaner and a gardener.

In a letter to his sister on 3 June 1993 the earl wrote: '*I see your need for a country retreat and I am happy to help provide it as long as there aren't too many disruptions on the estate. The Garden House seems to suit your needs perfectly. It would also make sense to have your own pool.*' He even suggested erecting a new security gate to keep press photographers at bay.

As she read that letter, the princess was mentally decorating the little cottage. So excited was she that, in early June 1993, she set off to Althorp at nine a.m. with Dudley Poplak and a picnic lunch, prepared by her chef, dreaming of idyllic weekends at her new home with William and Harry.

Fifteen days later, the dream was shattered when her brother suddenly withdrew his offer. He wrote: '*I'm sorry but I've decided that the Garden House isn't a possible move now. There are many reasons, most of which include the police and press interference which would inevitably follow. I am now bringing in a senior agent and need an extra house for him. I know I am doing the right thing for my wife and children. I'm just sorry that I can't help my sister! In theory, it would have been lovely to have helped, and I am sorry I can't . . . If you're interested in renting a farmhouse (outside the park) then that would be wonderful.*'

The princess read that letter over and over again, mystified by his volte-face. 'How can he do this to me?' she raged, then dissolved into tears. What puzzled her most was that he knew she had set her heart on moving into the Garden House. When he telephoned the palace a few days later, she slammed the phone down on him. 'I cannot bear to hear his voice,' she said. Almost immediately, she spilled her anger on to her red-edged, headed writing-paper, telling the earl exactly what she thought of him as a brother and how hurt she felt. Earl Spencer, probably suspecting the vitriol contained within the envelope, returned the letter unopened. He posted it back with a third letter he wrote on 28 June: '*Knowing the state you were in the other night when you hung up on me, I doubt whether reading this* [the princess's letter] *will help our relationship. Therefore, I am returning it unopened because it is the quickest way to rebuild our friendship.*'

But that friendship had been damaged for ever. How ironic, then, that after her death Earl Spencer chose to accept his sister and bury her on an island grave. Suddenly, the outside interference that had so bothered him no longer seemed a concern. Nowadays he encourages the press and thousands of visitors each year to pour through his gates to see his own Diana museum and buy souvenirs.

The 1993 rift widened as the princess refused to take her brother's telephone calls. Earl Spencer had to resort to writing to her private secretary, Patrick Jephson, to communicate with her. Then, in September, he dealt his sister another crushing blow by demanding the return of the Spencer family tiara, which she had worn on her wedding day in 1981 and which was precious to her. As Princess of Wales, it was an essential part of her regal uniform and she wore it to state banquets at Buckingham Palace, state openings of parliament and diplomatic receptions. When he wrote to Patrick Jephson, Earl Spencer made it clear that the tiara had only been 'on loan' to the princess because his grandfather had bequeathed it to him in the 1970s. '*It should now be returned to its proper owner,*' he wrote. For twelve years, possession of the tiara had not been in question, and the princess felt the timing of the request related directly to their disagreement over the Garden House. The earl felt that his new wife, Victoria, should wear it.

It was not merely a symbol of the princess's royal status, it was a memory of her wedding day. But the princess would not give her brother the satisfaction of knowing it bothered her. That October the tiara was handed back to him and it was my duty to remove it from the safe where it had sat in a box alongside what she called her 'spare' – the lovers' knot, pearl and diamond tiara that the Queen had given her as a wedding present. At least she was able to keep the Windsor tiara.

Meanwhile, in the KP household, there were staff changes that affected life at the Old Barracks. Maria, who had been a maid with little responsibility since we moved from Highgrove, was promoted to dresser following the resignation of Helena Roache. She would work part-time alongside the senior full-time dresser, Helen Walsh. The appointment posed some domestic difficulties in the Burrell household because Maria suddenly went from nine-to-one house-maid duties to an erratic timetable, sometimes having to rise at six, or work in the evenings. We had to arrange our lives so that when she worked evenings I swapped shifts with Harold Brown to be at home with the boys. Maria knew it would be a strain but she wanted to help the princess. She said she would try the job for a year and thought that was an established agreement with the princess. The Boss proved flexible, even allowing Maria to wake her with a telephone call at seven a.m. instead of walking in personally as normal duty would have required. But the daytime hours got longer and longer. Maria had never before spent an evening away from Alexander and Nick and she missed them. When she went shopping for the princess late in the afternoon, she would see the boys playing on the green in front of the Old Barracks. More often than not, when she worked evenings the boys were asleep by the time she finished. But if Maria was working hard, Helen was toiling harder.

The princess recognized the sacrifices they were both making and attempted to compensate. She gave Maria bags full of unwanted designer shoes – Chanel, Jimmy Choo, Ferragamo or Rayne – because they were the same size six-and-a-half, plus handbags and discarded suits by Catherine Walker, Versace and Chanel. Helen also found herself the grateful recipient of unwanted clothes and gifts. It was the princess's way of making space in an ever-expanding wardrobe and saying thank you. Her sister, Lady Sarah McCorquodale, also benefited from this generosity.

Generosity in a royal household was nothing new. In my time with the Queen I had been given gifts from foreign tours. In my time at Highgrove, Prince Charles had given me a table carved from a redwood tree trunk, books, a silver box with an enamel lid and a pair of Lalique crystal grouse. The only time I had ever helped myself to the prince's possessions was when I joined the princess on a prearranged Highgrove raid. Harold Brown, Dudley Poplak, the Boss and I went there, post-separation, to remove items of furniture, lamps, pictures and ornaments. 'This is our one and only chance to take what we want!' We piled the items high in a removal van.

Prince Charles was placing his own decorative stamp on his home, bringing in more dark-wood furniture. The princess was in hysterics when Dudley commented: 'It looks like he's returning to the womb!'

If 1993 had got off to a flying start for the newly independent princess, it ended in a series of blows. First, came the falling-out with Earl Spencer. Then, in the November, the *Sunday Mirror* published photographs of the princess working out in her leotard at the LA Fitness Centre in Isleworth, London. Gym owner Bryce Taylor had planted a secret camera in the ceiling. The princess instructed lawyer Anthony Julius of Mishcon de Reya, and the newspaper was condemned for a blatant breach of privacy by the Press Complaints Commission. It also led the princess to make a dramatic announcement that she was retreating from public life on 3 December during a speech she was giving at a charity lunch for head-injury victims. She stunned the world when she said: 'I hope you can find it in your hearts to understand and give me the time and space that has been lacking in recent years. When I started my public life twelve years ago, I understood the media might be interested in what I did . . . but I was not aware of how overwhelming that attention would become.'

The royal household, which felt it was an unnecessary, melodramatic statement, offered its usual amount of sympathy: the princess's name was withdrawn from the Court Circular and she was not invited to Royal Ascot. The princess had only asked to step away from the spotlight into the shadows, but found herself unceremoniously ejected from the stage door.

The breach of privacy at LA Fitness – which was settled out of court with an apology from the *Sunday Mirror* in 1995 – had deeply upset her. When she was hurt, she would retire to her bedroom where she knew no one could get to her. She cursed herself over the gym pictures because, in co-operating with the media over the years, she felt she had given them the inch that had been extended into a mile. I was reduced to leaving messages on pieces of paper in her sitting room and on a stool at the top of the stairs. She surfaced for her meals but they were subdued occasions. When I was downstairs in my pantry, she reflected alone on what she felt were her mistakes, playing requiem masses at full volume. When that happened, I knew she was drowning her sobs, which were ridding her of the hurt. As she often said: 'I only feel fully protected when retreating into my shell. No one can hurt me there.'

But she bounced back every time, which was why her withdrawal from the public stage was never going to last long. The people who mattered to her most, the general public, were shouting, 'More, more,' the moment she walked off.

With all official public engagements cancelled, the blank diary for 1994 allowed the princess to do what she enjoyed most: socializing over lunch. The afternoons from January through to the spring were filled with appointments at her favourite eateries: San Lorenzo, Le Caprice, the Ritz, Claridges, the Ivy, Bibendum or Launceston Place. Australian television presenter Clive James and friend Lord Attenborough were regular fellow diners, and she must have seen Lucia Flecha de Lima and Rosa Monckton twice a week. KP became her luxury decompression chamber and I could almost see the stresses of her high-profile life lifting. The coiled spring unwound, played lots more tennis, went to the ballet or the cinema, stayed with friends. Warm, carefree, energetic and good company, she was back on top form. For one full day, she treated her staff to a trip to Alton Towers theme park because William and Harry wanted to try out Nemesis, the new thrill ride. It was one of her 'let's-be-normal' days out and there were thirteen of us, including me, Maria, our boys, nanny Olga Powell, chauffeur Steve Davis, and the young princes, shadowed by their police protection officers, Graham Craker and Chris Tarr. One notable absentee was fellow butler Harold Brown, who was rapidly falling out of favour with the Boss. As if to emphasize the normality of the day – which was never going to be achieved – the princess decided we should travel to Staffordshire by public transport. Dressed in a green and white American football jacket, she marched the party to Euston railway station and we boarded a first-class carriage. The princess joked that the at-seat trolley service was almost as good as being on the Royal Train. Maybe it was the continual keep-fit programme she was on, but I didn't realize until that day how fast she could walk. Keeping up with her around the park was like being on a non-stop ride in itself. Nick was the only one in the party who got respite because he rode on the princess's shoulders. She stopped once, for lunch, tucking into beefburgers and fries with the rest of us.

No matter that the day was intended to be normal; the press had got wind of her visit and followed us everywhere.

'Come on, Mummy, come on this ride,' said Harry, tugging at his mother's sleeve.

She looked skywards to the twisted metal of the suspended rollercoaster, Nemesis, and shook her head. 'No, I'll be sick,' she said, and stayed with Maria. The sedate pace of the River Rapids was more her style.

Another little person tugging on her arm was Nick. All he wanted to do was go on the Mad Hatter's Tea Party ride. 'Giant teacups, I want to ride on the giant teacups, Princess!' he begged her. That was why the princess, the young princes and our boys appeared in the following day's newspapers whizzing around in the giant teacups. Sadly, nowadays Nick cannot remember being carried around by the princess, even though a framed photo of them takes pride of place in our house.

The newspaper coverage showed that the press would never give her the time and space she had requested the previous December. Denied images of the princess performing her duty, 'Her Majesty's Reptiles', otherwise known as the press, spent every day searching for her going about her everyday life. Journalistic curiosity intensified and, day after day, the newspapers were full of images: the princess at McDonald's; arriving at the Chelsea Harbour Club fitness centre; walking along the street; eating in a restaurant; shopping with friends; in the back of a taxi; driving her car. If the princess stepped outside KP, it was a picture. In 1994, the media, with its voracious appetite, ratcheted up Di-mania to another level.

If there was a time when the princess attempted to 'find herself', it was 1994. I seemed to open the door to an ever-growing band of lifestyle gurus, health experts, healers, astrologists and psychics. Friends offered counselling services, ears and shoulders to cry on. She placed the well-intentioned advice from people who genuinely cared in the same melting pot as the zodiac information, the power of the crystals, the messages from the spiritual world and the 'energies' around her. She mused about them long and hard while undergoing acupuncture, massage or keep-fit. Even Dudley Poplak used to send phials of Bach Rescue Remedy, calming herbal drops.

The scent of incense from burning joss-sticks in the princess's bedroom wafted through the first floor, overriding the air-fresheners the maids had used earlier in the morning. I became used to the immaculately turned-out astrologer Debbie Frank arriving at the KP front door. The floor of either the drawing room or the sitting room became scattered with zodiac charts as Debbie and the princess sat on the carpet, plotting the movement of the planets and what it all meant for the royal Cancerian. She felt that Cancerians, like their symbol the crab, had a hard outer shell, a soft centre and wanted instinctively to skulk sideways into the shadows. She also felt that it explained her fascination with water and her dream to live, one day, in a house on a coast. She told Debbie: 'This house is full of Geminis. William's Gemini, Paul is Gemini – and it's not easy!'

Debbie was keen to offer me the expertise of her readings but I declined. 'You really must have your chart read,' implored the princess. 'It's riveting stuff.'

Once, an acupuncturist from whom the princess had just returned telephoned. If acupuncturists are meant to be calming, this call was anything but. In fact, the practitioner was on the verge of panic. 'I'm a needle short. I think I may have left one in the princess's head!'

I walked up the staircase and into the sitting room where she was writing at her desk, half expecting to find an antenna protruding from her scalp. I started to chuckle, and the princess looked up.

'I've just taken a call,' I said. 'Apparently, you might have an acupuncturist's needle still in your head.'

The princess patted it all over, then burst out laughing. 'Put the poor woman out of her misery and tell her I'm okay. I feel a lot better for seeing her again!'

The princess never failed to see the funny side of her therapies and treatments. Some were more bizarre and self-punishing than others. Twice a week it was my duty – and not the chauffeur's (because of its private nature) – to drive the princess to a clinic in North London for colonic irrigation. 'You *don't* want to know, Paul!' she said.

She drove herself to the home of Susie Orbach, the psychotherapist who specialized in eating disorders and played an important part in helping the princess bring her bulimia under control. Dr Mary Loveday, a small, softly spoken lady, addressed the chemical balance in the princess's body and prescribed vitamin supplements that she would take three times a day.

The growth of the human spirit and the spiritual side of life, 'the other side' as she called it, fascinated the princess. Psychic Rita Rogers, based near my home town of Chesterfield, was a constant guide to her, and Simone Simmons, a faith healer, was always on the telephone. Some nights, it was not unusual for the princess to spend up to five hours on the telephone to her. I had Simone to thank for the smell of joss-sticks.

My view was that these alternative therapists provided the Boss with a release that made her happy, each in their own different way. But a fascinating pastime turned into an over-reliant addiction that disturbed me. What was also disturbing was the way the paparazzi stalked her wherever she went. Once, when she was leaving the London home of Susie Orbach, the princess, wearing dark glasses, was reduced to tears as freelance photographers, working for foreign magazines and agencies, surrounded her, poking fun at her and bullying her with comments such as 'Look at you, you're a wreck' or 'You're nothing but a tart, Diana.' When the princess burst into tears and ran to her car, the next day's headlines screamed, 'DIANA WEEPS', and suggested she was sobbing over her marriage.

Few women would have coped in the eye of those daily storms.

On many occasions in central London I witnessed what it was like to be at the centre of the mêlée. I would park the car on a meter and wait for the princess to return from a health clinic, shop or restaurant. I would catch her eye in the wing- or rear-view mirror as she was pursued by the 'rat-pack', lean over, with the engine running, and push open the door so she could leap inside: 'Drive, Paul, drive.' But the photographers were already around us, leaning from both sides across the bonnet, banging on the windows. The princess, holding a hand to her bowed head, said once: 'We're going to kill somebody one day.' She found it all extremely distressing.

The best times when I was driving with the princess came on sweltering summer days when we stopped at traffic lights with the Mercedes roof down. She loved the shock on motorists' faces when they glanced to one side and recognized her; glum faces were suddenly brightened with delight. Once, the traffic lights turned red and we pulled up alongside a building being renovated in the Mayfair district. One of the builders on the lowest level of scaffolding noticed the princess. Within seconds, word had leaped up to every level and it seemed as if the entire site's staff had downed tools and burst into a chorus of wolf-whistles and colourful support.

The princess was embarrassed and pretended not to hear, but when we drove off, she lifted a hand into the air, waved, and giggled all the way home.

One image the press never captured was when the princess turned up at Maria's surprise fortieth birthday party held at Café Rouge, a short walk from the palace, on 1 February 1994. The fancy-dress theme was 'famous people'. Maria and I went as Antony and Cleopatra. Former Highgrove housekeeper Wendy Berry was Cruella de Vil, brother-in-law Pete Cosgrove was Al Capone, and my brother Graham and his wife Jayne came as Napoleon and Josephine. When the princess walked through the door to join us, my other brother Anthony, masquerading as General Custer, shook hands with the Boss and asked her, rather bluntly: 'What have you come as?'

In a black trouser suit with a black and gold embroidered waistcoat, she replied: 'A princess, of course!'

That Saturday afternoon, as fellow staff and friends prepared their costumes, the princess had gone secretly to meet Mother Teresa, but she was keen to join the revellers because many would be household staff she knew from either KP or Highgrove. Even her old friend from Buckingham Palace, retired Palace Steward Cyril Dickman, was there. The princess wanted 'to do something normal for a change', she said. But when you are the Princess of Wales, freed from police protection, walking through a public restaurant and into a private room is never going to be regarded by anyone else as normal. Perhaps it was my Roman centurion-style outfit, but I assumed the role of protector for the evening, and arranged to meet the princess with a small group of other costumed guests at the police barrier on the palace drive at eight o'clock.

The princess appeared out of the darkness and couldn't believe the sight before her. 'Look at you all!' she said, and doubled up with laughter. She walked to the venue in the middle of this crowd: the Princess of Wales encircled by Antony, the Three Musketeers, Batman and Robin.

Friends and family had travelled south from North Wales, and their false moustaches and wigs almost dropped off when the princess walked through the door. A senior royal at a fancy-dress party in a public restaurant! Stuffy courtiers trapped in a different age might have disapproved but I had never seen the princess have such fun at a social event. She sat in a chair drinking water, giggling over the high-spirited antics as the crowd sat in a row on the floor, performing the boat dance before a conga snaked its way round the upper floor.

Then, the princess took centre stage near the red DJ booth: she had agreed to hand out the prizes for the fancy-dress competition. It made my brother Graham's night when he won first prize as Napoleon and she presented him with a CD-player.

After two hours, the princess decided to leave, and, still enthusing about what a wonderful time she had had, I walked her home – the Princess of Wales walking through Kensington with a Roman centurion at her side.

It was a joy to watch the princess joining in with Maria's birthday celebrations, especially when she was dreading her own. She hated the birthday focus turning on her: she felt uncomfortable because she feared that friends and associates might feel compelled to spring treats or give generously. She gave generously to so many people on their birthdays – she noted her friends' on a calendar. But receiving presents embarrassed her. As she said so often: 'It's much easier to give than receive. There's no strings attached to giving.'

Each 1 July, knowing her enjoyment of WH Smith's humorous cards, I would slip one, signed by the Burrell family, on to her desk. In fact, there was light-hearted rivalry among the staff as to who could buy the funniest, most daring greeting. She opened them after breakfast and stood them all on the round table in her sitting room. Then the flowers started to arrive. Twenty-four long-stemmed yellow roses, boxed from Edward Goodyear, the florist in Mayfair, from a secret admirer the world never got to know about. Red roses arrived from friends. Then white flowers – tulips from Elton John and more roses from Gianni Versace – arrived in vased displays. Anna Harvey, the editor of *Vogue* in London, sent a gift-wrapped blouse or dress. There was always a generous gift from Catherine Walker and from Jo Malone. All her female friends sent flowers or presents. At the police box, well-wishers left cards, presents and flowers. By the end of the day, apartments 8 and 9 resembled a florist's shop and every conceivable flat surface was covered with cards.

If the princess dreaded 1 July, so did her butler. I would be running up and down those stairs for hours on end. A delivery from Selfridges, from Harrods, from the royal grocers Fortnum & Mason, from Harvey Nichols. And then, without fail, a bunch of flowers from Prince Charles who addressed every letter and card he sent, every year until her death, 'Dearest Diana'.

For the remainder of her birthday, from late afternoon until she went to bed, she wrote letter after letter to say thank you to relatives, friends, associates and organizations. I have never seen anyone write so many or respond so quickly. But the princess never forgot the strict discipline instilled into her as a child by her father, who made his family sit down and write thank-you letters religiously.

In the KP sitting room, she removed sheets of her red-edged paper, with a scrolled D below a coronet, from the central drawer of her mahogany desk. She sat there, with her back to the window, as if it were a correspondence production line: write, fold, envelope, seal; write, fold, envelope, seal. Hour after hour she sat there, dipping her black fountain pen into a pot of blue-black Quink, penning her appreciation in the distinctive handwriting that flowed across the paper. Then, after underlining her signature as she always did, she flipped over the letter and pressed it lightly on to the pink blotting paper, which, by the end of the night, was smudged with black. I had to ensure that a pristine sheet was in place for the morning. She folded the letter in half, popped it into a cream envelope lined with red tissue, addressed it then placed it on top of an ever-growing stack. 'I *have* to write thank-you letters. If people take the time and trouble to send a gift, the least I can do is thank them,' she said.

Before she went out for dinner on any other day of the year, she prepared her thank-you letter to her host or dining companion. The envelope would be addressed and propped against a silver ink stand, and on her return she would write the letter, regardless of the hour, so that it could be posted the following morning.

After six months away from the official world stage, the princess began to tread, gingerly, back into the spotlight. The Red Cross, through its director-general Mike Whitlam who became a firm ally, coaxed her into joining a special commission to advise the International Red Cross Federation. In May 1994 the role took her to Geneva. Her private secretary Patrick Jephson claimed that the princess's eyes were glazed with boredom so she soon stepped down. The real reason for her departure was that she didn't want to be an executive pontificating in the boardroom but among the people, having a hands-on approach. She left because of frustration, not boredom, and, as time would prove, she maintained strong ties with the organization in future missions.

The princess returned to London and attended the unveiling of the Canadian War Memorial in Green Park and then, on the eve of the fiftieth anniversary of D-Day, she went to a church service in Portsmouth before joining other senior members of the family on the Royal Yacht *Britannia*. The princess was slipping back into the groove, but never forgot the causes she was passionate about: she attended the launch of the thirtieth appeal of the mental-illness charity Turning Point, went to a concert to raise money for AIDS charities, supported the homeless charity Centre Point and then, later in the year, was at the Palace of Versailles near Paris for a French Foundation for Children dinner, drawing a standing ovation from almost a thousand guests.

She still walked beneath the halo of world-wide acclaim. Crowds cheered wherever she went. At dinners, galas and state functions she dazzled everyone, from presidents to ordinary people. She demanded no special treatment yet her presence, her magical aura, commanded respect and attention.

Yet all the support and encouragement did little to boost her confidence. At KP, she needed constant reassurance. Her inner strength remained, though, and she counted on it to build her confidence. She needed it on 29 June 1994, when an eagerly anticipated television documentary about Prince Charles, made by broadcaster Jonathan Dimbleby with the co-operation of the prince, was screened ahead of a book. Entitled *The Prince of Wales*, it was a riposte, with the royal seal of approval, to the Andrew Morton book of 1992. It had been in the making for eighteen months. So, as the princess had faced royal wrath for her denied co-operation with Morton, Prince Charles's office, with his say-so, had been making his friends available to speak on his behalf, dressed up as a twenty-fifth-anniversary celebration of his investiture as Prince of Wales.

Jonathan Dimbleby claimed later that the prince had not wanted anything to go in the book that would hurt the princess. But he confessed on television to adultery with Camilla Parker Bowles. The princess had no idea that such an admission was coming. How on earth that could be construed as not hurtful to her was bewildering to all at KP. As the documentary was trailed in the preceding days, the princess had worried about the programme's content. She found refuge and advice in the company of Lucia Flecha de Lima, Annabel Goldsmith, Susie Kassem and the Duchess of York, who came to KP to support her. On the day of the evening screening, there came crucial support from another quarter: St James's Palace. That afternoon, the Duchess of Kent – a shining example of warmth and grounded humanity – visited the princess, urging her to be strong. 'How am I to go out there and face everyone?' the princess said that afternoon. If only the misinformed cynics who painted her as a hard-nosed media manipulator determined to make the front pages could have heard her.

That evening, as Britain settled down in front of the television, she was committed to a long-standing engagement to attend a dinner at the Serpentine Gallery in Hyde Park. She was the gallery's patron, a friend of its chairman, Lord Palumbo, and guest of the then newly appointed chairman of the Arts Council of England, Lord Gowrie. She prepared for the engagement racked with nerves, half of her mind on the documentary, the other half on whether her chosen dress was suitable. Outside the gallery, television cameras focused on her arrival, desperate to capture her reaction to the Dimbleby documentary.

The princess was dressed and ready to go an hour before her intended departure, pacing up and down the first-floor landing. In the pantry downstairs, my ears monitored the creaks in the floorboards.

Then they stopped. 'Paul, are you there?'

I bolted up the first flight and stood looking up to the landing where the princess stood, hands on hips, wearing a midnight blue cocktail dress, nipped into the waist with a belt, white satin cuffs and a tight white collar that hugged her neck. 'Well, do you like it?' she asked. My response wasn't spontaneous or enthusiastic enough. 'You don't, do you?' The hands dropped off her hips.

Despite the expert female dressers, a male opinion in the household became her most reassuring sounding-board, just like in Pakistan or Czechoslovakia when she asked Mervyn Wycherley's or my opinion of an outfit. She wanted to gauge the wow-factor. At KP it was usual for her to appear half-way down the stairs, posing like a model in a new hat or suit. 'What do you think?' Or draped in a new dress, with one leg in a pair of tights and one leg out. 'With tights or without?' Or one foot in a flat court shoe, one in a high heel. 'Heels or not?'

Once, during a dress-fitting with designer Jacques Azagury, the princess stood with him in the sitting room as his fitter, a lady called Solange, was pinning the hem of a red dress with matching chiffon scarf. 'Isn't it beautiful, Paul? Isn't Jacques clever?' she said, having called me in.

It was virtually impossible not to give a favourable reaction when the princess was dressed to impress. But I had warned her: 'If you want an honest opinion, ask me. I'll give it. If you don't, don't ask me.'

The evening of the Serpentine Gallery event was a time for

unfavourable honesty. 'Tonight of all nights I think you should look a million dollars and that isn't the dress. Sorry,' I said.

'Well, I haven't got anything else to wear!' she protested.

I flew up the remaining two flights of stairs and, with the princess, went into the wardrobe room. We slid back hanger after hanger of evening wear. 'What about this one?' I asked, pointing out a sparkling black dress.

The princess screwed up her nose. 'No. Too much of an old friend.'

Then, in the black section, I found a short cocktail dress designed by Christina Stambolian. The princess liked it but doubted whether she would still get into it because she feared her constant workouts at the gym might have broadened her shoulders. 'There's one way to find out.' She left the room in midnight blue, holding the latest suggestion by its hanger.

She reappeared in off-the-shoulder black silk crêpe. And she looked spectacular.

'Now *that* is the dress,' I said.

'You don't think it's too much?' she said, jabbing a finger towards her cleavage.

'It's perfect,' I said, and then we went to the safe near her bedroom. She pulled out a choker of pearls, which bore a large oval sapphire surrounded by two rows of diamonds, an engagement present from the Queen Mother.

As departure time neared, she was still pacing the landing. 'Why do I feel so nervous?' she said, irritated with herself.

Reassurance was needed. 'You look fantastic. You'll knock them all sideways,' I said.

'Mmmm.' It was incredible that she didn't think so.

The princess had long drilled into me how to arrive and how to depart: 'Arrivals and departures – *the* most important times of any event.' I reminded her of this just before she left. Then I added: 'Remember, when you arrive, stride out, walk tall, firm handshake and say to yourself, "I am the Princess of Wales." Don't forget that.'

There was a characteristic sharp intake of breath. 'Here goes then, Paul.' I followed the chiffon fishtail down the staircase and along the hallway to the front door. As I shut the rear door of the chauffeur-driven car, she beamed. I waved as the car pulled away.

I watched the television bulletins later that night showing her arrival on that balmy summer's night: striding enthusiastically out of the car, bounding over to Lord Palumbo, shaking his hand and smiling as if she didn't have a care in the world. It became one of the most famous images of the princess and was captured on all the front pages the next morning. 'TAKE THAT!' said the *Daily Mirror*. And Charles? 'NOT FIT TO REIGN,' it cried.

The princess returned to the palace, already aware of what Prince Charles had said about being unfaithful. There was no hint of triumph. She was quiet. No snack. No hot drink. She went straight to her bedroom and I turned off all the lights. Bar one.

9. 'The Boss'

No one could ever pretend that duty within the walls of KP was easy. Like life itself, it was never easy for staff corralled by the walls of apartments 8 and 9. Like in countless other relationships – in family, marriage, friendship or business – happiness can sometimes wrestle with the reverse. Life with the Boss was a rollercoaster ride. Those with weaker stomachs would describe it as a white-knuckle experience. The highs were tremendous but the lows were desperate and, for many, the ride went too fast, turned upside-down once too often and seemed out of control. But the princess *was* in control, and she decided, with the capricious ruthless streak that was part of her character, who rode with her and whom she left behind. The key to longevity with the princess was emotional stamina; you did not judge or question, just accepted the whole package, warts and all, as the complex, flawed but loving, wonderful human being that she was.

Unswerving support and loyalty carry no conditions, especially when they are expected. The going clearly got tough for those who felt sidelined and they jumped ship far too readily, some before they were pushed; they will have convinced themselves that they never saw the writing on the wall. Others, with a consuming devotion, tried to hang on but their P45s arrived through a misunderstanding of their motives; their exits were terrible to witness. Some true friendships were terminated for good with a knee-jerk based on misunderstanding or misinformation. There was always an inherent risk in growing too close to the princess: the heartbreak of knowing, loving and then losing the intoxicating friendship of a phenomenon, either by choice or otherwise.

I know that heartbreak because Maria experienced it between late 1994 and 1995. Maria had said she would try the post of dresser for a year but the hours got longer, the demands greater and she could not bear another year of hardly seeing Alexander and Nick. The boys were used to Dad working all hours but not Mum. 'It will get better. Don't give up,' I implored her time and again, trying to avoid the inevitable. I knew that if she stepped down the princess would view it as abandonment. In her life, she saw such rejection as if it were an enemy stalking her. She had felt rejected by her family, who had yearned for a boy, rejected in marriage by Prince Charles, rejected in the search for refuge by her brother, Earl Spencer. The saddest irony of all was that the princess could be equally harsh in handing out rejection. With Maria's experience, I found myself – not for the first time in a royal duty – caught in the middle of the crossfire between the two women I cared most about.

When my wife went to meet the princess at KP to announce her reluctant resignation because she wanted to spend more time with her family, I was the coward who fled and hid, unable through fear to act as peace-keeper. I placed my hands over my ears in the hope that the inevitable din would disperse by itself. Later that night, in December 1994, the conversation was relayed to me by a devastated Maria.

'What? After all I've done for you?' said a livid princess. 'I've bent over backwards to accommodate you and be flexible, and this is how you repay me.'

Maria attempted to get a word in edgeways and explain that the agreement had been for a year and she had honoured that, but her boys came first. 'But she wiped the floor with me. She had me in tears,' she told me that night.

The following day, the fall-out was still evident from the black cloud that hung over the breakfast table.

'Good morning, Your Royal Highness,' I said, armed with a pot of coffee.

On this occasion, there was no bright response. 'Paul. Can you have a word with your wife?'

For once, I had hoped for a huge headline in the papers to divert the princess's attention, but there was nothing. Meekly, pathetically, I said Maria had made up her mind, tried to explain the family-based reasons and reassured the princess that it had been a difficult decision for my wife but that she had made it in the full knowledge that I would be giving 200 per cent effort for both of us. The princess was unforgiving. For the remaining four weeks of Maria's notice period, she never said a word to her. It was known as a 'no speaking spell' among palace staff.

By 1995, others had fallen out of favour and it was sad, as well as unfathomable, to see chef Mervyn Wycherley leave KP after a nine-month no speaking spell. Another casualty later that year was my fellow butler Harold Brown who leaped before he was pushed after enduring his own no speaking spell. He landed comfortably in the service of Princess Margaret and, therefore, kept his living quarters in apartment 6. His departure left me as the sole butler, with an ever-shrinking staff and an ever-increasing trust with the Boss.

But even I was not immune to criticism and the princess's cold shoulder. The blackest period of my time with the Boss was when she began to tighten her financial belt at around the time of her divorce. The expense of running a household dawned on her, and I think she saw the KP telephone bill for the first time. She had a printout of the itemized bill and all staff were asked to write their names next to personal calls they had made. My fraction came to around £300. I wrote a cheque and thought that would be the end of the matter. But it wasn't.

My usage of the telephone had clearly rankled with the Boss. As I presented the cheque, she wanted to know why I had been running up such a bill. I made the mistake of speaking my mind. 'As I am working such long hours, I don't see the harm in me ringing my family. I'm working almost sixteen-hour days, Your Royal Highness.'

It was taken, wrongly, as a moan. For the next two weeks, she blanked me, and refused to say a word to me. It was a deeply upsetting time. I felt cut off, deprived of her special friendship, and isolated.

It became so bad that I had to resort to leaving Post-it note messages around the apartments. She, in turn, wrote her replies by memo.

The obvious silliness of the situation came to a head when an important message went astray, and she asked for an explanation: 'Why couldn't you just tell me, Paul, instead of writing it down?'

'Your Royal Highness!' I said, in exasperation. 'How can I? You haven't been talking to me!'

She looked almost resigned to the point I had made, so I kept on.

'I cannot do my job properly like this. I don't know what I have done but, please, let me assist you so I can function properly.'

The ice melted there and then. A huge wave of relief swept over me as I was brought back in from the cold. From then on I was careful about how often I used the KP telephone.

'IN FROM THE COLD,' said the *Daily Mirror* headline to mark the defrosting in relations between KP and Buckingham Palace when the princess was invited to spend Christmas with the rest of the Royal Family at Sandringham in December 1994. The press believed, wrongly, that it was Her Majesty's private secretary and the princess's brother-in-law, Sir Robert Fellowes, who had extended the invitation. The truth was much warmer. In a handwritten letter, the Queen said that both she and the Duke of Edinburgh would like the princess to stay with them on Christmas Eve with Princes Charles, William and Harry.

My eyes became used to witnessing important correspondence: from the Queen, the Duke of Edinburgh, Prime Minister John Major, Elton John and numerous other people, including the princess's family. I was her permitted witness to many things, even her will and legal divorce papers that she didn't want her private secretary, Patrick Jephson, to see. I wasn't the only friend to view the correspondence. She took advice on speeches and letter-writing from her journalist friend Richard Kay. My 'correspondence sessions' took place either on the stairs or in the sitting room where the princess sat at her desk. Letters composed officially by Patrick Jephson would be sent round for her perusal in a folder. She would shout my name from the top of the stairs and we would meet half-way and sit down. Her on one step. Me on another. 'What do you think about this?' she would say, or she would shriek, 'Have a look at this!' Or she would leave a letter on the desk in my pantry with an attached note, saying, 'Let me know your comments on this.'

It was on such an occasion that she showed me the letters from the Duke of Edinburgh and her brother Earl Spencer. In time, she wrote private letters to me: thoughts she wanted to get down on paper, truths she wanted to record and leave in my trust; or philosophies about inner strength that she wanted to share. My duty evolved until the princess would share her most sensitive letters, and let me listen to her most private phone calls. In witnessing all her lines of communication, I know that, until her death, the Queen and the princess were in touch and on the best of terms. And, as an independent witness, I know the history, the traumas, and the nightmares she lived.

The Queen's Christmas invitation led the princess to take to Norfolk a present for every member of the Royal Family. In the weeks before the holiday, she had sent me to Kensington, Knightsbridge and Mayfair to buy gifts for family, friends and staff. Her generosity knew no bounds so, with her approval, I spent thousands of pounds. Relying on my knowledge of and time with the Queen, I chose for her something practical – a cashmere cardigan, a Hermès scarf or a tartan rug; for the Duke of Edinburgh, a cartridge case, a shooting stick or hip flask. I spent hours wrapping the presents, leaving the princess to write a personal note for each before she left for Sandringham. Privately, she loved the build-up to Christmas even if the actual day was, by her own admission, 'a bit grim'.

Had I failed to put up a tree two weeks before the big day, she would have been the first to complain. Each year, I ordered an eighteen-foot Norwegian spruce from the royal estate at Windsor, which took pride of place on the staircase, positioned on the flat level between the first and second flight of stairs. It was decorated with ten sets of white lights, adorned with crystal and glass ornaments with white cotton icicles dangling from each branch, topped with a silver star. There was a smaller spruce for the nursery on the second floor. William and Harry were in charge of its decoration, using hand-made ornaments crafted at school.

Away from the palace, Christmas was a magical time at our home, and our tree, decorated in red, green and gold, sat in the corner of the sitting room, which looked out towards the palace. I dressed up as Father Christmas and, in a carefully choreographed routine, delivered the boys' presents from behind a huge white beard and red-hooded tunic, complete with black wellington boots. They didn't guess it was me (until they spotted the same wellington boots in the outside shed!). Nick, then six, wanted to be the centre of attention, doing cartwheels in the bedroom, shouting 'Look at me! Look at me!' Those few magical minutes gave Maria and me, and our annual Christmas visitor Betty, Maria's mother, so much pleasure.

But I knew that, come mid-afternoon on Christmas Day, the princess would be back at KP alone, having left her boys at Sandringham. By the time she arrived, I was waiting at the door because the thought of her returning to an empty home on such a day seemed so sad. 'You can't spend Christmas here by yourself. Come down and spend some time with us,' I urged her.

'No, Paul. You don't want me spoiling your Christmas. It's a family time. I'll be fine here.' She wanted to be alone.

Then the princess did what she always did every Christmas afternoon. She sat at her desk, got out the fountain pen and bottle of Quink and started writing thank-you letters for the presents she had received. But first, before I left, she penned me a festive greeting. 'To Paul, Wishing you a very Happy Christmas, with love from Diana'. Then she addressed her first envelope and wrote her first letter: to Her Majesty The Queen, Sandringham House, Norfolk.

I returned home almost reluctantly. 'If you want anything, just call me,' I said.

The princess's address book was packed with names from all walks of life. Whenever she met anyone for the first time, she could make them feel as if they had been a friend for life. Articles began to appear in newspapers, detailing her 'charmed circle'. If the princess was spotted socializing with someone or attending a therapy session, journalists concluded there was a deep, lasting, best-of-friends association. The Boss had many friends, but there was only a small inner circle, headed by Lucia Flecha de Lima, who was best friend, mother-figure and counsellor rolled into one. Lucia's husband, Paulo, had been transferred from London to the Brazilian embassy in Washington but even the different time-zones failed to send the friendship out of synch. Lucia would set her alarm for three o'clock in the morning so that she could talk to the princess at the start of her day. If the princess needed advice or consolation, she rang Lucia. I faxed a never-ending stream of letters and messages across the Atlantic to her. Being a friend to the princess meant being a friend on twenty-four-hour call and Lucia accepted this. She was there every single time for the princess.

'I couldn't cope without her. She's marvellous. She's like a mother to me,' the princess said, time and time again. In August 1994, the princess went to Washington. In May 1995, Lucia came to London. At Christmas 1996, the princess stayed with Lucia. Back and forth across the Atlantic, that friendship bridged its long-distance divide and became stronger as time went on.

In London, the princess's surrogate family came in the form of Rosa Monckton, Susie Kassem, Lady Annabel Goldsmith, Richard Kay and Dr Mary Loveday. These people, like myself, saw the princess at her most raw and knew *everything* in return for non-judgemental friendship. They understood her better than anyone else and loved her for the person she was.

The Duchess of York's presence was a guaranteed pick-me-up for the princess. Wide-eyed and bounding up the stairs full of energy, she was a survivor, like the Boss, and there were constant phone calls of support between the two.

They sat in the sitting room, deep in serious conversation or laughing, comparing the knife wounds left in their backs by the royal household. I built up a vicarious trust with the duchess through the princess and a friendship developed. Even when she knew the Boss was out, the phone would ring in the pantry and the familiar, Sloaney voice would cheerily say: 'Hi, Paul, it's the duchess.'

She could be as confused about people's motives as the princess. 'Why do people say such hurtful things about me all the time? I don't know what's expected of me,' she would say.

Like the princess, she believed in karma. 'What comes around, goes around,' they both said.

I listened to her like I listened to the princess, and felt terribly sorry for her. 'Look,' I said, 'remember what the Boss says – kill people with kindness and never let them know they're getting you down.'

I recall those conversations, over the phone or at KP, fondly every time I look at a framed picture the duchess sent me at the end of 1994, showing her with her little daughters, Beatrice and Eugenie. At the bottom, she wrote a special message: '*Dear Paul and Maria, thank you so much for your incredible kindness and support. Words are not enough but thank you. With bestest wishes – Sarah.*'

Outside the trusted circle of the princess's closest friends, she knew exactly what to tell and what not to tell each person. Each one brought a specialism or an experience to the table, which meant she counted on their advice or wisdom. The princess compartmentalized her friendships and preferred to meet individuals one-to-one. Her friendships were like an assortment of boxes and I knew which box she was opening, why she was opening it and where it was ranked in her life. Being at the centre of her world meant becoming a trusted messenger. When the princess was away, she gave me permission to look through her address book, find a name, ring a number.

With Harold Brown gone and the princess wondering who around her she could trust, my role as butler began to evolve in 1995 into personal assistant, messenger, driver, delivery boy, confidant. I stepped in at times when she chose not to use her chauffeur, PR guru or private secretary because she didn't want professional eyes witnessing certain friendships, messages or private missions.

'Paul, stand by the fax machine now and don't leave it until it's all come through.' The voice of the princess travelled down from the first-floor and reached me in the pantry.

1995 was the year when the princess trusted me to handle her correspondence, from the professional to the most personal and secret. She started to shield information from Patrick Jephson's eyes and divert faxes from his office at St James's Palace. She had heard a rumour that he was growing dissatisfied and seeking employment elsewhere. She confronted him with it and his response didn't convince her that he would remain at KP indefinitely. She became wary and put a distance between them that was never bridged again. 'How does he expect me to communicate with him on highly delicate and detailed discussions regarding my marriage and my future when I don't even know whether he will be here in the future?' she said. A new fax machine for the princess's personal use was installed in her sitting room, placed on the carpet under her desk, hidden by the sofa positioned directly in front. There were numerous occasions when I walked into the sitting room to see her and found no one there.

'Your Royal Highness?' I called, turning to go into the drawing room.

'I'm down here,' said a voice from out of nowhere. The princess was on her hands and knees under the desk, trying but failing to operate the fax machine. Technology, like cooking, was not one of her strong points.

'It's hopeless. I'm hopeless!' She would laugh with self-mocking humour.

After a few more weeks of facsimile frustration, the machine under the desk was abandoned. Instead, she started to utilize my machine downstairs, underneath my desk in the pantry. She handed me sensitive documents to send and wait for the replies to come through. She sent personal mail overseas by fax to ensure immediate receipt, instead of having to rely on drawn-out communication via the post.

On one occasion, she trusted neither the fax nor the post. 'Paul, I would like you to deliver this letter by hand,' she said, handing me a letter. I looked at the sealed envelope. The name was familiar. And so was the address – overseas.

My eyes conveyed my surprise at such a long-haul mission. 'I know it's a long way but it *is* important,' she said.

'Consider it done,' I told her, and kept hold of the envelope until she left on a visit abroad. In the time she was away, I boarded another plane to a different destination for a two-day trip and dropped the letter into the hand that would pen the reply. By the time the princess returned to KP, I was back on duty to welcome her home.

'Mission accomplished,' I said.

In January 1995, the chattering classes were still ruminating over Prince Charles and his relationship with the mistress with whom he had confessed to having an affair, Camilla Parker Bowles. Speculation intensified when, eleven days into the new year, her divorce was announced from Brigadier Andrew Parker Bowles following a two-year separation. But the princess's attention and serious concern had been diverted elsewhere – to the relationship between her husband and his assistant Tiggy Legge-Bourke. Even the press was training its sights in her direction, further arousing the suspicions of the princess.

'THE KISS' was the front-page headline in the *Daily Mirror*, showing Prince Charles skiing with friends, which included Tiggy Legge-Bourke. In a series of photographs the prince, wearing a red bobble hat, put his arm around her and kissed her 'in a show of affection'. His private secretary Richard Aylard explained to reporters: 'It's not unreasonable for him to kiss her on the cheek, it is perfectly ordinary.'

The princess didn't agree and she felt the relationship was crossing the line far too soon after the assistant's recruitment. In fact, so suspicious was she that she regarded Camilla Parker Bowles as yesterday's news. She felt Tiggy Legge-Bourke was getting too close to

Prince Charles as well as to William and Harry. As far as the princess was concerned, she was still married and two other women were circling dangerously around her territory.

Don't ask me why I did it, but as everyone sent me cards and presents for my thirty-seventh birthday on 6 June 1995 I decided to send a gift to Mum in Grassmoor. I wanted her to receive a little something to mark the anniversary of my birth. Via a garden centre in Derbyshire, I arranged for the delivery of a stone trough filled with flowering plants to last the summer. A simple message dictated over the phone was written on a card and placed among the greenery.

When she opened the door of the same terraced house where I had grown up, she was, typically, wearing her pinny. 'I think you've got the wrong house, duck. It's not my birthday,' she said, as Dad later told me.

Then she started to read my message and was overwhelmed. It wasn't often Mum received flowers. It was the first time she had ever received them from me on my birthday and my words had moved her. When I heard her tearful joy over the telephone at KP that afternoon, I vowed to do the same every year. Two weeks later, she was raving about her blossoming trough in the garden when she and Dad came to the Old Barracks for the night before I drove them to Heathrow airport and waved them off on a dream holiday to America and Canada.

When the telephone rang at two o'clock in the morning on 15 June, my subconscious state told me it would be the princess, who was away on an engagement in Russia. She was the only person who ever phoned at such an unearthly hour. A crisis, personal or otherwise, must have happened. Maria got up to answer the telephone. Moments later, she was sobbing. 'How am I going to tell him? How am I going to tell him?'

The princess! What's happened? I shot out of bed and bolted across the landing into the sitting room where Maria was still on the telephone.

It was my brother Graham. Mum had collapsed in the street in Ottawa, Canada, and died instantly from a massive heart-attack. She was fifty-nine.

The next morning, the princess rang to check on life at KP where she was due to return two days later on the Saturday to be with William and Harry. As soon as I heard her voice, I broke down. 'What on earth's the matter, Paul?' she asked.

In my devastation, I explained how Mum's heart had given way, how she had seemed so healthy before she left. Then I told her how lost Dad was, stuck in Canada, struggling to organize the release of Mum's body to return home.

'Leave it to me, Paul. We'll get on to it straightaway.'

One call from the Princess of Wales's office to the British High Commission in Canada sorted all the technicalities that surround a sudden death in a foreign country. In the middle of a hectic schedule in Russia, the princess took charge of events in Canada to help the grieving in England. She even took the trouble to ring and speak to Dad in his hotel room in Ottawa. She spent around thirty minutes comforting him, reassuring him that someone from the high commission would be with him at all times, the release of the body was being organized and his flight back to Britain was paid for.

'On your return, I would like you to come to London with your sons. I would like to see you,' she told Dad.

As soon as the princess arrived back at the palace that Saturday, I was with her in the sitting room. I sat on the sofa, cried and apologized, and she sat down with a comforting arm round me. I had known how good, how strong, how compassionate she had been with others and there I was, embraced by that caring nature that had touched so many strangers over so many years.

She spoke about fate, the meaning of life, the meaning of death, her spiritual beliefs, the final moments she had shared in that hospital room with her friend Adrian Ward-Jackson, experiencing 'the journey of his soul'. 'Paul, the spirit stays around after death. Your mum is still with us. Believe in that. You're strong. You need to be strong,' she said.

The next day was Father's Day. Dad and my brothers Graham and Anthony drove to the palace for that desperate weekend. Mum's body was still in Canada, due to return the next day.

We met the princess at the police barrier on the drive. She was wearing a sweatshirt, purple cycling shorts and trainers, and she had left William and Harry in the nursery. She embraced Dad and my brothers one by one. Then, linking her right arm with Dad's left, she said: 'Let's go for a walk.'

On that warm afternoon, Dad and the princess walked in front, we three brothers walking close behind. We went into Kensington Palace Gardens, up the Broad Walk running through the centre of the park towards Bayswater Road, then turned right within the park to the Italian Gardens, continuing through Hyde Park, past the Serpentine Gallery, towards the Albert Memorial, then back full circle to the palace. We were walking and talking, all five of us, for forty-five minutes.

Without a baseball cap, the princess was instantly recognizable. When a passer-by tried to take a photograph, she extended her arm politely and asked: 'Please don't.'

Despite his grief, Dad was concerned about the princess being exposed in a park. 'You don't have to do this for us. You're being noticed. We should go back to the palace,' he said to her.

'Graham, I think I'll be okay with your three strapping sons around me.' I think that was the only time Dad raised a smile all weekend.

We walked back with the princess to the orangery beside the state apartments. 'If there is anything I can do, Graham, just tell Paul.' She embraced my family one last time, then disappeared through a door set in the brick wall. Dad couldn't get over how kind the princess was, and how much time she had spent with us all.

Later that evening, Dad wanted to be alone and he went outside to sit on the bench on the green that stretched out in front of the Old Barracks. I looked down from the first-floor sitting-room window and there he was, with his back towards us. And the princess was beside him again. She had been returning home in her car when she spotted him from the drive. She had pulled over and walked across the green to join him. I looked down, thinking how odd it was to be watching my dad with her. I watched his head moving as he talked, wiping his eyes with his handkerchief. Then he broke down, weeping on the princess's shoulder.

Mum came home on the Monday. We buried her that same week. On the eve of the funeral, her coffin rested on the altar at Hasland Church where she was christened and married, and where Grandma and Grandad Kirk were buried. We filled the church with white flowers of every description. We lit candles in her memory. Each one of us then had a private moment. I stood and placed my hand on the polished wooden lid, bowed my head and closed my eyes, remembering what the princess had said: 'Your mum is still with us.'

At the funeral we couldn't see the coffin because it was covered with a wild garden of flowers. As the other relatives and friends drifted away after the service, I stood by the graveside with Graham. That was when he told me Mum's secret: her decision to burn Cunard's job offer.

We went back to No. 47 Chapel Road. Mum's handbag and knitting were on a chair in the back near the fire.

As Dad flicked on the kettle and my brothers, sisters-in-law, nieces and nephews milled around the house, I sat down and opened her handbag. Inside, there was a powder compact with a Royal Yacht *Britannia* crest on the lid, a present from my days with the Queen, and a lipstick. The only other item was her battered red purse, which, typically, contained not one penny. But there was a folded card. It was the message I had sent in the stone trough on my birthday: '*Mum, just a little something for suffering so much pain to bring me into the world on this day 37 years ago. With all my love, from your eldest – Paul X.*'

Family was important to the princess, but it was unfortunate that hers was not as close-knit as her inner circle of friends. Her sister, Lady Sarah McCorquodale, was a regular visitor from Lincolnshire. Out of all the Spencers, she was the closest. Her mother, Frances Shand Kydd was a virtual recluse on the Scottish island of Seil but visited when she could. In fact, the princess saw more of her stepmother, Raine Spencer, than she did of her own mother and lunched with her at least once a month, sometimes at Cecconi's, just off Bond Street, because that was her late father's favourite restaurant.

But while there was a constant stream of visitors to KP, it did nothing to fill the silence in the late afternoons and early evenings when the princess might find herself alone. With William and Harry away at school or at Highgrove, the void had to be filled.

'I hate the silence in this home,' she said, as she sat reading *Vogue* or *Harpers & Queen* on a Saturday morning. Music filled some of the space but she missed the physical presence of what she called 'the small people'. 'Paul, ring your boys and ask them to come up,' she said.

The sound of feet running around the apartment, the childish screams, the videos playing on the television, Harry's PlayStation being hijacked, it all helped take away the loneliness. Alexander and Nick got the free run of a palace without knowing that, just by being there, they made the princess feel happier. 'Do you want something to eat?' the princess would ask them, leaning against the doorway of her boys' sitting room, and she would go to Darren McGrady in the kitchen and ask him to feed two hungry boys their usual – burger and chips.

Alexander and Nick loved going to KP. They ran up the front drive, racing each other to the back door and into my pantry before bolting up the stairs to where the Boss would be waiting, more often than not on the telephone to a friend.

'Hi, Princess.'

'Hi, Princess.'

The double yell of my two boys would echo back down to me in the pantry.

With each visit, they returned home full of excitement to the Old Barracks where Maria was still frozen out by the princess. These visits thrilled the boys but hurt Maria. 'She's got you up there and now she's got my boys,' she cried, one night.

It didn't help one Sunday morning when Nick, with a child's innocence, asked Maria: 'Why don't you work for the princess any more, Mummy? Why don't you like her?'

'Paul, whatever she has been saying, it's got to stop. Why did Nick ask me that?' demanded Maria. It was as if I was caught in the middle of family politics between an ex-wife and a new girlfriend. Later that summer, though, Alexander and Nick effectively brought the old friends back together. Somewhere along the mad dash between KP and the Old Barracks, our sons became keepers of a royal peace.

Nick was sitting with the princess, and she asked after his mummy. 'She wants to be here too, Princess,' he said.

That night, I was released early from duty and the phone rang. Maria answered. It was the princess. In a marked change from previous calls that year, she didn't immediately ask for me. She started chatting and the two were soon talking as if nothing had happened.

Maria had been brought back in from the cold. She was one of the lucky ones.

Bridges needed to be strengthened between KP and Fleet Street, so the princess, who was intent on avenging her husband's public admission of adultery, went on a charm offensive to woo the media. She invited newspaper editors and columnists to private lunches at the palace. She felt it was a good opportunity for her to be seen in her natural environment, and would give journalists a chance to understand her a little better. She, in turn, would attempt to discover what made them tick, what they knew and why certain angles had been adopted in certain articles. It was a mutual fact-finding mission.

'If BP [Buckingham Palace] find out, the press office will go into its usual blind-panic mode!' She laughed.

The great, the good and the not-so-good of Fleet Street wiped their feet at the front door of apartment 8 and, no matter how brave they had been with their newsprint columns within the safe confines of their empires, it was fascinating to watch them walk with clear trepidation into the disarming territory of the Boss. For so long, she had been only a captivating image that, day after day, had helped them shift their headlines from the news-stands. Now it was her turn to confront them in the drawing room and over lunch. She was in brilliant form. How she and I laughed as we dissected each guest after they had left.

'How funny to see that I can make such powerful people so nervous,' said a bemused princess, then added, 'How enjoyable!'

One by one, journalism's luminaries arrived on different days: Charles Moore, editor of the *Daily Telegraph*; Paul Dacre, editor of the *Daily Mail*; Piers Morgan, editor of the *Daily Mirror*; Stuart Higgins, editor of the *Sun*; Lynda Lee-Potter, columnist on the *Daily Mail*; and even the BBC's royal correspondent Jennie Bond. It had been pre-arranged with the Boss, who was dressed to kill on each occasion, that I linger in the doorway of the dining room. We had secret signals, which had been well rehearsed – and well used over the years with any dinner guest. One furtive look of those blue eyes beneath a raised eyebrow was her way of telling me to serve the three courses quicker. One unfortunate lunch guest, a famous TV personality as well as newspaper columnist on non-royal issues, was served the fastest lunch on record. He was received, fed, watered and dispatched in forty minutes, never to be seen again.

'I almost slipped into a coma through boredom, Paul. He was *so* boring!' She was disappointed because her illusions had been shattered.

Editors and columnists enjoyed the off-the-record opportunity to chat to her and ask questions. The princess was the perfect diplomat. When Stuart Higgins of the *Sun* asked about her thoughts on Camilla Parker Bowles, she responded, 'Well, I actually feel quite sorry for her.' He had been expecting scorn and bitterness to pour forth and nearly fell off his bamboo chair. Then the Boss added, 'The woman has lost almost everything in life and gained what, exactly?'

When Piers Morgan of the *Daily Mirror* pitched in with his forthright 'Do you think Charles will become King?', she answered: 'Well, he thinks that but I think he would be happier living in Provence or Tuscany.'

The lunch and good-natured banter with the *Daily Mirror* editor was joined by William. He sat beside his mother, listening intently, and his age belied the maturity he showed.

Piers Morgan turned to him: 'What do you think of the press?'

William looked up to his mother, who gave him a nod for him to answer. 'They are okay. I have begun to recognize them and know where they will be so that means I can avoid them. It's not the British press that are annoying, it is the photographers from Europe. They sit on the riverbank at Eton, watching me rowing, waiting for me to fall in!'

The BBC's Jennie Bond was the only journalist lunch guest who benefited from the princess's generosity. In what was probably the most relaxed conversation of them all, the off-the-record chat turned into women's talk as the well-groomed royal correspondent took advice from the world's best-dressed woman. Jennie had commented on the stunning sheen of the princess's hosiery and, later that evening, I had to gift-wrap six new pairs of tights and forward them with a note. During that lunch, the princess also advised Jennie on the best colours to wear for television. On another occasion, the princess's private courting of the media backfired and handed her sternest critics a golden opportunity to whip up an anti-Diana storm. She had been photographed in a car, secretly meeting *Daily Mail* reporter

Richard Kay down a side-street. The hysteria that followed represented rank hypocrisy. The princess, for so long in her life, had been briefed against by officials from the royal household or Prince Charles's catty friends. All she was doing was taking charge of her own PR machine, ensuring she was understood, not misunderstood, and she chose to channel truth through a trusted ally. She was doing no more than Prime Minister Tony Blair's team of spin doctors or Prince Charles's one-time aide Mark Bolland who, by courting the media after the princess had died, led a PR strategy to 'sell' Camilla Parker Bowles to the public. What clearly rankled with the press offices at Buckingham Palace and St James's Palace was that the princess was one step ahead – and winning the game.

As the car crossed the Shepherd's Bush roundabout and headed on to Bayswater Road to the north of KP, the male passenger with the furtive eyes dived rather dramatically to his right on the back seat and lay on his side, pulling the green tartan rug over him. I rolled my eyes as I concentrated on the road ahead. It wasn't the first time I had to sneak a secret visitor past the police, but this passenger seemed to enjoy the cloak-and-dagger operation more than most.

I flicked the indicator and turned right, passing the foreign embassies on the 'Millionaires' Row' running parallel to the palace. To anyone looking on, I was alone in the car, heading as normal to my workplace.

'Where are we now? Have we gone past the police post yet?' asked a muffled voice from under the rug.

'No. Stay under. I'll tell you when,' I said impatiently, keen on sticking to the strict instructions from the princess to 'keep him hidden on entry'.

As the car slowed up at the security barrier, the uniformed guard recognized my car and face and waved me on.

'I can't believe they never stopped you,' the muffled voice said.

I drove under the arch of the clock tower at the side of the palace into Clock Court and parked adjacent to the secret doorway into apartment 9.

'I can't believe how easy that was!' exclaimed the passenger, casting aside the rug and stepping out. Martin Bashir patted out the creases of his jacket and shirt, picked up his briefcase and followed me through the door, up the stairs, past the princess's bedroom, down the corridor and into the boys' sitting room where she was waiting for him. It was midsummer 1995, and the wheels were being put in motion for the filming and broadcast of a royal *Panorama* interview for BBC1.

I have to be honest, I had no idea then that the *Panorama* project was being planned. It seemed that only Bashir and the Boss shared this secret. But getting the television journalist in and out of KP became a well-rehearsed routine, no questions asked, small-talk exchanged.

It was a mission carried out in either my blue Vauxhall Astra or the princess's dark blue BMW. 'The beauty of a BMW is that it melts into the crowd in London,' she always said.

The instructions were easy to follow. Park outside the white office building that sits alongside BBC Television Centre, wait in the car park and Martin Bashir would emerge and get into the left rear seat. When approaching KP, 'keep him hidden'. I had become expert at keeping other visitors hidden, visitors a lot more sensitive than Bashir; visitors who made much less fuss than he did. But in delivering him unnoticed to the princess, my job was done and I returned to the pantry until I was needed for the return leg.

'Paul, are you there?' shouted the princess.

'Yes. Is he ready to leave?'

'Mr Bashir, your chauffeur awaits,' smiled the princess.

On those visits, there was never a hint that a project was being covertly planned. It was one secret the princess was not going to share with me. Not until it was 'in the can'. But Bashir was a clever man and, in time, he knew the insecurities of the princess, and no doubt convinced her of the wisdom of doing such a frank television interview. The princess listened to the charming, smooth-talking operator. Instinctively, the princess *wanted* to trust him. He played the pity card and talked to the princess that summer about how life 'hadn't been great' for him recently, his marriage and the pressures of living in a terraced house in the Wimbledon area of London. As she told me afterwards: 'He's not had an easy life. I enjoyed talking to him.' I think she even convinced herself that he was a friend.

What she didn't know was that Bashir phoned me regularly, on the hunt for inside information. What he didn't know was that, once, when he rang, the princess was standing next to me in the pantry, some time after the interview's transmission.

As I went through the routine of batting away his small-talk, she mouthed to me: 'Who is it?'

Covering the receiver mouthpiece, I mimed back: 'Martin Bashir.'

'Put it on the speaker.' She pointed at the button on the telephone. I pressed it, and within seconds, the irreverent voice of the journalist echoed round the pantry. After that conversation, the princess saw her 'friend' in a different light.

With the *Panorama* programme, Bashir had tapped into the princess's vengeful streak: at the time she wanted to get even with Prince Charles over his adultery confession on the Dimbleby documentary. Filming took place on a Sunday when she could be assured of being alone. No dresser, no chef, and it was my day off. The princess had to cope with salads in the fridge and notify the police of visitors she expected. The camera crew, under the direction of Martin Bashir, set up its equipment in the boys' sitting room. The next morning when I asked why the furniture had been moved, the princess said it hadn't been.

Then, a week before transmission, the princess told me she had filmed *Panorama*, it was all top-secret stuff and she felt Britain would understand her better at the end of it. 'I'm sure many people will support you. As long as you are happy with the end product,' I told her.

On the night of Monday 20 November, I sat at the Old Barracks and joined more than twenty million viewers in watching the princess speak about how she wanted to be 'the queen of people's hearts', how Prince Charles would not suit the 'top job' of being king, how there had been 'three people in our marriage', how she had adored James Hewitt, and how she would not go quietly. The interview told me nothing new. No views were expressed that I didn't know already, but my concern for her image was great as I watched *Newsnight* on BBC2 and saw Nicholas Soames, the politician friend of Prince Charles, tear into her with the kind of hypocrisy that both she and I had come to expect and loathe. When Prince Charles needed defending, Nicholas Soames would be wheeled out to make an articulate argument with his anti-Diana ramblings. The next day, the princess was in high spirits, buoyed by the adrenaline rush of her latest surprise move and also by the positive reaction, and sympathy, she had received in the morning newspapers. She had taken a huge PR risk, and her reputation among the British public as a royal survivor was intact. But in her headstrong decision to co-operate with Bashir, she had never considered, perhaps naïvely, the implications that *Panorama* had for her marriage. Divorce would be rushing to her door. But, momentarily, she was on the crest of a media wave. There was almost an air of invincibility about her. She felt she could take on all comers, and next in line was Tiggy Legge-Bourke.

It was 14 December 1995 and the staff Christmas lunch, combining the offices of both the Prince and the Princess of Wales, was being held at the Lanesborough Hotel on Hyde Park Corner. It was the day when the Boss was going to come face to face with Tiggy Legge-Bourke.

'Come with me in my car,' the princess said. We drove the short distance together, past the Knightsbridge Barracks, through Hyde Park and the stone arch, pressing the button inside the car that remotely activated the barrier in the archway. 'I love this little short-cut.' She beamed. By the time we arrived we were late, and the hundred or so guests were already enjoying the pre-lunch reception.

As we entered the room, heads turned to the princess. 'Keep standing by me and just watch,' she said, through her smile. Those elegant legs strode purposefully through the crowd. She was making a bee-line for Tiggy Legge-Bourke, who was chatting at the far end of the room. I was walking in her wake.

'Hello, Tiggy. How are you?' said the princess, smiling. Before she could answer, the princess adopted an air of mock-sympathy. '*So sorry* to hear about the baby.'

Horror paralysed Tiggy's face. Tears welled in her eyes, and she left the room, accompanied by Prince Charles's valet Michael Fawcett. I turned to find the princess. She was mingling with the rest of the crowd. Her message had been fired across the bows of her husband's camp. Job well done, she thought.

'Did you see the look on her face, Paul? She almost fainted!' said the princess afterwards.

The thunderbolt delivered at the Lanesborough had sent tremors across Hyde Park and into both St James's Palace and Buckingham Palace. Prince Charles was livid. Word even reached the Queen, and she was aghast. The fall-out of the princess's barbed greeting sent after-shocks through the system for the following week as Tiggy Legge-Bourke instructed lawyers to deny the allegation, and a statement said, 'that a series of malicious lies are circulating . . . which are a gross reflection on our client's moral character. These allegations are utterly without the very slightest foundation.'

The actions of the princess had the desired effect, precipitating the most discreet behind-the-scenes investigations, led by the Queen's private secretary, Sir Robert Fellowes. He personally telephoned the princess, also his sister-in-law, four days after the confrontation to get to the bottom of whatever it was she had been alluding to during the conversation with Tiggy Legge-Bourke. She had put the cat among the pigeons and, during the phone call, she reported her allegations to Her Majesty's right-hand man: that Tiggy had been having an affair with Prince Charles, and she had undergone an abortion. She even furnished the Queen's office with a precise date.

'There, now it's all official. Robert has promised to investigate the allegations,' she told me after the phone call.

Back at Buckingham Palace, Sir Robert Fellowes was the perfect man to handle such a sensitive issue. After putting down the telephone to the princess, he set out to ascertain the truth.

He discovered that Tiggy Legge-Bourke – who was 'carefully questioned' – had been to see her private gynaecologist twice, once in the summer, once in the autumn of 1995, for what was described as 'women's problems'. She had been to hospital on two separate occasions in the autumn of that year.

But Sir Robert concluded that the allegation made by the princess was false. His dismissal of her claim was delivered by a uniformed orderly who rang the bell and handed me the official letter.

The princess opened it with her silver paper knife and shook her head disapprovingly as she read the words. 'Typical!' she said. 'Paul, look at this.'

He had written:

> Your allegations concerning Tiggy Legge-Bourke are completely unfounded. Her relationship with The Prince of Wales has never been anything but a professional one.
>
> On the date of the supposed abortion, she was at Highgrove with William and Harry. It is in your own best interests that you withdraw these allegations. You have got this whole thing dreadfully wrong.

The thorough inquiry was emphatic that there was no truth whatsoever in these allegations. Indeed, Robert Fellowes attached his own personal note to his sister-in-law to emphasize how wrong she was: 'This letter is sent from one who really believes that you've got this whole thing dreadfully wrong, and that you *must* realize it – please.'

With hindsight, and on any objective assessment of the fact, the princess could simply never have been right.

By the end of 1995, the princess's own private secretary was drafting a letter. Patrick Jephson had decided to quit KP. Another member of staff who leaped before he was pushed. All lines of effective communication had been cut between him and the princess. It was sad to witness the demise of that relationship because not only had he been expert at his job, he had been close to the princess. I was once dispatched to Asprey & Gerrard, the Crown jewellers, to choose a pair of gold links for him, bearing his initials. The princess also allowed him to leave the office early on Friday and not return until Monday so that he could spend more time with his family in Devon. But by 1995 he felt snubbed by every private decision she had taken, and was blind to the correspondence she had diverted through my fax machine. There is no future for an unhearing, unseeing employee in a royal household. The *Panorama* interview and the Tiggy Legge-Bourke incident had been the final straws. His curt resignation letter, which dropped into KP one day, summed up his bitterness: he told the princess that she had denied him all normal means of communication with her, leaving him to feel unwanted.

'The rats always jump ship, Paul,' she mused. 'Looks like you'll have to be butler, lady-in-waiting and private secretary rolled into one. You're at the helm now!'

The Herculean task of managing the princess's PR was, thankfully, not my responsibility. That burden fell to a new recruit, Jane Atkinson. She was charged with handling the continued fall-out from the Tiggy Legge-Bourke incident. Prince Charles's assistant demanded an apology but the princess refused to back down. By then, her mind was elsewhere. She had received her own bombshell, hand-delivered by a uniformed orderly. The Queen and Prince Charles had fired a double salvo into KP just before Christmas. A divorce was demanded by both the sovereign and the heir to the throne.

Divorce was a word and not a prospect to the princess. It was something she had often used to threaten Prince Charles during the latter years of their marriage. She had screamed it to get his attention, to wound, like a child in a tantrum threatening a dismissive parent that she was going to run away, knowing she didn't really mean it. In getting to know and understand the princess, I talked with her about how misunderstood she felt, how much pain she had endured, how she felt her 'personal torture' – because that was what she called it – had helped her grow into a stronger person. But one thing that shone through each heartfelt conversation was the love that lingered for Prince Charles, no matter how much hurt she felt he had caused. She had found freedom and relief in the separation but she was adamant about one thing: 'Divorce is a non-starter.'

Then, a week before the princess was due at Sandringham House with William and Harry for Christmas, she received a lengthy letter that made first official mention of a divorce. It did not come from Prince Charles, but from the Queen. It arrived as a crushing blow on 18 December 1995. It was the first time the princess had ever heard the word 'divorce' on Windsor lips.

The Queen had seen one book from the princess, another from the prince; one television confession from her son, another from her daughter-in-law. The disintegration of the marriage between the Prince and Princess of Wales was being played out in public. As head of state, she felt she had to take control. I had taken this letter to the princess in her sitting room, and returned to the pantry. Minutes later, a familiar cry travelled down the staircase: 'Paul, come here.'

She was on the sofa, and looked on the verge of tears. With an air of resignation, she rolled her eyes, beckoning to the desk behind her. 'Look what's arrived,' she said.

On the desk, left exactly where it had been read earlier, was a letter with the red crest of Windsor Castle. I recognized the distinctive handwriting of the Queen. It began, as always, 'Dearest Diana' and ended, 'With love from Mama'. This letter, though, was different from any other I had read and, as the Queen's former footman, I felt uncomfortable as I read it.

I was talking to the back of the princess's head as she remained on the sofa but I needed to express my discomfort. 'I'm not sure I should be reading this, it says "in the strictest of confidence".'

'Oh, Paul, just read it. What am I going to do? What will everyone think?' She sighed.

As I read the letter, she jumped up, agitated, and began pacing. 'The Prime Minister and the Archbishop of Canterbury! My divorce has been discussed with John Major and George Carey before it has been discussed with me.'

The princess was infuriated that the Queen had consulted the government and the Church first. The constitutional issues did not concern her. 'This is my marriage and it is no one else's business!' she yelled. Recalling another part of the letter, she said: 'In the country's interests, is it? What about the interests of me? What about the interests of my boys?'

She felt that her divorce, just like her marriage, was being handled as if it were a business matter. The tone of the Queen's letter was sympathetic, delicate and devoid of anger, but it did smack of a mother-in-law frustrated with the behaviour of both parties, emphasizing that a divorce could not inflict further damage on the two sons who had suffered enough over the previous years.

The princess was having none of it. She immediately telephoned the Queen at Buckingham Palace. In a polite conversation, the princess questioned the haste for such a monumental decision. The Queen calmed her and tried to reassure her that she would not be rushed into any decision.

The Boss was not reassured. She sat down at her desk and dipped her fountain pen into her bottle of Quink. She penned an instant reply to the Queen, telling her that she needed time. But there would be little time to reflect. The next day a second bombshell landed on the doormat: a letter from Prince Charles requesting a divorce.

Again, I was invited to read it. Prince Charles said the marriage was beyond repair and that that represented both 'a national and personal tragedy'. Divorce was inevitable and it needed to be done quickly, he wrote. The princess suspected that the letters were a two-pronged assault from Buckingham Palace and St James's Palace, intended to make her buckle under the pressure.

She placed both letters on the desk, the red of Windsor and the blue of Highgrove side by side. 'What do you see?' she asked. The obvious didn't strike me. 'Look.' One finger underlined a sentence used in the Queen's letter. Then the same finger pointed to a sentence in the prince's letter. Both were the same, word for word, referring to the 'sad and complicated situation' of the royal marriage. 'Those letters have been drafted and advised by the same people,' she said, with the excitement of someone who had just made a vital discovery. 'They must think I'm stupid.'

She sat down and fired off a response to her husband, unable to write fast enough to keep up with her anger. Her response was unequivocal: '*Your request has utterly perplexed me. I do not consent to an immediate divorce!*'

That week, events and emotions reached boiling-point, with the Tiggy Legge-Bourke allegations coming to nothing, and the letters from the Queen and Prince Charles. Ahead of her, there was another difficult festive period, made even more awkward by the divorce request. In that week before Christmas, I doubt I had ever seen the princess so heartbroken and her reaction summed up the dichotomy in her: loving Charles on one hand and resisting a divorce, but having briefed against him with the Morton book and the *Panorama* interview. In seeking to hurt him into a reaction, I suspect the princess wounded herself. Prince Charles had clearly reached the end of his tether.

Communication between the prince and princess was at its weakest. The princess requested one-to-one meetings, but the prince wanted someone to sit and take notes. She refused, and 1995 ended in stalemate. The prince wanted a divorce. The princess wanted to remain married.

At this time I became a crutch that the princess leaned on. She was despondent and felt her world was about to be turned upside-down, her role taken away from her. The divorce letters left her in pieces. She curled up on the sofa, put her head in her hands and sobbed. As butler, what was I supposed to do? Stand there?

In William's absence – he was a great source of comfort to his mother when she was distressed – I made sure the supply of Kleenex was plentiful. I made sure I was there to listen. I made sure she was not moping in her loneliness. I didn't see the Princess of Wales crying: I saw a vulnerable, hurt woman crying and in need of comfort. The Queen would never have displayed such emotion before me, and no footman would ever have had the temerity to place an arm round her. But I had a much warmer, closer relationship with the princess who was a tactile person. When she was hurt she was like a little girl, and the sight of her hurt compelled me to do something other than stand awkwardly by. I sat beside her, put an arm round her and tried to tell her that everything would be all right, that she was strong, a survivor, that the British public were behind her. I listened for many hours and, as we did when we watched *Brief Encounter*, we ended up laughing.

As I got closer, I would remain with her until I knew that she was going to be all right by herself. But even when I left to return home, I worried endlessly. On some occasions, she would wake at two or three, and feel the need to talk. I would listen, and be back at work for breakfast.

That Christmas, the princess penned me a letter, dated 27 December 1995, which I treasure to this day. When the misinformed, the embittered and the ignorant attempted, during my Old Bailey trial in 2002, to suggest that I was nothing more than a butler to the princess, that my closeness was a figment of my imagination, I read this note over and over again. At the toughest time of my life, it was the turn of the princess, through her own words, to comfort me:

A letter that is long overdue to thank you profoundly for everything that you've done for me and, in particular, since August. Your presence through the tears and frustration has proved invaluable, and I did want you to know how enormously I appreciate your support. 1996 will be a happy one and I look forward to it . . . thank you, with love from Diana

10. Handling the Divorce

Facing the Queen in a one-to-one meeting at Buckingham Palace, the princess knew she would never have a better opportunity to ask the one question that had constantly chipped away inside her mind since Prince Charles had publicly confessed to an affair with Camilla Parker Bowles. 'Does this mean that Charles is going to remarry?' asked the princess.

'I think that very unlikely,' replied the Queen.

If the Boss had gone into that meeting looking to emerge with concessions, that one reassurance from the highest level made her feel more secure about the future if it involved divorce.

It was mid-morning on 15 February 1996, and the princess had come to Her Majesty's sitting room for a discussion that Prince Charles hoped would end the stalemate over the divorce that everyone but the princess wanted. On the previous day, she had sent her estranged husband a Valentine card, signed 'With love from Diana'. Cupid had long since deserted them as a hopeless cause, but the princess was defiant until the end, even as the system prised away her fingers off a marriage on which she had so stubbornly refused to loosen her grip. She never stopped loving Prince Charles. She felt she was being forced to let go. Even when she stared irreparable damage in the face, the inevitable never dawned on her.

But the summit with the Queen was her first opportunity – since the divorce letters had dropped on to her mat – to speak openly and frankly to her mother-in-law, and she didn't want to leave anyone under any illusions. 'I do not want a divorce. I still love Charles. None of what has happened is my fault,' said the princess. Her stance was crystal clear from the outset in what turned out to be a businesslike but friendly discussion. It couldn't be anything other than businesslike because the Queen's deputy private secretary Robin Janvrin was there to take notes. The grey suits at Buckingham Palace had been worried because 'Bulimics rewrite history in twenty-four hours.'

The princess didn't want a note-taker at a private family discussion but it was feared that she might brief allies in the media. The Queen had Robin Janvrin by her side to preserve the truth. When she got back to KP, the princess had me for the same protection.

As the princess spoke of her profound upset over the marriage break-up, the Queen apparently listened sympathetically. Indeed, she emphasized how, over the years, she had tried to do everything she could to help, as had the Duke of Edinburgh.

But the princess, who never doubted that her parents-in-law had made a substantial effort even if their son had not, felt that others were only too happy to see her cast adrift, that they had been jealous of her work in public life. She unbottled years of suspicion and emotion before the Queen, and not for the first time. She knew she could talk to the Queen. Answers and solutions were rarely forthcoming, but Her Majesty always provided a sympathetic ear, even when the complexities of the situation frustrated her. Over the years I despaired when journalists and 'in-the-know' royal 'experts' had claimed that the princess and the monarch spat venom at each other or, as the *Daily Mail* once suggested, 'Diana spurned the Queen's hand of friendship . . . turning the two women into enemies'. They were never enemies.

Until the princess's death in 1997, the Queen and the princess exchanged numerous letters. Two different royal icons from different generations tried hard to understand each other. The one area on which they shared common ground was the welfare of William and Harry. In that meeting, the Queen reassured the princess that she must not worry about the welfare or custody of the two young princes. 'Whatever may transpire in the future, nothing will change the fact that you are the mother of both William and Harry. My concern is only that those children have been in the battleground of a marriage that has broken down,' she said.

As the meeting continued, and Mr Janvrin's pen remained poised, the princess ultimately agreed to a divorce, but she wanted to record her hurt too. She said: 'Mama, receiving your letter and Charles's letter on almost the same day before Christmas was tough. It was the first time Charles had actually mentioned divorce, and the letters I have received since have not helped.'

The Queen agreed. 'The recent exchange of letters has not led anywhere, but what I wrote before Christmas remains my view. The present situation is not doing anybody any good, either country, family or children.' The monarch was insisting, at her diplomatic best, that divorce proceedings should start soon. There was no turning back.

But she more than understood the princess's concerns for the future. Afterwards, the princess said that she had displayed the sensitivity and kindness that the Duke of Edinburgh had shown in his letters in 1992. By the spring of 1996, the princess felt she had had far more constructive talks with her mother-in-law than she could ever have had with her husband.

Then the meeting had reached the point about the future and title of the princess, a sensitive issue that became the subject of intense media speculation in the following days. The princess insisted that she had not offered to drop 'HRH' because it was too important to her. Then Buckingham Palace issued a statement stating: 'The decision to drop the title is the Princess's and the Princess's alone.'

It is true that the princess first raised the issue of her future role. She said to the Queen: 'I have worked hard for sixteen years for you, Mama, and do not want to see my life taken away from me. I want to protect my position in public life. I want to be able to stand up for my own life.' She then added: 'I have real concerns about the future, and all the answers lie with you, Mama.'

The Queen accepted that, but said: 'I would like to decide things in consultation with Charles. The title is also a matter to be discussed with Charles.' Then she added: 'Speaking personally, I think that the title "Diana, Princess of Wales" would be more appropriate.'

The issue of HRH status remained uncertain until both the Queen and the princess could discuss it with Prince Charles. What is certain is that the idea for the title by which the princess would later be known was a seed sown by the Queen.

Many things were discussed that day: the princess was refused an office inside Buckingham Palace and she told the Queen the reasons behind Patrick Jephson's departure. As the lengthy meeting continued, the princess expressed her concerns about William's safety. She was worried about her eldest son and Prince Charles flying on the same aircraft: if a disaster or mid-flight incident occurred, they would both be affected.

The Queen replied: 'That is only a problem on holiday and then it is only a question of who flies on public aircraft. The royal aircraft are safe. That is probably not a big worry.'

By the end of the meeting, the Queen was anxious to let the princess know that she was always there for her. 'This is a very difficult issue for me personally but the situation does need resolving for everybody's sake,' she said.

Duty and protecting the country's interests had placed the Queen, yet again, in an unenviable position as mediator between son and daughter-in-law. The princess accepted that the Queen needed to be firm but she could not get over how considerate she had been. 'I just want an amicable agreement, Mama,' said the princess. 'I do not want to be difficult.'

I couldn't imagine life without the princess.

'Diana's rock' is a phrase some will believe, and others will pour scorn on but it was a label she attached to me in conversation with her friends. Yet she never expressed it directly to me. In KP, she described me as: 'You are my third eye, Paul'; 'You are at the helm of my ship.' Or, when she was with her friend Susie Kassem, I was 'Magic Merlin'. It is also true that she often said to me, 'Oh, you're such a pain in the arse!' when I offered an unpopular suggestion, fussily arranged the flowers in the sitting room or just got in the way.

But I also knew when to be there when she wanted company and to talk. It was the same instinct that told me when she wanted coffee or carrot juice. The art of being a good servant is to anticipate the next move and to know what the master or mistress wants before they know it themselves. Or, as housekeeper Mrs Wilson put it in the movie *Gosford Park*: 'To be the perfect servant is to have no life.' Maria would probably have agreed with that.

I knew when the princess was down, when life was getting on top of her. At those times, I would merely make my presence known: appearing in the sitting room as she sat on the sofa, waiting by the arch leading into her dressing room, standing near the sideboard in the dining room as she ate, leaning against the banister on the first floor as she dashed from bedroom to sitting room. At these times she called me her 'emotional washing machine'. 'I can come home, tell you everything and tip it all out,' she said.

She went out and sucked up grief, pain, plight and suffering on her visits to the homeless, the sick, the dying and the poor, and returned to KP burdened with it but satisfied that, in a day's work, she had showered love and affection on the people who mattered. Put that with her own insecurities, fears and problems, and emotional overload was the result. She used to arrive at KP and rush up the stairs, shouting: 'Give me five minutes. I must talk to you – I *must* talk to you.'

I flicked the kettle switch and made two cups of coffee, and we would sit for beyond an hour, chatting. Or, rather, I would listen as the princess told me of the saddest things she had witnessed, or of a thrilling moment when a sick child's eyes widened to look at her. The princess's eyes often welled as she recalled traumatic experiences at a hospital, hospice or medical centre. It was as if talking to me became an emotional release. Then, she would pick up the phone and call a friend, or ring healer Simone Simmons or psychic Rita Rogers.

As William grew up, the princess decided to have serious mother-to-son conversations with him. She felt he was a wise head on young shoulders, and she had brought up both her boys to be sensitive, caring and in touch with their emotions. But she confided in William about her problems and her life. He got used to comforting her and had a mature outlook that belied his years. He had to take on board a lot of his mother's emotions at a tender age but the princess didn't want to hide anything from him. She wanted him to know all there was to know so that he wasn't presented with a distortion of the facts from either the press or the wider family.

One Friday, William came home as usual on an exeat from school, accompanied by his friend Sam. Police protection officer Graham Craker had brought them to the palace and William darted through the front door and up the stairs, shouting, 'Mummeeee!'

By then, he was almost as tall as the princess and his smile showed off his metal braces. His mother, who had been listening out for the car's wheels on the gravel, rushed out on to the landing and gave him a hug. No matter how old they were, the princess mothered her boys with love and hugs. That weekend, he bounced off his mother and dashed into the boys' sitting room to slouch on the green sofa stationed in front of the television with his friend. The noise of an action-packed PlayStation game and competitive shouts suddenly broke the quiet of KP. The princess loved it when her sons came home, their natural exuberance bringing joy back into the apartments.

William's friend Sam saw the world of KP through a young outsider's eyes. William and Harry were used to me – I was part of the furniture. It was their schoolfriends, people like Sam, who seemed to find it odd that the butler was a regular face in the private living quarters of the princess. From Friday through to their departure on Sunday, Sam saw me here, there and everywhere. William burst into the sitting room, unannounced, with Sam trailing behind him. 'Oh, sorry, Mummy,' he said. I was sitting on the sofa beside the princess, who was perched on the edge of the seat, half facing me. We were deep in conversation.

As William retreated politely, we heard Sam ask: 'Why's *he* always in there?'

William's reply was matter-of-fact: 'Oh, that's only Paul. He's here all the time.'

The one place to find the princess was her writing desk. As a prolific letter-writer, she was at home there. In our conversations, she sometimes struggled to articulate an experience or her emotions. But with a pen in her hand she found the words to express herself. If she taught me anything, it was the same lesson she taught William and Harry: always write thank-you notes for people's time, gifts, hospitality, advice or friendship. She said that the one thing I taught her was to write down her thoughts at the end of one of our many conversations. 'Let yourself know how you feel. It can be therapeutic,' I had said. I knew the importance of writing everything down because the Queen kept a diary, with her unique perspective on history. The princess was living extraordinary episodes as a royal icon, no more so than in the mid-nineties. When it seemed that many were briefing against her, she needed to keep an accurate record of the truth.

On the morning after one of our sessions, I would walk into the pantry and find an envelope on the green leatherbound blotter on my desk. Inside, the princess had written her thoughts on her red-edged paper. She had mulled over our conversation, the advice given, the opinions she refused to change. Those letters became an official addendum to our talks.

Often, she would show me a letter, like the divorce letters from the Queen or Prince Charles, and take it back but, on occasion, when she felt 'the truth needs to be kept safe', she wrote it down and gave it to me. I became the repository for royal truths; quite separate from the intimate secrets that were never written down and remain locked inside my head. Each letter invariably started: 'As I sit here today . . .' Those notes are her legacy and are crucial to the truths that enshrine her memory and debunk the damaging myths that seem to have been peddled since the day she died.

On 28 February 1996, KP issued a statement: 'The Princess of Wales has agreed to Prince Charles's request for a divorce. The Princess will retain the title and be known as Diana, Princess of Wales.'

The announcement followed a meeting between Prince Charles and the princess. But it was a letter from the prince, received earlier that week, that had finally convinced the princess to raise the white flag. Nothing would change his mind and he was exhausted from arguing about what had gone wrong and who was to blame. *'Let's move forward and not look back and stop upsetting one another,'* he urged her, and the princess agreed. With mutual obduracy removed as an obstacle, lawyers began work on the severance of the fairytale. Throughout that spring, the princess maintained communication with the Queen.

Once a decision had been reached the Boss seemed mentally stronger. After years and months of being in denial over divorce, she seemed to have garnered some extra mental strength from somewhere. 'I'm focused, Paul,' she said. 'I have a strong sense of public duty. I am clear-headed and motivated and want to get on without obstruction.'

In May, as the lawyers thrashed out an agreement and divorce settlement, the Prince and Princess of Wales put on brave faces as they attended the annual parents' day at Eton for William. The princess wanted to be there for her elder son but had been dreading the occasion because she knew that her husband's friends, the Knatchbulls and the Romseys, would also be there because they, too, had children at the school. The princess had wanted to arrive with her husband but her request was declined. 'I was cold-shouldered the moment I got there by everyone, including Charles,' the princess told me afterwards.

At the pre-luncheon drinks, she had mingled by herself, smiled and chatted with everyone, every inch the strong and confident princess, masking how uncomfortable she felt. At the concert that followed, a seating plan was the final straw. She had wanted to sit next to Prince Charles but she found herself beside the provost while the prince sat on the other side of the aisle with the provost's wife. I'm not having this, she thought.

The princess got up, crossed the aisle and approached the provost's wife: 'Excuse me, do you think I could possibly swap places with you so that I can sit next to my husband?'

The provost's wife could hardly refuse and the princess had deftly pulled off a little coup that had gone unnoticed by everyone but her husband. Nor had she finished upstaging him. The humiliation was not going to be hers. She made sure of that outside the school, where the BBC and ITN television camera crews were waiting.

As the Prince and Princess of Wales emerged outside as proud parents and parted to go their separate ways, the princess rushed to her husband's car, placed a hand on his shoulder, kissed his cheek and whispered: 'Goodbye, darling.'

The moment of a rare, united front made all the news bulletins that night and the following day's headlines screamed: 'A KISS IS JUST A KISS.'

'Now Camilla knows what it feels like to be on the receiving end,' said the princess, at breakfast the next morning. She was civil throughout divorce proceedings but she didn't have to be forgiving as well.

On 30 May 1996, the divorce of the Duke and Duchess of York became absolute. The duchess came bounding into KP, stripped that day of her HRH status and living with the new title of Sarah, Duchess of York. She laughed over that morning's headlines. 'We'll show 'em!' she said. At what was a sombre time for both ladies, their shared laughter was a tribute to two people who refused to lie down and give up before 'The Firm'.

Like the princess, the duchess felt liberated by that sense of new-found freedom. She, too, had an inner resolve that helped her survive against the 'grey suits', who, she felt, continually undermined her.

The duchess was big enough to accept that she had struggled to cope with the expectations heaped on her shoulders. She had been 'wandering lost without a compass' and had faced a poisonous press and vicious enemies within the royal household. But she was always one of life's survivors. She seemed to know that even on the day divorce was granted. 'We'll win in the end, won't we, Paul?'

'Just keep smiling and hold your head up high,' I replied, and she breezed into the sitting room to join the Boss. That summer, the princess and the duchess went on holiday to a mountain hideaway in the South of France with their children. In sharing their experiences, their struggles and their pain, they had never been closer. More sisters than one-time sisters-in-law, each learning how to survive in their own indomitable way. Besides, both had new men in their lives and seemed happy again.

Part of the princess's own survival plan was to find a new future and head off in a different direction. She would always be anchored in London and KP for William and Harry, but she began to search for a holiday home and a foreign base from which she could project a humanitarian campaign on a global scale. 'Do you like Australia, Paul?' the princess asked me, at the start of an exceptionally hot June in 1996. She asked me what I thought about a life down-under, and I reminisced about my travels to the other side of the world on tours with the Queen. 'I've been to every state and New South Wales is probably my favourite,' I told her.

She was sitting on the sofa flicking through a collection of brochures and property magazines sent to her by her herbalist friend Eileen Whittaker – also a friend of the Duchess of York. 'Would you ever consider living there?' she asked.

I knew the princess liked to shock but over the years nothing she had done had truly shocked me. Until then. I looked at her as if it was a joke. 'I'm serious!' she added.

'Well, it's a bit too far away from home for me,' I said.

'I know, I know,' she said, clapping shut the brochure, and then she changed the subject.

The laughter of KP was in sharp contrast to the silences at the Old Barracks. With no second butler to fall back on, no full-time lady-in-waiting and no private secretary, work was like a constant treadmill that kept me running around and away from home. I was, and I knew it, spending far too much time at work: out of our home by eight o'clock in the morning and not back until beyond eleven. When I returned, all Maria welcomed home was an emotionally drained, exhausted and irritable husband. Alexander and Nick only saw me on Sunday or when the princess invited them to play at the palace. Family life was suffering. Since the day the princess had announced in February that she had agreed to a severance of her marriage, I had lived, eaten and slept the divorce drama by her side, sharing with her the traumas, the legal meetings, and the unsettled feeling that the imminence of tumultuous change can bring.

'While you watch over the destruction of one family, this family will need to be reminded what you look like,' said Maria. 'Forget about there being three people in the marriage of the Prince and Princess of Wales. There are three people in our marriage: you, me and the princess. I'm sick of it, Paul.'

Another Burrell marriage was in a far graver state. My brother Graham had confessed to an affair, and his wife Jayne had left the family home with the two children. He rang me in my pantry, full of remorse and shedding tears, and the marriage seemed well and truly over. We were a close family and that marriage breakdown occupied my thoughts more than the divorce of the prince and princess. The Boss noted that I was down when I served her dinner on the day Graham had telephoned. She knew, from the barbecues we had shared at Highgrove, how close I was to my brother.

When she had finished, she said: 'Can I have Graham's telephone number? I will ring him.'

That night, she sat at her desk and dialled his home in Grassmoor, Chesterfield. My brother was on the sofa in front of the television when he answered.

'Hello, Graham, it's Diana. Paul's not all right so I don't expect you are either,' she said.

Graham could not believe who was speaking to him, and no one at work would believe him if he told them the Princess of Wales had rung him at his terraced home to act as a virtual marriage counsellor, he said. The Boss was brilliant. She listened and offered words of comfort, sharing her own feelings about how difficult it can be when a marriage falls apart. She asked him about love, marriage, his other woman, the future, and she telephoned him on three more occasions over the following fortnight. She didn't mince her words. She told Graham how foolish he had been but, if he still loved his wife, he should persuade her to come back. Assisted by the princess, Graham did just that. To this day, my brother credits the princess for helping save his marriage.

One marriage that could not be saved, to her eternal regret, was her own. Each Tuesday night since February, Lord Mishcon had arrived at the front door. He was a small, gentle man who, according to the princess, had a genius of a legal brain. He was also extremely charming. In those early winter months, I opened the door, he stepped in and removed his hat. When he shook the princess's hand, he often said, 'Excuse the cold hand of an old man, ma'am. I assure you that the heart is warm.' Before he had issued his latest briefing on negotiations with her husband's office, he had already got her smiling. By the summer, Anthony Julius, another lawyer from the same firm, was the bearer of good and bad tidings. By the end of June, only small technicalities had to be ironed out.

The divorce settlement stated that the princess would receive a £17 million lump sum payment. In return, the Prince of Wales had made his demands clear: he wanted back a pair of watercolours of distant German relations, a pair of chairs (*circa* 1780) and all of the George III silver, which we had used on a daily basis.

On 1 July, there was a constant stream of flowers, presents and cards for the princess's thirty-fifth birthday. One smitten individual sent two bunches of long-stemmed red roses, thirty-five in total. But two days earlier, on the Saturday, there had been an even greater surprise. The front doorbell rang. No one was expected and I turned the brass knob, wondering who it could be.

The last person I expected was the heir to the throne. Prince Charles had popped in, unannounced. 'Hello, Paul, may I come in?' he said. He had been due to catch a helicopter from the paddock beyond the upper stables at the rear of the palace but was early, so he had decided to visit his estranged wife.

'Your Royal Highness, I think you know the way.' He smiled and went up the stairs. If I was surprised, I couldn't wait to see the reaction of the Boss.

'Diana, are you there?' Prince Charles called, walking up the stairs as I followed behind.

He was met by the rather stunned princess on the first-floor landing and they greeted each other with a kiss on both cheeks. She looked over his shoulder at me and her eyes widened with mock horror. Then she couldn't resist breaking the ice with her usual humour. 'I suppose you've come to take the furniture away, then, Charles!'

Husband and wife, in the throes of a rather awkward divorce, laughed together for the first time in an age. If only they could have done that more in public, I thought. These two people got on, even if it was as friends. It was a bizarre scene, and also sad: I detected a surge of excitement in the princess. I could see her re-energizing on the spot. It was all very cordial, relaxed and civil. I went downstairs to make the prince a cup of tea, just how he used to like it at Highgrove: Earl Grey, strong, with a dash of milk.

In mid-July Buckingham Palace announced that a decree nisi had been granted. It left one outstanding issue: the princess's HRH status. The Queen had first suggested the title Diana, Princess of Wales, but the matter of HRH had remained unresolved. What I do know is that the princess rang her brother-in-law, the Queen's private secretary, Sir Robert Fellowes, to ask that she be allowed to retain the title HRH. Her request was declined. She would receive a £17 million lump sum payment but the price would be the loss of her royal status. The princess was not someone to stand on ceremony but it was an important title because, in her eyes, it was a special title given to her upon marriage and it seemed spiteful to take it away. It was, she felt, part of her royal identity and she had worked tirelessly as a royal highness for many years. When the final decision was taken behind the scenes, the princess was devastated.

She turned to William in her distress. She told me how he had sat with her one night when she had been upset over the loss of HRH, put his arms round her and said: 'Don't worry, Mummy, I will give it back to you one day, when I am king,' which had made her cry even more.

When the tears had subsided, the princess began signing more than a hundred typed letters to charities, regiments and organizations to which she had an affiliation, explaining that, because she would no longer be HRH and a member of the Royal Family, she felt unable to be a royal patron. She severed links with the Red Cross and Help the Aged. Instead of spreading herself so thinly, the princess felt she would be more effective concentrating on a small nucleus of organizations so she kept her ties with the National Aids Trust, Centrepoint, Great Ormond Street Hospital, the Leprosy Mission and the English National Ballet.

Meanwhile, the princess's office moved lock, stock and barrel from St James's Palace to the ground floor of apartment 7 in KP. She had been refused an office at Buckingham Palace because the Queen felt it was better that she remained independent. So apartment 7 became known as the office of Diana, Princess of Wales, headed by the comptroller Michael Gibbins.

One of the complications that the loss of HRH brought the princess was that protocol dictated that she would be an outsider required to curtsy to those members of the Royal Family who still carried the title. The one-time future Queen of England now faced the humiliation of curtsying to the Duke and Duchess of Gloucester and Princess Alexandra. But she found support from an unlikely corner of the Royal Family. Her next-door neighbour from apartment 10, HRH Princess Michael of Kent, wrote a sincere letter that touched her. 'Paul, look at this. What a sweet, sweet thing to say,' she said.

> I was horrified to learn in the Press that after your title was removed, you would be expected to curtsey in public when meeting me . . . I insist that this would cause me the greatest embarrassment, so please do not even consider it. I have always admired your courage and strength. If only Charles had loved you from the beginning, then this situation would never have happened. You will always have my support.

The letter from Princess Michael of Kent was a shot in the arm. All I could do, together with the rest of her friends, was reassure the princess that she was far greater than any combination of three initials. I told her: 'You don't need a title. Wherever you go in the world, you are known as Lady Di – and no one can take that away from you. Besides, you will always be HRH in my eyes.'

And I remained true to my word for what would be the final year of her life. Each morning, when I greeted her at breakfast, I placed the coffee-pot on the table and said: 'Good morning, Your Royal Highness.'

If there was one blessing in disguise in the loss of her HRH status, it was that she was free to chart her own path in life and concentrate on her humanitarian projects. But others, in the world of movies and cosmetics, had different offers to throw her way.

One evening in July, the telephone rang. It was the film actor Kevin Costner. The call came through on the direct line into my pantry. As I placed him on hold, I rang the princess on her extension in the sitting room. 'It's Kevin Costner. He would like to speak to you,' I told her. There was a shriek of excitement. 'Put him through, Paul, and come up.'

I walked into the sitting room and the princess was at her desk, listening intently. She saw me and waved me over. 'But I can't sing!' she said, giggling. 'What would I be expected to do? . . . I'm not sure but, yes, okay, send it and I promise I will have a look.' When she ended the call, she told me: 'He wants me to star in his next film – *The Bodyguard II*!' It was the sequel to the first film, starring Whitney Houston. She would play a princess. He would save her life. He promised it would be tastefully done. He would look after her. He would send her the script in the post from America. 'Can you believe it?' she said. 'He was so charming but he cannot be serious.'

Mr Costner could not have been more serious. It had been an informal approach but the princess, while it flattered her ego and she had been charmed by him, dismissed it. 'It is simply impossible,' she said.

The proposed script for *The Bodyguard II* eventually arrived. I'm not sure that she managed to read it.

The movie offer followed a more suitable suggestion from the American cosmetics giant Revlon. They had approached the princess with a proposal for a multi-million-dollar deal to head a charity organization on their behalf. 'Cindy Crawford will continue to be "the face". They want me to be the "spirit and style",' she told me.

★

From mid–February, we had all been working towards and building ourselves up for the morning of 28 August 1996, the day the divorce became absolute; the day the Prince and Princess of Wales became single again. When that day dawned, the atmosphere was a mixture of sadness and anticipation. As I stood in the corridor waiting for the princess to come for breakfast, it struck me that while she was letting go of her marriage I was cutting ties with the royal household I had joined in 1976 and beginning a new adventure, so the sadness was balanced with the excitement of a new challenge.

When the princess appeared, she was full of energy, determined to make a success of her independence. She tucked into grapefruit and honey and talked about the tours that were planned: Washington in September, Australia in November. She was still thinking about moving to Australia.

Later, she paced the sitting room, preparing herself for a day of being besieged by the world's media outside. The telephone rang. It was Sir Robert Fellowes, in his capacity as her brother-in-law rather than as the Queen's private secretary. 'I wanted to ring just to say good luck for this difficult day ahead. It is a tragic end to a wonderful story,' he told her, but the princess was in no mood to wallow in pity or sympathy.

'Oh, no,' she said, looking at me. 'It's the beginning of a new chapter. And remember, Robert, I do still love my husband. That will never change.'

The princess looked so elegant that day in pastel blue. She picked up her handbag, took a deep breath and strode along the landing, down the stairs and to the front door with determination, still wearing her engagement and wedding rings. 'I'll take them off eventually,' she said, 'but not now.' She remembered only too well her reaction when divorce ended the marriage of her mother and father, and how traumatic it was for her as a child to see the rings removed. 'A ring is so small but it signifies so much,' she said. She walked out of the door to fulfil an engagement at the English National Ballet.

She returned later that day, wanting to talk. Over coffee in her sitting room, she said, 'I'm now a very rich lady and I think you deserve a wage rise.' My salary was increased from £22,000 to £30,000, and the rest of the household – chef Darren McGrady, secretary Caroline McMillan, comptroller Michael Gibbins and

239

personal assistant Victoria Mendham – were rewarded too. The Boss was thanking us for sticking with her over the past few months, through thick and thin.

She seemed quiet when I left her. We had spoken about the significance of the day, her love for Prince Charles, how she wished the British public knew how much she hadn't wanted a divorce, how she wished things could have been so different. She delved into the myriad philosophies that, as she put it, 'help me to do the mental house-cleaning'. Philosophy arrested her insecurities, worries and doubts, and the words of others gave her strength.

> Be more concerned with your character than your reputation, because your character is what you really are while your reputation is merely what others think you are.

> The self must know stillness before it can discover its true song.

> Success is the result of good judgement. Good judgement is the result of experience. Experience is the result of bad judgement.

> Use problems as opportunities to change our lives.

> Problems call forth our courage and wisdom.

> Learn to adapt yourself to the demands of such a creative time.

> From a correct relationship to yourself comes a right relationship to all others and to the divine.

Or she quoted Benjamin Franklin: 'Those things that hurt, instruct.'

On the night of the divorce she repeated another to convince herself that she had done the right thing. ' "There needs to be a meeting of heart and mind which allows one to love and let go." I know that, Paul. I know that now,' she said.

So much nonsense has been written about the princess and her divorce. So-called friends and advisers have lied to the world that she had wanted to divorce Prince Charles from as early as 1990. So much nonsense has been written about a hatred for her husband that never existed. 'Charles and I are friends and are civil to one another. I think he realizes what he lost in me. I have no hatred for him. All the suffering has made me into the person I am,' she said. When it came to her views on Camilla Parker Bowles, she harboured

240

resentment but not hatred. She had to fall back on her philosophies again to come to terms with her feelings towards her husband's mistress. She referred to one in particular: 'Resentment is trying to change something that is just what it is. When we can't change it, we resent it.'

The princess spent many hours trying to fathom why her marriage had failed. We spoke about it many times. Even more than that, she spent hours analysing herself, trying to understand her own mind. In doing so, she would become a better person, she said. It was easy and convenient for her husband's friends to deal with her problems by explaining them away as 'Diana is being unstable again.' The princess didn't operate in such shallow waters. She often went in search of deep self-analysis. In doing so, she learned a lot about what had gone wrong, and where, perhaps, the rot had set in. The bottom line was that she suffered from low self-esteem, which ate away at her, then at her marriage. As she explained it: 'High self-esteem doesn't protect you, but it does allow you to entertain self-doubt without being devastated!'

She felt her low self-esteem had taken root in childhood when she had acquired many of her ideas about herself. She had taken that poor self-image into the marriage with Prince Charles. In him, she focused solely on deriving a boost to her ego, through his recognition of her achievements. When it was not forthcoming, she said she felt rejected. 'As if the entire foundation of my self-esteem had been demolished,' she said. Citing someone she called Mevlana, 'the best poet and mystic ever' apparently, she said, 'It is said that "patience is the key to joy" – if only I knew that back then!'

The princess also needed to realize, and I think many people told her this, that anger was a natural emotion, but she felt many women found anger distressing. I told her that Prince Charles did too.

She even hired a boxer to come to KP with his punchbag so that she could rid herself of her anger. Diana, Princess of Wales, could certainly pack a mean punch.

We discussed all those emotions that night of the divorce. After our discussion, I left to go to the kitchen. When I returned to the pantry, there was a little note saying 'thank you' on top of another piece of A4 lined paper, her thoughts at the end of our conversation.

All she had ever wanted was for the British people to understand what she had gone through, how difficult it had been. And while she felt that Prince Charles had truly made her suffer, she had learned from her suffering. She went to her grave loving the prince. I know that because it is the truth she left on my desk that night. Prince Charles has often said that, within the next twenty-five years, the royal archives will prove the truth of his relationship with the princess. It seems wrong to allow the world to labour under illusions for the next quarter of a century. The princess's own words can debunk the lies now. That night, she wrote to me:

It's the 28th August 1996 – 15 years of marriage have now been signed off. I never wanted a divorce and always dreamed of a happy marriage with loving support from Charles. Although that was never meant to be, we do have two wonderful boys who are deeply loved by their parents. A part of me will always love Charles, but how I wish he'd looked after me and been proud of my work.

It has been a turbulent 15 years, having to face the envy, jealousy, hatred from Charles's friends and family – they have so misunderstood me and that has been painful and brought enormous heartache.

I want so much to become Charles's best friend as I understand more than anyone what he is about and what makes him tick.

11. A Matter of Trust

'Hurray, you're home!'

Those words leaped from the burgundy-edged cream paper. We had pushed open our front door at the Old Barracks, dragging our suitcases behind us, after a two-week holiday to Kentucky, which had given me the chance to catch up on lost time with Maria and the kids. Amid the mail spread out on the mat was an envelope that immediately grabbed my attention. It was addressed to 'Paul' in the princess's handwriting.

On the eve of our return, she had nipped down and pushed the letter under the door. As I read on, there was clearly lots to tell: *'Dramas galore during the past two weeks and you'd be impressed by these ones! It's wonderful to know you've returned. See you Monday! love from Diana.'*

I returned to work with a tan that sickened the princess. We both had tans that needed to be topped up, and the princess went on her sunbed at least twice a week. It was as big as a space-ship, situated on the ground floor next to the dresser's room and the wardrobe room. 'You go and warm it up, Paul, I'll be down in half an hour,' she used to say. She never liked using the machine cold and the benefit of being the official 'warmer-upper' was that I had a fifteen-minute stint in it before leaving it ready for the princess. She once remarked that she felt 'like a sandwich in an ultraviolet toaster'.

When William and Harry returned from their summer vacation at Balmoral, his mother thought William had been placed on a rack and stretched. He stood next to her in the sitting room and she couldn't believe how much he had grown: he was fractionally taller than she was when they stood back to back. He needed new rugby boots and I was sent out to purchase a size-thirteen pair for a boy who was aged fourteen and still growing.

'Height. It's a Spencer gene,' said the princess. 'The Windsors are PORGs – People of Restricted Growth.'

William knew he was growing fast too. 'I couldn't believe it at Balmoral. Granny and Aunt Margot seemed to have shrunk. And I'm taller than Papa now,' he boasted.

Little Harry looked up at his brother and mother. The princess looked down at him. 'Oh, Harry, you've got the Spencer gene too. You'll be as big as your brother one day.'

William will be king one day, King William V. In the summer of 2003, in an interview to mark the celebration of his twenty-first birthday, he spoke of how seriously he took his role, and how much he wanted to become king. I knew the boy, so it was heartening to hear him say this. I suspect it would also have been a nice surprise for his mother because she knew how much the shy, introvert schoolboy had dreaded the prospect of ascending the throne. He was reared with huge expectations and yet he didn't want the spotlight. As he went around Wales on his twenty-first-birthday engagements, I know the princess would have been brimming with pride at the adjustment he seemed to have made. I know how proud she would have been because of her concern for his future. 'William doesn't want to be king, and I worry about that,' she told me, one night in the sitting room. 'He doesn't want his every move watched.' She went on to telephone her American friend Lana Marks and express the same worries.

The princess empathized with her son who, like his mother, was naturally shy and retiring. He had been born second in line to the throne. At the time Harry's attributes and attitude almost made him more of a realistic prospect to take on the onerous duties of the monarch. He was more outgoing and pragmatic.

'Harry would see no problem in taking on the job,' said the princess. 'GKH. That's what we'll call him. GKH, for Good King Harry. I like that!' From then on, whenever Harry was visiting for a weekend, we used those three initials to refer to him. It was an affectionate nickname she shared with two other close friends, even if Harry never knew. 'Where's GKH?' she'd ask, when looking for him around the house.

Of course, whenever the boys were in the house, staff had strict instructions on how to address them. We were not to bow, despite their HRH status. We were not to call them 'Your Royal Highness'. We were not even to refer to them as princes. They were, quite simply, William and Harry. It was all part and parcel of the princess's determination to ensure they were treated normally.

As a teenager normality was all William wanted. He longed to be cool and ordinary, not unique and destined for a life of privilege and duty. His mother had been thrust, unprepared, into the royal spotlight as the future Queen of England, so she understood his fear, but she didn't want it to take root and grow into his adulthood. That was why she coached him, prepared him, and spoke at length to him about his birthright. William could also count on the wisdom and support of Prince Charles and the Queen. At Eton, he regularly crossed the bridge across the Thames into Windsor and walked up to 'Granny's castle' to have tea with Her Majesty, joining her for lengthy discussions about what the future held, what his role would entail, how important his duty was to the country and its people.

The princess began the life-of-duty grooming process at an early stage, as it was for generations of royal children. But she did not want advisers from the royal household moulding her son. She wanted to do it her way, just as she had taken charge of his upbringing, virtually making the nannies redundant.

I was at KP when the princess encouraged William to make his first ever speech at the age of ten. It was Christmas 1992, and tradesmen and servants had gathered in the state apartments for the annual staff cocktail party. Earlier, William had drafted a few words to say to us. He had sat at the princess's writing desk in the sitting room, giggling nervously as he wrote his début speech on a sheet of pink paper. Then his moment came. He stood on a box so that he could be seen, and around a hundred people fell quiet. 'Ladies and gentlemen . . .' he started. His mother's eyes were on him. '. . . I know how busy you must all have been,' and he had the room laughing at the ironic remark, aimed at a notoriously overworked joint household, 'so I would like to thank you all for coming.' Then, in a reference to the protection officers in the room, he said, 'I should warn you there are enough policemen in here to breathalyse you all twice over! Merry Christmas and a Happy New Year.' The place erupted into a roar as he stepped down to a hug from his mother and a ruffle of his hair from his father.

Harry's trademark was his kindness. Once, when Alexander went to play on the prince's PlayStation, he said that he was saving for a console of his own. Harry, who appreciated that royals wanted for nothing, said he felt sorry for him. He went to his bedroom on the nursery floor and returned a few minutes later with a five-pound note. 'Here you are, Alexander. Put this towards your savings.'

Meanwhile, William was still joining the princess at KP lunches at which she encouraged him to join in conversation with adults: with Elton John, discussing and asking questions about AIDS; with *Daily Mirror* editor Piers Morgan, to foster better relations with the media; with Sarah, Duchess of York, chatting about the problems and pressures of duty.

One day, William received special permission to take the afternoon off lessons at Eton because his mother had arranged a surprise. As he waited upstairs, a black stretch limousine pulled up outside the front door. Out stepped supermodels Naomi Campbell, Christie Turlington and Claudia Schiffer, who were in London to open their Fashion Café. William, who had posters of them on his wall, had longed to meet them, so the princess had arranged for them to come to KP, just a few months after she had organized a meeting for him with Cindy Crawford.

William, excruciatingly self-conscious about his brace, sat down uncomfortably on a sofa in the drawing room as Campbell, Schiffer and Turlington all leaned in around him, posing for the camera the princess was holding. William blushed: 'Mummy, stop it!'

The supermodels tried to put him at ease with polite conversation and the princess was delighted with how her son coped. If he can handle himself in the company of beautiful women today, I suspect that is down to his mother.

When Claudia Schiffer asked him about Eton, he replied, 'I don't much like the heavy mashed potato, but the lady maths teacher, Miss Porter, is very attractive,' which she and the others found very funny. He went on to talk about life at Balmoral, the Queen's corgis and his likes and dislikes. When the supermodels swept out of the front door, the princess asked him what he thought. 'Not as nice as Cindy Crawford,' he said.

William shared the desire to be normal with his mother. The most photographed woman in the world longed to taste anonymity. She loved doing 'what everyone else does'. If she walked around a zoo or park unnoticed, she was delighted. Sometimes, she went out at seven a.m. to jog or roller-blade around the paths of Kensington Palace Gardens, knowing she could glide gloriously in a rare freedom when no one was around.

When she was feeling particularly daring, she opted to wear an elaborate disguise, and kitting her out soon became part of my duty. Once, I was sent out to buy a shoulder-length straight brunette wig from Selfridges. Then I had to go to an optician in Kensington High Street and purchase a pair of large, round-rimmed spectacles, asking the optometrist to ensure that he fitted clear glass for the lenses. When I got back to KP, the princess couldn't wait to try on her new look.

I was in my pantry when she came downstairs as a different person. She tried to keep a straight face but I couldn't help gawping. 'Nobody's going to recognize you! Look at you!' I said. The princess was shrieking with laughter, tears rolling down her face.

That night, in wig, glasses, black Puffa jacket and denim jeans, Diana, Princess of Wales, joined a queue with friends outside Ronnie Scott's jazz club, in London. The next morning, she couldn't wait to talk about it over breakfast. 'The smoke in that club got into my eyes – even with the glasses on!' she explained. She went on: 'When we were standing outside, we queued far too long for my liking. I started to chat up a man next to us and he didn't have a clue who I was. It was so funny. I could be me in a public place!'

The paradox was evident to me even if it was lost on the princess, because she wasn't 'being me' at all. She had needed to become a different person before she could be herself, and as she marvelled at the freedom of disguise, I thought how terribly sad her statement was.

'Come on, I want to show you something,' said the princess in late September 1996. I followed in her wake, trying to keep up with her rapid strides downstairs and into the dressers' workroom and wardrobe room, with its floor-to-ceiling white doors. She flung them open one by one, exposing rails of long evening dresses, arranged in the colour spectrum, starting with black at one end, through colour in the middle and white at the end.

'Just look at all these dresses!' she said. 'How many ballgowns do you think there are in this room?' She began walking down the line, using one finger to count them all on their velvet hangers. There were sixty-two in that room alone, which did not take into account the dresses that hung in the L-shaped wardrobe room on the first-floor.

'Each one of these is a memory and an old friend,' she said, 'but now is the time to sell them all.'

In late summer this represented shock number two. First, the suggestion about moving to Australia; then selling off her wardrobe. The princess was taking charge of her world. Out with the old, in with the new. It had been a conversation with William, and then Elton John, that had prompted her into thinking about a charitable dress auction. The divorce settlement had left her with millions. Auctioneering her dresses would ensure that others benefited too, especially AIDS charities, which needed money for hospices and research.

We stood in that room as the princess picked out dresses and reminisced. She took a hanger, held a dress high, arm extended. 'Ah. My *Gone With the Wind* dress!' She held out a full, off-the-shoulder floral-print gown. Then she pulled out another. 'Worn at the White House, dancing with John Travolta when it was someone else I had my eye on!' It was an ink-blue velvet creation.

Then she spotted an oyster satin dress with a bolero jacket, made by Victor Edelstein, and worn at the Élysée Palace, Paris, at a state banquet given by President Mitterrand. 'Not sure I can part with this. When I wore it, I actually felt like a princess.' The following June her reluctance was clear when the final selection was made for the New York auction: that dress was the last lot, no. 80.

Nostalgia did not stop the princess in her mission. She grabbed two hangers, I did the same, and we went upstairs, back and forth, back and forth.

'Ring Maria and ask Betty to come and join us,' said the princess, knowing that Betty was staying with us at the Old Barracks.

By the time Betty arrived, my shirt was stuck to my back. I had been up and down those stairs as I carried around fifty dresses to the first floor, then dismantled and reconstructed a rail in the boys' sitting room. It now resembled a cluttered second-hand-clothes shop. The princess treated the auction idea a little like she did her personal life: she wanted advice from everyone. Betty, an expert with knitting needles at home in North Wales, suddenly found herself as the voice of reason on *haute couture* at the palace. How the princess laughed! Betty was not ruthless enough for the task: all she saw was the most beautiful collection of dresses being thrown out and she was horrified. She had visions of them appearing at a jumble sale, like the ones she attended at Kenyon Hall run by the Women's Institute. 'Ooo,' she said, visibly shocked, her hand at her chest, 'you mustn't throw that one out!'

One by one, I held up the dresses and the ruthless selector, the princess, disagreed with the hoarder, Betty.

'Ooo, no. You don't want to be giving that one away either!' Betty kept saying. 'Oh, now, that's a nice dress. What a waste!' she went on . . . and on. Before long, the princess was crying with laughter.

That weekend, William brought some tough decision-making to the process. He flicked back the hangers on the rail that had appeared in his room and made his selection. Another person whose input was precious was Aileen Getty, daughter of American billionaire Paul Getty. She had full-blown AIDS and came to lunch several times at KP. The princess couldn't wait to show her the dresses that were being sold to raise money for people in her position.

Christie's sent its costume expert, Meredith Etherington-Smith – to whom the princess took a shine – to catalogue and describe each dress. As there was no lot thirteen, seventy-nine dresses – cocktail and evening wear – went under the hammer and raised $3,258,750, around £1.85 million, for AIDS and cancer charities on both sides of the Atlantic.

One cupboard in the downstairs wardrobe room was left untouched. On the day of the auction's conception, she had lifted back the tissue covering one particular dress: the wedding gown she had worn in 1981. 'This is one dress I can't sell,' she said, and remembered how her mother Frances Shand Kydd had paid for it in guineas. 'I want to donate it to the Victoria and Albert Museum for its national dress collection,' she said. She expressed that wish a year before her death. She did not mention it exclusively to me: during a lunch with *Daily Telegraph* editor Charles Moore she had told him too. Today, that wedding dress stands on display in the Diana museum at Althorp, her ancestral home.

Some dresses were never destined for auctions or museums. Some unwanted designerwear went to female staff, but other suits and dresses were taken to second-hand-clothes stores in Knightsbridge or Chelsea where they would be handed over in exchange for cash when sold. This was done at the princess's behest, to raise spending money for her because royals rarely carry hard currency. The princess tended to use a credit card, which she signed as 'Wales', not 'Diana'. By generating cash, she could spend it as she wished without trace, and take William and Harry to the cinema or to McDonald's. In the biggest paradox of their opulent royal life, the young princes were fascinated by money and how the Queen's face adorned every note of every denomination. A five-pound note became known as a 'blue Granny'; a ten-pound note was a 'brown Granny' and a fifty-pound note was a 'pink Granny'. When the princess handed out money, it was a joy to watch the boys jumping up and down, clutching the notes, invariably a 'pink Granny'.

Both personal assistant Victoria Mendham, who left palace service in early 1997, and I took around twenty outfits to the second-hand-clothes shops, which suddenly had labels such as Catherine Walker, Versace, Chanel, and Armani hanging on their rails, without knowing the name of the donor. An outfit worth two thousand pounds would be sold for around two hundred, and somebody, somewhere, would be walking around in the princess's clothes.

These regular sales netted the princess around eleven thousand pounds, which she kept stuffed into an envelope in a bottom drawer. One day, in April 1997, she decided to hand it over to comptroller Michael Gibbins, whose jaw hit the floor when he opened the envelope, the princess said. He took the money and banked it, unaware of how such a sum had been raised. Even the accountant had been left in the dark about the princess's most private finances – until then.

The problem with being a newly divorced princess and the most beautiful woman in the world is that men across the globe are aware that you are single again. By the end of the summer of 1996 many high-profile or wealthy men began to make their intentions known to the princess. She was flattered, of course, but she already had feelings for someone. Not that her suitors were aware of that because her recent happiness was a secret. They kept knocking on the door, undeterred by polite refusals or constant excuses. Being butler at KP at this time was like being a flatmate to a platonic female friend, sharing with her the flattery and thrill of the chase, knowing that she was unattainable. My duty now involved fielding calls from the smitten, the downright persistent and the unhappily married. It was my job to know whom she wanted to speak to and whom she didn't, who had to be let down gently, who had to be told 'No!'

One day, out of the blue, fifty long-stemmed red roses arrived with a rather over-familiar message attached. The princess first sought my opinion, then gossiped about the gesture with Katherine Graham, who was nearing her eightieth birthday but never lost her elegance as publisher of the *Washington Post*. The princess admired her strength – 'She went out into a man's world and came out on top' – and Miss Graham became a key ally in America along with Anna Wintour, editor of *Vogue*, Barbara Walters, the doyenne of US television interviewers, and New York-based photographers Patrick Demarchelier and Mario Testino.

The princess adored life in Manhattan: shopping on Fifth Avenue, lunching at the Four Seasons, staying always at the Carlyle Hotel. She became a regular visitor to America, spending a lot of time in Washington where, of course, she stayed at the Brazilian embassy with her number-one friend, Lucia Flecha de Lima. It was Lucia who introduced the princess to Lana Marks who became a friend in the final year of the princess's life – a psychiatrist's wife who lived in Palm Beach, Florida, and ran exclusive leather boutiques across the States. She shared the princess's sense of humour as well as her passion for fashion and ballet. When Lana first came to stay in London, it was my job to smuggle the princess into the Lanesborough Hotel for a discreet lunch: the princess lay down on the back seat as I drove my blue Vauxhall Astra into the portico at the front door.

'Is the coast clear?' she asked.

Not one photographer in sight. 'All clear,' I said, and she got out of the car and dashed into the hotel.

One Oscar-winning Hollywood actor's confident image suddenly disappeared when it proved he was too shy to ring the palace himself and ask the princess for a date: he got a friend to write a letter on his behalf. When the princess wrote back, politely refusing, he returned with another request a month later. She had a drink with him and chose never to meet him again.

He wasn't the only one with honourable intentions. There was a sporting legend, who made a living out of racing in a field of competitors; a leading musician; a novelist; a lawyer; an entrepreneur; a billionaire who ran his own empire, and one extremely famous politician. The unfortunate thing was that while they might have provided the princess with enthralling company, her heart lay elsewhere.

The princess called me the 'steward of the racecourse' because I helped control the men in her life: deciding, after some serious consultation, who was a live runner in the race and who was lagging behind at the back of the pack. I was now organizing virtually every aspect of her life, but I carried out the duty in a light-hearted manner. I teased her. She teased me. Just as she had compartmentalized certain friendships, she controlled the position of her gentleman friends. We called it 'the trap system', as if the men were competitors on a racetrack, running round after the princess with their gifts and flowers. The occupant of trap No. 1 never changed. He remained in pole position in the princess's eyes, not threatened by those on the periphery. Throughout the day, I kept the princess informed about which trap had rung, and at what time. 'Trap No. 5 has rung, he wants you to ring him back. Trap No. 8 wants to speak to you, shall I put him off again?' On her writing desk, the princess kept a list of the traps and their occupants. In my pantry, a duplicate of the same list, which changed as men fell in and out of favour, was tucked into the back of my desk diary.

Sometimes, the princess could not believe how many suitors were making their intentions known. She used to joke that the racecourse was getting 'a little overcrowded'. Once I wrote to her: '*There is still serious overcrowding on the racetrack. After further consultation, I have been informed that Traps 8 and 9 are void and have been declared non-runners. One failed the random drug testing; one failed the strict medical examination.*'

Then the princess wrote to me: '*Due to serious overcrowding on the racetrack, the judges have asked for a re-evaluation on the contents of the traps and have asked Mr Paul Burrell for his valuable assistance on this sensitive issue!!*'

Following what I would call 'a steward's inquiry', it became rather empowering to strike a line through the traps containing the lawyer and the politician.

The drawback of being sucked into this royal vortex, and being so close to the princess, was that my life merged into hers. When friends said they would always be there for her, it meant on call twenty-four hours a day. Being butler and friend placed an even greater expectation on my time. In September 1996, I had got home late, beyond eleven o'clock again, and was sitting down to a bottle of red wine with Maria at the Old Barracks. Just after midnight, the princess rang in tears after a little setback in her personal life. As I spoke to her, Maria tutted. The princess was asking me to go out and deliver a message to someone following an altercation over the telephone.

Hearing how upset she was, how could I refuse? Even at that late hour, even though I was exhausted, I had to – I wanted to – oblige. As I put down the receiver, I had to tell Maria that the princess needed me to run an errand.

'That's it. I've had enough. You – are – pathetic!' she spat.

'But, chuck, you've got to understand that she needs me. No one else can help at this hour,' I said.

'Paul. You baby her. She clicks her fingers and you go running. Well, I've had it. I've had it with you and I've had it with her!' Maria stormed off to bed as I put on my shoes, pulled on my jacket and went out into the night.

Mission accomplished, I got to bed in the early hours. That morning, I went to work as usual for eight o'clock, wondering if I had ever been to sleep. But the tiredness was worth it when I reached my desk in the pantry and found a note from a far happier boss.

Dear Paul. Not many people would venture out late at night to sort a heart out ... but then, not many people have the kindness and qualities you possess ... I am profoundly touched by your actions last night, and very much wanted you to know that. Times are challenging in this particular home, but one thing is for sure, that is without you at the helm of this ship, we'd all be in bad shape and the laughter gone! So thank you very much for coming to my rescue once again, love from Diana.

I had gone into work almost looking forward to discovering whether or not she had left me a little note. Notes were left on a daily basis around the apartment: instructions, requests, messages or thank-yous – she still took time to write down what she could have said to my face or over the telephone.

Once, one of her suitors had persuaded the princess to accept a dinner invitation when she didn't really want to go, and I teased her endlessly about being on her guard. 'Don't worry, Paul, I can look after myself,' she said.

When she left, I stayed at the palace and spent half the evening worrying about her, wondering if she was going to be okay. I had told her to ring me on her mobile, which she kept in her hand-bag at all times, if there were any problems. She was due back by eleven o'clock so I decided to leave a mischievous note on her pillow, wondering, as a man, if I could second-guess the suitor's every move. The princess often said I had an annoying habit of always being right.

When she got back, she filled in my joke questionnaire and left it on a stool at the top of the stairs to ensure it was the first thing I saw when I arrived before breakfast. My questions were written in black; the princess penned her answers in green.

YRH . . .
IF . . . you had a candlelit dinner for 2? Correct!
IF . . . there were roses on the table? Correct!
IF . . . he had lizard lips and drooled all evening? Deaf instead.
AND insisted on you drinking a glass of champagne? 2 glasses.
THEN I WAS RIGHT!

That morning, at breakfast, we laughed so much. After serving her, I pulled up a chair, sat down at the dining-table and said: 'Come on, then, tell me about it.'

Those were exactly the same words used by one national-newspaper journalist who had obtained the telephone number for the direct line into my pantry. He rang to inquire about a tip-off he had received that I had been offered a position as butler, in America, to movie actor Mel Gibson. By 1996, the press was beginning to analyse the relationship between me and the princess. First came the

News of the World on 14 January with a headline 'BUTLER IS THE ONLY ONE DI TRUSTS' followed by a full page in the *Daily Mail*, asking, 'IS THIS THE ONLY MAN DIANA REALLY TRUSTS?' and telling how I was assigned 'to stand guard over her fax machine back home and act as her most personal of go-betweens' even when she was away on holiday. But the unexpected call about Mel Gibson was the first time I had been put on the spot by someone I didn't know.

The truth was that an American agency had tentatively suggested that I might work for Mel Gibson but I wasn't going to tell that to this persistent reporter. In a ten-minute phone call, he pressed for the truth, but I said: 'I am happy working with the princess.'

The reporter kept on: 'But will you deny that Mel Gibson has approached you to be his butler?'

'I am happy working with the princess,' I repeated.

It threw me, and I panicked because I hadn't told the princess about the Mel Gibson idea because it was a non-starter. Now the newspapers could cause trouble for me, I thought. I went upstairs and immediately told the princess about the call.

She was furious. 'I'm not having this! I'm not having them ring you here like that!' and she stormed downstairs, out through the back and into the adjoining office where she made Caroline McMillan ring back the reporter, scolding him for breaching accepted protocol, asking him to refrain from contacting her staff and repeating that her butler was going nowhere. I dreaded the next morning's newspapers and, with the princess, I read the rather embarrassing headline across two pages that announced, 'I'M DI'S GUY', telling how I had snubbed Mel Gibson to pledge my future to the Boss. A potentially negative situation had been turned into a positive story, and the princess spent the day teasing me about being her guy.

I thought all talk about being poached was over, until the day American chat-show host Oprah Winfrey came to lunch at KP. The princess was really nervous about meeting her because, she said, 'She is such a big name.' It didn't cross her mind that perhaps Oprah would be nervous too.

I took Oprah into the drawing room and offered her a drink. She accepted a glass of water. Then I returned to the princess in the sitting room. 'What's she like?' she whispered.

'She's taking everything in, not missing a trick. She's extremely smart and wearing the *most* enormous diamond studs in her ears!' The princess seemed impressed.

She made her typical confident entrance. 'Sorry to keep you waiting, sorry, sorry,' she said, as she walked over to greet the US television star.

I served lunch in the dining room and soon became part of the proceedings as conversation turned to America.

'We love America, don't we, Paul?' the princess said. 'He goes there every year for a holiday.'

Cue Oprah to the princess: 'So, would you ever consider living in the United States?'

'It would be a wonderful place for my boys to visit,' she said diplomatically, not mentioning that she was still considering a move to Australia.

Then I chipped in: 'I would pack my bags and go and live in America tomorrow.' I looked at the princess and winked.

Oprah saw her opportunity. 'We could do with a butler. Why don't you come to Chicago and look after me?'

The princess suddenly straightened in her chair. 'Look, Oprah,' she said, laughing, 'he's my butler and he's staying here.' It became a friendly tug-of-war all the way through to coffee: Oprah kept returning to it to embarrass me.

After lunch, the princess and I walked her to the front door where her car was waiting. Just before she pulled away, Oprah opened the window, leaned forward and said: 'This is your last chance, Paul.'

The Boss stood beside me at the front step, threw a possessive arm round me and shouted out: 'Hey, he's mine – and he's staying here with me,' and the lunch appointment ended on laughter as we stood there, waving her goodbye.

I seemed to be constantly beside the princess, morning, noon, late at night.

'Come on, Paul, we're going for a drive,' said the princess, one summer's evening after dinner.

We jumped into her BMW. She headed out down the back-streets of Bayswater and Queensway, towards Paddington Green, near the railway station. Right. Left. Right. Left. Side-street after side-street. She knew all the short-cuts. 'You don't need to do the Knowledge!' I joked.

'I could take on any London cabbie.' She smiled, the peak of her baseball cap shadowing her face.

We arrived at a street corner. The princess pulled over but kept the engine running. Then she dropped the electric window on my side. Two heavily made-up girls in short skirts had been talking to each other on the corner. When our BMW pulled over, they stopped, looked, caught my eye and tottered over in their high heels. The ladies of the night were working their patch.

The larger one maintained eye-contact with me as I shuffled in my seat. She placed both hands on the roof of the car, bent down and leaned in. 'Hi, Princess Di. How are you?' she said, speaking across me.

My head swivelled right and the princess was leaning in towards me. 'I'm fine [name]. Have you been busy?'

The second, slimmer girl bent down to join in the conversation. 'Nah, it's been quiet but we'll stick around. Gotta work, Princess,' she added.

Good God, I thought. The princess knows them.

'Who's this, then?' said one, looking at the rather nervous character who was saying nothing.

'This is Paul.' She introduced me. We shook hands. It was all very polite.

The Boss reached into her pocket and got out two crisp £50 notes. 'Look, girls, have the night off. Go home to your children,' she said, stuffing the notes into two eager hands. The princess asked about their children. One had been coughing. Was he better?

After a brief conversation, the larger woman patted the roof of the car, and the two girls were off, lured away by a pair of braking headlights a few hundred yards down the road. A load of good that £100 hand-out just did. What a waste, I thought. 'This is absolutely crazy. You cannot afford to be here, Your Royal Highness,' I said. 'DI AND BUTLER CAUGHT KERB-CRAWLING' was the imaginary headline that had raised my voice by a panic-stricken octave or two.

'Oh, Paul,' said the princess, as she pulled away, 'lighten up. Those girls need help and that's all I'm doing – helping them.'

The naïvety of her mission was astonishing but her heart, as always, was in the right place. If the princess had been faced with an avalanche, I think she would have tried to stop it. She wanted to help everyone. The sick. The poor. The homeless. The starving. AIDS sufferers. The infirm. Prostitutes. Drug addicts. Drunks. If it was up to her, and increasingly it seemed that it was, her mercy missions would have been endless. How many times during my duty did I hear those earnest words: 'I feel I can help . . .' or 'I want to go where hearts need mending'? She wanted to mend the world and society on a scale that was a mercy Mission Impossible.

We returned to the Paddington area several times in the summer and winter of 1996. In November, we pulled over at the same street corner. This prostitute had two children at home, was working the streets to provide for them, and couldn't even afford a coat on such a cold night.

The princess, in one of her roadside 'counselling' sessions, had given this woman £100. 'Now, buy yourself a coat, and I want to see you in that coat the next time I'm here,' she said, almost motherly. Within a few weeks, we saw the woman again looking a lot warmer – wearing a thick waist-length black coat.

In the princess's wardrobe, there was a floor-length fur coat that she had once been given. She had accepted it graciously as a gift but she never wore fur. One afternoon I saw her leave KP with it tucked under her arm. She returned home without it. She told me how she had been driving through Victoria when she spotted a skip on the side of the road. She stopped the car, dropped the window and hurled in the coat. 'You never know, a tramp might pick it up. That should keep him warm!' she said.

I got used to sitting in that BMW, sometimes in the passenger seat, sometimes behind the wheel, often after midnight. There was a practical reason for making it so late: not only were the streets of London quieter, the princess knew that photographers, should they be watching, could not get sneak photos with long lenses in the dark.

Parked in an alleyway just round the corner from the Royal Brompton Hospital in Chelsea, I could be waiting for an hour, listening to late-night radio. I had dropped off the princess who left, armed with magazines, videos and CDs for the heart-and-lung transplant patients or those suffering from cystic fibrosis. These hospital visits were not new, even if cynics dismissed them as publicity stunts. The princess was there because she had a contact at the hospital, and she genuinely cared and took an interest. She was doing nothing more than she had done when Adrian Ward-Jackson died in 1991 or when I was in hospital in Swindon in 1992. She knew that, for some people, her visits could be more of a tonic than any medicine and that was all that mattered.

Sometimes waiting in the car for the princess was not so boring. Once, when she was lunching with her friend Lord Attenborough at Tante Claire in Chelsea, sitting in the window, I arrived in the BMW to pick her up at two thirty. Luckily, there was a parking space directly in front of the restaurant, and I could see Lord Atten-borough's back with the princess facing the window. She had seen me pull in.

The car stereo was playing the CD soundtrack from *Aladdin*. Our family friends in Florida, Chuck Webb and Ron Ruff, regularly sent the princess CDs of the latest Disney movies: *The Lion King*, *Pocahontas*, *Beauty and the Beast* and *Toy Story*. I have long been a collector of animation art and visited New York for its annual animation sale to purchase 'cells' – individual frames from the movies with their original production backgrounds. The princess had her own cells, most famously from *Who Framed Roger Rabbit?*, presented to her at its royal première in Leicester Square, London. She also bought William and Harry all the Disney videos, and she often drove to Disney soundtracks – *Beauty and the Beast* and *Aladdin* were her favourites. The in-joke between butler and princess was one particular track on *Aladdin* – 'A Whole New World' – which she played over and over again. She knew the lyrics off by heart and, whether with me or alone, she sang them out loud when driving. This song was playing as she was finishing her meal with Lord Attenborough. I started to mouth the words and gesticulate in an exaggerated manner. When she saw me, she giggled, and no doubt Lord Attenborough thought his jokes were working a treat. On the way back to the palace, we sang that track together. Not quite Rachmaninov but another memory nevertheless.

By November 1996, after the princess had visited Sydney, Australia, to help raise $1 million for the Victor Chang Cancer Foundation, she returned and waved goodbye to dreamy thoughts of living down under. Australia and its people fell in love with her but, unfortunately, she was not in love with Australia. She felt it was 'primitive' compared to London, New York and Washington, and said she would have felt so isolated there. Instead, her attention turned to a new potential home: South Africa.

Christmas 1996 would be the princess's last Christmas, and she spent it in another corner of the globe, in the Caribbean. The press was convinced that she was heading to Australia to enjoy the festive period with a male companion so it was my job to keep them under that illusion, booking two seats on a Qantas flight for Sydney, knowing that reporters would be checking the flight passenger list. As the media stalked the Qantas desk at Heathrow, the princess sloped off on Christmas Eve to the opposite side of the world and the exclusive K-Club complex on the tiny island of Barbuda, near Antigua, accompanied by her personal assistant Victoria Mendham. The ploy worked, but only for a day or two.

William and Harry had delved into their Christmas stockings on the Sunday before Christmas. William was overjoyed with his stereo system. Harry started hooking up his PlayStation 2.

On Christmas Day, the telephone rang constantly at the Old Barracks. Maria insisted that I didn't answer it. We both knew it would be the princess and, for once, I obeyed a command from my wife so that I could give all my time to my family.

On Boxing Day, I took the calls. The princess rang every day for a chat until her return on New Year's Day, and she couldn't wait to get back. Unlike Harry, who had gone to Klosters in Switzerland with Prince Charles and had the time of his life skiing, despite the presence of the press which he later described as a 'nightmare' to his mother. William had refused to go with them: aged fourteen, he was already beginning to loathe the media spotlight. I had no choice about my next destination: Angola. I would walk beside the princess as she came into her own as a true philanthropist, championing the humanitarian causes that meant so much to her.

12. Side by Side

I followed on the heels of the princess as we walked out of the squinting brightness of the African sun and into the gloom of a village hospital. I say 'hospital' because that was what it was to the locals, but really it was a bare room with around six metal-framed beds. The walls had once been plastered but never decorated. With the media pack jostling and shuffling behind us, we walked to the bedside of a young girl, a thin white sheet pulled up to her neck, her wide eyes staring up at us.

Then a nurse pulled down the sheet to her waist to expose the most horrific sight. Her entire insides were spilling out of her gaping abdomen. She had gone to fetch water for her family and stepped on one of the ten million landmines that remained buried and live under Angola's scorched soil.

It was impossible to connect the two sights: the pretty face on the pillow, the bloodied entrails at the midriff. The most instinctive thing to do was recoil, but the princess forced herself to focus on the girl's eyes. She didn't want this young patient to think she was unbearable to look at, even though she was beyond help. The princess placed her hand in the girl's and bit her lip to stop herself crying. Then she pulled the sheet up to the girl's neck, turned to the press and said: 'Please, no more.' The camera lights flicked off.

It was 15 January 1997. The day is remembered for that famous image of the princess walking through a minefield being painstakingly cleared by the Halo Trust, treading along a safe path in her white shirt and cream chinos, wearing a green flak jacket and helmet with clear visor. It was a photo-opportunity that led cynics back home to suggest that the princess was meddling on the political stage, and call her a 'loose cannon'. Her endorsement of the anti-landmine campaign would sharpen the world's focus on the forgotten victims of war, the innocent civilians killed or maimed for taking one wrong step in village streets littered with deadly devices as deeply entrenched as the global landmine treaty that had seen Britain, Canada and America stalling.

The cynics in Fleet Street accused her of having seized another well-rehearsed, attention-grabbing photo-opportunity in the mine-field. But they hadn't seen that little girl in the hospital bed because the princess didn't wish them to see her. It was one of thousands of profound moments I witnessed during my duty when the princess, privately and away from the cameras, genuinely made a difference to what she called 'real people'. One brief moment in a simple African clinic could not restore life to the girl but it brought hope to those who had been forgotten and, quite rightly, she drew attention with the Red Cross to a hidden tragedy. Those who don't want to believe that she made a difference should have read the *Sunday Times* article filed by its reporter Christina Lamb. That day she stayed behind to interview the little girl.

The journalist, hardened by war-zone experiences, cynical by nature, had tried to explain to the child who had just visited her bedside. 'She is a princess from England,' said Mrs Lamb.

'So is she an angel?' the little girl asked, and that afternoon she died from her injuries.

Outside, the princess provided her own answer. Responding to reporters' questions about being 'a loose cannon', she replied, 'I am a humanitarian – always have been, always will be.'

I had not been on a tour with the princess since Egypt in 1992 but she had asked me to join her on the four-day trip to Angola from 12 to 17 January. The request came out of the blue. 'There will be just you, me and people from the Red Cross,' she said, as well as two police protection officers, on whom the government insisted on an overseas trip.

I wondered what use I could be.

'You will come everywhere with me, my assistant, lady-in-waiting, secretary and dresser!' she joked. So I woke her, ironed her clothes and shadowed her every move on engagements. My enforced versatility once again provoked the press to ask questions about the significance of the butler being the princess's constant shadow and I sensed, among other royal household staff, that my role was putting a few noses out of joint.

The princess had rebuilt bridges with the Red Cross since her withdrawal as its patron, and had consulted Mike Whitlam, its then director-general, about its anti-landmine crusades. He had sent literature and videos for her to watch, and that was what had fired her desire to do something. In Angola mines killed one in four of its twelve million people and the country became the launch pad for the princess's anti-landmine crusade with Mike Whitlam by her side.

Armed with the itinerary for the trip, I had gone shopping for the dress-down clothes the princess would require. First stop was Ralph Lauren in Bond Street for shirts, chinos and three-quarter-length trousers. (She even bought me some new shirts.) Then there was Armani for jeans, and Tod's for flat leather footwear. All had to be packed with the dresses and skirts needed for the embassy and dinner with the first lady, Ana Paula dos Santos. I also went to Boots for the essentials, including vitamins.

Bill Deedes, a veteran columnist from the *Daily Telegraph*, was to join the press pack in Angola but the princess insisted he travel with us to and from the capital, Luanda, because he had been such an influence on her thinking, having been involved with the anti-landmine cause since 1990. He had been a regular visitor to KP where we had a standing joke about the difficulty of the *Daily Telegraph* crossword. 'My butler still thinks your crossword is so unfair,' the princess said, every time she welcomed Bill, highlighting my intellectual shortcomings for the puzzle rather than her own.

On the flight to Luanda, she was endlessly scribbling notes and redrafting her speech, which was delivered amid the rubble of the run-down airport. She declared that she wanted 'to ban, once and for all, antipersonnel landmines'.

As we drove to the British embassy, bumping around the potholed roads in a Landcruiser, the princess was shaking her head at the pitiful sights she witnessed: almost every other person we passed had just one leg; only the façades of buildings remained – homes, shops, offices – peppered with craters from mortar fire. It was like driving through a movie set.

It had been a long road that the princess had travelled since she had visited Calcutta in 1992 and Mother Teresa's home, which focused its work on the starving, the sick and the dying. That trip had been a life-changing experience for her, giving her hope and placing her on a humanitarian and spiritual path at a time when she had found zero fulfilment in an ending marriage. 'That was when I found my direction in life,' she told me.

We had spoken about the significance of Calcutta many times, but before we left for Angola, she presented me with a copy of a record of her thoughts and emotions on that trip to India, as if she wanted me to understand what the humanitarian cause was all about and why such work was important to her. She had also given it to acupuncturist Oonagh Toffolo, whose husband Jo had received many visits from the princess at the Royal Brompton Hospital. The princess's vivid account explains how she experienced a spiritual awakening in Calcutta that became the driving force behind every caring act she carried out, every mission and campaign she worked towards.

She had gone to visit Mother Teresa's home, and when she arrived sisters sang the Lord's Prayer in the chapel, then knelt with the princess to pray.

The princess viewed those women as saints. She never considered herself to be one, regardless of some of the labels attached to her image by others. Sisters like those in Calcutta were the true saints. Princesses in England were not. But she wanted to bring to her public the warmth and compassion she had felt in those women.

Angola 1997 would mirror Calcutta 1992, in how the princess reached out to the sick. India acted almost as a template for her to rely on in future humanitarian missions, because she could never forget how important a simple, sincere gesture could be when dealing with the young, the sick and the poor.

She carried with her in her heart the lesson she had taught herself in one instinctive moment when, as she visited Mother Teresa's home for children, she picked up a blind and deaf boy. As she wrote later: '*I hugged him so tightly, hoping he could feel my love and warmth.*' She spoke about the experience with passion, belief, and with a conviction that made me understand where she was coming from.

Her written account of her experiences in Calcutta told of a visit to a hospice for the dying. On reading it, I knew that her time there, coupled with the experience of witnessing the death of her friend Adrian Ward-Jackson in 1991, had made the greatest impact on her, which was why she gave me such strength after my own mother's death. In sharing it with me, she wanted me to understand better the roots of her humanitarianism.

In that hospice, she was confronted with row upon row of beds, each filled with a man, woman or child facing inevitable death with courage. 'Dying with dignity', she called it; individuals were 'happy' to pass away under Mother Teresa's roof.

I doubt the princess had ever been so overwhelmed by any other scene in her travels around the world. She went to each bedside, and offered everyone a box of chocolates. One man was so weak with tuberculosis that she placed a chocolate in his mouth for him.

I read what she had written about the entire experience, and how it had so profoundly changed her outlook on life – and death. On returning from Calcutta, she was driven by a deep need to help the sick and dying on a global scale. It had been her awakening. You only have to analyse the princess's speeches post-1992 to realize how she talked more and more about spiritual beliefs. She truly felt that her most rewarding time was when she helped the sick and dying. She felt 'replenished' by doing it. It was also her responsibility, she felt, to use her position as the Princess of Wales to make a difference.

In Angola, I read that account over and over again. Each morning, the princess couldn't wait to get out and see the victims of the landmines. Eager, once more, to make a difference.

'Come on, let's get to work,' she said, and we went to visit the villages of Huambo and Kuito, following the path that she had embarked on five years earlier.

Later that year, in June, the princess visited New York to meet Mother Teresa in the Bronx. A headline in Britain read: 'ANGELS IN THE BRONX'.

Angola represented the apogee of my years in royal service, when I transcended all personal and professional expectations. It was the time when, with encouragement from the princess, I felt confident enough to leave behind the self-imposed limitations of being 'butler' and become her virtual right-hand man. I finally discarded the remnants of the butler's uniform in the second week of January at the British embassy in Luanda where I went front-of-house instead of remaining backstage. When the princess told me that she intended to take me everywhere, she meant it. I just didn't realize that it would involve walking through marble corridors of the government building to meet the country's first lady, Ana Paula dos Santos, and the foreign minister.

In Pakistan, Czechoslovakia and Egypt in 1992–3, I knew my place on the sidelines as an observer. In Angola, I became a participant, beside Diana, Princess of Wales, and was received after the princess by our hosts. I don't think the first lady even knew my job title was 'butler'. As far as anyone in that room was concerned, even the Angolan staff, I was her private secretary or equerry-in-waiting. It was a bizarre feeling for me because I knew exactly who I was.

A private secretary should be doing this, I thought, but she didn't have one. A lady-in-waiting should be doing this, but she didn't have one. So, it was left to the man who had pressed her dress, carried her luggage and handwashed her garments to have a formal audience with the first lady, listening intently to the discussions on landmines and the country's politics.

At least my training stood me in good stead. I had been well used to announcing the heads of Commonwealth countries to the Queen on the Royal Yacht *Britannia* so I knew the protocol and exactly how to behave, one step behind the princess.

As I stood there in those first few anxious minutes, I remembered my first duty at Windsor Castle back in 1976, and how I hadn't been trusted to handle the meat or vegetable trays. And there I was, standing and then sitting beside the Boss, the woman who had engineered my career advancement. I felt proud. And, if I'm being honest, rather smug too, knowing that if the royal household could have seen me, they would not approve. It made the experience even more enjoyable, imagining the suits sniffing down their noses that I didn't 'belong' or didn't 'know my place'. It was an accusation I would face when working for the Diana, Princess of Wales Memorial Fund.

I'm not even sure Her Majesty's Ambassador Roger Hart grasped what on earth my role was. As we stayed in his official residence, he often saw me emerging from one-to-one meetings with the princess. Then there was dinner when the princess requested that my name be included on the seating plan. So there I was, making polite conversation at the dinner table with Her Majesty's representative in Angola, his wife and the princess.

The best bit for me, and what made the princess really giggle, was when it came to the end of the evening and she announced that she was going to retire for the night. It was a rehearsed departure so, as she stood and pushed back her chair, so did I, and we retreated simultaneously and broke into raucous laughter as we remembered the raised eyebrows we had left at the table. She loathed the claustrophobia of stuffy formality even though the ambassador and his wife were great company.

We only had a formal dinner once. After that, it was a cold snack in her room. Every other night, the princess, wrapped in a towelling robe that covered a swimsuit, went with me through the official residence, down the passages, through the kitchen and out into the garden to the swimming-pool. I sat on the tiled edge with my feet dangling in the water, counting the lengths the princess swam. End to end, motoring along in front crawl, she did twenty before stopping to catch her breath.

Then she stood in the shallow end, pushing back her drenched hair. 'How do you think today went?' she asked, leaning against the side of the pool. We discussed how it had gone, what tomorrow would bring, and her private concerns. Then, she did another twenty lengths beneath the stars and the moon.

Lord Attenborough was about to release his latest film, *In Love and War*. At its première in London in February, it would be trailed by a ten-minute documentary to raise money for the British Red Cross Landmines Appeal. That was why a production team had exclusive access to our Landcruiser to shadow the princess in Angola.

On this occasion, the princess didn't mind having a camera crew breathing down her neck because she knew it would highlight the cause around the world, but it required one technical practicality: the princess had to be 'miked up'. A microphone was attached to the front of her shirt, leading to a transmitter pack on her belt at the back of her trousers. I think it was on day two of the trip that the sound recordists got more than they bargained for. Forgetting that she was wired for sound, we made what the princess referred to as 'a pit stop' at a remote garage. I wandered off with her for a private chat away from the cameras, behind the building. She wanted to discuss personal issues and whom she would call when we got back to the official residence. Then we gossiped about the camera crew: the characters, the way they worked, the silly incidents, and she was giggling mischievously. Finally I spotted the microphone and it dawned on her at exactly the same time. Her laughter turned to horror.

'Check it!' she panicked.

Sure enough, the little light on the transmitter pack was blinking red. Our gossip had been transmitted live.

Returning to the vehicle like two naughty schoolchildren, we felt out guilt was as glaring as the sun, but all the princess could do was purse her lips to restrain a fit of giggles. To this day, I still don't know if the production company picked up on that moment. We never dared ask.

Angola was an exhausting, emotionally draining experience, but everyone involved returned with a feeling of triumph that we had bounced an important issue on to the world stage. At the end, the princess, with her usual generosity, demonstrated her gratitude to all those who had participated and made the trip such a success. All the staff at the British ambassador's residence, the drivers, the chef, the maids, the office staff and the ambassador himself, received wallets and leather memo pads, embossed with D and a coronet, and signed photographs of her. When I returned to KP, a gift from her was waiting for me: a marble bust of an African woman that she had been given in Angola.

The generosity of the princess ultimately led me into the number-one court at the Old Bailey when the outside world, and especially Scotland Yard, could not grasp how much senior royals gave to members of their staff. It was incomprehensible to those who had no knowledge of a world behind closed doors.

The previous September, my son Alexander had gained a place at the London Oratory School beside the mighty stadium of Chelsea Football Club. The princess asked about his progress at school. I happened to mention that he seemed to have a lot more homework.

'So he's locked away in his room for hours on end, is he?' she asked.

'No. He sits at the kitchen table while Maria's making tea,' I said.

The princess couldn't believe that he didn't have a desk. Kitchen tables were for family eating. Desks in a quiet corner were for homework. 'I have just the thing,' she said.

In 1981, to mark the marriage of the Prince and Princess of Wales, the city of Aberdeen had presented them with an upright writing bureau, but it was never used. It had been in storage for all those years so the princess saw the opportunity to put it to good use. My brother Graham and I went down to a storage cupboard in the inner hallway on the ground floor at KP and loaded the desk into the back of my Vauxhall Astra. It was one of the items I was said to have stolen after the death of the princess.

In the final year of her life, the princess was constantly getting rid of items that reminded her of her marriage. The carpets and china bearing the Prince of Wales feathers had already been thrown out. Now circumstances were different. While part of her would always remain in love with Prince Charles, a fresh clearing-out process began of the more sentimental items, as if she was mentally shedding a past that had been crammed into her emotional baggage. Genuine happiness lay with someone else. She had finally persuaded herself to move on and let go. It wasn't a process carried out with any animosity because relations with Prince Charles had never been more civil. As with the dress auction that would be held in June 1997, the princess was giving up her past. And what a personal triumph it was for her to accept that she was 'giving up my past'. Because its significance was vast and showed how far she had come in her personal growth. For at the height of her bulimia, the past had haunted her and she said the condition made her 'bring up my past'. The distinction is important to recognize. She had triumphed. She had survived. She had grown strong. And she was heading in a new, exciting direction.

'In our new world, we won't be needing all this,' said the princess, standing in the boys' sitting room. She was emptying boxes full of clothes, trinkets, ornaments, CDs, books, cassettes, unwanted gifts. This was her 'nesting' process, which took place either late in an evening or on a Sunday afternoon.

She gave me a Cartier clock. It had been bought by Prince Charles but she thought its mother-of-pearl face and orange and black marble base were 'hideous'.

A pile of jumble was heaped in the centre of the room and the princess invited members of staff to help themselves. Lily Piccio, a Filipino maid, could not believe her eyes, and carried whatever she could to the modest flat she shared with her sister. Aromatherapist Eileen Malone, mother of the cosmetics entrepreneur Jo Malone, also received another ornate carriage clock that had been a wedding gift. 'It will always remind you of me,' said the princess. Psychic Rita Rogerts was presented with a beautiful eighteen-carat-gold Van Cleef and Arpels necklace in the shape of intertwining hearts, worth at least £8000. For her eightieth birthday *Washington Post* publisher Katherine Graham received a silver box from Asprey jewellers with K inscribed on the lid, and inside, 'Devotion and admiration, from Diana'. Even Christie's expert Meredith Etherington-Smith knew the kindness of the Boss. As a thank-you for cataloguing and supervising the dress auction, the princess, who knew her love of starfish, had the Crown jewellers at Garrard create a solid gold starfish scattered with diamonds and inscribed on the underside 'With fondest love from Diana'.

Black bin-liners filled with clothes went begging and healer friend Simone Simmons, who was visiting the princess almost every day, was another beneficiary. One afternoon when Simone was there, the princess asked her to help herself. 'What? You want me to take all these bin-bags of clothes?' said a somewhat surprised Simone.

'No,' said the princess, 'those bags are for Paul,' and I took at least three filled with clothes, handbags and shoes for Maria while our sons slipped into William and Harry's cast-offs.

The princess gave even to complete strangers. Once, my sons were playing on the green with an American teenager called Bill. The princess and I were walking down to the high street when she stopped to talk to him. Then she told me to provide for him a photograph of herself, which she signed and I framed.

Like the Filipino maid, Scotland Yard could not believe its eyes, or the truth, when officers entered Maria's and my bedroom and found designer suits, which the princess had once worn, hanging in the wardrobe; when it found CDs in a box; when it found ornaments on our shelves; when it found the writing bureau. When it found around four hundred items that the princess had given me.

Nor could the Spencer siblings judge as credible the prodigiously giving nature of their own sister towards non-relatives. Lady Sarah

McCorquodale later said that she expected me, as the butler, to have nothing more than a signed photograph and a pair of cuff-links. They wonder why I have always maintained that friends knew the princess better than her own family did.

At Easter, the princess returned to the K-Club and Barbuda with William and Harry. In May, she went on a three-day trip to Pakistan to visit Imran Khan and his wife Jemima, daughter of her friend Lady Annabel Goldsmith. The princess wanted to learn more about Islam. On each visit, she rang me three times a day as, I'm sure, she did other friends. I honestly don't know what she would have done if she had lost her mobile telephone. It seemed to be permanently attached to her right ear.

While she was away, I was showing a new recruit the ropes at KP. The princess had hired an under-butler to carry out the duties I no longer had time to perform. Craig Weller, then twenty-three, had been trained by the team at Buckingham Palace and his arrival made my life much easier.

The princess returned from Pakistan and I learned a big secret. It was one that she should not have told me, but one that she was bursting to share. I think she managed to keep her lips sealed for all of five minutes.

'Paul! Paul!' she shouted from the first-floor landing before she ran down the stairs to my pantry. 'I've got a secret! I've got a secret!'

By the time she reached the bottom step, it was a secret no longer. I was perplexed. This was not the normal manner in which she imparted information. She was wearing a pale blue Chanel suit when she told me: 'You're going to get a medal, Paul!' Then she broke the news that I was to be decorated by the Queen at Buckingham Palace with the Royal Victorian Medal, Her Majesty's personal order. 'And it's about time too. It's all supposed to be a secret but, hey, you know all my secrets, I had to tell you. I'm so pleased for you, Paul,' she said.

I was stunned. The Queen was going to decorate me in her birthday honours, to be announced in June, in recognition of my twenty-one years in royal service. Finally, she was rewarding me for all those years of walking nine recalcitrant corgis.

The princess seemed more excited than me. She told me: 'After the investiture, I'll take you out to lunch and we will have champagne to celebrate at Mara's [San Lorenzo restaurant]. We'll make an occasion of it.'

When the official announcement was made on 17 June, the princess was in Washington attending the eightieth birthday party of Katherine Graham, but she still sent a congratulatory telemessage. It read: '*A million heartfelt congratulations on your RVM – it's wonderful news and the boys and I are absolutely thrilled for you! Love from Diana, William and Harry.*'

On the morning of my thirty-ninth birthday on 6 June, I walked into my pantry and found an envelope on top of a gift-wrapped box on my desk. Inside was a gold, black-leather-strapped Longines wristwatch and the attached note read: '*Happy, Happy Birthday, with love from Diana*'.

On 1 July, as the princess turned thirty-six, KP resembled a florist's shop again: around fifty separate arrangements of fresh flowers, dried flowers and plants took over every vase and pot. They included sixty white roses from Gianni Versace and a dozen trumpet lilies from Giorgio Armani. The Prince of Wales sent a perfumed candle from Highgrove. Mohamed Al Fayed, owner of Harrods, sent a leather handbag. The princess's stepmother, Raine Spencer, was the first telephone caller of the day, followed by Lucia Flecha de Lima – waking in Washington at three a.m. so she could be among the first to wish the princess a happy birthday at eight, British time. That is the devotion of a true friend.

If my duty involved being one step ahead of the princess, it also required me to act on instinct for the young princes. William and Harry knew that every Christmas their mother and I would choose their presents and, at the same time, I would be secretly selecting presents from them to the princess. I acted on their behalf for her thirty-sixth birthday. I knew exactly what to buy. Her collection of crystals was growing as she tapped into their healing and calming 'energies', encouraged by friend and healer Simone Simmons, who always wore a huge crystal pendant round her neck. On her advice, I went to a fossil and crystal expert in Chelsea, beside the London Oratory School, and entered a multicoloured crystal maze. On a shelf stood an eighteen-inch stone tower, whose front section had been removed to expose its sparkling purple and violet crystal interior. I knew immediately that that was the gift, even if it did cost £500. On a weekend prior to her birthday, William was back from Eton and he sneaked down to my ground-floor storeroom while the princess sat upstairs in the sitting room. With both hands, I lifted this thick icicle-like rock out of its box, and William's face lit up. 'That's brilliant, Paul!' he said.

Once it was wrapped, William cradled it in both hands and heaved it up the stairs. 'Are you sure you can manage it, William?' I said, as he staggered under its weight.

Minutes later, I heard the tearing of paper, the rustling of tissue and then a shriek of delight. That crystal stood to one side of the fireplace in the sitting room, a prized possession.

Down at the Old Barracks, my son Nick treasured his own crystal collection, inspired by what he had been shown by the princess who had sat with him in the sitting room, leaving him spellbound with tales of the magic crystals could bring. He had taken his little box, with tiny crystals embedded in cotton wool, to show to the princess. It made me smile to see my nine-year-old son in conversation with the princess. She sat on the edge of the sofa, peering into Nick's box. Both of them were engrossed. Nick told her how important it was to wash, clean and re-energize the crystals.

'They need to be put under a bright light, Princess,' he advised her.

So the princess decided to give her butler's son a duty to perform. She gave him some of her crystals and he arrived at the Old Barracks to wash them in a bowl of warm, soapy water. At night he left them to dry under the bright light of his bedside lamp. The next day, he rushed up to the palace to tell the princess that her crystals were fully recharged.

As a reward, the princess gave him a rose crystal and told him to place it on his bedside table where it would soothe him as he slept. 'I have exactly the same rose crystal next to me when I sleep,' she told him, 'so now you can have one too.' Then she made him a promise. 'After we all come back from our summer holidays, I will take you to the crystal factory and we will choose a nice big crystal for you.'

Nick couldn't wait.

★

For her birthday, dress designer Jacques Azagury had created the most stunning, sparkling, beaded black evening gown, with low-cut neckline and black satin straps and bows. 'You *must* wear that to-night!' I said, as she paraded up and down the sitting room. I went across the landing to the safe and pulled out some sapphires and diamonds.

'No, Paul, not those. I want to wear emeralds.'

That night, she wore the Jacques Azagury dress to the centenary dinner of London's Tate Gallery, wearing the emerald and diamond bracelet Prince Charles had given her as a wedding gift, the emerald and diamond earrings he had bought for her twenty-second birth-day, and Queen Mary's cabochon emerald and diamond choker, a wedding present from the Queen.

It was decided, after much discussion between the prince and prin-cess, that Harry should follow in his brother's footsteps and go to Eton after he finished at Ludgrove.

'He will look good in a tailcoat, won't he, Paul?' said the princess. 'Like a little penguin!' Harry had longed to go to Harrow so that he could be with a friend from the van Straubenzee family, so the news that he was going to look like a penguin at Eton hardly put a sparkle in his eyes.

Nor was William getting his own way: there was a pro-hunting rally in London and the young prince was eager to get out there, join the crowds, talk to the people and mix, but the princess would not allow him to go. She didn't 'feel it was appropriate'. Strangely, Tiggy Legge-Bourke joined the crowds and her presence made the next day's headlines instead. William realized his mother's point.

There were three children who couldn't smile enough inside the palace, though. A sweet family came to visit for tea: a mother, a father and their ten-, seven- and five-year-old children. Since the age of four, the seven-year-old girl had had a brain tumour. It had been removed twice but had returned and her parents had been told it was inoperable a third time. It had been the child's wish to have tea with the princess so the Boss decided to grant it. I was sent out to get Barbie balloons and little toys for the table. That family left with their memories captured in a disposable camera.

The treat for William and Harry was a summer holiday in

St Tropez on 11 July after the princess had turned down an invitation to holiday with them on the island of Phuket in Thailand. Mother and sons jetted off to the South of France and the coastal home of Mohamed Al Fayed, his wife Heini and three of their youngest children. The princess was taking up an invitation extended to her in the spring. She had decided to say yes after lunching with her stepmother Raine Spencer at the RAC Club in the first week of July.

The Harrods owner – who lived the high-life in London's Park Lane, complete with his own butlers – was by no means a close friend of the princess. He had been on the periphery of her life with strong links to her family: he had been a friend of her late father, Earl Spencer, and Raine. Indeed, Raine was a regular visitor to his residence in the Bois de Boulogne district of Paris. This property was known as the Villa Windsor because it had formerly been the home of the Duke and Duchess of Windsor following the duke's abdication in December 1936.

Al Fayed's fascination with all things royal led him to purchase the impressive property when the duchess had died in 1986. Eleven years on, he was making his move on another figure blamed for bringing turbulence to the Windsor dynasty: Diana, Princess of Wales. For many years, he had made known to her his presence and hospitality. Whenever she shopped at his Knightsbridge store, he always popped up at her side. Every Christmas, without fail, he sent a Harrods hamper to KP. On birthdays, he sent the princess and the young princes a generous gift. In the eyes of the Boss, he was a true gentleman. He had learned from Raine Spencer all about the difficult times the princess had faced in the mid-nineties. All he wanted to do was help and be there if she needed him – out of respect for his friend, her late father, he had always told her.

Until that summer the princess had always politely turned down his offers of hospitality. But the offer of a break in a villa overlooking a bay on the Côte d'Azur, with rigid security and private staff, proved irresistible. For William and Harry, there was also the prospect of jet skiing, speedboat rides and scuba-diving. A 200-foot yacht, *Jonikal*, serviced by its own crew, awaited them. It was the Egyptian multi-millionaire's own version of the Royal Yacht *Britannia*. What the princess didn't know as she flew out there was that it had been specifically bought to accommodate her and the princes. No sooner had she said yes to his holiday invitation than Mr Al Fayed took out his chequebook and purchased it for an estimated £15 million. Nor did the princess realize that her host would be providing something else to help lift her spirits: the presence of his eldest son Dodi, a film producer who was engaged to be married later that year to American model Kelly Fisher. Mohamed Al Fayed requested his son's company on the boat on 15 July.

When Dodi Al Fayed arrived on the *Jonikal* on 15 July, the press besieged the princess from a hired boat. I was holding the fort back at KP, overseeing a refurbishment of the princess's sitting room. She had brought in her old friend Dudley Poplak once more to work his magic and transform her favourite room from pink and cream to something 'a little more professional and mature' – creams, golds and blues. The striped sofas were reupholstered in cream; peach cushions replaced with blue and gold. A new cream-upholstered long stool arrived, on cabriole legs. The princess had loved pink – even the paper used for her internal memos was pink – but that summer she was erasing it from her world.

As the upholsterers, carpet-fitters and curtain-makers moved into the sitting room, the princess rang me constantly. She was regretting a spontaneous drop-in she had made on the press boat to ask them how long they intended to remain in position taking photographs. Before leaving, she had teased them, 'I'm going to shock the world when I make my next announcement!'

At KP, comptroller Michael Gibbins was dealing with the fall-out and the princess instructed him to issue this statement: '*Diana, Princess of Wales wishes to make it clear that she did not give any exclusive interviews to reporters yesterday. Her purpose in talking to some journalists was merely to enquire how long they intended to remain in the South of France as the oppressive media presence was causing great distress to all the children. There was no discussion of the possibility of any statement being issued in the future.*'

The princess was ringing me at KP up to eight times a day from the *Jonikal*. In one typically marathon call, she told me that she was going to get back at the media – using her leopardskin-print swimsuit. 'I'm going to wear it for the rest of the holiday. That will annoy them because they'll get the same picture every day!' she said. Sure enough, the papers were filled that week with her on the beach, on the boat, on the jet-ski, diving into the water wearing her leopardskin swimsuit.

What shattered the fun was the news that her friend Gianni Versace had been shot dead outside his mansion in Miami. At the end of the autumn, he had been due to send an entire winter wardrobe to the princess. For that month's *Vanity Fair* magazine, she was pictured wearing a Versace dress on the front cover. News of his death sent the princess into overdrive. Every hour, I had a frantic call from her. 'We must get hold of Elton John!' she said. 'He's somewhere in the South of France. His home in Windsor will have the number.'

I didn't get the chance to say that Elton had called KP the previous day, leaving his contact details. The tragedy of Versace's murder had ended a nine-month silence between the princess and the singer, and brought about a long overdue reconciliation. She had fallen out with him after a donated photograph of her and her sons had been used 'inappropriately' in Versace's book, *Rock and Royalty*. The princess was horrified when she saw that the family image had been used among photographs of semi-naked male models. She was deeply worried about what the Queen would think. The use of the photograph had nothing to do with Elton but because he had been the go-between she had blamed him, and the dispute had festered on both sides. That rift was healed in shared grief, and the princess comforted Elton at Versace's funeral on 22 July as she sat with an arm round him.

In a phone call, she told me that speaking to Elton again was 'like old times'. She added: 'He has been so understanding and told me that isn't it ironic that we can make something good out of tragedy and mend our friendship. He said Gianni would like it. Wasn't that sweet of him?'

The Boss was panicking. The private jet that was due to bring her and the boys home had a mechanical fault on the airport Tarmac in Nice. 'I must come back, Paul. I have a serious public engagement at a hospital tomorrow,' she said, on Sunday 20 July. They should have been back for six o'clock but she was on the phone, stranded, at eight thirty. Eventually, they made it back at midnight. 'Oh, it's so good to be home,' she said. She always liked coming home.

'So, how was it?' I asked.

'Wonderful. We had a great and normal time.' Then she went to bed.

The next day normal duty would resume: Meredith Etherington-Smith for lunch, and Mike Whitlam from the British Red Cross for tea.

That late summer I read the tabloid newspapers with incredulity as two names occupied all headlines, DIANA AND DODI, and with disbelief the journalists' assertions that this was the princess's 'first serious relationship since her divorce'. It was an absurd thing to suggest and the princess was worried that many people 'would read too much into this'. She had known Dodi for less than two months, and she *never* rushed into making up her mind about any man.

All the princess's closest friends know the identity of the only man with whom she had enjoyed a happy, long-term, serious relationship since her divorce. And it was *not* Dodi Al Fayed. It was someone whose relationship with her was formed on foundations far deeper and more meaningful than the brief spiritual connection she had made with the softly spoken Harrods heir. He spent a total of ten minutes at KP in their entire time together. It is wrong, and therefore not true to the memory of the princess, to allow the world to accept the notion that the princess had decided Dodi was 'The One'. It is true that she was captivated by his company, enthralled by his charm, excited at the novelty of his lavish romance. But 'The One' he most certainly was not. In fact, while her head was dizzy from jetting around Europe, her heart was, I am convinced, still in London.

Mohamed Al Fayed himself joined the speculative frenzy. He was reported as saying, 'I'm like a father to Diana.' With all due respect to him, that was never the case and, in the solitude of KP, it seemed to me that this entire Diana-Dodi relationship was heading into Fantasyland. Lucia Flecha de Lima's ambassador husband Paulo was a father-figure. Lord Attenborough was a father-figure. Mr Al Fayed could only claim, at best, to have had a distant avuncular role in her life. He was exceedingly kind but he was as much a father to the princess as Dodi was 'The One'.

In fact, to me, Dodi wasn't even Dodi. He was called 'Sister'. That was the code-name given to him by the princess so that we could refer to him openly. When the princess said, 'What do you think my sister would say?' or 'Has my sister called?' she was not referring to Lady Sarah McCorquodale or Lady Jane Fellowes but to him.

She had been swept off her feet, intoxicated by Dodi's extravagance and his spoiling nature. He had a jet-set life and toys that offered a royal lifestyle without the suffocating restrictions.

'Can I take you to dinner?' he had asked in a phone call to KP.

'Of course,' replied the princess. 'When?'

'Tomorrow night.'

'Where are we going?'

'Paris,' he said, and the princess was high with excitement.

Dodi was going all out to impress her: arranging a helicopter to whisk her across the Channel, accommodating her in the family-owned Ritz Hotel's Imperial Suite. I packed everything she would need into her Versace shoulder-bag. She left for the night, leaving nanny Olga Powell and me to look after William and Harry.

That Saturday evening, 26 July, she rang me from the suite. 'Oh, Paul, it's wonderful. Wonderful!' she squealed. 'And he's just given me a present. I couldn't wait for him to leave so that I could tell you. He has bought me the most beautiful gold watch surrounded by diamonds. I've *never* seen anything so beautiful.'

She was like a sixteen-year-old girl, and her happiness was contagious.

It was on that day that she had visited Villa Windsor – where it was suggested that she and Dodi had been making plans to live. Not according to the princess. 'We didn't stay long. The rooms are like a mausoleum. I couldn't live there! It's full of ghosts,' she said. She asked me to buy a black crocodile picture frame from Asprey so that she could send Dodi a photograph of herself. He had requested one.

'You can't dedicate the photograph to him. You don't know who it will be shown to,' I warned her. The frame was bought and she put the photograph in it. But, tellingly, she heeded my cautionary advice and didn't personalize it with a message or her signature.

She arrived back at KP bearing gifts for Maria and me. She pulled out of her shoulder-bag two peach towelling robes, each with an embroidered crest of the Ritz Hotel. 'I'm sure they'll suit Maria. Just not sure how you'll look in peach!' she joked.

In that final week of July, the princess chose to make a hard decision. Her head told her to draw a line under her previous relationship. Dodi, too, had decided to call off his engagement to Kelly Fisher. Both were single adults again. William and Harry were to spend August with Prince Charles in a vacation that would end at Balmoral. The princess joined Dodi, this time alone, from 31 July to 4 August, back aboard the *Jonikal* in the Mediterranean, cruising from Corsica to Sardinia, then returned home to get back on the humanitarian path.

A global map peppered with red pins was affixed to a piece of card and propped against the back of a chair in the corner of the KP sitting room. With the help of Mike Whitlam, the princess had identified the most landmined countries of the world – from Georgia to Korea, Angola to Vietnam – and each pin denoted a danger area, and a mission to be accomplished.

Following up the Angola triumph, the princess had planned to take her anti-landmine crusade to Georgia in southern Russia but the British government had deemed the trip too risky, so plans had to be cancelled. Instead, the tour switched to the former Yugoslavia and Bosnia from 8 to 10 August, accompanied by the Landmine Survivors Network (LSN) and Bill Deedes, from the *Daily Telegraph*.

On the first night, we stayed in private accommodation provided for us in the hills of Tuzla. That night, the capacity of princess and butler to deal with anything remotely hi-tech was put to the test. Give me a knife, fork and seating plan, and I will take on the best. Give me an electronic gadget, and I'm useless. When Dodi provided a satellite telephone for the princess to keep in touch from Bosnia, the two of us had looked at it helplessly. There we were, outside a mountaintop house, the princess holding out a compass to tell me the direction of the satellite, while I, having unpacked and aligned the machine, rushed into the undergrowth to find a signal.

'IS IT WORKING YET?' I called, and the princess could hardly speak for laughing. Then, at last, we found a signal and she made contact.

'I'll give you a couple of my mild pills before you go to bed after all that excitement,' she said, as we packed the machine away.

'I might never wake up!' I said.

'Don't worry, I'll make my usual amount of noise. You'll wake up.'

The next day, we travelled in a group of five in a Landcruiser, and the princess insisted on riding in the front passenger seat. Beside me in the back seat were Americans Jerry White and Ken Rutherford who had founded the LSN after they had become civilian victims of landmines. Jerry had lost a leg; Ken had lost both. They shared the princess's sense of humour. As she got into the front seat, they would start to clamber awkwardly into the back, and she would swivel round and say to them: 'You can take your legs off, boys!' and that broke the ice for two men, who felt that because she was 'royalty' they had to keep their artificial limbs attached.

As we travelled towards Sarajevo along dusty, primitive roads, the princess nibbled fruit or sipped Evian water from a plastic bottle. Talk focused on the known fact that a landmine victim can recall exactly where and when – date and time – their accident happened. 'It is etched on their memories for ever,' the princess added.

Jerry told of his accident, then Ken recalled his. The princess said: 'My accident was on 29 July 1981.'

There were puzzled looks all round. Not even I knew instantly what she meant. Then the penny dropped and everyone laughed. Until the princess spotted a lady carrying a bunch of flowers and walking through the gate of a cemetery. 'Stop! Stop now!' The vehicle pulled into the side of the road.

The princess slid back the door, jumped out, and galloped through a hole in a brick wall, then wove through the rows of headstones until she reached the lady. It transpired that she had lost her eighteen-year-old son in the former Yugoslavia's civil war. While the grieving mother arranged the flowers at the graveside, the princess sat with her and talked. After about five minutes, the princess stood up and both women cupped each other's faces in their hands and said farewell.

We went on to stay at the Elephant Hotel in Sarajevo. The princess wanted to use the satellite telephone again, so I spent half the evening hanging out of the window, waving the receiver around. 'No . . . yes . . . no . . . yes,' said the princess, indicating whether or not she had a signal.

Dodi had been shopping for a new car, even though he had enough to fill a car park. Now he wanted to buy a silver Lamborghini and he told her that he was going to buy her a surprise present. His father was parading himself at the Craven Cottage home of Fulham Football Club, which he had purchased for around £7 million, pledging to invest more than £20 million in the transfer market. On a less grand scale, he sent a £5000 wide-screen Sony television from Harrods to KP as a gift for William and Harry, together with two laptop computers, one of which the princess gave to my boys. With Mr Al Fayed making it clear that money was no object, and his son flaunting his extravagance, a niggling doubt wrestled with the princess's excitement. It was all becoming a bit too much.

We drove into Sarajevo and visited a hillside shanty town with a priest as our escort. There, we met a fifteen-year-old girl in a home crudely constructed out of brick and topped with corrugated sheeting. She had no parents and had lost a leg while foraging through a refuse tip to find a meal for the younger brother and sister in her care. The press, and indeed the princess, thought the plight of this teenage girl was harrowing. But while the reporters and photographers focused their attention on one more landmine victim, I caught the princess's eye and drew her attention to a curtained-off back room. The two of us sloped off into it without being followed by a lens. As our eyes adjusted to the darkness, we saw the teenager's skeletal four-year-old sister on a stinking mattress in a corner of the room. She was severely mentally handicapped. She had soiled her bed. She was drenched in her own urine. Her eyes were closed.

We didn't say a word. I just watched as the princess walked over to the bed, crouched and picked her up. She cradled the tiny frame to her and stroked the wasted arms and legs.

The child opened her eyes, which had no pupils. She was blind. As I stood at the Boss's shoulder I realized there and then that I was witnessing something very special. There were no photographs to record the moment. I was the only witness to a simple act of humanity, an action that personified the woman I knew so well. Now I could see for myself the worth of those notes she had given me from Calcutta 1992 when she had written about a blind and deaf boy: '*I hugged him so tightly, hoping he could feel my love and warmth.*'

She performed countless other humanitarian acts on that brief mission but that one, and the girl in the hospital bed in Angola, I shall never forget.

On the flight back to Britain, the princess, Bill Deedes and I sat together. The Boss decided to make a short toast. Raising a glass, she said: 'Here's to our next country.'

When we returned to KP, she was already focused on her next landmine mission: to Cambodia and Vietnam, in October 1997.

13. Goodbye, Your Royal Highness

Rapturous applause erupted around me as 'Beauty' and 'the Beast' took their bows on stage to a standing ovation at London's Dominion Theatre.

It was the night of 30 August 1997, my final chance for relaxation, and I had taken in a musical with my family before the Boss returned from Paris the following day. She was spending her last night of an impromptu summer holiday with Dodi in the Imperial Suite of the Ritz Hotel.

Back at the Old Barracks, Maria, my brother Graham, his wife Jayne and I sat in the lounge, clasping mugs of coffee, reliving the highlights of one of the princess's favourite musicals.

I was the first to retire to bed, ready to return to seven a.m. starts at KP, looking forward to seeing the princess for the first time since 15 August and catching up on all her gossip. She had plenty to tell me. She had made that clear on our last telephone conversation. There was also a lot to be planned before an autumn of more landmine missions.

Shortly after midnight, the telephone rang. It was Lucia Flecha de Lima, and she was frantic. She had been at home in Washington when Mel French, chief of protocol for President Clinton at the White House, had rung to inform her about a car accident involving the princess. She had seen reports on CNN. Lucia did not yet have the new number for the princess's mobile. I knew that the princess never went anywhere without it so I rang it, not even considering that she wouldn't answer. She always answered. It rang, then clicked on to the automated answering service. Maria made more coffee. I rang again. And rang. We sat around the kitchen table. I rang and rang and rang.

Over the years, I had repeatedly told the Boss that if she was ever in trouble, she should get to a public restroom, lock herself in a cubicle and ring me. 'I will always come and get you, no matter where you are,' I told her. Now she was in trouble, her phone was ringing out, and I felt helpless.

I left the Old Barracks and ran across the green, up the road alongside the palace and into the office. Comptroller Michael Gibbins, personal assistant Jackie Allen, driver Colin Tebbutt and secretaries Jo Greenstead and Jane Harris were there. Anxious faces everywhere. Someone made coffee. Michael, who was chain-smoking, manned the telephone on the desk in his private office, liaising with the Queen's private secretary at Balmoral, while Jackie and I sat outside in the general office.

The first call came through about twelve thirty a.m., and it confirmed there had been a car accident in Paris. It didn't seem to have been serious.

Within the hour, there was a second call. It *was* serious. Dodi was dead. The princess had suffered injuries, believed to be a broken arm and a fractured pelvis. I must get there, I thought. She'll need me. Jackie Allen started to book flights for me and driver Colin. He was chosen because, as a former royalty protection officer, he was well used to making unemotional decisions. All British Airways offices in London were closed so the tickets had to be booked via its offices in New York.

At four o'clock, Michael picked up the telephone again. Jackie went into the room. Minutes later, she emerged. She told me to take a seat, and put an arm round me. 'Paul, you're going to have to be strong. I'm sorry to have to tell you this but the princess has died.'

The princess had been pronounced dead an hour earlier, at three a.m. British time, four a.m. Paris time, after failing to survive emergency surgery. An invisible force knocked me back and winded me. If I had screamed, no sound would have come out. Complete emptiness. Raw pain. Jackie and I sat there and cried together. Then duty, engaged on some kind of auto-pilot, kicked out emotion. She needs me more than ever now, I thought.

I rang Maria at the Old Barracks. 'Chuck, the princess has died. I'm going to Paris.' I left her sobbing. The plane tickets were booked. I rushed home to pack a small overnight bag, then ran back to apartments 8 and 9. I walked through the back door into a home that had been expecting her. Its silence hit me. Within twelve hours, her voice and giggling would have filled that void. Now nothing. I walked around. Everything was how she had left it. I went to her desk. All neat and tidy: three miniature clocks ticking quietly, telling the same time; a dozen pencils in a beaker; the Quink bottle to one side; the fountain pen in the inkstand; a memo sheet containing her 'word list' of good vocabulary to use in correspondence. She had no qualms about being a bad speller.

Then my eyes found what I had gone searching for: the rosary beads given to her by Mother Teresa, draped round a miniature marble statue of Jesus Christ, which stood next to two statuettes of Our Lady, one white, one ochre, beneath the lampshade. I picked up the rosary beads and slipped them into my pocket. I went into the dressing room and approached the table in front of the mirror where she got ready every morning, where the hairdressers styled her hair. There was the miniature clock, which told her whether she was late or not; half-used bottles of her favourite perfumes, Faubourg 24 by Hermès, and Heritage by Guerlain; her Pantene hairspray; a glass full of cotton buds; rows of lipsticks in a plastic container. I took one lipstick and a powder compact off her dressing-table and placed them inside a leather Gladstone bag with the gold D and coronet emblem, especially made for her in the previous year. I did *not* take any clothes. I drew all the curtains, then took the princess's jewellery and placed it in the safe.

I walked outside to join Colin Tebbutt. There was one last thing I needed to do because I knew we couldn't leave these most private rooms – the sitting room, bedroom, dressing room – unguarded as we flew to Paris. It was her world. It needed protecting. Colin and I went around shutting the doors and sealing them with thick parcel tape, adding a sticky label, which we then signed, denying access to the all and sundry I feared would come marching through within the next twenty-four hours.

Colin and I drove to Heathrow for the first flight to Paris. Thank God he was there, with his knowledge of the protocol of VIP airport procedures. On the flight over, I hardly said a word. All I could hear was the princess's voice. The last conversation. The last time I had seen her. Her laughter. Her eagerness to come home and see William and Harry.

How would I find her? How would I cope?

Paris. She hadn't even wanted to go to Paris.

Why? Why? Why?

As I flew across the English Channel, Lucia Flecha de Lima was boarding the first available plane from Washington to London.

Maria was waking our sons. Twelve-year-old Alexander had heard the news from the conversations on the landing, and was sitting up in bed, saying nothing. Nine-year-old Nick had also heard. He was lying on his front, the pillow over his head, sobbing his little heart out. 'She was going to take me to the crystal factory. She was going to take me to the crystal factory.'

That Sunday, Maria never got dressed: the telephone rang constantly.

I arrived in Paris to do what the princess would have expected.

Britain's ashen-faced ambassador to France, Sir Michael Jay, and his wife, Sylvia, met us at the British embassy. After coffee, I took Mrs Jay to one side. 'I am worried that the princess will be dressed in an awful shroud, and she wouldn't like that,' I said.

Mrs Jay understood. 'Come with me, and we'll do something about it,' she said.

She took me to a rather grand suite of rooms, and opened a large Louis XIV-style wardrobe. 'If there is anything suitable in here, please take it,' she said.

'It has to be black, and possibly three-quarter length with a high neck line,' I explained.

Mrs Jay rifled through her hangers and pulled out a black woollen three-quarter-length cocktail dress with a shawl collar. 'That's perfect,' I said, and we slipped a pair of black shoes into the princess's Gladstone bag. The dress was placed in a hanging-bag, and we set off on the short journey to the Pitié-Salpetrière Hospital. As we arrived at the front entrance of the eight-storey hospital, Mrs Jay, who had seen the princess in the early hours of the morning, squeezed my hand. 'Be brave,' she said.

I remember the muggy heat and endless empty corridors, as if the whole place had been evacuated. On the second floor, we walked out of the lift into a hive of activity. Doctors milling around in white overalls. Nurses rushing around. Policemen standing guard. We were ushered into a small office. In broken English, the chief surgeon expressed his sympathy, and explained that nothing could be done to save the princess. Then we were led down yet another corridor with empty rooms at either side. At the end, two gendarmes stood to either side of a doorway. That's where the princess is, I thought.

We passed the policemen, entered the next room on the right, and were introduced to a Roman Catholic priest, Father Clochard-Bossuet, and an Anglican priest, the Reverend Martin Draper. It had been Father Clochard-Bossuet who had administered the last rites, and he told me how he had anointed the princess with holy oil. My mind flashed back to all those times when the princess and I had gone down to the Carmelite Church in Kensington Church Street, lit candles and prayed together.

In Paris, Colin and I drank coffee and waited with the priests. Chief nursing officer Beatrice Humbert walked into the room, wearing her white coat. It was about eleven o'clock. She told us we would be going in to see the princess shortly. Nurse Humbert, a small, tidy, exact lady, handled the situation as a consummate professional.

I said: 'I really do not want this to turn into a peepshow. I need to be informed of everyone who wants to enter the room where the princess is lying.' She understood my anxieties about privacy, and left the room to make sure the instructions were kept.

Eventually it was time to see the princess. I don't know how I stood up. Nurse Humbert held my hand tightly and Colin took my arm. We went out and past the two gendarmes, who bowed their heads. The door opened into dimness. Daylight sneaked through the slits of the almost-closed Venetian blinds over the windows. One wall light provided the only illumination. A lady and a gentleman undertaker stood like statues in the corner. The silence was broken only by the whirring of a large fan.

Then I saw her. The woman I had looked after for so long was lying on a bed with its headboard to the wall. A white cotton sheet was pulled up to her neck. Nurse Humbert and Colin took my weight as I leaned into them, wanting to look away, needing to be by her side.

The reality struck me in that room, and I sobbed. I approached the side of the bed, wanting her to open her large, blue eyes, wanting to see her smile, wanting her to be asleep. What I witnessed before me was indescribable, and it is not appropriate to explain further.

But, regardless of how she looked, I wanted to hold her, as I had so many times before. I wanted to make things better, as I had so many times before. The draught of the fan came across me as it turned slowly: the princess's eyelashes moved. What I would have done for those eyes to open.

I looked up and noticed that the only flowers in the room were two dozen roses from the former French president Valéry Giscard d'Estaing and his wife. All that kept me strong in that room was the spiritual belief the Boss had fostered in me. She had not been afraid of death since she had witnessed the passing of Adrian Ward-Jackson in 1991, which had marked the beginning of her spiritual enlightenment, her fascination with the soul. *'When a person dies, its spirit hangs around to watch for a while,'* I heard her voice say, from long ago when my mum had died. That thought was my only comfort. I believed that her spirit was still in that room above her broken body, a soul waiting to begin its journey, as she would have put it.

I wiped my eyes, gathered my strength, and informed Nurse Humbert that I had brought a black cocktail outfit and shoes to dress the princess, with her lipstick and powder. Then I took Mother Teresa's ivory rosary beads out of my pocket and gave them to the nurse. 'Can you please place these in the princess's hand? Thank you.'

I had another task to perform: I had to go to the Ritz Hotel and collect the princess's possessions from the Imperial Suite. Colin Tebbutt, who was selflessly dealing with my grief and shock before his own, had organized transport. It was only a short drive through Paris, and we were soon at the reception. I asked if Mr Al Fayed could be informed that I was there to collect the princess's belongings. Reception told me he was upstairs. We were left waiting in the main reception corridor for around forty-five minutes. Eventually we were informed by a messenger that Mr Al Fayed was too busy, and the princess's belongings had already been dispatched to England, via his country estate, Oxtead.

We headed back to the hospital, which was thronging with press. Colin and I sat in the room where we had met the priests. A telephone rang on a side-table. I picked it up and recognized the voice of the Prince of Wales, ringing from Balmoral.

'Are you all right, Paul?' he asked.

'Yes, Your Royal Highness, thank you.' I remember thinking what an idiotic thing it was to say. I had never felt so bad in my life.

'Paul, you will come back with us on the Queen's Flight. We will be with you about six o'clock. Jane and Sarah [the princess's sisters] are coming with me,' he said.

Then he said something that left emotion strangling my goodbye. 'And William and Harry send their love, and the Queen wants me to extend her sympathy to you.'

I asked Nurse Humbert if I could see the princess again. I composed myself, this time knowing what to expect. Yet, when I walked in, a different sight confronted me, one that brought dignity in death – something else the princess would have said. She now wore the black dress and shoes, her hair had been beautifully blow-dried and, in her hand, she held Mother Teresa's ivory rosary beads.

That afternoon Prince Charles arrived. He walked up to me, and the grief we both felt didn't need to be expressed. He stood opposite, touched my lapel and said: 'Are you sure you're all right?' I managed a nod.

When Lady Jane Fellowes and Lady Sarah McCorquodale saw me, they ran up to me, flung their arms round me and sobbed. In a way, one Windsor, two Spencers and a butler were a great comfort to each other.

Shortly before six o'clock, I entered the room for the last time. The princess's body had been placed in a coffin. Much nonsense has been written, on both sides of the Atlantic, that she had told me she wanted to be buried in a casket with a window so that her face could be seen. She never said any such thing. Her body *was* placed inside a grey casket with a window, which was then placed inside a French oak coffin with a solid lid; I was told that the window was to meet French Customs regulations.

I boarded the Queen's Flight BAe 146 with Prince Charles, Colin Tebbutt, Lady Jane and Lady Sarah. All of us bringing the princess home.

How ironic that I took my seat on the plane next to Mark Bolland, the prince's aide, who was then his deputy private secretary; the man the princess called 'the fruit in the suit'; the media Svengali who, in later years, would be charged by St James's Palace with a deliberate proactive press strategy to make Camilla Parker Bowles acceptable as the partner of Prince Charles. I wondered what on earth he was doing on the plane, and hardly said a word to him. As tea was served in the cabin, I felt sick at the thought of the princess below us in the hold. Reduced to precious cargo.

The plane touched down at RAF Northolt, west London. We disembarked from that sombre flight, stepping down the metal stairs into a stiff, warm breeze that lifted everyone's hair. The evening sun was shining. We stood in a silent line on the edge of the airfield's apron. Almost in slow motion, eight airmen gently pulled the coffin out of the belly of the plane, the Royal Standard draping it. They walked in slow steps across the Tarmac to the waiting hearse. Prince Charles headed north to be with William and Harry. Two sisters and a butler were charged with ensuring that the princess reached her next destination: first an undertaker's, and then the Chapel Royal at St James's Palace.

The three cars in our cortège pulled away from the airfield and out on to the A40 dual carriageway to take us into the centre of London. The most amazing sight brought me out of the blur and back into focus. As we drove, other cars braked and stopped. Every single motorist, on both sides of the road, on one of the busiest routes into the capital, stopped, turned off their engines, climbed out and stood by their vehicles, heads bowed. People lined the footbridges and dropped flowers into our path. All I could think of was what the princess would have thought. 'They're not stopping for me! Oh, no!' She would have curled up with embarrassment.

We arrived at an undertaker's in London, and the next person I saw was the princess's doctor, Dr Peter Wheeler, who comforted everyone. He took me to one side, concerned at what I had witnessed in Paris. 'If you need anything to help you sleep . . .' I nodded. I wasn't the only one having to be professional in duty at the loss of a dear friend, and I did not envy Dr Wheeler the duty he had to perform. 'I have to attend an autopsy now,' he said, 'and it is not going to be easy.'

'Why does she need another autopsy?' I asked, knowing she had already undergone one in Paris.

'The one performed in Paris was conducted on French soil, under

French law. For our government's satisfaction, we have to do the same,' he said, mentioning something else about forensic inspections and necessary procedures. An autopsy was held in 1997, and yet, by the end of 2003, no British inquest has been held. The princess's body rested overnight at the undertaker's.

The next day, there was only one place for me to be – back at KP as usual. Butler to a household without a mistress. At eight o'clock on that Monday morning, my first duty was to remove the parcel tape from around the doors. I was now back to guard her world. I was the only person who remained in apartments 8 and 9, save for Lily the maid, who tried to keep cleaning but sat there, breaking down.

Michael Gibbins came to see me, armed with a difficult task. 'Paul, I've been asked by St James's Palace to collect all back-door keys.'

Less than twenty-four hours after bringing the princess home, I was being asked by those unfeeling suits in the household to hand over the keys to my world, and they were getting our comptroller to do their dirty work. There was no way I was handing them over. I refused, and it wasn't challenged.

The cold-hearted treatment of the princess's staff was evident later that day when I learned the fate of dresser Angela Benjamin – whom the Boss had admired for her fresh approach, casual manner and sense of humour. When she turned in for work like the rest of us, she had found herself being escorted off the premises by policemen. She was told to gather her belongings, and was even watched as she unloaded her laundry from the tumble-dryer. Her own grief didn't seem to matter. She was back on the train to Devon by lunchtime, wondering what on earth she had done wrong. The answer is clear: she was a warm human being with genuine feelings in a robotic world run by a cold, unfeeling household, which brings about banishment as easily as it commands loyalty.

That morning, I was unaware of what had happened to Angela. I had been at my desk in the pantry, staring out of the window into the courtyard. The desk diary was open in front of me. William and Harry's tailor was due. Then the Armani fitting. From upstairs, all I could hear was the princess's telephone ringing. Then, within the next hour, mine began to shrill: two lights blinking for both direct lines into the palace. I answered calls all day long. No sooner had I placed the receiver on its hook than it rang again. Another friend, turning to me as the closest person to the princess, to share their grief: the intimate friends, celebrity friends, alternative therapists, astrologers, psychics, fitness instructors, hairdressers, dress designers, members of the Royal Family. The list was endless. Anybody and everybody who had shared the princess's world rang that day. Even her own family, Lady Sarah, Lady Jane and her mother Mrs Frances Shand Kydd, came to me with their grief, all wanting to offload their feelings, ask their own questions, what had been the princess's innermost feelings about them. Some remembered. Some smiled at the memories. Some felt guilty and needed almost to absolve themselves. It was like being a priest listening to a day of confessions and thoughts.

Eventually, by the second day, it was all becoming too much. Michael Gibbins and Jackie Allen decided, for my own good, to take messages on my behalf.

That week was the most distressing period of my life, and only a sense of duty got me through. I had much more important things to occupy my mind than embittered family politics. From the very beginning, the Spencers included me in *every* decision, trusting my judgement and knowledge. I drew up my recommendations for the guest-list for the funeral at Westminster Abbey, taking the princess's address book and detailing to her family all her friends. Lady Sarah looked at the list and doubted the attendance of some high-profile names: George Michael, Chris de Burgh, Tom Hanks, Tom Cruise, Steven Spielberg. 'But they *are* friends of the princess,' I told her.

I felt it summed up everything that I, the butler, not the family, knew who the princess's real friends were.

Back at the Old Barracks, Maria was attempting to comfort Mrs Shand Kydd, who had descended, chain-smoking and drinking copious amounts of wine, saying how her daughter should never have been on that boat with the Al Fayeds; how, as a family, the Spencers were in control of arrangements, not the Windsors, how her son Charles was going to make a speech 'to be proud about'; what a good mother she had been to the princess.

But I knew the truth of this family's relationship with the Boss – and it emerged some years later. If ever there was a real mother-figure in the life of the princess, it was Lucia Flecha de Lima. There is no doubt that the princess viewed the relationship she shared with her as that of mother and daughter. Lucia treated the princess as if she was one of her own, and the comfort she gave the Boss in her most troubled times was enormous. On the Monday morning, the one person I longed to see was Lucia, and she arrived at the palace to be with me, accompanied by her daughter Beatrice.

Over four nights of that week, the princess – by now in an English oak, lead-lined coffin – lay in the Chapel Royal at St James's Palace, whose rear walls backed on to the Mall where mourners from all over the world began to gather, laying flowers and lighting candles. It was a public vigil that mirrored those that took place outside the gates of Kensington Palace.

I couldn't think of another person I would rather have been with at that time than Lucia, and we decided to go together to the chapel, she in a black dress, me in a black suit. The door creaked open and we looked down the nave with its wooden pews on either side. There, ahead of us, in the chilly grey of that holy place, was the coffin, resting on a trestle before the altar. It struck me how lonely, cold and unfamiliar it all was, but Lucia had spotted something else awry. Not one candle was lit. Not one flower was to be seen. Outside, the most spectacular remembrance garden was being laid by the public, and there were more flickering candles on the grass verge than there were stars in the night sky. Inside, there was nothing.

Lucia immediately found the Queen's chaplain, the Reverend Willie Booth. 'Please, please, put some flowers from the people in here,' she said. He said he would see what he could do.

For Lucia, it was not an emphatic enough response. The ambassador's wife clicked into assertive diplomacy. 'I can only say that if there are no flowers in here when we return tomorrow, I will walk outside and tell the people that the princess has no flowers!'

At a time when the Queen had not yet travelled south from Balmoral, and harsh questions were being asked about the Windsors' distance from the mourning capital, the prospect of Lucia revealing the cold bareness of the chapel was the last thing a troubled monarchy needed. To ensure that her polite but firm request was met, she took it upon herself to arrange for bouquets to be brought in by the princess's florist John Carter. He provided them free of charge. The next day, a bunch of white trumpet lilies lay on top of the coffin, sent by Prince Charles, and Lucia brought more flowers; white roses arrived from the garden of Lord and Lady Palumbo. Lady Annabel Goldsmith spoke to me every day by telephone, and Rosa Monckton, who was a best friend and sister rolled into one for the princess, came to KP with her husband to sit with me. We reminisced and cried together, and she, too, visited the chapel.

Susie Kassem came to the palace. She brought with her a candle. Together we went to the stairs, to a landing point on one of the turns. We stopped beneath the huge Nelson Shanks portrait of the princess. Susie bent down and placed the lit candle on the carpet. We knelt together and prayed, sharing our own memories in silence.

Sources of strength from within the princess's inner circle were around me. Her friends, the people who knew her best, were rallying round as a team, ensuring that the farewell went perfectly.

Michael Gibbins told me that William and Harry were coming home with Prince Charles. As they met the crowds outside, and inspected the flowers left in tribute to their mother, I was waiting for them in the inner hallway. Harry rushed through the door and hugged me, his tears soaking my shirt. William reached out and shook my hand. The outward courage both boys were displaying was incredible, and they suddenly seemed so grown-up in their black suits and ties.

'We've come for a few things. We're just going upstairs,' said William, and the two brothers went to the nursery and their sitting room.

'How are you coping, Paul?' said Prince Charles, who was clearly struggling with the enormity of events. He spoke politely and calmly, but he looked distant as he wandered around the apartment, lost in thought. He went upstairs. I followed, without being asked. At Highgrove, this would have been the height of presumption because, when I worked under his command, my presence was requested, or expected, at lunch or dinner. But in a domain that was no longer his, I could not be dismissed. He was now in *my* territory. Whether a friend or the future King of England, no one was left out of my sight. I followed him into the sitting room, and he walked to the writing desk, standing over it. He opened a top drawer, looked up, saw me watching his every move, and closed it again.

William's voice broke the awkwardness. 'Are you ready, Papa?'
All four of us went down the stairs together.

'We'll see you soon, Paul. We'll be back,' shouted Harry, before they all disappeared out of the front door.

A clear, forensics-like bag arrived at KP. It contained the clothes the princess had been wearing when the chauffeur-driven Mercedes smashed into the thirteenth pillar of the Place de l'Alma. Lucia was with me at this most harrowing time. We now had something of the princess from Paris: a black top and white trousers. We stood at the bottom of the stairs with the bag. It didn't seem to matter that they were bloodstained and shredded by the surgical procedures. It was her. In my grief, I couldn't let go. I placed that bag in the refrigerator on the ground floor.

Preserving the princess's dignity was imperative. 'Dignity in death', as she would have said. Somehow, the thought of her spending the eve of her funeral in the Chapel Royal didn't seem appropriate, and I made my feelings known to both Lady Sarah McCorquodale and Michael Gibbins.

KP was the princess's home: it was where she had spent most of her adult life. It seemed only right that she should come home for that final night and leave through the front door *en route* to Westminster Abbey. 'Let me look after her one final night, and let her leave from the front door one last time,' I pleaded. Lady Sarah wanted to bring her sister home, too, and the Queen approved the request.

The princess would spend her final night in the inner hallway on the ground floor. On that day, I had asked the police to bring flowers in from the street. I spent two hours arranging those flowers with the bouquets sent by friends – white lilies, white tulips and white roses. There were flowers in urns, perched on ornate pedestals, and on the carpet. I brought out every candlestick in the house, interspersing them among the greenery.

Then Roman Catholic priest Father Tony Parsons, from the Carmelite Church where the princess and I had prayed, arrived. He had with him two huge ivory church candles, which I placed on silver stands, and anointed the room with holy water. He handed me photocopies of appropriate prayers to read, and a biblical text from the Gospel according to St John. The two of us said a prayer together before he left.

I was left by myself in the middle of that room in my black suit, breathing in the thick scent of the flowers. In those silent minutes before the princess arrived, it was like waiting for her to come home on her birthday, with flowers everywhere. The double doors of the front entrance were open, and I heard the tyres of the hearse approach. Her Royal Highness, because that was what she was to me, was carried into her home, the coffin draped in the red, gold and blue of the Royal Standard.

I didn't light the candles, not then, I kept the ceiling lights on. Mrs Shand Kydd visited with her grandchildren, spending time beside the coffin with Lady Jane and Lady Sarah, but there was no Earl Spencer that night.

The one person who wanted to be there – who *should* have been there – was Lucia. All week she had been asking to join me for the vigil. 'Can I come and join you in prayer, Paul?' she asked, over and over again. But when I told Lady Sarah how important Lucia was to the princess, and how much she needed to be there that night, Lucia's request was denied. Lady Sarah felt it appropriate for only family to attend. The one woman, in my opinion, who was more family than any of them was refused her final, most personal farewell.

Maria didn't want me to be at the palace by myself. 'You look exhausted, chuck, it's a big day tomorrow. You need to sleep,' she protested, knowing it was in vain.

'She cannot be on her own. I *have* to be there.'

All relatives had visited the princess by ten o'clock that night. I closed and bolted the front door, ready for the long night ahead with the princess for the vigil I had so meticulously planned. Instead of Lucia by my side, there was a stranger: the Right Reverend Richard Charteris, Bishop of London. He sat in prayer on a chair in the corridor leading to the front door. In the inner hallway, I turned off the lights and lit the candles, all fifty of them, creating dancing shadows on the surrounding yellow walls. I sat on a chair with my back to the Bishop, my left hand on the coffin, my right hand supporting the prayers and biblical text on my lap. Despite my grief, and knowing that around thirty thousand people were praying for her outside, I felt like the most privileged person in the world to be able to spend that last night with the princess. I never slept a wink because it was my duty to stay awake. I had a final special conversation with the princess, knowing she was listening. I talked to her, read to her and prayed for her until seven a.m.

When morning came, I left for the Old Barracks, showered and changed for the funeral, then returned to the palace. It was a beautiful morning. The flowers still gave off a scent. The candles had burnt out. I waited to hear the slow, rolling wheels of the King's Troop gun-carriage pull up outside. Eight soldiers, in scarlet Welsh Guards' uniforms, filed in, lifted the coffin on to their interlinked arms and took the first steps on the two-mile journey to Westminster Abbey. It was ten past nine on that Saturday morning as they prepared to leave.

It was a sight to behold on our front doorstep. Six black horses, mounted by men in ceremonial uniforms, wearing caps with a single protruding gold feather, the First World War gun-carriage behind, carrying the coffin, white lilies spilling over its sides. Then came the 1st Battalion Welsh Guards, standing to attention in their red tunics and bearskins. I looked across the road. Maria, Alexander and Nick were huddled with the rest of the household staff.

The horses moved off and the wheels of the carriage began to turn. I had stood in that same spot two weeks earlier, waving off the Greece-bound princess in her BMW. Now she was leaving again. For the last time. I didn't wave: I bowed.

14. A Very Strange Business

Earl Spencer stood looking down on the coffin from his elevated position in the ornate pulpit at Westminster Abbey. As he spoke, his words rattled around in my mind: words he had directed at his sister: '*Your mental problems . . . Your fickle friendship . . . I was a peripheral part of your life and that no longer saddens me . . . Our relationship is the weakest I have with any of my sisters . . .*'

That was what *I* heard as he delivered his emotionally charged masterpiece of oratory, speaking, 'as the representative of a family in grief, in a country in mourning, before a world in shock'.

My ears weren't listening to his public funeral address delivered on 6 September 1997. I was recalling the private words he had delivered to the princess a year earlier on 4 April 1996; words the world should have heard before it jumped to its feet in a tearful ovation after his funeral speech.

As his voice echoed through God's house, I sat in the choir stalls, head bowed, suppressing disbelief as his carefully crafted words leaped from the pages in his hand and grabbed the monarchy by the throat, leaving the crowds outside applauding its public humiliation, while the master of the 'blood family' seized the most inappropriate moment to claim the moral high ground. The hypocrisy masked by his eloquence was only known by the princess's real family: the people like me who knew her best, the surrogate family of chosen friends and confidants who knew the truth of this alienated brother-sister relationship.

I didn't see the closest of brothers walking into the pulpit that day. I saw a distant cousin who was once close in a faraway child-hood; someone speaking on behalf of a remarkable adult he clearly loved but didn't know. By his own private admission, he had only seen the princess around fifty times since she got married in 1981. He expressed that statistical truth in a rambling letter, which she read with me on the stairs at KP in the spring of 1996.

299

As the abbey and the nation were riveted by his funeral address, I found myself caught between two flashing images: the earl speaking fondly in the elevated pulpit above me; the princess on the stairs, holding one of his letters, entirely different in tone.

In the abbey in 1997, he said, 'Fundamentally she had not changed at all from the big sister who mothered me as a baby.' Then my mind flashed back to 1996: '*After years of neglect on both sides, our relationship is the weakest I have with any of my sisters . . . perhaps you have more time to notice that we seldom speak.*' And '*I . . . will always be there for you . . . as a loving brother: albeit one who has, through fifteen years' absence, rather lost touch – to the extent I have to read Richard Kay* [in the *Daily Mail*] *to learn that you are coming to Althorp . . .*'

Back in the abbey: 'Diana remained throughout a very insecure person – most childlike in her desire to do good for others so she could release herself from deep feelings of unworthiness of which her eating disorders were merely a symptom.' In 1996: '*I fear for you. I know how manipulation and deceit are parts of the illness . . . I pray that you are getting appropriate and sympathetic treatment for your mental problems.*'

The princess felt she was over her bulimia, but what upset her most was the suggestion that she was mentally ill. 'Mental problems' was a phrase she had thought she would only ever hear from the sniping friends of Prince Charles.

Back in the abbey: 'The world sensed this part of her character and cherished her vulnerability, while admiring her for her honesty.' In 1996: '*I long ago accepted that I was a peripheral part of your life, and that no longer saddens me. Indeed, it's easier for me and my family to be in that position as I view the consternation and hurt your fickle friendship has caused so many . . .*'

Then he referred to William and Harry. 'We will not allow them to suffer the anguish that used regularly to drive you to tearful despair . . .' Another flashback: '*I'm sorry but I've decided that the Garden House isn't a possible move now. There are many reasons, most of which include the police and press interference which would inevitably follow.*'

That letter had driven the princess to tearful despair. His request for the Spencer tiara had upset her, and his letter of April 1996 had brought tears again.

Many commentators viewed his speech at Westminster Abbey as

the expression of his pain for a sister badly treated by the system. In my eyes, it was the words of a man riddled with guilt, focusing on childhood because of the distance that had come between them in adulthood. But he included some apt tributes, too, describing the 'unique, the complex, the extraordinary and irreplaceable Diana, whose beauty, both external and internal, will never be extinguished from our minds'. And he captured the 'joy for life, transmitted wherever you took your smile, and the sparkle in those unforgettable eyes . . .'

I couldn't help feeling, though, that this man, who had caused his sister so much heartache in recent years, was not the man to speak on her behalf, to be the standard-bearer for the princess. He had turned down her plea for sanctuary at her ancestral home, yet was preparing to accept her into the grounds now that she was dead. I sat there thinking, how can he be so hypocritical in God's house?

Nor could I believe that, on a day of remembrance for a remarkable life, the earl had chosen such a moment to make a veiled attack on the Royal Family, reminding the world that he, his sisters and mother were the blood family who would protect William and Harry 'so that their souls are not simply immersed by duty'.

At that point I lifted my head and looked over at the Queen. Harry was stroking his face. William gazed ahead: pawns in a Spencer v. Windsor tussle. I thought how the princess would have cringed at such a public declaration of ownership when she, of all people, respected the influence that Prince Charles and the Queen had over her sons.

I stared at the coffin draped in the Royal Standard, with a candle at each corner. On it, propped in a wreath of white roses, was a card from the young princes: 'Mummy' had been written on the envelope. I clutched Maria's hand to my right and Nick's to my left. He was crying his heart out, and Alexander, on the other side of him, was doing his best to be strong. I looked straight ahead of me and saw Hillary Clinton. Then came another flashback: the princess telling me how, on a visit to the White House earlier that year, she had talked to Mrs Clinton about one day living in America, and how the first lady had spoken about how much the American people would embrace her. I choked back the tears once more.

Then Earl Spencer finished his address, and there came the sound of rippling applause, rolling in from the streets, through the Great West Door and down the nave; a Mexican wave of clapping. I looked around and saw Elton John and George Michael clapping. Euphoria was greeting a travesty of the truth, and the Queen's humiliation was complete.

An emotional outburst from a Spencer was received warmly by a people who, that week, had turned like never before against the House of Windsor. I felt a profound sense of injustice. The Queen had been a firm favourite of the princess, who corresponded with her until her death. She admired the Duke of Edinburgh for his cruel-to-be-kind mediation during the separation in 1992. But if that year had been the Queen's *annus horribilis*, then the six days before the princess's funeral in 1997 were the worst of weeks for a family that dithered in its transfer from Balmoral to London, hesitated over whether the Union Jack should fly at half-mast over Buckingham Palace, and was paralysed by the enormity of the grief at the loss of the princess.

Never, it seemed, had the monarchy been in such a perilous state, thrown into a state of rare introspection and a review of its protocols. The address by Earl Spencer, followed by its rousing reception, exacerbated an undoubted crisis. Commentators rambled on about how the death of the princess had crystallized the gulf between an anachronistic monarchy and its modern-day people; how in death the princess had brought the House of Windsor to its knees, having proved to be no more than a nuisance in life. Even more dangerously, the republican arguments gathered momentum.

In the maelstrom of that week, the saddest thing, and the truth that no one stopped to consider, was that the princess would have been turning in the coffin that had not yet been laid in the ground.

Columnists and television pundits seemed to relish the thought of her looking down from above, gleeful that an institution perceived as at the root of her isolation and suffering was floundering. Yet no one could have been more devoid of hatred than the princess, and no one wanted to see the House of Windsor survive more than she.

The fundamental point is that she did not blame the Royal Family for her isolation. The cause of her suffering and misery was Prince Charles, but she harboured no hatred towards her ex-husband or his parents. Indeed, if the princess could have spoken up that week, she

'Let's have a happy snap, Paul' – despite Prince Charles making fun of her sense of style

'The Boss and her
right-hand man' on
a landmine mission
in Angola

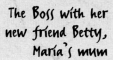

The Boss with her
new friend Betty,
Maria's mum

No chauffeur required, no police protection, just the princess and me

A month before her death, the princess returns from a break with Dodi,
about to tell me all

The final goodbye,
6 September 1997

In Westminster Abbey

Stepping off the royal train to go to Althorp for the private burial service

Outside the front door of apartments 8 and 9 at KP, before the Queen bestowed on me the Royal Victorian Medal

The Old Bailey trial of October 2002. Maria and I arrive for the first day

The princess's sister, Lady Sarah McCorquodale

Mrs Frances Shand-Kydd, the princess's mother

The royal conversation that led to the collapse of my trial

Walking to freedom ... and into a media scrum

That infectious giggle ... how I remember her best

would have *defended* the Windsors. That is why the vengeful tone of Earl Spencer's speech was so wrong and inappropriate. Had he known his sister, he would have known the truth.

Of all the speeches that could have been made that week, the princess, in her simple terms, would have taken the attitudes of the mourners in a totally different direction. 'I can never find the words to do justice to what I want to say,' she often moaned (hence the 'word list' on her desk). But in the October before her death, we had sat on the stairs at KP trying to do just that. Over an hour, we had sat, ruminating over her future, her fears, and the state of the monarchy. Teasing out her thoughts, putting them on paper. The next day, as was becoming usual, an envelope lay on the desk in my pantry. It contained a letter, written on her burgundy-edged paper.

If that letter could have been produced at her funeral, it would have thrown the weight of the 'People's Princess' behind the Royal Family at a time when it needed it most. I reproduce it now to remove all doubt, and they are the thoughts, devoid of animosity, of the only Spencer whose views count:

I just long to hug my mother-in-law, and tell her how deeply I understand what goes on inside her. I understand the isolation, misconception and lies that surround her and feel very strongly HER disappointment and confusion. I so want the monarchy to survive and realise the changes that will take [sic] to put 'the show' on a new and healthy track. I, too, understand the fear the family have about change but we must, in order to reassure the public, as their indifference concerns me and should not be.

I will fight for justice, and fight for my children and the monarchy . . .

The Royal Train was waiting for us in London, and I was invited to the family-only burial service, seventy miles away at Northamptonshire at the Althorp estate. As the hearse carrying the princess collected a shower of flowers on its crawl through London and up the M1, I joined the Spencer family, Princes Charles, William and Harry aboard the train with its smart burgundy carriages, pulled by the two locomotives named 'Prince William' and 'Prince Henry'.

It was a strange, subdued, awkward journey, which took one and a half hours. I must have nodded off as soon as we pulled away, catching up on the sleep lost during the all-night vigil. I woke up at a station near Althorp. After a short drive to the family estate, we assembled in the drawing room before being taken into the grand dining room. It struck me, as we walked through the hallway, that the black-and-white chequered marble floor was similar to that at Westminster Abbey.

Earl Spencer stood at the top of the long, rosewood table, telling everyone where to sit. I found myself positioned rather awkwardly between the Boss's mother and ex-husband, Mrs Frances Shand Kydd to the left, Prince Charles to the right. It wasn't easy for the prince to be sitting there on Spencer territory, having endured the anti-Windsor tone of the earl's funeral address, knowing that all eyes were not looking at him kindly.

Conversation was difficult and stilted but – as the only one around that table who knew how civility had been restored between the prince and princess – I kept the small-talk rattling along, knowing that a conversation about Highgrove and its gardens would see us through the three-course meal.

'You must come down and see the gardens some time,' said Prince Charles.

'I would love to, Your Royal Highness,' I replied, knowing that it was unlikely.

William and Harry sat on the other side of their father, nearer the bottom of the table. Both boys were quiet, chipping in with polite conversation now and again.

As coffee was being served, a butler approached the earl and whispered in his ear. He stood and left the room, and he must have been gone for about five minutes. When he returned, he announced, 'Diana is home.'

We crossed the chessboard hallway. I was walking just behind Prince Charles and the boys. Looking down the hallway from over their shoulders, I saw the hearse – and something else. The Royal Standard that had been draped over the coffin was gone, replaced by the white, red, black and gold of the Spencer flag, which only half covered it. In the five minutes when the earl had been out of the room, he had made the swap. Until my trial in 2002, everyone had

304

believed that the princess had been buried as they had last seen her, her coffin wrapped in the standard. Buried as a royal. Buried as a princess. As she would have wanted. Yet the carefully orchestrated dignity of that day altered when the earl switched flags, and the pitiful inappropriateness of such a petulant gesture seemed lost on him. For the princess had been proud to be royal, and had wept over the loss of her HRH status. It seemed ironic that the Royal Family, having denied the princess her HRH status, had respected her role and given her a royal send-off with a state funeral. Yet, there was her brother, exercising his control and devaluing the day's significance.

Eight soldiers from the Princess of Wales Regiment suddenly appeared, and carried the princess on their shoulders, one step at a time, down towards the lake, across a temporary pontoon and on to an island where a grave had been prepared. There was no carpet of flowers, only grass and the shadows of the trees, as shafts of sunlight shot through the canopy of leaves. All I could think was, What a lonely place to bury a woman who couldn't bear loneliness. It was as if a stranger had been planning the funeral of the woman I knew best, and was getting it all so terribly wrong. There is not a friend from the inner circle of the princess who agrees that it is an appropriate place for her to be buried. When she wanted refuge in life, the earl turned her away. When she needed a final resting place, he accepted her – and placed her in the loneliest of locations. But this was the goodbye, and I knew I would not be back. As for all her true friends, there would be no return to this island for me. No graveside to visit, as the princess had said she would visit Princess Grace's in Monaco, as I had visited my mother's on countless times.

The burial service was thirty minutes long. What happened and what was said should remain private. All I will say is that at the end I crouched down, picked up a handful of earth and dropped it on to the gold plate that read, 'Diana – Princess of Wales 1961–1997'.

Then I stood, and said aloud: 'Goodbye, Your Royal Highness.'

Afterwards, I sat with Mrs Frances Shand Kydd in the little white temple overlooking the lake. She smoked a cigarette and reflected, 'Well, at least I had her for nine months, Paul. All on my own. She was mine for nine months.'

I unknotted my black tie and undid the top few buttons of my

305

shirt. Then I removed the gold cross and chain that she had given me to wear on the eve of the vigil. 'This has protected me, but now it belongs with you,' I said, and it fell into the palm of her hand.

After she had finished two cigarettes, we all reconvened in the drawing room for a cup of tea. Everyone stood huddled in little chattering groups. Then Earl Spencer approached the television in the corner of the room, and switched it on. All eyes turned to the screen. The highlights of the funeral were being shown on one channel. Prince Charles and his sons stood there in silence. The room was silent. Why are we watching this now? I thought.

Then Earl Spencer's voice came out from the back of the television, filling the room. His echoing voice from Westminster Abbey. His speech from the pulpit. I have never been caught in such an awkward moment. But Prince Charles was clearly not standing for a repeat performance of the humiliation.

He put down his cup and saucer, and said to William and Harry, 'I think it's about time we were leaving.' As the earl's speech carried on in the background, the Windsors politely shook hands and said goodbye. I left shortly afterwards.

I must have wandered, lost, around apartments 8 and 9 throughout September and October. I wasn't sleeping well, and when I did, I had a recurring nightmare: the princess was with me at KP, saying, 'When are we going to tell people that I'm still alive?' and I would wake, convinced she was there. Or Maria told me I would cry in my sleep. At that time, I couldn't sit and grieve at the Old Barracks. I *needed* to be up at KP for comfort. It was the only place where I felt close to the princess.

I went from room to room and stayed there for hours on end, imagining the princess everywhere. In the sitting room curled up on the sofa. At the piano playing Rachmaninov. At the dining table wrapping her towelling robe tight around her at breakfast. In the wardrobe room doing a catwalk pose. At her desk, head down, writing letters. I sat on the newly upholstered sofa, holding a cushion with a D embroidered on it. I looked across at the fireplace and saw signs of the princess's humour: a red and white 'I LIKE DI' sticker slapped incongruously on to the grey marble surround; a sign above it saying 'CAUTION: Princess On Board'. Two pairs of pink ballet shoes hung on the hook on the back of the door. In one corner on the floor, there was her school tuck-box, with 'D. Spencer' on the lid.

I sat on the stairs, imagining her leaning over the banister – 'Paul, are you there?' – the times we had composed letters together, the sound of the door closing, of her rushing in with her latest piece of gossip.

I sat on the *chaise-longue* in her bedroom, staring at the small mountain of teddy bears on a sofa against the wall, with a gorilla, a panda, a rabbit, a frog, a pink elephant, a black panther, a hedgehog. There must have been about fifty.

On both bedside tables, there were pictures of William and Harry. And then I went over to the round table near the window, where there were five framed photographs of her husband with the boys, and one just of him, with other treasured images: her beloved father, Earl Spencer, a night out with Liza Minnelli, dancing with Wayne Sleep at the London Palladium, her sisters Jane and Sarah, her friends Lucia and Rosa.

Maria came up to visit me one day with a sandwich. 'Chuck, it's not doing you any good being here,' she said. But it was. Somehow.

In the middle of one night, after experiencing the usual nightmare, I left the Old Barracks and went up to KP. Having just dreamed about the princess, I needed to sense her. Those who have experienced loss might understand what I did next. Those who have not might consider my action to be that of a madman. It seemed right at the time. I went into the L-shaped wardrobe room, pulled back the curtains where her dresses hung, crouched in the gap between the floor and the clothes. I could smell her scent. In that position, I fell asleep for the night.

In mid-October, I was in that same wardrobe room with the princess's sisters and mother, Lady Sarah, Lady Jane and Mrs Frances Shand Kydd. The family was going through the clothes, deciding what to take. They asked me to fetch the princess's luggage, a matching set of three black leather suitcases. Each one was packed with blouses, skirts, cashmere cardigans and shoes, cosmetics, bubble bath and perfumes, then loaded into the back of estate cars outside the front door. None of these items had been valued before probate but, as executors of the estate, the family was doing as it wished.

I had already been busy cataloguing the entire contents of the apartments, linen, ornaments, jewellery, clothes and personal effects. It was a painstaking task carried out with the help and expertise of Meredith Etherington-Smith from Christie's, who had catalogued the princess's dresses for the hugely successful auction in New York earlier in the summer. David Thomas, the Crown jeweller, also visited, to finalize an inventory of the princess's collection. As I stood beside Lady Sarah in the wardrobe room, she removed a silk blouse that the princess had worn. Still attached to each sleeve were silver and red enamel heart-shaped cufflinks. Without saying a word, Lady Sarah removed them, pressed them into my hand, and smiled. 'If there is anything else you want, Paul, you only have to ask,' she said.

I clasped the cufflinks and said, 'I have all that I need, and the memories are in my heart, but thank you.'

Lady Sarah, who I knew had been closest to her sister of all the family, was an executor of the will together with her mother. Such was their generosity at the time that they had used their discretion to vary the will, bequeathing to me £50,000 'as recognition of your duty and loyalty towards the princess'. Lady Sarah continued rummaging through the clothes. Then she took out a black Versace dress and jacket, handed them to me and said: 'That's for Maria. She can wear them for the investiture.'

The date had come through. The Queen was going to decorate me with the Royal Victorian Medal on 13 November. I would return to Buckingham Palace for the first time since I had left the Queen's service ten years earlier.

It was strange to drive through the front gates of Buckingham Palace, across the forecourt, through the archway, and into the quadrangle, the red gravel raked flat for another event. I got out of the car, looked up to the top-floor windows and showed Alexander and Nick where Dad's first living quarters had been. I arrived there as a recipient in morning dress like everyone else, not as a servant in livery. I had not felt so nervous since my first day at work as a footman in 1976.

It was a bright, crisp winter's morning as we approached the glass veranda of the main entrance and entered the palace. Maria and the boys peeled off to take their places in the Ballroom. I could hear a string orchestra playing in the background as I joined the hundred other recipients of honours, all gathered in the Queen's Picture Gallery – where I had seen the princess cuddling her bridesmaids at her 1981 wedding. That day, the memories stalked me down every corridor and in every grand room as clocks and watches ticked towards eleven a.m. Then, in groups of ten, people were called to proceed through the gallery and wait at the threshold of the Ballroom where an audience of five hundred people was witnessing a very British spectacle.

As I waited, I noticed a young lady sitting all alone on a sofa, directly beneath a Van Dyck portrait of King Charles I. 'So what are you here for?' I asked, after introducing myself.

'The George Medal,' said the quietly spoken twenty-two-year-old.

It is the highest medal that can be bestowed on a civilian for bravery, and this young, attractive, blonde-haired woman in a smart light red dress and coffee-coloured hat was to receive it. I wondered what on earth she had done. She was Lisa Potts, a nursery nurse, who had used her body to shield children at a picnic while a deranged intruder wielded a machete, slashing her in the playground at St Luke's infants' school in Wolverhampton.

I looked at her hands, which were terribly scarred. 'That's nothing compared to the injuries suffered by some of the children. Some of them were cut from their mouths to their ears,' she said.

Burrell and Potts were asked to proceed to the Ballroom together. She was the star of the investiture, and it was a privilege to share the occasion with someone so courageous. I watched and waited as she approached Her Majesty and said a few words.

Then it was my turn to accept an honour that the princess had said was in recognition of my twenty-one years in royal service, serving the Queen, Prince Charles and herself. But then I got a surprise.

The Lord Chamberlain's voice came across the microphone: 'To be decorated with the Royal Victorian Medal for services to Diana, Princess of Wales, Mr Paul Burrell.'

No one had told me, but the Queen had felt it fitting that the award should focus on my loyalty to the princess. I bowed, shook her hand, and she pinned the medal to my lapel. 'You don't know how happy I am to give this to you,' said the Queen. 'It means an awful lot, and thank you for all that you have done. What are you going to do now?'

I glanced over her shoulder and spotted an old colleague, Christopher Bray, the Queen's page. 'Perhaps Christopher might need an extra hand, Your Majesty?' She chortled. We shook hands again, I took two steps back, turned and walked out of the room.

That night, a group of ten family and friends went to celebrate with me at San Lorenzo restaurant. Just as the princess had planned.

Two weeks later, a letter arrived at the Old Barracks from the Chancellor of the Exchequer, Gordon Brown, informing me that I had been chosen as a member of the Diana, Princess of Wales Memorial Committee to help advise the government as to how the life of the princess could best be commemorated; I would be working alongside the princess's friends Rosa Monckton and Lord Attenborough. It was set up to complement the work of the independent and recently established Diana, Princess of Wales Memorial Fund.

If there was a moment when the critics believed that I was nothing but a butler with 'ideas above his station', then I suppose my appointment to the committee was when people who were not close to the princess began to snipe behind my back rather than to my face, misunderstanding my relationship with her.

Such a misunderstanding perhaps wasn't helped by a comment piece in the editor's leader column of *The Times*, headlined: 'BUTLER POWER: Paul Burrell is the best man to select the Diana memorial'. It read:

> No man is a hero to his valet . . . nor no princess either a heroine to her butler . . . but the butlers and valets are the unsung and offstage heroes. They are among the select few to be admitted to the private reality behind the public masks of ceremony and razzmatazz. So the appointment of Paul Burrell . . . is a rare instance of life imitating art. For once, the butler is being consulted officially . . . Jeeves would have approved. But this is a problematic assignment . . . the Government is following wise precedents of fact, folklore and fiction. When in doubt, consult the butler as the discreet insider who really knows.

I think understandable pride made me somewhat deaf. I couldn't hear the knives being sharpened behind my back.

★

William and Harry returned to KP two weeks before Christmas 1997. I had prepared the apartments with flowers and plants, to make them look as homely as possible, and nanny Olga Powell was with me in the sitting room, awaiting their arrival. The boys burst through the front door in a jolly mood, looking forward to Christmas at Sandringham.

I walked round the apartment with them, holding a handful of yellow Post-it notes to label what should go where, and who owned what item. The boys were moving, with Prince Charles, within St James's Palace, from an apartment to York House, their new London base. William and Harry scurried from room to room, gathering books, cuddly toys, photographs, posters, videos and paintings, then decided which sofas, chairs and rugs they wanted to take with them. William was the more methodical of the two. He mentioned jewellery, then dismissed it. 'Oh, we can do that in the new year, there is no rush,' he said.

The one thing that struck me was how polite he was, even when it came to selecting his *own* possessions. 'Can I have this . . . Would it be all right if I have this?'

'William,' I said, 'everything here is yours and Harry's. You can have whatever you want. There is no need to ask.'

He walked into the L-shaped wardrobe room, and stood facing a collection of Chanel, Versace, Jacques Azagury and Catherine Walker creations. 'What should we do with all of Mummy's clothes?' he asked.

'I'm not sure whether you are aware,' I said, 'but the Spencers are planning an exhibition at Althorp, and they very much want key possessions and costumes to be included in that – including the wedding dress.'

'No!' William retorted sharply. 'I definitely do not want them to have that.'

'Why not?' said Harry, chipping in.

'I just don't, that's all,' William snapped, 'but they can have some of Mummy's dresses. We can do that in the new year too.'

It was the princess's wish for her wedding dress to be sent to the National Dress Collection at the Victoria and Albert Museum. Her elder son was making it clear that he didn't want it to go to Althorp. So where is it today? It's on display at Althorp.

Then William continued around the nursery corridor. 'I'd like that rug, that sofa, that chair . . . those curtains, that drinks table . . .' and we remembered how the princess had spent £30,000 on new carpets two years earlier.

It was poignant to watch the two brothers going around their rooms, selecting items, and watching William take charge of his younger brother.

'Can I have my bed, please, Paul,' Harry asked, 'and that chest of drawers?'

'Oh, you don't want that, Harry!' said William, getting all paternal. 'There's not enough room for *that*.'

'Yes, there is,' Harry shrieked, and I could see the princess shaking her head and smiling.

There was no dispute when they entered their sitting room downstairs, location of their huge wide-screen television. 'It's far too big for Highgrove. Can it go to York House, please? It will fill one wall!' William said. He was always in charge of the electronics and visuals. I smiled because I sensed that Prince Charles would not approve. He hated the boys sitting in front of the television watching mindless programmes. He rarely watched television unless an informative documentary was being screened.

Then we entered the sitting room, and I think that was when memories stopped them in their tracks, because this had been their mother's room, and they felt it. Silence descended. William stood looking at the photographs on the table. Harry stood over the writing desk, touching everything in a daze.

After a few minutes, William's voice halted the reflection. 'I want the giant hippo, Paul,' he said, pointing at it. Mother and sons would all lie back against the huge cuddly toy on the floor to watch television.

When the tour was finished, the apartments were littered with yellow Post-it notes, items of furniture labelled 'W–York House' or 'H–York House'.

As they searched through the video collection and flicked through the CDs, I remembered that 1997 was to be the first year *ever* that the princess would have had the boys to herself for Christmas Day: she had agreed in the summer with Prince Charles and the Queen that they could break away from the tradition of Sandringham. She had planned to spend Christmas with her sons at the K-Club in Barbuda.

But even though the princess was no longer with us, I still wanted them to have a reminder of a KP treat: a tradition they could take with them to Sandringham. I had prepared a Christmas stocking for each of them. As the boys were saying goodbye and rushing down the stairs, I stopped them. 'Because I have always been responsible for making up your stockings every year, I could not let this year pass by without doing the same,' I said. Surprise registered on both their faces. 'I have even sewn up the tops so that you cannot get to the contents! I rather doubt they will survive, though, until Christmas morning,' I said, handing over the knitted stockings the princess had used every year.

'Oh, they will, Paul,' said William, 'and thank you so, so much.' Harry ran into me and gave me a hug.

Together, we walked to the front door. 'Now, you know exactly where I am. If you want *anything*, then all you have to do is call me,' I said.

'We will, Paul,' said Harry, 'and we will see you in January when we return from skiing with Papa.'

When their stockings were tucked safely into the back of the Land Rover Discovery with the rest of the belongings they had collected, they wound down their windows, William in the front, Harry in the back. ''Bye, Paul!' they shouted, as protection officer Graham Craker drove them away.

I had stood there so many times with the princess, waving them off. She always turned to me and said: 'The house will be quiet now. I'll miss ma boys.'

From the centre of the princess's world at KP, I looked outwards with dismay.

In its infancy, the Diana, Princess of Wales Memorial Fund was run by the princess's divorce solicitor Anthony Julius. It seemed to me that he was taking charge of every aspect of her life, with Lady Sarah McCorquodale and Michael Gibbins following in his wake. I saw three people who didn't know the Boss intimately suddenly running her affairs. An independent charity set up in memory of the princess had none of her closest inner circle of friends helping to steer the project. After being in charge of the princess's *entire* life when she was alive, I suddenly found myself on the periphery.

At the palace, I was getting used to visits from Mrs Frances Shand Kydd. She would be in the sitting room with a bottle of wine, going through her daughter's correspondence, taking unilateral decisions over what should be destroyed. She shredded more than fifty letters, and I witnessed history being destroyed by a family that was already intent on seizing control of her world from the Windsors. I felt it was wrong.

The fund. The shredding. By the end of 1997, I felt I was losing control over a world the princess had expected me to control for so long. I had never felt so helpless. Suddenly *The Times* newspaper's leader article about 'consulting the discreet insider who knows' seemed to count for nothing. It was not in my nature to stand by and watch everything roll out of control. It was, in my eyes at least, my duty to do something about it, yet I found myself in a dilemma about who I could discuss my concerns with. None of the Spencers would understand: I wasn't family. William and Harry were too young, and the Prince of Wales was an impossible counsellor to seek. I'm not sure he would have listened, let alone understood. There was only one person who *would* listen: Her Majesty the Queen. I wouldn't need to go through the pompous royal household to get an audience. I knew that.

I picked up the telephone and rang someone close to the Queen, someone discreet whom I could trust. 'Do you think the Queen would see me, and spare me five minutes?' I asked.

'Leave it with me, and I will let you know.'

The following day, the answer was delivered. 'The Queen would be delighted to see you at two o'clock on Thursday, 19 December. I think you know your way here.'

In through the side door off Buckingham Palace Road. Past the policeman, who was expecting me. Down through the tiled underground corridors. Past the stores, wine cellars, linen room and flower room, and into the tiny two-person lift. I knew my way around Buckingham Palace, even after such a long time away from its warrens.

As the lift doors opened, I stepped out into a familiar utility area before opening a huge oak door and walking out on to the red carpet of the Queen's corridor, timing my arrival for exactly one fifty-five p.m. I approached the narrow Pages' Vestibule, half-way along the corridor, where I had waited to serve the Queen so many times. I sat and waited now until she had finished her coffee after lunch. Then, virtually on the stroke of two o'clock, a page said: 'The Queen is ready for you now . . . It's Paul, Your Majesty.'

There she was in her private sitting room. The diminutive figure stood at her desk in the bay window, wearing her half-rimmed spectacles. Government papers and red boxes were strewn across it. Nine or ten corgis were littered around the room. Some, from a generation I did not know, raised their heads and growled.

The Queen walked across to me, and I bowed before she extended a hand and said: 'Hello, Paul, how are you?'

The smile was as warm as it ever had been, even if the lady was slightly older, slightly greyer. She was dressed in blue, wearing three rows of pearls, and a huge heart-shaped diamond brooch.

She saw I was clutching a small offering. 'A bunch of flowers, Your Majesty.'

'How kind of you,' she said, taking them, 'and they do smell good.'

She was relaxed, friendly, unguarded, and she knew from the informal briefing she had been given that certain matters regarding the princess were troubling me.

'It is a very strange business,' she said, starting the conversation, and handing the flowers to her page.

'I know, Your Majesty. There is absolutely no one whom I can confide in. You are my only answer, and thank you for affording me the opportunity to speak with you. It means such a great deal to me.'

We remained standing. One does not sit when in the presence of the Queen at a private audience. I knew that. Her Majesty asked me how I was coping. I said I was keeping myself busy. She asked about Maria and the boys. I provided the update. Then I got to the point: sharing with her the internal politics at KP, how I felt the Memorial Fund was being handled, the characters involved, the problems I perceived. We spoke about Anthony Julius, about Lady Sarah, about Patrick Jephson, about my future, about the huge legal costs the fund was incurring: £170,000 alone for October. Then we spoke about Dodi Al Fayed, and the princess's fascination with him.

It seemed the Queen was under the same impression as the rest of the country: that the relationship was the start of a long-term union rather than a summer fling.

'Your Majesty, this romance would have ended in tears. The princess was aware that he had problems: money, drugs, drink and even prostitutes, which will, I have no doubt, come out in the end.' I continued: 'I always said to the princess, "Be in charge of your own environment." But the truth was that she was not in control on that boat. He had the air-conditioning on full, he chose the boat's destination, he chose the food, he decided to go to Paris. She wanted to come home, Your Majesty. She wanted her independence back.'

The Queen listened intently and, as she did on many subjects that day, gave a frank and honest opinion. She then told me how Mrs Frances Shand Kydd had occasionally called her since September.

'May I say, Your Majesty, that you were very brave to be in!' I joked.

With that name raised, there was no better time to express my concerns about what I had witnessed at KP: the seemingly indiscriminate shredding of documentation, letters and memos that, I felt, could have historic importance. 'Your Majesty, I cannot allow history to be erased. I intend to protect the princess's world and keep safe her secrets, and I intend to keep documents and artefacts she gave me.'

Again, the Queen listened. She did not object, and I think we both understood that I felt it was my duty to do something. I didn't need to go into detail about what items would be secured and where I would take them. The absence of a frown from the Queen was enough to tell me that I would simply deal with the matter in a way I felt appropriate.

I think she could empathize with what I was experiencing. She told me: 'I remember that when my grandmother died, I went across to Marlborough House to find stickers on everything. They had all descended like vultures – and that, I know, is the most awful part following a personal loss.'

It was then that we spoke about William and Harry, including their visit to collect possessions from KP.

I had never had such a long conversation with the Queen, and it was a privilege to be in her company for what turned into a personal

316

and intimate meeting that lasted, to the best of my recollection, from two o'clock until shortly before five. Standing throughout. We did have ten years to catch up on, and it was like a reunion with a long-lost relative. It felt that informal.

Of course, the prospect of a butler having a near three-hour audience with the Queen was 'fanciful rubbish', according to the newspapers in the days following the collapse of my theft trial at the Old Bailey in 2002. Incredulous royal experts, who could only dream of such a conversation with the Queen, appeared on television and played down my recollection of that meeting, dismissing it as 'unthinkable' and 'highly unlikely' and 'pure fiction'.

'The Prime Minister only gets fifteen minutes, so it is unlikely that a butler would be granted such an audience,' scoffed one disbelieving former member of staff.

The *Sun* newspaper waded in with its usual amount of accuracy, trumpeting how the meeting was three minutes long, and never went beyond an hour.

Then Buckingham Palace issued a statement to clear up the truth and enlighten a few people. The Queen's personal recollection was that 'The meeting lasted *at least* ninety minutes.'

Whatever the version, we seemed to be standing there for an inordinate amount of time. We might as well have been feeding the corgis.

Of course, we spoke at length about the princess. In fact, I told the Queen that Prince Charles was the one man she had truly loved all her life; knowing that the princess had, herself, relayed that same message in that room in February 1996.

As we spoke about the princess, the tone of the conversation changed. I could almost sense the Queen wishing the clock to turn back. 'I tried to reach out to Diana so many times. I wrote many, many letters to her, Paul,' she told me.

At that moment, I could visualize the princess and me on the stairs or in the sitting room, reading the kind correspondence from Buckingham Palace or Windsor Castle. 'I know. I saw those letters and the princess always replied. But the trouble was, Your Majesty, that you spoke in black and white, the princess spoke in colour.' I was suggesting that they were from different generations, speaking different languages.

For the first time in my life, I felt like embracing the Queen but, of course, she wasn't the princess, and it was impossible. I just stood there, listening to her and thinking that if Britain could have seen how genuine and warm she was towards the princess, there would have been no controversy about her distance in the immediate days after the princess's death.

I remembered the note the princess had left me about the Queen: '*I long to hug my mother-in-law.*'

I was witnessing the genuine concern of a mother-in-law, not a distant sovereign; someone who had sincerely tried to help, and the Boss knew that. Which was why she never regarded the Queen and the Duke of Edinburgh as enemies.

The Queen knew that much, but she added, 'My gestures were either not welcomed or simply misunderstood,' and her sad frustration was evident – 'and all I was attempting to do was help.'

As the meeting neared its end, the Queen said one more thing to me. Looking over her half-rimmed spectacles, she said: 'Be careful, Paul. No one has been as close to a member of my family as you have. There *are* powers at work in this country about which we have no knowledge,' and she fixed me with a stare where her eyes made clear the 'Do you understand?'.

'Well, it has been fascinating talking to you again, Paul,' she said, 'do let me know how everything turns out, won't you? I really think it is time that I took the dogs for a walk now.'

We shook hands. I bowed, and left the room.

Ever since the end of my trial when I first detailed that meeting with the Queen, there has been much speculation, and again scoffing, over the tone and meaning of the 'Be careful' message from Her Majesty. So, what did she mean? All I know is what I heard. It wasn't quantified or expanded upon, neither was it melodramatically delivered. I walked away and accepted what had been said as it had been intended: as sound advice to be vigilant. In my opinion, she was telling me to be careful of everyone because no one more than the Queen understood the position in which I found myself, and the closeness I had shared with the princess.

The reference to the 'powers at work in this country about

which we have no knowledge' has often played on my mind in the intervening years and, yes, I have worried about it too. The Queen might have been referring to the power base of media barons and editors who can topple individuals from their pedestals. She might have been referring to that unknown quantity called 'the Establishment', an undefined, invisible network of interlocking social circles of the great and the good. She might have been referring to the domestic intelligence service MI5 because, have no doubt, the Queen does not know of its secret work and darker practices but she is aware of the power it is capable of wielding. Like the royal household, the intelligence services are given *carte blanche* to act in whatever way is considered to be in the best interests of state and monarchy.

All I do know is that, within four years of Her Majesty's warning, I was arrested and sent to trial for a crime I never committed in a case that barely had the legs to stand up. All the time, the under-currents running beneath the surface of that case were about the secrets of the princess. Who had them? Where were they? But, in all honesty, I cannot pinpoint what the Queen was referring to. I have beaten myself up mentally many times over why I didn't ask her at the time what she meant. I, like you, can only speculate. No one is more aware than I of the knowledge locked away inside my head. In choosing to impart certain information to me, the princess ensured I shared a historic knowledge. I was her independent witness to history, in the same way that I was her witness to the letters she wrote and received, the divorce papers she handled and the will she made.

She also shared with me her concern that she was constantly monitored. It is naïve of anyone to think that the princess, from the moment she married Prince Charles, would not have had her telephone calls bugged, or that the associations she made were not checked. It is a matter of routine that members of government and the Royal Family are monitored. She knew that. So, in that regard, 'the powers' were discreetly at work in all my years at Highgrove and KP. She made me constantly aware of it, and the need to be vigilant. If there was one thing about life at KP that the princess loathed it was the inescapable feeling of constantly being listened to or watched. It was one of the reasons why she shed her police protection. She didn't trust the police as tools of the state. In fact, she had a deep-seated suspicion about anything and everything to do with the state.

When both of us were away from the palace, she even suspected that listening devices had been planted in apartments 8 and 9. Once, both of us moved all the furniture to one side in her sitting room and rolled up an Aztec-style rug, the blue fitted carpet and its underlay. Then, we prised up the floorboards with screwdrivers. She was convinced there were listening devices in the palace but we found nothing. She worried about devices being placed in plug sockets, light switches or lamps. Some will dismiss this kind of worrying as outright paranoia. If such worries were in isolation and devoid of rational reasoning, I would tend to agree. But the critics who were far too eager to dismiss her as paranoid didn't realize that she had good reason to be concerned. She was being cautious, not paranoid, because she was acting on sound information received from someone who had worked for the British intelligence services; a man whose expertise, advice and friendship the princess came to rely on.

Even another member of the Royal Family warned the princess: 'You need to be discreet – even in your own home – because "they" are listening all the time.' (Before my trial at the Old Bailey in 2002, I witnessed, with my legal team, documented evidence that even my telephone lines, during the course of the police inquiry, had been 'intercepted' without my knowledge and at least twenty telephone numbers had been monitored.)

Armed with such advice, I defy anyone in the princess's position not to go on the hunt for the devices. When she found none, she called on the help of her ex-intelligence-services friend. One weekend afternoon, he visited the palace, using a pseudonym. He carried out a sweep of the apartments to detect listening devices. Every room was checked. Nothing was found. Then, in demonstration after demonstration, the princess and I were given a sharp lesson in hi-tech surveillance techniques. But what startled the princess most was to learn that 'monitoring' did not necessarily require devices to be planted in a household. So hi-tech were the intelligence facilities that a conversation could be listened to from a surveillance van parked outside, transmitting a signal into the building and using mirrors to bounce it back. As a result, she took down the round convex mirror that hung above the marble fireplace opposite the window in the sitting room. She was not paranoid: she was being advised.

In the final two years of her life, the princess grew increasingly concerned about the security around her. Ever since the separation in 1992, she felt she had grown in stature, and she was ready to take on the world in her humanitarian mission. But, rightly or wrongly, she felt that the stronger she became, the more she was regarded as a modernizing nuisance who was prepared to go out on a limb and do the unconventional. She was later to be proved right, to some degree, when her humanitarian work in Angola in early 1997 led to suggestions that she was a 'loose cannon' who was doing more harm than good. In the autumn of 1996, she had an overpowering feeling that she was 'in the way'. She certainly felt that 'the system' didn't appreciate her work and that, for as long as she was on the scene, Prince Charles could never properly move on. 'I have become strong, and they don't like it when I am able to do good and stand on my own two feet without them,' she said.

In one particular period of anxiety, in October 1996, the princess called me from my pantry. I met her half-way down the stairs. A question of self-doubt led to reassurance from me, and one more question led to us sitting on the stairs and talking through her concerns. She felt there was a concerted attempt by what she referred to as the 'anti-Diana brigade' to undermine her in the public's eyes. We spoke about the continuing role of Tiggy Legge-Bourke. We spoke about Camilla Parker Bowles and whether Prince Charles really loved her. Inevitably, we spoke about how the princess felt undervalued and unappreciated. But the basis of the conversation seemed to be her worries about what the future held. She said she was 'constantly puzzled' by the attempts of Prince Charles's sympathizers to 'destroy me'. It was a 'down day', and the princess needed to talk. With all sorts of jumbled thoughts racing through her mind, we went into the sitting room to write it all down and then make sense of it. Again, the pen put her thoughts into some form of therapeutic order.

As the princess sat at her desk, I sat on the sofa, watching her scribble furiously. 'I'm going to date this and I want you to keep it

. . . just in case,' she said. For she had another reason to write down her thoughts and present them to me that day. She was, rationally or irrationally, worried about her safety and it was preying on her mind. She wrote down what she was thinking but didn't articulate her justification for doing so. I think she would have felt silly, or perhaps embarrassed. She just wanted to put it down. It was, in a way, her insurance for the future.

When she finished the letter, she popped it into an envelope addressed to 'Paul', sealed it and handed it to me. I read it the next day at home, and thought nothing of it. It wasn't the first time, or the last, that she would express, verbally or in writing, such concerns to me. But, with the benefit of hindsight, the content of that letter has bothered me since her death. For this is what she wrote ten months before she died in that car crash in Paris.

I am sitting here at my desk today in October, longing for someone to hug me and encourage me to keep strong and hold my head high. This particular phase in my life is the most dangerous. [The princess then identified where she felt the threat and danger would come from] is planning 'an accident' in my car, brake failure and serious head injury in order to make the path clear for Charles to marry.

I have been battered, bruised and abused mentally by a system for 15 years now, but I feel no resentment, I carry no hatred. I am weary of the battles, but I will never surrender. I am strong inside and maybe that is a problem for my enemies.

Thank you Charles, for putting me through such hell and for giving me the opportunity to learn from the cruel things you have done to me. I have gone forward fast and have cried more than anyone will ever know. The anguish nearly killed me, but my inner strength has never let me down, and my guides have taken such good care of me up there. Aren't I fortunate to have had their wings to protect me . . .

That letter has been part of the burden I have carried since the princess's death. Deciding what to do with it has been a source of much soul-searching. All I can say is, imagine if that letter had been penned to you by a loved one and then, within the next year, they died in a car crash. In trying to make sense of it, you tend to waver from considering it a wild coincidence to more bizarre, paranoid explanations. I had hoped that the matter would be put to rest by an inquest into the princess's death – a full examination by a coroner and court in the UK of the events of 31 August 1997. But, for some inexplicable reason, there has not been an inquest. If it were anyone else, an inquest would have had to be held and yet that essential, inquisitorial process has been pushed to one side.

In the late summer of 2003, it was announced that an inquest was being planned in Surrey to examine the circumstances, primarily, of the death of Dodi Al Fayed. It was unclear whether that hearing's scope would include the death of the princess. Whatever the situation, the lack of an inquest to date, and the attempt by Scotland Yard and the CPS to destroy my reputation with my Old Bailey trial in 2002, has led me to make the contents of that note public. I agree that it may be futile in what it achieves because it can do no more than provide yet another question mark. But if that question mark leads to an inquest, and a thorough examination of the facts by the British authorities, it will have achieved something. Perhaps there is a desire to allow the matter of a British inquest to go away, but that cannot be allowed to happen.

15. A Knock at the Door

If the princess was happy to have me at the helm when she was alive, then those charged with enshrining her memory in death would have preferred to see me thrown overboard. In what would become the story of my life between 1997 and 2002, few people grasped the nature of the privileged relationship I shared with the Boss behind closed doors at KP, and the implications of that misunderstanding would ultimately conspire with ignorance to haunt me for years to come.

The problem with sharing such an intensely private world is that its unique qualities are not witnessed by outsiders. When something is not witnessed, especially when ordinary codes of conduct are breached, it is misunderstood. I was a butler who had done his duty, nothing more, nothing less. But in some people's eyes, perhaps, I was a butler with delusions of grandeur who was getting too big for his boots.

An overwhelming desire to cut me down to size, and squeeze me back into some sort of livery where I belonged, became apparent not long after February 1998, with my appointment to the Diana, Princess of Wales Memorial Fund as its salaried fundraising and events manager.

I was catapulted from a quiet and secret area of a palace into offices at Millbank Tower in south-west London. I wanted to harness the new role I had been given and help steer funds in a way that would have made the princess proud. I was receiving cheques galore: from $2 million from the manufacturer of Ty Beanie Babies to £26,000 from Tower Records, to a few hundred pounds from a young farmers' group near Highgrove. I opened charity events all over Britain, including the Junior National Disabled Games in Birmingham, and went to meetings with the Memorial Committee in Downing Street. There would be no problems on the committee. The power struggle would come on the Fund.

I felt I could bring a unique perspective to the table, and inject the princess's wishes into the Fund's work. I had known the princess inside out, understood how her mind worked, had been alongside her on her humanitarian missions, had dreamed with her on paper about future missions and charity work that were close to her heart.

One evening at KP, the princess and I were in the sitting room, jotting down ideas about the way forward because she felt her good intentions were being misunderstood.

> I have been given a quality, much to the horror of Charles, and it is a quality I must nurture and use in order to help those in distress. I will never let down those who believe in me, and I will always bring love wherever I go in the world, to whomever: leper, Aids patient, King, Queen or President.
>
> I have a path of fate to follow, and tread it I will with pride, dignity and abundance of love and understanding for those in need and that I give with open arms . . .

I knew the humanitarian direction in which she was going. In sharing her thoughts about the way forward when she was alive, I honestly felt I was qualified to lead the way forward on her behalf, ensuring that her wishes and way of thinking informed the work of the Memorial Fund. The princess's personal assistant Jackie Allen, and secretaries Jane Harris and Jo Greenstead, each brought their own passionate beliefs to the table of what it was right and wrong to do in the princess's name.

Like me, they, too, would find themselves distanced for being too emotionally involved. I felt I was treated as the butler who was fast becoming a nuisance, with his convictions about what the princess would have wanted. But what really started putting lofty noses out of joint was when the press began identifying me as 'the voice and face of the Fund'. Especially when Lady Sarah McCorquodale was its president.

'Remember where you come from, Paul.'

'Look, Paul, stop walking around like the walking wounded. We are *all* grieving, you know.'

'I'm afraid he's an emotional cripple. Emotional people don't make the best decisions.'

'Paul, wouldn't you rather find employment elsewhere, and get away from all this? There are some rather nasty rumours circulating about you.'

Such comments, to my face or behind my back, were becoming commonplace in London circles. But I remained focused on unfinished business. If my duty had been to serve the princess in life, then I was intent on serving her memory in death.

I remembered what the princess used to say about putting her head above the parapet. 'You always get shot!' But she stood up for what she believed in and stubbornly dug in her heels. I could only do the same.

The princess's leatherbound green address book had been left on my desk in a locked room, separate from the main general office at Millbank Tower. Jackie Allen and I had locked that room every night. Then, one day, during the infancy of the Memorial Fund, the address book went missing. It contained the names and numbers of all the princess's friends. It was a directory of her life. I had read it to her during the all-night vigil.

With Jackie, I reported it stolen to the then office manager, Brian Hutchinson. He, in turn, reported it to Lady Sarah McCorquodale. The police were not called. There was not even an internal inquiry. The theory in the office was that it could have been taken by a cleaner, a night-watchman, or a security guard. It was never investigated, and that alone made me suspect that something wasn't quite right.

Dr Andrew Purkis arrived as the Fund's chief executive, and we never did see eye to eye – because the princess would never have seen eye to eye with him. He made it clear that he was the 'voice of the Fund if there was going to be one'. He had not even *met* the princess, so my bewilderment at hearing this stranger talking about her memory was profound. He had been the Archbishop of Canterbury's private secretary at Lambeth Palace. He was the High Church and the Establishment rolled into one: everything the princess had rebelled against. He had been given the position because he had a good brain and an excellent management pedigree. Yet I felt that he had no conception of how this precious legacy should be managed.

He could never empathize with the passion or conviction that ran through the majority of her friends. A charity in memory of a special someone is starved of essential inspiration and guidance if it is incapable of harnessing or understanding the personality of the name it operates under. Surely.

Whenever I made a passionate defence of the princess's remarkable personality, I felt I was screaming from behind a thick glass wall.

Dr Purkis had known I was not going to hang out the bunting to mark his arrival. 'I know you may resent me taking this post, but I will try and work alongside you the best I can. I do not want there to be any animosity,' he told me.

By the start of July 1998, apartments 8 and 9 had been stripped bare. No carpets. No silk wallpaper. Not even a lightbulb. It seemed as if no one had ever lived there. The Royal Collection had gathered its fine furniture and paintings. Jewellery had been returned to Buckingham Palace. William and Harry's requests for their possessions had been carried out. The Spencers took away the rest to Althorp, including the Nelson Shanks portrait on the stairs and the wedding dress. Even the princess's BMW was sent to a secret location to be destroyed so that no one could benefit from its provenance.

The erasure of everything I knew meant that my inevitable departure from KP was imminent; I had put it to the back of my mind ever since the previous December when Maria and I were given notice that, because I was no longer employed by the royal household, we did not qualify for grace-and-favour accommodation at the Old Barracks. On 24 July we said goodbye to so much: the palace, our home, the boys' schools, their friends, our friends, our parish priest, my pension scheme. We lost an entire lifestyle. But, more than anything, I finally had to let go of the private world at KP to which I had clung since the princess's death. This was the physical letting-go, although I knew that the mental letting-go would not be possible. I'm not sure it ever will be.

When Mrs Frances Shand Kydd learned of our eviction from royal accommodation, she offered to give us £120,000 towards an apartment in London on the conditions that the deeds were in her name and that we would allocate her a room so that she could stay there whenever she was in the capital. It was an incredibly kind offer, but we had our little cottage in Farndon, Cheshire, so we decided to move north and start afresh. Maria and the boys would live in that village, surrounded by family, while I spent the week working with the Memorial Fund in London and staying with a friend.

On our final day at the Old Barracks, Maria and the boys packed up the boxes and cleared out the flat. They left me to make one final visit to KP. Across the green. Up the road alongside the palace. Past the cottages on the left. Along King's Passage and into the back door of apartment 8. I wandered through the ground-floor workroom, past the empty wooden pigeon-holes, and into my pantry where the cupboards had been cleared, the telephone and the fax had been removed. My mere presence – the footsteps, the opening of doors, the creaking floorboards – seemed to leave an echo in a house that I remembered to be so full of life. I roamed around the apartment, standing in each room for ten or fifteen minutes, reflecting on what had happened in that space. I was mentally projecting images over a blank background, replaying and fast-forwarding five years of life at KP, all condensed into that hour in which I was lost in complete silence. It was a shell but, in my mind, I was visualizing everything as it had been.

I carried these thoughts with me on the long journey up the M6, to a new life in the North.

I lived, breathed and slept my role at the Memorial Fund. I was up and down the country helping to raise money in memory of the princess: at a London Lighthouse fashion show; at a golf club in Telford, Shropshire, with former England goalkeeper Peter Shilton to host a disabled sports day; at a charity cricket day in Retford, Lincolnshire; at the Great North Run in Newcastle-upon-Tyne; at a bagpipe competition in Glasgow. I travelled the length and breadth of Britain, and the Fund didn't seem to care that I was working for those causes on my weekends off. I went to accept cheques personally because I felt it was important for someone from the Fund to recognize the efforts of the people who had raised money for the princess.

By October, the offices had moved from Millbank Tower to

County Hall at Westminster, and I had an office with stunning panoramic views of the Thames, the Houses of Parliament and Big Ben.

My horizons were not looking so good, though, because I wanted to run in the New York Marathon in November. Dr Andrew Purkis wrote to me, making it clear that he was not going to allow my profile to get out of hand:

> If and when you go to New York . . . you will be doing so as a private trip . . . to fulfil a personal ambition. You are not representing the Fund . . . and you will not do anything or give any interviews relating to the work of the Fund. Even any media interview, which started off purporting to be about Paul Burrell the person, would in fact, pretty soon, start highlighting the fact that you work for the Fund.

So I completed the marathon in four hours forty minutes. In my own capacity.

Later that month, a Masquerade Ball was held at the Grosvenor House Hotel in London's Park Lane to raise money for the Diana, Princess of Wales Memorial Fund. A host of celebrities turned up in her honour, and the rock star Bryan Adams donated a signed guitar, which was auctioned by former soccer-player-turned-actor Vinnie Jones. But after such a night of glitz and glamour, I could almost hear the sniping that I was 'star-struck' and 'too interested in the showbiz side of life'. The writing was on the wall.

In the last week of November, I was asked to attend a one-to-one meeting with Dr Purkis. The neatness of his brightly lit office symbolized how efficient this man was in his capacity as chief executive. Wood panelling covered the four walls up to dado height; not a piece of paper was out of place on his desk. Above where he sat hung a photograph of the princess, taken by Mario Testino for a CD compilation in tribute to the Boss.

Dr Purkis, a small, nervous-looking man, soon got to the point. He suggested I should start to look elsewhere for a career because they were intending to close down the fundraising and events department. 'The future for you within the Fund is rather limited,' he said.

All I heard was an insignificant voice, droning in the background. I didn't grasp what he was saying because I was focusing on the Mario Testino portrait of the princess. This man does not have a clue about you, I thought.

I interrupted him in full flow. 'Are you telling me that you're going to make me redundant? Because I will not be tendering my resignation. This is what I know and do best. You'll have to surgically remove me from this Fund, and then out I will go with the dirty laundry and –'

'Paul, I don't like to use analogies like that, but I do feel that it is time for you to move on.'

How dare he? 'It's all very well for you to sit there and say that,' I said, 'but you're not affected publicly in the same way that I am. If you push me out, it will affect the work of this Fund.'

Dr Purkis wasn't listening.

A few days afterwards Lady Sarah McCorquodale rang me. 'Are you all right, Paul?'

'No, I'm not. Not really,' I replied.

'Let's have lunch next Tuesday. I'm at Mishcon de Reya's for a meeting, so we can meet up and talk,' she said.

When I agreed, I had expected it to be a one-to-one informal lunch. So, after receiving one more cheque at County Hall from the organizers of a charity day, I went to the arranged rendezvous at a wine bar near Southampton Row on Tuesday 8 December. In the corner, I spotted Lady Sarah at a corner table – with solicitor Anthony Julius, one-time interim chairman of the Fund who had remained as a trustee.

'I had no idea that the big guns were coming,' I said light-heartedly, in a vain attempt to break the ice. I looked at the rather serious face of Anthony Julius and, true to legal form, he was in no mood for banter. I knew a lot about him because the princess had told me more than he would ever know, but at least we had one thing in common: he and I had been the only people trusted to handle her divorce papers.

He opened the conversation by stating that both he and Lady Sarah had been instructed to explain the current situation. As he rambled on towards the inevitable regrets that people often express when kicking you up the backside, I thought how funny it was that the person doing all the talking was the one I had not arranged to meet. Lady Sarah was quiet as a mouse.

'You have two alternatives, Paul,' he said. 'One is to leave with acrimony, which will hurt you, your family and the Fund, and which you would bitterly regret in a few years' time. The other is to accept the hand of friendship, which is being extended to you now. We will utilize the tremendous goodwill and resources of the Fund to find you alternative employment.'

A hand of friendship, he called it. All I felt across the table was the cold aristocracy of Lady Sarah and the arrogant legal might of Anthony Julius strangling me.

I pointed out that I still felt there was much more work to do.

Then Lady Sarah came to life. 'But *what* do you want?' she said, clearly irritated. 'Your job is redundant!'

Anthony Julius waded in again: 'Remember, Paul, when the money began to arrive at Kensington Palace, Lady Sarah, myself and Michael Gibbins decided to set up the Fund. If it hadn't been for us, you would not have had this job to go to in the first place.'

I think he wanted me to be grateful. 'But you can't say "if" because "if" is a very big word. "If" the princess hadn't died, you wouldn't have needed to give me a job,' I pointed out.

'Oh, yes, you can, Paul,' said an indignant Lady Sarah. 'Oh, yes, you can say "if".' Then she tried another argument. 'Wouldn't Maria and the boys rather you were with them than here in London?'

When in trouble, dig deep for the emotional screws. 'Look,' I said, 'my family are, and always will be, behind me in whatever I choose to do.' I had to bite my lip on what I knew about the value the Spencers placed on close families.

'Paul, all we want to do is help you make a decision,' said Anthony Julius.

I asked him if the meeting was on or off the record. 'It's on the record, unless you specify otherwise,' he replied. 'The trustees are aware that we are meeting and expect a report of this conversation.'

Lady Sarah was fiddling with her salad. I hadn't even started tackling the fish on the plate in front of me. I felt myself becoming emotional and tried to control it, but I couldn't. 'I don't recognize the two people I'm sat with, I cannot listen to this any more.' My voice cracked. 'You will have to excuse me for being rude, and leaving the table.'

I got up, grabbed my coat from the back of the chair and headed for the door. 'So we'll see you later, Paul?' Lady Sarah's voice chased me out of the wine bar. Her sister would never have treated me so badly, and that thought sent tears rolling down my cheeks as I dashed into the open air.

I flagged down a taxi, and jumped into the back. I could not contain a roar of grief.

'Are you all right, mate?' asked the driver, looking into his rear-view mirror.

'I'll be fine. I've just had some bad news. Can you take me to Kensington Palace, please?'

It was the only place I could think of going. I could no longer have access but I could walk around Kensington Palace Gardens. There, I managed to compose myself, then headed for the Dome Café in the high street where I met up with the *Daily Mail* reporter Richard Kay: someone else who had known the princess better than anyone on that Fund; someone who would understand the injustice of it all. Not one word appeared in the *Daily Mail*. But by Friday the *News of the World*'s royal reporter, Clive Goodman, was on to my imminent redundancy.

When I was called into the office of Dr Purkis on the Monday after the *News of the World* had printed its story, the weekend's press coverage was spread across his desk. He told me that he had confirmed reports that I had met with the media 'to discuss the Fund's business'. I was beyond caring. After one more heated conversation, he told me: 'Right. I will ring you later in the day to tell you of my decision.' Those were his final words to me.

To quell the press furore over my impending dismissal, Dr Purkis put the matter into context in a memo to all staff: 'This episode is a piddling storm in a teacup being generated by the lower end of the tabloid press.'

On 18 December, the Friday before Christmas, Dr Purkis rang me at home to explain that he had 'no alternative but to give you a month's notice'. I returned to work on 21 December to clear my desk, and speak my mind to a chief executive who was attempting

332

to be conciliatory. I walked into his office and said: 'I have come to say goodbye.'

Dr Purkis replied: 'I want to thank you for everything and for all your hard work during the past ten months.'

'I did what I did for the princess. In memory of her, not for anyone else,' I said.

'I know how upset you must feel.'

'No, you don't. I doubt whether you have any idea. You and the trustees have totally mismanaged my role ever since I arrived here, not once realizing the potential I had to offer,' I said.

Dr Purkis mounted his defence. 'That is not true, Paul. The trustees have fire in their bellies for this Fund.'

'Andrew, this Fund bears no resemblance to the person whom I knew. It does not fulfil her wishes or her requests!'

'We believe that it does, and we will do everything we can to make sure that it continues, Paul,' he said.

'Andrew, I leave here with a heavy heart, but I wish you all the luck for the future.' I placed an unopened Christmas card on the table. 'And if this card is from you, then I have to return it.'

Outside, Jackie Allen gave me a hug on the steps as the press were waiting to capture my departure from the Fund. It was a sign of solidarity. In time, she, Jane Harris and Jo Greenstead would also be leaving: three more passionate voices lost from the Fund.

'How do you feel, Paul?' yelled one reporter.

'Very sad.'

'Will you continue the princess's charitable work?'

'I'll do my best.' Then I scrambled into a waiting car, and I was away. Lady Sarah McCorquodale no longer had a meddlesome butler on the Fund. But it wasn't going to be my final confrontation with the princess's sister.

We would come face to face once more. Four years later. In courtroom number one at the Old Bailey, London's Central Criminal Court.

On New Year's Day 1999, Clive Goodman, of the *News of the World*, rang me at home. 'I have been told that a pair of earrings which belonged to the princess have gone missing. Would you like to comment on that?'

'Can I ask where you got that information?'

'You know I can't tell you that, Paul, but, needless to say, it's a very good source,' said Clive.

My concern was obvious. David Thomas, the Crown jeweller, Lady Sarah McCorquodale and I had carefully dispatched all of the princess's jewellery to Althorp. I catalogued all of the earrings and saw them leave.

I rang the Fund's press officer, Vanessa Corringham, to inform her of the conversation that had taken place with Clive Goodman.

In a letter, dated 2 January 1999, to my friends in Kentucky, Shirley and Claude Wright, I wrote: '*It has occurred to me that someone might be trying to damage my reputation, particularly that I come from the Fund with such good press, and my profile is riding high. Someone might wish to see my name tarnished, or am I getting paranoid?*'

Aged forty-two, I found myself adrift with no attachment to a palace or a princess. For the first time since joining the household staff at Buckingham Palace in 1976, I felt out on a limb. I decided to put to good use my years of royal training. I published a book on social etiquette and manners, entitled *Entertaining With Style* (*In the Royal Manner* in the USA), and found that I could still rely on my trade. The proceeds of that book allowed us to move from the then £110,000 Old Barn property in Farndon to a larger, Georgian house, on the market for £185,000. On the back of that book, I started to give lectures on entertaining, royal style, occasionally charging £3000 but a lot of the time without a fee at charity events.

It was an income, based on royalties and lectures, that would ultimately grab the attention of Scotland Yard. With regard to my bank statements, the figures didn't add up. Two and two would equal five.

Someone had pulled back the brass knocker and rattled it against the blue front door. It was still dark outside. Maria was already up, making breakfast downstairs. I rolled over in bed, and the bedside clock told me it was shortly before seven. It was Thursday, 18 January 2001, and Scotland Yard's 'Special Inquiry Team' – a unit known as SO6 – had arrived.

'Chuck!' Maria shouted up the stairs. 'There's some people who want to talk to you.'

I pulled the white dressing-gown around me, left our second-floor bedroom and went down the steep, narrow, right-turning staircase. At the bottom, I saw Maria, still in her blue nightshirt. Her entire body seemed to be shaking.

'It's the police,' she mouthed.

I dropped off the bottom step of the stairs, went past the kitchen through the next doorway off the narrow hallway, whose peach walls are lined with group staff photographs from the royal tours I spent with the Queen, or the Prince and Princess of Wales. Two smartly dressed, stern-looking individuals greeted me: a rather buxom woman with blonde hair, DCI Maxine de Brunner, and a tall, debonair man with thick black hair, DS Roger Milburn. A warrant card flashed out of a leather wallet. 'I am arresting you on suspicion of the theft of a golden dhow. You do not have to say anything but it may harm your defence if you do not mention, when questioned, something which you later rely on in court. Anything you do say may be given in evidence,' said DS Milburn.

They had arrived to arrest me in connection with an inquiry, which had begun the previous year, into the theft and sale of an eighteen-inch-long jewel-encrusted Arabian dhow worth £500,000, a wedding present to the Prince and Princess of Wales from the Emir of Bahrain. It had been offered for sale at an antique shop called Spink in London. The police 'had been told' that I instructed its disposal, and that tall story had brought them to my door. It set in motion a personal nightmare for myself and my family, and a process that would be recorded for its embarrassment factor in the books of British legal and political history.

Perched on the arm of the sofa, I could smell the sausages Maria had been frying in the kitchen. The boys were still asleep upstairs. Belle, our West Highland terrier, waddled in and began to sniff the strangers' shoes.

Did I have anything in the house that had been removed from Kensington Palace? Did I know the whereabouts of the dhow? I was asked.

Then DS Milburn asked me two bizarre questions: 'Do you have a manuscript of the memoirs you are writing?'

If there was one moment when I knew the officers were stabbing in the dark, that was it. No such manuscript existed. I only began

335

writing this book, *A Royal Duty*, in April 2003, and this book is the *result* of that arrest, a response to the confusion and doubt Scotland Yard raked up over my true closeness to the princess. But in January 2001 I had no idea what 'manuscript' they were talking about.

Then came: 'Lady Sarah McCorquodale has said that you had a box which belonged to Diana, Princess of Wales. She would like you to return the contents of that box.'

The questions kept coming. 'Did you ever remove this box from Kensington Palace?'

What? I thought. Lady Sarah McCorquodale was the last person to have it. Wasn't she? I knew exactly what they were referring to: the deep, mahogany box that the princess had kept in the sitting room as a storage place for her most sensitive papers and documents. The box Lady Sarah and I had opened together at KP after her death. The box that, to the best of my knowledge, was with her.

My manuscript. The princess's secrets. That was what Scotland Yard had come looking for, together with 'documentation relating to the sale of a golden dhow', which was something else that they would not find in my house.

Maria went into the kitchen, followed by DCI de Brunner. DS Milburn stayed with me. 'If you give us what we want, we'll be out of here. If you don't, we'll have to search the house,' he told me.

In the kitchen, DCI de Brunner was making the same point to Maria. 'I suggest, Mrs Burrell, that you speak to your husband and tell him to give us what we're looking for.'

At my Old Bailey trial in 2002, both detectives would deny that they had ever said such a thing. 'That is completely incorrect,' said DS Milburn. 'That is absolutely wrong,' said DCI de Brunner.

Three more detectives, who had been waiting in a vehicle outside, entered the house to carry out a robust search after I had insisted I had no material relating to a golden dhow, no contents of a box, and no manuscript for a book. Every cupboard, drawer, wardrobe, cabinet and shelf was searched. One officer was told to shadow me wherever I went: he was outside the bathroom as I showered, on guard outside the bedroom as I dressed. An officer rifled through every possession in every room: first floor, second floor, third floor, loft. Dozens of large polythene bags were being filled with unwanted possessions from KP: sentimental items given to me by the princess, gifts she had bought us, dresses, shoes, hats and handbags she had passed on to Maria, sentimental photographs, items she had entrusted to me, items she had discarded but which I couldn't bear to destroy. Precious memories and possessions were being bagged up as evidence, labelled as items that Paul Burrell had stolen from Diana, Princess of Wales the moment she was dead.

Not for the first time, I was losing control of a world I was meant to protect. The Memorial Fund had denied me a voice, and perhaps didn't want to attach any significance to my closeness to the princess. But now Scotland Yard was questioning the very thing that was sacred to me: my *duty* to the princess. The Fund may have thought I was emotionally handicapped but my devotion was never in question. Scotland Yard was rummaging through my home, questioning my loyalty.

Maria had to take her mother to an urgent hospital appointment. My niece Louise Cosgrove, who was then working as my secretary, turned in for work as usual at nine o'clock and walked in to chaos. Maria had got the boys off to school, having told them the police were 'carrying out certain checks'. I cannot remember seeing them that morning. Louise got on the telephone to speak to a legal firm. Shortly before ten, a solicitor, Andrew Shaw, arrived. He was a district judge who had happened to be the duty solicitor at his firm, Walker Smith & Way, in the centre of Chester. His support and no-nonsense approach, then his friendship, helped me survive that day, and for the next eighteen months.

I was at my desk in my office. An officer stood over me as I stared, in a trance, at everything around me: to my left on the wall, a photo of the princess wearing her blue 492 baseball cap; a 45 r.p.m. record of Tina Turner's single 'Simply The Best' signed 'Diana' – a fortieth-birthday present from the princess to Maria; to my right on the desk, a Lord Snowdon portrait of her in a pink, beaded gown. All I could hear was footsteps above, and the rustling of the police exhibits bags coming down the stairs. It was like witnessing a burglary in my own home.

Detectives had gone upstairs to pursue a hunch on the golden dhow, and they were finding what they considered to be a royal treasure trove that no servant should have: crockery, ornaments, photo-frames, clothes, photographs, paintings, CDs, handbags, hats, shoes, letters.

I heard a voice travel down the stairs: 'We're going to need more bags . . . MORE BAGS!'

'We're going to need a furniture van!' shouted another.

Good God, I thought, the children have been let loose in a sweet shop.

In the afternoon, I was arrested a *second* time. 'Mr Burrell, I'm now arresting you on suspicion of theft of the property we are finding in this search.'

Instead of receipts for the sale of a golden dhow, they were finding endless items with royal connections. Why that should have been a surprise was beyond me. Since the age of eighteen, I had only ever lived in palaces and castles where hard-working staff had received hand-me-downs, unwanted ornaments, generous gifts, discarded clothes. But Scotland Yard were oblivious. This was a royal find like never before. A servant caught red-handed, they thought. And they had only ever come in search of documentation relating to the sale of a dhow.

The random search went on from seven a.m. until eight p.m. My home was turned upside-down.

They found the writing bureau the princess had given to Alexander. Then they read its engraved plaque: 'Presented by the City of Aberdeen to HRH the Prince of Wales and Lady Diana Spencer on the occasion of their marriage on 29th July 1981'. Must be stolen, they thought.

They found an Indiana Jones bullwhip, which the princess had given to me, knowing my love of movie memorabilia. Then they read the attached documentation: 'Presented to HRH Prince of Wales at the première of *Indiana Jones and the Last Crusade* on 27th June 1989'. Must be stolen, they thought.

They found the biblical text I had read to the princess during the all-night vigil at KP, and thought it was stolen. The misunderstandings were endless, and the police were having a field day as they seized and bagged more than four hundred items.

I sat, crying, over my desk, shivering with fear. I had watched my world disintegrate and it was heartbreaking. In an instant, I knew –

even if no one else did – where it was all leading. At that point, I could see the consequences of raking over it all.

'What are they doing? They don't know what they're doing,' I cried to Louise.

Andrew Shaw came in to speak to me. He said I looked lost, and he was so concerned about my mental state that he called for the police surgeon. He duly arrived, noted my devastation but observed that I was 'fit to be detained'. All I could think about was that the detectives upstairs had no idea what they were opening up. There were secrets in that house that no one should know about. The princess's privacy was being compromised in the raid, which I was powerless to stop. Bundles of letters she hadn't wanted to be kept at KP were being scanned; sealed boxes I had taken from the palace for safekeeping in Farndon were being torn open. Strips of negatives were taken away to be developed and passed round. The police were ripping through the Boss's most personal items, and it was obscene. In my eyes, I had let her down by allowing them through my door. I have never felt so useless. So numb. So physically sick.

If the police were blind to the consequences of their actions, then I had never seen so clearly: the princess, Princes Charles, William, Harry . . . the Queen. The world I had been protecting was being dragged down a road to where exposure was inevitable: the police would make sure that my arrest, and the carloads of items they had seized, got maximum media exposure.

My devotion to the princess was not only being questioned in the course of a 'discreet' inquiry. It was going to be held aloft before the nation, doubted, then analysed. Everything I had stood for was about to be dragged into a humiliating, public arena.

'DI BUTLER ARRESTED' screamed the *Daily Mirror*, the following day, with a photograph of me being led into a police station in Runcorn. The humiliation was complete.

'You understand the charges that have been made against you, Mr Burrell?' asked the desk sergeant in the custody suite at Runcorn police station.

In that bare room, which was not dissimilar to a basement at Buckingham Palace, I didn't understand a thing as I began to empty my suit pockets on to the counter.

'Could I also have your belt, Mr Burrell, your shoelaces and your tie?' the sergeant added. Nothing that could form a ligature would be left in my possession. 'It is normal procedure, Mr Burrell.'

A female custody officer, with short, spiky blonde hair, then took my arm. 'Don't worry. I'll take care of you,' she said, in a Scouse accent. She led me down a tiled corridor to the cells. Kate Murphy's face was the kindest and warmest I had seen all day, after so many hours with the brusqueness of Scotland Yard.

Andrew Shaw was behind me, and the three pairs of heels echoed down the corridor. All around us, we could hear the other occupants of the cells shouting, moaning and banging. The fresh activity had roused them. We stopped when the officer faced a thick steel door. I could not believe what was happening as she heaved it open and I walked in. It was a soulless room, with bare, cream-painted stone walls, and one tiny square window. There was a stainless-steel toilet in the corner. 'I'm afraid we cannot offer you five-star cuisine. The food is microwaved, but I recommend the curry,' she said, with a reassuring smile.

When my solicitor had gone, urging me to be strong, I ate curry as my first meal of the day, out of a plastic container with plastic cutlery.

I tried to sleep but it was difficult to get comfortable on a 'bed' that was no more than a wide stone step. There was no pillow, no blanket. The 'mattress' was like one of those plastic mats gymnasts use.

The next morning, DS Roger Milburn returned. On instructions from Andrew Shaw, I said nothing to his volley of questions. Again, his curiosity seemed to focus more on the contents of a box, sensitive paperwork and a manuscript. It was almost as if the four hundred or so items taken from my house were a postscript to be addressed later. For five hours, I sat wondering what on earth was going on. Each time he asked me a question, I replied: 'No comment.'

Surely, this was a mistake. Surely when the Royal Family heard what had happened, this nonsense would end. When I was released on police bail, pending further enquiries, I honestly believed that somebody somewhere in the system – Scotland Yard, Buckingham Palace, Kensington Palace, St James's Palace, the Queen, Prince Charles, Prince William, someone – would realize there had been a misunderstanding. Gifts of royal provenance were in hundreds of royal servants' homes up and down Britain: sentimental symbols of time spent working for a senior royal. Gifts were an unwritten perk of the job, going back to George V's days. Everyone in the royal household knew it. Everyone in the Royal Family knew it.

But the silence was deafening.

16. Cloak and Dagger

'Paul, the eldest son would like to meet you,' said the voice at the other end of the mobile telephone. It was the discreet, household staff code-name for Prince Charles; 'the favourite son' was Prince Andrew, and 'the youngest son' Prince Edward.

In the weeks and months after my arrest the need for discretion was paramount. Twenty telephone lines of my closest family and friends were bugged, as documentation later proved. It was prudent, on a monitored telephone line, to use no names and keep the conversation deliberately vague.

After months of waiting, and wondering why the Royal Family had decided to leave me hung out to dry, the call came through to my house in Farndon on 2 August 2001. The well-spoken voice, ringing from London, was that of a trusted intermediary who had been in discussion with the most senior advisers to Prince Charles at St James's Palace. The wheels had been in motion for months. The go-between, who was acting on behalf of me and the palace, was caught between different sides who shared a deep concern about the implications of a potentially damaging, high-profile court case.

I didn't want to enlighten Scotland Yard about private issues concerning the Royal Family. I had wanted the chance to speak, privately and confidentially, to Prince Charles. To make him understand. To let him know the madness of what was happening. To make sure that he, William and Harry knew what a terrible mistake was being made.

One instructional telephone call had brought me hope. At long last something was about to happen, and it was going to happen at twenty-four hours' notice.

All I did was listen. 'A meeting has been authorized. What you should do is drive to Gloucestershire. You will be given further instructions once you've got there. The meeting will not be at the country house, it will be at someone else's house. The eldest son will meet you there. He is anxious to sort this out once and for all.'

After I had spent many months wallowing in self-pity, euphoria swept over me. Once Prince Charles had heard what I had to say, he would know my innocence. He would just *know*. For an entire spring and summer, I had been trapped in one of those nightmares when you are screaming to be heard but you emit no sound. Now the man who used to employ me, the father of the boys I had seen grow up, was going to do what no one from the House of Windsor had done since January. Listen.

It had taken several months to reach such an optimistic point.

The House of Windsor had made its first tentative, indirect contact within two weeks of my arrest. The media that had been camped outside my home had dispersed, and I was at home in Farndon when the trusted intermediary made his initial telephone call after starting discussions with Prince Charles's advisers. It was at a time when I was still trying to come to terms with the enormity of what had happened. He told me: 'The view which has been conveyed to me is that he believes his ex-wife's staff are being persecuted. You still hold a special place in the affections of his sons. There is deep concern within his family. It has been suggested that you write a letter to him, explaining why such property was ever in your house. This could be the first step towards sorting all this out.'

It was the last week of January 2001. The date is significant because, in the post-trial inquiry held by Sir Michael Peat into the conduct of the Prince of Wales's household in relation to my trial, the clear inference was that it was *me* who made all the approaches to St James's Palace, that I had made all the requests, in a cynical attempt to lay the foundations of a future defence. Indeed, in the absence of any further details, it was suggested that those approaches did not start until April 2002.

But the truth is that my telephone rang first. Not vice versa. It was my intermediary who, after one of many discussions about the case, relayed a message to me to pen a letter. That request came from the prince's deputy private secretary Mark Bolland, a shrewd aide whose loyalty to his employer was as strong as mine to the princess. Both he and the prince's private secretary, Sir Stephen Lamport, were fully up to speed with the police inquiry, and were acutely aware of the potential public-relations nightmare of a high-profile court case. But the suggestion that it was me making the approaches is not true. The truth was that it was *his* idea for me to write to Prince Charles, just as it would be his idea for me to write, in a similar vein, to Prince William.

Mr Bolland would inform Fiona Shackleton, the prince's solicitor, that he was in communication with me indirectly, but he could not divulge the identity of the intermediary who was running as a go-between on behalf of both sides. Prince Charles, it was clear in those early days, was keen to avoid a prosecution. I harboured faint hopes that he would know my innocence. But I also had a dilemma.

The constraints of the legal process – I had been bailed by the police – had taken from me the freedom to express myself candidly in any proposed letter. A full and frank explanation would be a defence in court, so any correspondence had to be carefully written. I sat in the Chester office of solicitor Andrew Shaw, and together we penned a letter outlining how my intentions had been honourable and my loyalty should not be questioned. I had wanted to say so much but, instead, it became a letter couched delicately in legal language. On 5 February it was in the hands of the intermediary. In time, he personally delivered it to Mr Bolland. My letter had arrived at St James's Palace.

It was, I thought at the time, the most important letter I would ever write, and would rescue me from a nightmare that made no sense. Prince Charles would understand, surely, when he read it.

> Your Royal Highness,
> I am most grateful for the opportunity to convey my thoughts to you concerning the recent situation . . . I have been bailed to return to answer further questions on 27 February.
>
> As you know, Maria, my sons and I received tremendous generosity from the Royal Family during our years of service. Specifically, we were given gifts by the princess and I was entrusted with confidences, both verbal and written. The police have taken from my home many gifts and items of sentimental value given to me by members of the Royal Family. Most sensitively, some material which was entrusted to me. There are also a number of 'family' items which, quite simply, I incarcerated firstly in storage, and then recently in my attic for

safe-keeping . . . I have not been charged with any offence at this stage.

It is terrible to be accused personally and publicly of dishonesty, and I cannot bear the thought of you, Prince William and Prince Harry thinking that I have let you, or the princess, down in any way. All I ever wanted to do was 'take care' of what I considered to be 'my world'.

Perhaps a meeting would help to resolve any misunderstanding and stop this sad episode escalating beyond control.

I remain Your Royal Highness' humble and obedient servant – Paul

It was a plea that fell on deaf ears, as would all my pleas for common sense over the following months.

My intermediary telephoned with news that made my heart sink. 'It doesn't tell him anything. It is not explanatory enough. I'm afraid the letter is not going to be forwarded.'

Mark Bolland had wanted to be enlightened. Instead, he had got a plea of innocence. The letter was returned to me, its envelope slit open. It had reached St James's Palace but had not, I was told, been seen by Prince Charles.

It was a missed opportunity – because when my trial ultimately collapsed, the prosecution said I had not told anyone of my intention to retain items from KP for 'safekeeping'.

But they could not have been more wrong. I had told the monarch in my meeting with her in 1997. I had told the heir to the throne in that letter on 5 February 2001. And in April I would send a letter to Prince William, the second in line to the throne, and that was certainly seen by royal eyes. I could not have made it clearer to a more powerful trio in the land. Yet no one listened. Indeed, no one *would* listen to me until my livelihood, health and sanity had been taken right to the wire.

On 3 April Sir Stephen Lamport, Fiona Shackleton and Sir Robin Janvrin, the Queen's private secretary, met at St James's Palace with the Spencers, Scotland Yard and the Crown Prosecution Service. One of the CPS officials made it clear that, if convicted, I would be sent to jail for five years or more. 'An aggravating feature would be the serious breach of trust,' the meeting was told. There was one

345

other interesting note taken that day: because the items found at my house were not the property of Prince Charles, the final decision over the continuance of a prosecution lay with the executors of the princess's estate. The Spencers were in the driving seat of the Scotland Yard express – and there was no prospect of them applying the brakes.

It didn't seem to matter that Lady Sarah McCorquodale and Mrs Frances Shand Kydd were oblivious to the lifestyle and generosity of the princess. All that mattered was their blinkered view: that Paul Burrell should have nothing more in his possession than a pair of cufflinks and a photo frame. He *should* be prosecuted. In having the executors on side, the police felt they were on a sure-fire conviction. The *real* family of the princess, those closer to her than her mother and sister, could have enlightened them because, unlike the Spencers, those friends knew the whole picture:

Lucia Flecha de Lima, mother-figure: 'The princess told me she entrusted private correspondence to Paul.'

Debbie Franks, astrologer to the princess since 1989: 'Diana considered Paul to be family.'

Rosa Monckton, sister-figure: 'The princess frequently gave gifts . . . she couldn't function without Paul.'

Lady Annabel Goldsmith: 'Diana said Paul was her rock . . . she talked to him like a girlfriend.'

Susie Kassem: 'Paul was the third person she trusted the most after William and Harry.'

Lana Marks: 'Diana told me that she gave Maria dresses and accessories.'

Even if they had asked the shoemaker Eric Cook: 'Paul and Diana were more like brother and sister than employee and employer.'

But Scotland Yard sat on the periphery and listened to the Spencers who, at the time of the princess's death, were not even aware of who her closest friends were. Detectives cast aside the need to get to the heart of the matter with the princess's inner circle when the first golden rule in any walk of life is 'know your subject'. Officers from SO6 didn't have a clue about Diana, Princess of Wales, in a case that revolved around her very world.

In the first two weeks of April, Mark Bolland made another suggestion to the intermediary: that I should now write a letter to

Prince William. The young prince was away on his gap-year travels but a letter, when it had been received at St James's Palace, could be faxed confidentially for his attention. On 19 April, I penned this letter to him:

> I so wish that I could have spoken with you in confidence during the past few months. There is so much to explain. Items which have been taken from me, many of which were given to me for safe-keeping, should be returned to you. I know that you realise that I would never betray the trust and confidence which your mother placed in me, and that I remain the person you have always known – Paul.

With that letter, I had again made clear my safekeeping role. So it baffles me that the prosecution case at my trial in October 2002 had proceeded, in the words of its counsel William Boyce QC, on the premise that 'Mr Burrell had never told anyone that he was holding anything for safekeeping.' Yet the CPS, the very institution Mr Boyce was representing, had seen my letter to Prince William eight-een months before the trial. One of its own lawyers, as the Sir Michael Peat inquiry made clear, '*said the letter reflected Burrell . . . trying to lay the foundations for a defence . . . and this letter may need to be exhibited*'.

The CPS had clearly read that letter, but come the time of my trial, they would claim not to have seen it.

The main thing for me was that I knew Prince William had read it. 'The letter was delivered. It has been effective this time,' my intermediary told me over the telephone. That letter would also be read by Prince Charles. As his solicitor Fiona Shackleton said in a meeting on 30 April: '*Mark Bolland got that letter written . . . we knew it was coming, someone told Prince Charles it was coming.*'

At that very meeting, which was attended by both the CPS, Scotland Yard and Lady Sarah McCorquodale, the crucial question then arose, in the light of the letter I had sent, whether Prince William would lend his support to the prosecution. When Lady Sarah pointed out that she had the final decision, Fiona Shackleton '*said she did not want Prince William to move out of tandem with the executors, adding that it needs to be all or nothing*'.

Prince Charles had the opportunity there and then to vouch for me and confirm my bona-fides role as a safekeeper of the princess's belongings. He chose not to do so.

In his defence Prince Charles said that he made it clear that he would *'prefer it if the prosecution did not go ahead'*. He seemed to think it was enough to tell the muggers to back off while watching his former butler being beaten up in the street.

As his palace's own post-trial inquiry would later make clear, if it had been one of *his* members of staff, it would have been different. DS Milburn's recollection was that *'Sir Stephen Lamport indicated that the household would support a prosecution which did not involve an employee of the Prince of Wales's household: the implication being that there might be less enthusiasm if a member of that household had been intended to be prosecuted.'*

If it seemed that I was friendless in royal circles, then I was a pariah in professional terms. The telephone was suddenly silent – it had never stopped ringing since publication of *Entertaining With Style*. No one wanted to hear lectures from a butler accused of the biggest betrayal. No one wanted to employ me, even the charitable organizations that had asked me to do free after-dinner speeches. Only one company remained true: Cunard. How ironic that the company whose job-offer my mother had thrown on the fire in 1976 was the one who stood by me, continuing to employ me on the lecture circuit on the transatlantic voyages of the *QE2*.

But it didn't lessen the impact when the real blows came. For others who had hired my services decided to wash their hands of me post-arrest. The *Daily Mail* dropped me as household-management columnist in its Weekend supplement. It no longer wanted my advice on how to be the perfect host, guest or cook. Then the household-products giant Proctor and Gamble viewed me as a PR disaster. I had signed a lucrative television-advertising deal to promote its disposable Bounty kitchen rolls. A promotional photo shoot had taken place at a private house in London, and filming was due to begin. But its executives couldn't wait to wipe the Burrell stain from the company image. My arrest had apparently brought 'disrepute' to its door, and I was sent packing with a £20,000 fraction of the money they had been going to pay me. That, combined with our savings, would be enough to see us through until the end of the year.

God knows how much money I must have wasted on knocking back bottles of Merlot and Chianti at a time when we were supposed to be cutting back on luxuries. Maria had selflessly given up her treats, refusing to buy makeup. Then she got a friend to pay her by the hour to clean her house – she fell back on her royal-household skills. And I was falling into a more morose state with each new day, lying in bed until beyond eleven, then sitting at my desk doing nothing but thinking, and then in the sitting room, knocking back three bottles of wine a night just so that I would sleep.

I would wake at four, sit on the edge of the bed and peer through the curtains to see if any strange vehicles were in the street. I woke up sweating and fretting more times than I care to remember. I was convinced, for nearly two years, that Scotland Yard would come back. Even to this day, if a postman knocks on the door with a package, I am sent back to 18 January 2001.

I did nothing but wallow in self-pity. So, thank God for my wife's strength. Maria's strength, support and sacrifices had always been there: the time when she moved, against her true desires, to KP from Highgrove; the constant occasions when she 'lost me' to the princess; the years when she had brought up our boys while I did my duty; or when I lived away from home to work for the Memorial Fund. I only woke up to her remarkable support when I was at my lowest. During the years when the princess had been leaning on me, I had been subconsciously falling back on Maria. Forget the fact that the princess called me her rock. The only rock, in all that time, had been mine: Maria. She pulled me out of my despair, and took those wine bottles away on so many nights.

'Look!' she would say. 'Stop feeling so bloody sorry for yourself. There are two boys upstairs who need you to be strong. They don't need to see you falling to pieces. You have responsibilities here as well.'

'But I can't cope with it!' I would scream.

Then Maria would pick up one of the many photographs of the princess and yell back, 'You chose *this* path. Now you have to get on with it. So get on with it – like I'm having to get on with it. She had you by the balls in her lifetime, and she's still got you by the balls now!'

For so long, Maria had wanted to move on, but I was happy to remain in 1997 with the ghost of the Boss. Her photographs were everywhere, in every room, and that made me feel better. Even when she had been dead for four years, I was still putting her before my family.

In October 2001, Scotland Yard pounced again and arrested another 'suspect' – my brother Graham. As before, it was a dawn raid, and the Special Inquiry Team officers searched his house high and low. He was arrested and taken away for questioning on the basis of a signed photograph of the princess, two plates bearing the royal cypher, a naval painting of HMS *Sirius*, and a framed print of a polo match. The paintings had been gifts to me from Prince Charles, which I had given to Graham when I had been living at Highgrove. We even had a photo showing that HMS *Sirius* painting on a wall at the cottage, hung there in 1994. But Graham was dragged away on suspicion of handling stolen goods in 1997.

Graham, like me, attempted in vain to educate the officers about the royal world, and the kindness of the Boss. He told them how he had chased her around Highgrove having water-balloon fights and how she had rung him three times at home to console him over his marriage difficulties.

He might as well have told them he had just landed from Mars.

'And what would an ex-miner be doing mixing with a princess exactly?' scoffed one of the detectives.

Graham was never charged but his ordeal of waiting, of being under suspicion, lasted ten months before the police realized they had no evidence against him. But I was condemned as a royal outcast.

In late May I was out shopping in Chester when the mobile rang. 'You'll never guess what's come in the post,' squealed Maria. 'An invitation . . . to Windsor Castle!'

When I arrived home, it was on the kitchen worktop: a white envelope bearing the seal of the Lord Chamberlain's office in St James's Palace. Inside, there was a gold-edged, stiff card invitation with 'EIIR' embossed in gold. It read: '*The Lord Chamberlain has been commanded to invite MR AND MRS PAUL BURRELL to a service of thanksgiving at St George's Chapel, followed by a reception at Windsor Castle, to celebrate the 80th birthday of HRH the Duke of Edinburgh.'*

Maria was so excited, and I was thrilled for her. The duke had thought to invite his former maid to the event on 10 June. It was ostensibly for Maria, but the kindness had been extended to me, too. It wasn't just the recognition of his consideration that brightened our day, our week, our month, our year, it was that we had been invited when we had felt that everyone was against us. No one will ever know how much that lifted our spirits at a time when I was still on police bail and not charged. Letters to Prince Charles and Prince William had passed without acknowledgement, and that had hurt. I had been clinging to a fading belief that, if there was justice, common sense would prevail and the madness would end. After all, in my mind all I had done was take care of someone in life and in death. Was that such a crime? I didn't expect people to understand, but neither did I think that devotion was illegal. So, when that envelope arrived, it didn't just bring a rather posh invitation, it brought hope, and a hand of friendship from the Queen and the Duke of Edinburgh. Maybe it would mark the turning point.

Then the telephone rang on 6 June – my forty-third birthday. A rather pompous, grand, military voice asked to 'speak with either Paul or Maria Burrell'. It was a Brigadier Hunt-Davis, private secretary to the Duke of Edinburgh, and our former neighbour from the Old Barracks. He got straight to the point. 'After a great deal of deliberation, and after taking considerable advice, I have come to the conclusion that it would not be in your best interests, Paul, to attend His Royal Highness The Duke of Edinburgh's eightieth birthday celebrations this forthcoming Sunday.'

The silence of my disbelief encouraged him to continue.

'We have had a great deal of inquiries regarding your attendance and, as the media are going to be present, it would not be fair to detract from what is essentially His Royal Highness's day. I am sure that you understand that this decision was not taken lightly, and was taken with everyone's best interests in mind.'

Shock made it hard for me to say more than a few words. Or maybe the pompous voice had intimidated me. I put down the telephone after an awkward goodbye, and stood in the second-floor sitting room, staring out of the window, replaying the conversation.

No, I thought, the Queen and the Duke of Edinburgh had invited me. Regardless of this aide's advice, I would go. I had nothing to be ashamed about. I picked up the telephone and dialled Buckingham Palace. I told Brigadier Hunt-Davis: 'I have thought about your advice, and am still intending to attend the birthday celebrations on Sunday with Maria, but thank you for your concern –'

'Paul,' he interrupted, 'you don't understand. *Your* invitation has been withdrawn. You are no longer invited.'

Now anger replaced shock. 'And what would happen if I decided to attend, and brought along the invitation?'

'You would be refused admission,' he said, 'and that would be rather embarrassing for you and the Royal Family. I feel sure that you would not wish to put them in that position.'

Then he offered the most breathtaking olive branch, which, I think, was intended to mollify me. 'But if Maria wants to attend, she is, of course, still invited,' he said.

I couldn't wait to slam down the receiver. When I told Maria, I don't know who was more angry: me or her. 'Right!' she said. 'If that's how they want to treat you, stuff 'em,' and that was that. Another wound to add to our collection.

We knew immediately that the late decision had nothing to do with Her Majesty. It was the 'grey suits' of the household, who act in what they believe to be the best interests of the Royal Family. It is a discretion that gives many of them rather odd delusions of power as they attempt to keep the wheels of the system rolling along. Eventually I discovered who was behind the withdrawn invitation: it was the Keeper of the Privy Purse, Sir Michael Peat – the man who would lead the Royal Family's inquiry into the collapse of my Old Bailey trial. He had spotted the name 'Burrell' on the guest list, and had queried the invitation with the brigadier.

I also know with certainty that the decision was taken without consultation with the Queen. She had privately made it clear that week that she had been looking forward to seeing both Maria and me again. In Her Majesty's eyes, someone is innocent until proven guilty and she saw no complication in the Burrells being invited to a function, especially since I had not been charged at that point with any offence. It is another frustrating example of a system that is full of people who think they know better than the Queen; the same suits who suffocated the spontaneity of the princess.

When Prince Charles learned of what had happened to me, I heard that he had expressed his disgust. His point was that my name had been on that guest list for at least four weeks without objection, so what had changed? He was as nonplussed as his mother, but the household had ensured that my attendance was stopped.

On 24 July, the intermediary brought together the prince's deputy private secretary Mark Bolland and me. Again, it was Mr Bolland who had made the contact to ask if the rendezvous could be arranged in London. Subsequently, the intermediary and I travelled by tube to Covent Garden station on the Piccadilly line. We turned left through the crowds and walked to the front of the Garrick Club. Mr Bolland was waiting near two telephone boxes in the street outside an office of Channel 5. The three of us began to walk down towards St Martin's Lane, heading in the direction of Trafalgar Square.

As we approached the entrance of the Duke of York's Theatre, Mr Bolland's mobile telephone shrilled in his pocket. He answered it. It was clear whom he was talking to.

'Yes, Your Royal Highness . . . Yes, he is with me right now . . . Yes, of course I will . . .'

It was Prince Charles. It was clear that he knew the meeting was taking place.

The deputy private secretary, who continued to walk and talk, was listening intently. 'Yes, sir . . . and good luck with the Prime Minister, sir.'

By then, our walk had taken us down the length of the street, past the London Coliseum, and to a corner where the doorway of the Corney and Barrow pub seemed to be the most inviting venue. It was shortly before three p.m.

'I remember when I used to have informal chats like that with the Prince of Wales,' I told Mr Bolland, and he smiled knowingly. We got some drinks in, and sat on high stools around an elevated table in the window, no doubt looking like a trio of businessmen enjoying an afternoon drink in the middle of a hectic day. It was certainly a formal, businesslike conversation.

Mr Bolland said that both William and Harry were upset over what had happened, and that Prince Charles 'was keen to resolve this situation'. He added: 'The Prince of Wales is very concerned about you. He feels you have been out in the cold too long. But we need to know why you were in possession of the property the police found at your house.'

I told him what I had told my solicitor: that the items were either in safekeeping, my own, or had been given to me by the princess or the prince. I added: 'This is a big mistake. It shouldn't be happening. It is ruining me and my family and I do not understand why I have been arrested. If this continues, it is going to open a real can of worms. I need to meet the Prince of Wales to explain everything.'

We were in that wine bar for thirty or forty minutes. Mr Bolland talked as much as I did. Which is why I find it strange that he later described the meeting as '*Paul Burrell giving me a sob story in which he stated his life was in tatters.*' If it was the sob story he claimed it had been, then it was a sob story that had an effect: Mr Bolland was accommodating, not dismissive. He shook my hand, and departed after making clear that he would recommend to the Prince of Wales that he himself should meet with me the following week.

True to his word, Mr Bolland organized a meeting in Tetbury, near Highgrove. My intermediary called me on the mobile on 2 August with the words: 'The eldest son would like to meet you.' The rendezvous was set for the following day.

As the post-trial palace inquiry made clear, Prince Charles believed that '*if Mr Burrell apologized and confirmed . . . his earlier letter to Prince William . . . and agreed to return all the property and promise not to reveal information personal to the princess, it might be unnecessary for the police to charge Mr Burrell*'.

It was decided to keep Fiona Shackleton and Scotland Yard in the dark about the meeting.

As back-up, my brother Graham joined me on the journey south in my car. We set off at six a.m. on 3 August, with a flask of tea and some sandwiches. It was a warm, sticky day worthy of shorts and a T-shirt but I had to look my best in my smartest grey suit, worn with the blue D cufflinks that the princess had given me. I had no idea of the exact location of the meeting. All I knew was that it was going to be held after Prince Charles had finished a game of polo.

He had personally requested that it take place away from Highgrove to avoid the prospect of me having to pass through the permanent police security. We seemed to be travelling for an age, and had passed the county boundary for Gloucestershire on the M5 when the mobile telephone rang. It must have been some time around noon.

It was the voice of the intermediary. 'It's off. He's had an accident.'

With a sinking heart, I pulled the car into the next petrol station. 'You have got to be joking!'

Prince Charles had been playing polo when he fell off his horse and was knocked unconscious. He had been taken to hospital and, after a near five-hour journey, I had to turn the car round and drive back to Cheshire. 'Well, that's it, then. There's no stopping it now,' I said to Graham. All I could think was, How very convenient that a fall from a horse has stopped him making the meeting.

In time, my suspicions were further aroused. For on the morning of 3 August *before* the polo match, both DCI Maxine de Brunner and Commander John Yates of Scotland Yard had visited the prince and William at Highgrove to provide a briefing about the case. It was a briefing that included a gross misinterpretation of the facts – and one that had hoodwinked Prince Charles and his son into doubting my innocence.

On 8 August, the police moved in to ensure that no more clandestine meetings could take place between myself and St James's Palace. DS Milburn took a signed witness statement from Mr Bolland, which made him a prosecution witness. As such, it would make it very difficult for him to have any further contact with me.

As the post-trial inquiry by Sir Michael Peat concluded: '*The police candidly told me that their obtaining of this statement . . . was Machiavellian. By this device, they sought to inhibit or prevent further contact between Mr Burrell and Mr Bolland.*'

Scotland Yard had misled Princes Charles and William, and had ensured that all lines of communication were severed. They were going to drag the case kicking and screaming into court, and the blinkers that they were wearing were going to keep them focused on the job in hand.

On Thursday 16 August, I returned for more questioning to West End Central police station in London. With my solicitor Andrew

Shaw at my side, I took with me a prepared statement. Over thirty-nine pages and in twenty-six lengthy paragraphs, I detailed the closeness of my relationship with the princess, explaining why certain items had been in my possession, enlightening them about the trust placed in me. It was intended to be my final plea for common sense. From behind the sober legal language, a hysterical voice was shouting back at the police to stop, read and understand the damage they were about to unleash.

'This is the statement we would like to present to you,' Andrew Shaw announced, pushing it across the table in the interview room.

DS Milburn left the room to read it. Within one hour, their minds were made up. 'Mr Burrell, we are going to charge you with three counts of theft.'

My stomach lurched.

Charged with stealing 315 items from the estate of the late Diana, Princess of Wales.

Charged with stealing six items from Prince Charles.

Charged with stealing twenty-one items from Prince William.

All accusations based on a belief that, some time between 1 January 1997 – eight months before the death of the princess – and 30 June 1998, I had thieved a furniture-van load of royal items from Kensington Palace.

As DS Milburn charged me, it wasn't sinking in. Why is the Royal Family letting this happen? What on earth is going on? What the hell have I done to deserve this? were among the thoughts racing round my head. Then the detective sergeant sat opposite me across the table and his words hit me like a sledgehammer: 'I believe you have stolen everything, and in twenty years in the police force, this must be one of the largest breaches of trust I have ever encountered.'

But it was clear that he had read the prepared statement because I had spoken about the various personal relationships the princess had had, without naming names, as illustration of my knowledge and closeness. 'So, was *your* relationship with the princess purely professional?' asked DS Milburn. It seemed that even police curiosity couldn't be satisfied.

As I was led down a corridor and into another room, I turned to Andrew Shaw, trying not to cry, and said: 'I cannot believe it. I cannot believe it.'

A doctor told me to open my mouth. A lollipop-like stick was scraped along the inside of my cheek to take a DNA swab. In another room, my fingers and thumbs were pressed against an ink roller for prints. Then I was told to stand against the wall to pose for the camera: right profile, left profile, full face. Three flashes that captured my despair on camera. I felt like both a freak and a criminal; the infamous star of a royal peepshow that had the police rolling around and laughing at me.

One police flashbulb turned into a blinding floodlight the next day as the first act of this Scotland Yard farce was played out on the steps of Bow Street Magistrates' Court. As a bewildering scrum of media and police shuffled me into that building, I kept my head down. I didn't see the fist that connected with the right side of my head. I just felt the stinging blow it left on my ear. A member of the public had run in from the street and thrown a punch.

'Just keep walking, Paul,' shouted my brother Graham, doing his best with the police to fend off the crowd around me. It dawned on me that some people had already made up their minds that I *had* looted the princess's world, and public hatred would follow. But first would come the humiliation. You cannot help but feel like a criminal, no matter how innocent you are, when you sit in the dock of the court. I couldn't wait for the formal procedure of that first hearing to be over with. There is nothing like a legal arena to ram home the enormity and reality of a situation that has, until then, seemed horribly surreal. The innocence I had been clinging on to for so long was replaced by an overwhelming feeling of shame. This is what a dock does to you. It dresses you in shame, and prevents you looking up to see who is staring.

Just to ensure that my humiliation was complete, the police press office decided to trumpet the full scale of the case against me. Ordinarily, only a summary of the charge would be revealed: the three counts of theft as they appeared on the charge sheet. But not this time. The press was handed the full, detailed breakdown of the 342 items taken from my home: each strip of negatives, and the precise quantity; each CD title, and its artist; each piece of clothing or fashion accessory, complete with its colour and design. It went from '*Item 193: Black leather handbag, white metal handles, contains Boots receipt, black plastic lighter and blue lipstick*', '*Item 3: one white metal pepper grinder'* to *'Item 240: Biblical text'* (the one used on the all-night vigil) and *'Item 245: notepad with details of mine victims'*.

On 30 August, Sir Michael Peat, who had been appointed as private secretary to Prince Charles, met with Scotland Yard and questioned the strength of the case. His own post-trial inquiry concluded: *'Sir Michael's principal concern was the possible adverse repercussions of this court case . . . He was also worried that this was not a strong case, and that there was a risk of acquittal. He believed the police evidence against Paul Burrell was weak.'*

Despite that concern, there was going to be no turning back. The Spencers wanted to see me walk the plank.

I flew out of the country the next day to find refuge with eleven members of my family on a pre-booked holiday to Florida. All around Manchester airport everyone was reading the front-page headlines about me. 'DIANA'S ROCK IN THE DOCK' screamed the *Daily Mirror*. 'Diana butler on £5m theft charges' said *The Times*. 'DIANA TRIAL SENSATION: Butler on theft charges after Highgrove summit' said the *Daily Mail*. When we arrived in our rented villa outside Orlando, the pent-up emotions of the previous forty-eight hours were finally released. 'Wept like a baby' is how my brother Graham described it.

I could escape the spotlight in Britain but I couldn't escape the hell. The mental pressure was indescribable. There seemed to be no room for rational thought, and I felt constantly agitated. I could hardly sit still, let alone relax, in the sunshine. I was losing my mind with worry, and the very fact I had been charged seared its mark into the personal pride that meant everything to me.

Desperate to ensure that the family enjoyed their break, I went along with them all to Disneyworld and the NASA Space Center, putting on a brave front.

Half-way through the holiday I collapsed with exhaustion. A blood condition meant that all the skin on my feet peeled away leaving them raw. I was treated in a Florida hospital. Doctors told me it was a nervous complaint.

By the end of 2001, our finances were in a parlous state. Both the bank manager and the accountant warned that if there was no income within the next three months we would have to consider remortgaging the house. Maria sent back her favourite aquamarine ring, a Christmas gift from me to her, to a London jeweller's in an attempt to raise some extra money. Things were becoming desperate, and we were running into arrears with our mortgage payments. If it wasn't for the generosity of friends, I don't know what we would have done: the Edwardses from Wrexham, the Wrights in Kentucky, Susie Kassem in London, and the Ginsbergs in New York. When Scotland Yard traced a substantial cash amount in our bank accounts back to the Ginsbergs, they went to interview them in their apartment on Fifth Avenue, believing that, perhaps, there was an ulterior motive.

'It's a bit excessive to give such an amount, isn't it?' they were asked.

'We are wealthy people, officer, we were helping a friend in need. What is so hard to understand about that?' The British police were sent away with a flea in their ear.

We also plundered Alexander and Nick's life policies, which we had taken out when they were babies. Eventually we scraped together enough resources to open a florist's shop in the neighbouring village of Holt. I used the floristry skills I had learned in the basement of Buckingham Palace, and my 'little shop on the corner' became a lifeline – not just financially: it gave me something to focus on. I am a proud man so I appeared strong to the many customers whose support was incredible. But when that closed sign flipped over in the window at five thirty each evening, I would sit in the back room, and refuse to go home. Maria had so often wanted me to be strong for the boys. I wanted to be strong. But I wasn't. So, crying my eyes out in that room was my release, hidden from the family because they had endured enough upset. If I cried by myself, no one need know. Yet, of course, Maria knew. Some nights I wasn't coming home until nine. I lied about having to carry out essential bookkeeping and stock-taking.

One night, the telephone rang. It was Maria. 'Chuck, when are you coming home?' I burst into tears yet again. It killed me to know that she was hearing me so weak. Some people grow strong in the face of adversity, but I seemed to be weaker by the day, and because I am not a naturally angry person, the injustice of it left me with nothing but a soul-crushing depression. Maria sent round my brother-in-law, Peter Cosgrove, and he found me in pieces. He just put his arms round me and said: 'Come on, let's get you home.'

Writing this, I look back and scold myself for being so pathetic. My perspective is different now – but only because justice prevailed. At the time, I was no good to anyone, and the irony of that was not lost on me. I had looked after and taken care of the emotionally needy princess, and soaked up all her despair and tears. As she had said, I often had the right answers in her most traumatic of times. Yet in my own trauma there were none.

In such a downward spiral, thinking straight is not a possibility. I was a hopeless father. A hopeless husband. I had been an ineffective protector of the princess's world against Scotland Yard. My reputation was going to be pulled apart in public. Everything I had ever cared about was, seemingly, being destroyed. At my lowest point, nothing seemed to matter apart from the prospect of being with the princess again. I wanted it all to end. I wanted to stop crying. I wanted to die. Then I would find her again. It was calculatingly selfish, but it is what I thought. I knew exactly where to go: a lay-by set back off the A41 in Cheshire. A quiet spot in the countryside.

I told Maria that I needed to deliver some flowers, and left the shop without even thinking about goodbyes. After a ten-minute drive, I pulled into the lay-by. Mine was the only car. The sun was shining. The sky was blue, save for wisps of white cloud. In the field beside me, a horse lowered its neck to eat the grass. On the passenger seat beside me there was a bottle of water and a little brown bottle containing sixty paracetamol. I sat there, looking at that horse, thinking what a beautiful day it was, that at least Alexander and Nick had Maria, and her family, who were our neighbours, would be there for them. They all had each other. I thought about all this. About Maria having the boys. Me being with the princess. About the finality death would bring to the court proceedings. About the way it would swiftly end the ordeal, and spare me the shame of taking the stand.

I had taken a sip of water and was looking at the unopened bottle of paracetamol in my hand, wondering if sixty tablets would be enough. Then, all the emotions welled up again, and disrupted the calm. Cowardice – or something – jolted me to my senses as quickly as the wind changed direction. Because I started to think about the finality of death in a different way. I would die as someone whose guilt had forced him into suicide. Maria and the boys would be left with that stigma. And the princess *was* still with me. It was her legacy that I had to defend. I threw the tablets back on to the seat, started the engine, turned round and went home to Maria. When I walked in through the door, Maria asked where the hell I had been.

Calmly, I told her the rationale behind my warped thinking.

She grabbed me by both arms. 'You have to think of me!' she said, shaking me. 'You have to think of me and the boys.' She must have looked into my eyes and seen nothing. 'Paul!' she shouted. 'You have to keep going. We all have to keep going. How would we cope without you?'

If ever there was a turning-point in the hell that was 2001 and 2002, it was perhaps that moment. Call it a sudden realization. Call it what you will. Maria made me seek help, and help made the hell seem bearable.

The doctor put me on a course of antidepressants. Maria persuaded me to see a counsellor. Every Monday morning, in a private room at the doctor's surgery, I sat and talked to a lovely lady called Jill. For the first time since 1997, I sat down with someone and confronted the loss of the princess.

Jill listened. I rambled on. I had bottled up so much. I had felt guilty, especially for Maria, that I had been unable to let go of the princess. For so many months I had believed I was going mad because the smallest thing set me off crying. Even as I offloaded my mixed-up thoughts to Jill, I suffered the excruciating embarrassment of crying in front of her.

But Jill was an immense source of comfort: 'Your behaviour is perfectly normal, Paul,' she told me.

It was as near to 'normal' as I was going to get for a while, and we moved into 2002, wondering what the year would bring.

Scotland Yard had made its 'Machiavellian' move to ensure that there would be no contact between me and St James's Palace, but it was powerless to do anything about other channels of communication with the House of Windsor. By the spring, I was maintaining contact with a senior member of the Royal Family, and the discreet support of this long-time ally of the princess proved to be a huge source of strength for me. In the biggest boost to my morale, I was told in a letter: '*I would shout your innocence from the rooftops if I could.*'

I had first written to the royal figure, expressing how '*totally trapped and alone*' I felt, and venting my frustration at how the '*police could not comprehend the world in which the princess lived*'. In knowing the princess, in knowing the workings of KP, this royal knew much more than Scotland Yard ever could. In my letters I asked for nothing. I wrote: '*Why have I been abandoned by the Prince of Wales and Prince William? . . . Surely someone must realize that 14 October* [the trial] *will unleash a media feeding frenzy, completely out of control . . . There is little I would ask of you, but to pray that there is justice.*'

What I received in response was a letter promising a lot more than prayer. This senior royal penned me the warmest of letters, and reminded me of the duties I had performed and the innocence that others believed in. Then, in the same letter, came an overwhelmingly generous hand of friendship: an offer of a secret bolthole that would provide accommodation for the duration of my trial at the Old Bailey; an address that would offer me both security and privacy. The proposal was that I should stay at a residence used by senior royals. My refuge would belong to the Crown Estate while I stood trial in a case brought by the Crown.

I was getting secret support from within the House of Windsor, and it was an enormous relief. Someone reminded me in a telephone call, around this time, that the Queen believed that any individual is innocent until proven guilty. All of this acted as timely support when solicitor Andrew Shaw and my defence barrister, Lord Carlile QC – the erstwhile Liberal Democrat MP – and his junior counsel Ray Herman were spending hours in legal conference with me, working on the minutiae of my defence.

I remember that my first explanation to Lord Carlile was that 'My life will seem stranger than fiction.' There were many times when the jaws of solicitor and both barristers hit the paper-strewn tables as I spent hours detailing the closeness I had shared with the princess. I was trusting these exemplary professionals with my life, having to explain aspects of a unique role in the shadow of the princess to clear my name.

'Your liberty is on the line, and if we don't know anything, Paul, we cannot help you,' said Lord Carlile. As my duty at KP unravelled, the legal team began to realize the level of trust that had existed between the princess and me, and how my work went beyond the call of duty and deep into her personal life.

Lord Carlile said: 'Your story is almost like a Shakespearian tragedy. It is a ticking time-bomb. I think we can be quietly optimistic about a successful result.'

The correspondence with the senior royal continued to act as a fillip. '*Your Royal Highness, I do not want to cause you any problems,*' I wrote. The kind, warm-hearted offer of accommodation remained. Until Sir Michael Peat discovered what had been proposed. He was informed in the late summer of 2002 about the invitation that had been extended to me. Aghast, he made his opinion quite clear: that such an arrangement would be wholly unacceptable in the circumstances, especially for a former servant without authorization to stay in such a property. An ally in the Royal Family had been forced to back down in the same way that the invitation to the Duke of Edinburgh's birthday party had been revoked. Royal hands were tied once more by the influence of a grey suit.

On both occasions that grey suit belonged to Sir Michael Peat. So I found it consistent that it was he, with Edward Lawson QC, who, at the end of my trial, was charged with the responsibility of leading the inquiry on behalf of the Royal Family into the circumstances surrounding the collapse of the Old Bailey court case. It was an inquiry with which I refused to co-operate. As Sir Michael Peat stated in his report: '*I do not know what, if any, views on the topic are held by Mr Burrell, who declined to be interviewed by the Inquiry.*' And he wonders why.

Actress Amanda Barrie, who had formerly starred in *Coronation Street*, then stepped in with a kind offer to share her accommodation in London. It was an overwhelming gesture but I opted to stay with old family friends in Hampton, near Richmond.

The best witnesses I could ever have called for my trial were the two remarkable women I had served, and who knew me best. One had died five years earlier, and the other was legally untouchable. For, in one of the many ironies of my case, the Queen is the Law. As head of state, she is the only person in the country who cannot be called to give evidence.

It is, I suppose, one of the hazards of the job when you have been a personal footman to Her Majesty, and end up being accused of theft from the estate of Diana, Princess of Wales.

Not that my hand was weak. Scotland Yard had prepared its *de facto* case, and it had the Spencers – Lady Sarah McCorquodale, Mrs Frances Shand Kydd and Lady Jane Fellowes – all lined up as key prosecution witnesses. Detectives, and it seemed the CPS, were happy to rely on the word of the executors to the princess's estate.

In my defence, I would rely on the word of the princess's innermost circle of friends, who were all prepared to take the stand and defend me: Lucia Flecha de Lima, Rosa Monckton, Susie Kassem, Lady Annabel Goldsmith, Lana Marks, Richard Kay, Lord Attenborough, Dr Mary Loveday, Simone Simmons, Debbie Franks, Jacques Azagury, Father Anthony Parsons, US attorney Richard Greene, Sir Jimmy Savile and numerous others, whom I will not list for reasons of discretion. They know who they are, and know how eternally grateful I remain to them for joining what I considered to be the most formidable list of witnesses. I also remain convinced that, had the jury heard what these people had to say, the transparency of the prosecution case would have crumbled before the jurors ever reached the deliberation room.

But the concern at St James's Palace was the likelihood of Prince Charles and Prince William being called by the defence as witnesses. Indeed, the CPS was so concerned about the prospect of me calling the heir to the throne and his son to the stand that its officials began to examine the possibility of hearing their evidence *in camera*. A prosecution document stated: '*We have every reason to think defence lawyers will seek to explore the private lives of Diana, Princess of Wales, HRH the Prince of Wales and HRH Prince William. It may be necessary to restrict who would be in court, and [explore] whether it will be necessary for the court to sit in camera.*'

At one point in February 2002, as was established by the post-trial inquiry, Commander John Yates of Scotland Yard had assured the anxious St James's Palace legal advisers '*that the prosecution would avoid their being called and going as far as to say . . . that the prosecution would be stopped [before the trial] rather than doing that*'.

It seemed that both princes were being constantly reassured that they would not be called as witnesses because the majority of the items on the charge list were the property of the princess. But Scotland Yard and the CPS seemed to miss the point. Prince Charles knew how much time the princess had spent at my cottage at Highgrove. He knew how often I had been caught in the crossfire of their marital breakdown. He knew that she took me everywhere with her, because that used to puzzle him. What he didn't know was that the princess had used me as her independent witness to history as it unfolded – the separation, the letters from the Duke of Edinburgh, the divorce – and all of that would have had to be examined to illustrate the true closeness I shared with her.

As for William, he knew better than anyone how close I was to his mother: he had seen me sitting with her on the sofa and had witnessed the rapport that went beyond the employer-employee relationship.

For those reasons, and because of the dire circumstances that had forced my hand, St James's Palace could have been in no doubt that, going into the trial at the Old Bailey, on 14 October, Lord Carlile QC would have stood in courtroom number one at some point during my defence and said: 'We call His Royal Highness The Prince of Wales.' Not since 1891 had a member of the Royal Family been called into a courtroom to give evidence. But 111 years later, history might have repeated itself.

17. Regina v. Burrell

One of the questions most asked about me is: 'What makes that Paul Burrell tick?' Some, perhaps, see my perception of duty as an unhealthy, obsequious obsession. Others, like me, prefer to view it as a duty born out of dedication to a devoted friend, one of the most inspirational women of our times. But on going into the Old Bailey trial, I knew the focus and fascination was always going to concentrate on the intricacies of my relationship with the princess.

The paradox of my life, and I know this, is that I was selfless in my role as a butler yet selfish in my others as husband and father. All I can say in my defence is that we meet few people in our lives who are capable of making such an indelible mark on our souls. The princess was a truly remarkable one-off. She afforded me the privilege first of entering her world, and then of giving me her friendship. It was not a gift to be relinquished: you hung on to it, cherished it and ran with it. The problem for some is that I'm still running with it, refusing to let go.

I have never been one for deep introspection or psychobabble. Depending on your viewpoint, my duty to the princess, in both life and death, will either be healthy or unhealthy. But unswerving loyalty to others is something that can be misinterpreted as well as misunderstood by anyone who lives outside palace and castle walls. When someone becomes dependent on another to function, as many royals do, then the need to be needed and the knowledge that you control can become almost addictive. The closer the relationship, the more addictive it becomes. In the end, the royal and the aide need each other in equal measure.

No one is supposed to be indispensable, and the princess certainly did a lot of dispensing with her staff. But, as she told friends who would have told the court, she felt she couldn't function without me. Her words, not mine. If I'm honest, I could not have imagined life not working for her, no matter how rough the ride became. I was as dependable to her as John Brown was to Queen Victoria; as

Margaret 'Bobo' MacDonald was to the Queen; as valet Michael Fawcett was to Prince Charles. I have never been unique or original in that regard. But if Scotland Yard couldn't comprehend the concept of being at home with the royals, the giving of gifts to servants or the trust reposed in certain staff, would a jury? Would the behind-the-scenes account of life with Diana, Princess of Wales, seem to ordinary citizens too far-fetched to be true? That was my worst fear as we prepared our case: that my defence would appear as real as an account of life from *Alice in Wonderland*.

In an attempt to get inside my mind and understand my way of thinking, my legal team sent me to lie down for five hours on a psychiatrist's couch in Beckenham, Kent. Even to this day, questions about my state of mind are asked. It seems to me that the best way of understanding me is to read the words of the expert who examined me: Dr Andrew Johns, of the South London and Maudsley NHS Trust. It saves me the introspection, and provides you with an independent voice. After a five-hour examination, he concluded:

> Paul spoke several times fondly of his wife, and of her strong support for him. In relation to his relationship with Princess Diana, he told me that he had 'far more respect' for her, saying that 'she trusted me more than any other man'. He argued that his relationship with his wife Maria was 'in a different compartment'.
>
> The professional relationship between Mr Burrell and the princess became one of considerable closeness. She appears to have greatly relied upon him . . . He appears to have been responsible for much of her daily care and, also, companionship . . . The key features of their relationship were as follows: she appears to have confided in him to marked extent; he would console her when necessary; when she was on holiday, she would phone him on a daily basis; she discussed with him her personal problems, showed him her personal correspondence, and trusted him to make occasional arrangements to see her male friends . . . Mr Burrell derived considerable self-esteem from her intimacy and friendship, and appears to have been devoted to her care, to the extent of spending less time with his wife and sons.
>
> In my opinion, the death of Princess Diana in August 1997 had an overwhelming impact on Mr Burrell . . . he saw her traumatized body a number of times . . . The impact of these events was increased when

he received a bag containing the clothes and personal effects that the princess had been wearing when she died. Mr Burrell developed a range of psychological symptoms and behaviours. His initial response was of helplessness, and he functioned almost automatically. He slept . . . with recurrent nightmares . . . He cried uncontrollably, and felt low in his mood. He meets diagnostic criteria for a prolonged depressive reaction. It is not inappropriate to suggest that his emotional state was such that he has 'entombed' important memories and items of the princess.

In my opinion, Mr Burrell does not . . . show signs of material mental illness, or personality disorder. He is of normal intelligence.

I was declared fit to stand trial in the Old Bailey on Monday, 14 October 2002.

'*Forget the West End theatre, and take yourself to the Old Bailey to see the greatest show in town,*' heralded one newspaper.

The royal freak show – the case of Regina v. Burrell – was about to begin in London's central criminal arena. Even the press would get access by a ticket system, and almost fifty yellow media passes were issued. Outside, the queues stretched the full length of the building as the public lined up for entry into the public gallery, which looks down on the courtroom. The world had its eye pressed against the keyhole of Kensington Palace, a sneak viewing brought to them courtesy of Scotland Yard and the Crown Prosecution Service. From that moment on, a protected privacy would be exposed. My life, and that of the princess, would be open to close scrutiny, speculation, doubt and ridicule. In writing this book, I continued to protect the darkest, most intimate secrets. But the truth of life at KP, and the essence of my relationship with the Boss, is intended to correct the distortion and wild claims peddled by the prosecution, the police and, at the end of the case, by poisonous newspapers, speculative royal commentators and embittered ex-staff released from the employment of the princess. In the end, there seemed to be a stampede to turn me into an unreliable historian. From the outset, my word, my life, my account of history – and therefore of the truths the princess entrusted to my care – were going to be dragged through the mud.

On the eve of the first day in court, I stayed at a budget hotel near

Euston station. A mini army of family and friends arrived in London to support me and Maria. As we pulled up outside the Travel Inn, I noticed a huge BBC advertising billboard suspended above the pavement on the hotel wall. A giant smiling face of the princess, looking her glamorous best, stared down on us as a question asked: 'Who is the Greatest Briton?' Sometimes, even when I am not looking for her, there is no escaping the Boss.

A journalist friend joined us all in the bar that night, and I needed several pints of Guinness to calm the nervous shakes that the mere prospect of appearing in the dock had brought on. Maria chain-smoked as we sat in that room, bracing ourselves for the next day's media circus.

Solicitor Andrew Shaw ensured that a smart, chauffeur-driven Mercedes would take us to the court, followed by a minibus full of equally apprehensive but faithful supporters. In the back of that car, I can't remember anyone saying a word. Maria and I just gripped each other's hands. Andrew and junior counsel Ray Herman were lost in thought in the front seats. In that silence, as we neared our destination, I began to feel unwell. My mouth was dry, and every vein seemed to be throbbing.

We travelled up Ludgate Hill, with St Paul's Cathedral in the distance. It was the same route I had taken on a state procession with the Queen to attend the Queen Mother's eightieth-birthday thanksgiving service, but this time we would never reach the cathedral. We turned left, passing the Crown Prosecution Service offices on the corner. As the car straightened up, I could see a crowd milling in the distance. Within seconds, it had become more distinct. It was the media. Dozens of them. Television crews running across the road with cameras on their shoulders. Two separate groups of photographers stacked high, all of them crouched, kneeling, sitting or standing on small metal step-ladders. There were radio reporters, newspaper reporters, hangers-on, crowd barriers to hold them back, police to keep order. Maria clenched my hand tighter. As the Mercedes pulled into the kerb, I looked to my left and noticed a makeshift platform supported by scaffolding. It was the BBC camera point opposite the court's main entrance. Maria and I began to shake almost in unison.

'Come on, let's get this over with,' I said.

'Good luck, everyone,' said Andrew, and got out to open the rear passenger door for us. I took a deep breath, swallowed hard and waited a few seconds.

'*Arrivals and departures, Paul. Arrivals and departures . . .*' I heard the princess say.

Then we were out and on to the pavement. The first thing that hit me was the sound of the camera-shutters; a rapid chorus of fluttering as if a thousand birds had been startled from a tree. Then the flashbulbs. I stood beside Maria, and put an arm round her waist. She did not let go of my hand. Two policemen held open a door as Andrew and Ray Herman ushered us inside. It was horrible to know that Maria was enduring the ordeal but she had insisted on being by my side. As we got inside, she turned to me: 'You are my husband. I am standing beside you, no matter what.'

'Paul!' boomed a voice. 'How are you?' A friendly hand was thrust out to me. It was James Whitaker, the royal correspondent of the *Daily Mirror*.

'I've felt better, Mr Whitaker, but thank you.'

I always called him Mr Whitaker, even though the princess referred to him affectionately during tours as the Red Tomato. Then, on a corridor, I spotted the BBC's Nicholas Witchell, another of the court correspondents' true gentlemen, 'Carrot top', as the princess called him. But the first face I had looked for wasn't there. The BBC's Jennie Bond, long admired by the princess, was covering the Queen's tour in Canada. 'Look out for the ankle bracelet she wears!' said the princess. She was fascinated by it.

When it came to keeping abreast of the media, the princess never missed a trick. She knew everything about them: those she loathed, those she liked, those she knew found the royal pressure a bit too much. All of a sudden, the eyes who had followed the Boss around the world were now glued to her butler.

As the building's clocks ticked towards ten a.m., we took the lift to the second floor, and I followed the flowing black cloaks in front of me as my defence counsel Lord Carlile and his junior, Ray Herman, led the way, wigs in their hands. We walked from the more modern end of the Old Bailey, and through some double doors into the Victorian, marble-lined area outside the primary courts where several defendants and their legal teams stood in huddles, or sat on oak benches. It reminded me of the Natural History Museum. Large murals reminded me of the Titian paintings the princess had hung in KP. Daylight poured through the glass of the huge dome above us all. I craned my neck and read the words inscribed into the curved stone: 'The law of the wise is the fountain of life.' Gathered around the glass-panelled door of courtroom number one, reporters – from as far away as America and Australia – huddled in a tight, impatient group.

'Don't worry,' said Lord Carlile, as we walked to the door. 'Today is all about formality, and the jury being sworn in. It takes a while for the actual case to begin.'

I took my first steps into the courtroom: with its oak and the green-leather cushioned seats, it mimicked the House of Commons. The glass-shielded box of the wide, square dock would be my working base for the next two weeks. Maria walked with my dad to a relatives' seating area on the right. I walked to the dock, the seat for murderers, rapists and armed robbers.

A female security guard politely stopped me taking my seat. 'Mr Burrell, you will have to come downstairs with me,' she said. It was protocol, apparently: defendants should not be seen in the dock until the judge has entered the courtroom. Early in the case, Mrs Justice Rafferty dispensed with this formality.

Behind me, a small flight of steep steps led into a white-tiled cell. Once I had disappeared from view, the blue-jumpered guard stopped me. 'You're okay there. Just stay here with me,' she said, and we sat on the bottom steps. It was as if she had wanted to spare me the prospect of going into the cell. She saw my hands trembling. 'You'll be all right, you know,' she said. 'I've sat in here plenty of times. I asked to do this case because it was you . . . and I've got a funny feeling about it.' Her name was Michelle, and I shall never forget the sensitivity and kindness she showed me.

The chattering in the packed courtroom above was silenced by three loud knocks. Mrs Justice Anne Rafferty had entered. Michelle nodded to me. I walked up the stairs and took my seat. Eyes pierced me from every direction. Above me to my right, the public sat forward to get their first glimpse. Behind me, obscured from the judge's view by the dock, the media sat on three stepped rows of benches. In the left corner, a huddle of other reporters squeezed into the spill-over press benches. In front, Mrs Justice Rafferty stared

371

straight ahead. To the left, facing the counsel benches, were the empty oak benches where the twelve jurors would sit. Their eyes would take in everything: me, secrets, sensitive documents, the memories and hundreds of photographs of the Boss, William and Harry.

I was asked to stand as the indictment against me was read out as offences contrary to the Theft Act 1968. My legs went to jelly, and I tried to hold myself bolt upright. I had this feeling that, at any moment, I would topple over. I was a nervous wreck.

Count one: theft from HRH the Prince of Wales. Count two: theft from the estate of Diana, Princess of Wales. Count three: theft from HRH Prince William of Wales. In the formality of the Old Bailey, it all sounded so much worse than it ever had in the magistrates' court. To each count, I replied, 'Not guilty,' and I looked down to the right and saw Maria suppressing tears on my dad's shoulder as the jury was sworn in.

One thing had changed in the preceding months. The 342 items I was initially charged with had been whittled down to 310, but it was no reason for optimism. The jury only needed to conclude that *one* item had been dishonestly in my possession to be sure of my guilt. The prosecutor William Boyce explained that such a collection of royal items was something 'someone just should not keep and should not have'.

I was determined to hold myself with dignity at all times. Andrew Shaw had reminded me of the don'ts of being a defendant in the spotlight – he'd sounded like Cyril Dickman on my first ever royal duty at Windsor Castle. 'When you are in there, don't stare at the jury, don't fidget, don't pass too many notes to us, and don't let them get to you.'

What no one could see below the ledge of the dock was that I was constantly rolling two little quartz crystals between my fingers. I had borrowed them from Nick's collection; a reminder of the energies the princess relied on. I truly believed, throughout every day of those mentally draining proceedings, that both the princess and my mother were with me.

Beneath my shirt, my mother's engagement ring hung on a chain round my neck. In my right-hand trouser pocket, I kept my hand on Mother Teresa's miraculous medal, which the princess had given me after the trip to the mission in London with Maria's mother.

It was hard to listen to Mr Boyce detailing the layout of my house and the contents seized from it. He went on and on: 'Cool and calculating decision . . . What were these items doing in his house? . . . Mr Burrell's varying explanations are not consistent . . . Pause to consider the potential value of one autographed CD . . .' I wanted to scream. I had far more potentially valuable items in my house than a Michael Jackson or Tina Turner album that the princess had signed – she always labelled them as hers; it was a habit from childhood. Whenever anyone visited KP and expressed a fondness for a particular record or song that the princess was playing on the stereo she gave it to them. Besides, Mr Boyce had missed the point. I had never, ever sold an item that had belonged to the Boss so the potential value he was asking the jury to consider was irrelevant. Its origin, the fact that it had been hers, was what was valuable to me.

It was more interesting to watch Mrs Justice Rafferty. She became mesmerizing, making copious notes, filling her fountain pen from a bottle of ink.

I wonder if it's blue-black Quink? I thought.

Then she would fidget with her blotting paper, wiping the nib dry.

Is she listening to any of this? Or is she bored too?

She fascinated me as she sat there in her scarlet robes and white wig. A lady who was the image of elegance. Far too glamorous to be a judge, I thought.

She walked in procession into court every morning and afternoon with an almost regal presence; and while her smile was warm, her icy stare demanded silence if the press behind me shuffled or chatted before she had adjourned.

I switched my focus on to the royal crest carved into the wood above Mrs Justice Rafferty. I read the words I knew so well: 'Honi soit qui mal y pense'. How ironic to be looking from a dock at the lion and the unicorn protecting the royal shield, encircled by the Royal Garter.

Maria was a witness for the defence so she wasn't allowed to stay in court. We decided she should return home to Cheshire and keep herself occupied by working in the flower shop.

My refuge would be the home of our friends Kevin and Sharon Hart – the first people we ever met after returning from Highgrove to London. Their Victorian terraced house in Hampton, near Richmond, was an escape each evening from the madness of the court and the publicity. Kevin and my niece Louise's husband Tom McMahon were my friendly shadows on alternate days of the trial. During that fortnight, strong friendships saw me through.

The evening of that first day in court we avoided the BBC and ITN news bulletins. The television was turned off as the prosecution's assassination of my character was aired and reported. I was sitting at a table with the nicest of families eating spaghetti Bolognese. Just being able to get away from the pressure was a mighty relief because, inside court, every expression and action was noted by someone.

'*Wearing his second natty tie of the week – another £65 Hermès creation,*' wrote James Whitaker in his column on day two, then, '*. . . and I sat opposite him in the canteen and watched him eat a healthy meal of moussaka . . . He copies Prince Charles in his dress sense . . . and his handshake is firm.*'

Daily Mirror reporter Steve Dennis conveyed to me the attitude in the press room: 'You are smiling too much, and looking way too relaxed – and it *is* being noticed.'

Relaxed! I had never felt such a nervous wreck in all my life, but it seemed not even a brave face was allowed. At least at the Harts' home, with their son Joe, then seventeen, and daughter Amy, nineteen, we could unwind with a bottle of Merlot and I could be myself without my moves being watched and analysed. If Kevin ever spotted me slipping into a morose state, he would leap up and say, 'Come on, then, let's go for a pint,' and we walked to his local pub, the Nag's Head.

'This is all so not fair, Kev,' I moaned.

'Paul, life never has been fair. You've just got to hang in there and be strong,' he said.

That first week, I received the most heart-warming letter from the Sisters of Assumption convent in Galway, Republic of Ireland. Sister Teresa, who had met the princess with Maria's mother, ensured that all the nuns prayed for me every day. 'Never underestimate the power of prayer, and we are praying for you,' said the letter. So many people seemed to be rooting for me. I received literally bags full of mail. My friends know that my feelings for that go beyond appreciation, but I have to mention Richard Madeley and Judy

Finnigan. For Richard, too, had once sampled the bitter taste of injustice when he was scandalously branded a thief in a Tesco store while he was a presenter on ITV's *This Morning*.

In the months and weeks before the trial, he wrote many letters of encouragement. Even when things were hectic at work, he found time to scribble notes of support on the back of his scripts. They gave me a massive lift. His insight was crucial. He wrote: '*It will seem as if you are in the eye of a storm, and everything is happening around you. I have been there. Let the legal process happen and do what we did: remain close as a family and be strong – Richard.*'

It was heartening to know that others were on my side, because William Boyce, in his clever articulation of the prosecution case, made everything sound so damning. I had been spotted sneaking into KP at three thirty one morning. The Spencers had told police that I should not have any royal property in my home. I hadn't told anyone that I was taking things for safekeeping.

But I had. I *had*. In a letter to Prince William in April 2001. What was wrong with these people?

I vented my anger and frustration in a little legal conference room on the first floor. This was our 'safe room' where exhibits and papers could be stored, and our discussions could take place away from the ears of the police and prosecutors. 'Let's go downstairs and discuss the day's events,' announced Lord Carlile, at the end of each day's evidence.

I had watched my QC at work in the courtroom with growing fascination, deftly mixing eloquent charm with a sharp legal brain and eye for detail. But he came alive, and ultimately kept me sane, in that small room, surrounded by crates of files and books.

Andrew sat at the table, sharing his thoughts as the man who had done all the initial groundwork on the case. Standing behind him was Shona, the clerk, who scribbled away on a back bench in the courtroom. Then there was me, squashed into a corner, wondering what all the legalese meant, remembering what Richard Madeley had said about it 'all going on around you'.

I lost count of how many times Lord Carlile exclaimed, 'It's absolutely ridiculous!' as we all became engrossed in the prosecution case, the way it was being handled, and the evidence we had never felt was evidence in the first place.

But no sooner had we become engrossed in a particular point than his humour would change the mood. His take-offs of the characters in the courtroom were a hoot, and I'm glad that, on occasions, we were able to be light-hearted.

Sometimes I would leave them to it and walk the corridors, pacing up and down, looking at the names of the defendants in other courtrooms, wondering if any more innocents were being made to look guilty too.

On day two of the proceedings, the farcical nature of the trial was summed up when someone spotted a plain-clothes policeman enter the room, flash his warrant card and sit down in the public seats. He caught the attention of a female member of the jury, and they acknowledged each other. When this rather curious connection was brought to the attention of Lord Carlile, the jury was asked to retire, Mrs Justice Rafferty asked that inquiries be made, and we were sent home for the afternoon. The following day, courtroom number one was startled by the findings of those inquiries. Scotland Yard's crack detectives were about to strike another blow for their staggering levels of common sense.

William Boyce was forced to explain that the plain-clothes officer, a detective inspector, had acknowledged his *wife* on the jury. It was their wedding anniversary and he had come into court to take her out for lunch. But it emerged that the officer had worked as a member of the Royal Protection Group between 1986 and 1989: he had been with the Royal Diplomatic Section, looking after foreign embassies. Not only that, but he had carried out his duties in the embassies neighbouring Kensington Palace. *And* he had served as a police officer in Peckham, London, in the early nineties with none other than DCI Maxine de Brunner, the senior investigating officer on my case. They had also worked together on a Metropolitan Police Service inspectors' promotion study group. The male officer now worked for the Special Branch.

I was dumbstruck.

'But DCI de Brunner's recollection is that she has not spoken to him in the last five years. She could not now put a face to the man,' explained William Boyce.

Lord Carlile was having none of it. 'If there is a police officer's wife who has an allegiance on that jury, then there is a danger of that allegiance being translated to other members of the jury. There should not be any connection on that jury to the Metropolitan Police.'

After a day of legal argument, Mrs Justice Rafferty agreed. The jury was discharged. The trial of Regina v. Burrell had to start again with a fresh jury of five women and seven men.

Even as the princess's world was spilling out into the Old Bailey, I was desperate to do what I could to protect her secrets. Secrets I did not want to be aired in court. Secrets that have not gone into this book. When I handed over my thirty-nine-page statement to police at the time I was charged, it was only ever intended to be an explanatory document, to be seen only by the trial judge, the barristers and the jury. There were sensitive paragraphs of the most personal nature, involving medical issues and her love life, which summed up my role and unique closeness to the Boss. I did not want them to be aired in open court before the press.

In the initial prosecution opening, William Boyce had allowed the first jury to read the contents quietly to themselves. As he pointed out: 'It is the defence's wish for relevant paragraphs not to be read out, and the Crown is content to accept that course.'

But the media was not. It challenged my request. Thankfully, Mrs Justice Rafferty agreed with us and, using her 'judicial discretion', she made a ruling that certain contents within the blue folders in front of the jury would remain confidential to protect Princes William and Harry. 'CENSORED', screamed the *Daily Mirror* the next day. 'AFFRONT TO JUSTICE.'

The media and defendants use the same door to exit the court. As we shuffled out that day, one female reporter turned to me and said: 'I've never known a case shrouded in such secrecy. You don't know what's going to happen next.'

DS Roger Milburn was in the witness stand, and Lord Carlile was pressing him to shed some light on what they had initially gone in search of when they raided my home. Documentation in relation to a golden dhow, said the detective.

Then my barrister kept pressing him, curious as to the contents of a box the police had kept asking for; the mahogany box with the initial D on its lid; the box in which the princess kept her most sensitive documentation; the box I was supposed to have removed from KP.

'So, what did you know about the alleged contents of this box?' enquired a curious Lord Carlile.

The press seemed collectively to hold their breath, pens poised.

DS Milburn hesitated. 'Great parts of this case are very sensitive,' he said, before looking to the judge and asking her: 'May I write it down on a piece of paper?' and Mrs Justice Rafferty nodded.

The press exhaled a sigh of frustration; all pens dropped on to paper.

Then the case was adjourned for the first weekend, prompting next day headlines of: 'DIANA'S SECRETS' and 'WHAT'S IN THE BOX?'

By the following Monday, the intrigue was over. The full picture emerged with the judge's approval. Scotland Yard was looking for a signet ring given to the princess by Major James Hewitt; a resignation letter from her private secretary Patrick Jephson; letters from Prince Philip to the princess; and a tape, which became known after the trial as the Rape Tape. It was a recording made by the princess in 1996 when she informally interviewed former KP orderly and ex–Welsh Guardsman George Smith. He had alleged that after a night of heavy drinking he had been raped in 1989 by a male member of staff who worked for Prince Charles. It all came to a head because George, who had worked at Highgrove, St James's Palace and KP, had been suffering nightmares, was drinking heavily, and his marriage was falling apart. He blamed it all on an incident that he said he was bottling up.

The princess was fond of George, and when he confided in her, she was appalled. Armed with a dictaphone, she went to visit him at a clinic where he was undergoing treatment for depression. She wanted his allegations on record. (George Smith has since waived his legal right to anonymity.) The Boss made the tape to protect the interests of someone she cared about, and she vowed to do something about it. In her eyes, he was the victim, and the perpetrator was still at large, working for her husband. She had placed the tape, without writing anything on its label, in the box where she knew its explosive contents were secure. But she was determined to make sure action was taken, so she rang Prince Charles, relayed the incident as it had been explained to her and begged him to sack the man in question.

She made the call in the sitting room at KP. I was beside her as an independent witness, and listened to every word. She was almost trembling with exasperation at her husband's lack of urgency over a situation she felt was criminal. 'Charles, are you listening to me? This man is a monster,' said the princess.

I only heard one side of the conversation, but it was clear that the prince had little time for what he saw as his wife's unnecessary hysteria. He told her 'not to listen to staff tittle-tattle'.

'You have to let him go. You have to do something.' Her pleas fell on deaf ears.

The princess knew the member of staff in question. From that moment on she loathed him. 'I know what that evil bugger did. I know what he did to George, and I will never forgive him for that,' she seethed, after her futile attempts to bring about justice.

Little action was taken. In October 1996 George Smith received a visit from royal solicitor Fiona Shackleton. The upshot was that the alleged rapist was not sacked, and George's stress and depression were put down to Gulf War syndrome. He never returned to work, and accepted a settlement at the end of his employment of around £40,000.

The princess ensured that the tape never saw the light of day. But the mystery of its whereabouts, and the threat its contents posed, emerged during the police investigation of my case. Lady Sarah McCorquodale had asked that Scotland Yard 'ascertain' the contents of the box. The princess had shown me the cassette tape, but she never gave it to me. After her death, both Lady Sarah and I noticed the blank-labelled tape in the box but it was not removed, and it was kept under lock and key. Only Lady Sarah and I knew of the key's location. But the lock was later forced and broken, said the police.

In court, DS Milburn said: 'I was looking for the contents of that box.'

All of a sudden, the undertones behind the raid on my home became clear.

DCI Maxine de Brunner took the stand, and everyone in court-room number one went, in their minds, to Highgrove on 3 August

2001, when she and Commander John Yates briefed Princes Charles and William about their investigation of me – before I had been charged.

According to the female detective's notes, and as the post-trial Sir Michael Peat inquiry confirmed, both princes were told that police had a 'strong case' because they *were in a position to show that Mr Burrell's lifestyle and finances altered drastically after the death of Diana, Princess of Wales*' and that '*police are in a position to evidence that large quantities of items have been sold abroad to several dealers*'. The briefing also explained: '*In addition, an independent source has shown police photographs of several staff members dressed up in clothing belonging to Diana, Princess of Wales at a party . . .*'

None of that was true, and DCI de Brunner admitted they did not have a shred of evidence, and never had, to support the claims that painted me as a thief who sold the princess's items around the world and dressed up in her clothing. God knows what my former employer and the boy I watched grow up thought of me.

A briefing that was intended to paint 'the full picture' had been riddled with falsehoods, because it was presumed that my financial status had improved because of the sale of royal items from KP. But my finances had improved because of my book, *Entertaining With Style*, and the lectures I had given to promote it. As an illustration of just how exhaustive and thorough the police investigation was, DCI de Brunner said she was not aware of the book I had written or the lectures I had done. She said the briefing was based on 'intelligence that we had gained'.

Then Mrs Justice Rafferty, who looked as incredulous as the rest of us, stepped in and asked: 'Is it right that you allowed the two princes to remain under that gross misapprehension?'

DCI de Brunner, who had not once corrected the wrong information she had imparted, replied: 'Yes, it is.'

Lord Carlile carried on: 'You do not think that the failure to correct these falsehoods was grossly misleading and unfair to Mr Burrell?'

DCI de Brunner: 'All I can say is, I didn't inform him of the changes.'

Lord Carlile: 'It would not have been difficult, would it, for you to telephone the solicitor to the Prince of Wales, Mrs Shackleton, and tell her that he had been given some mistaken information? You could have done that, couldn't you?'

'I could have done.'

'And you did not?'

'No,' replied DCI de Brunner.

In the post-trial inquiry of Sir Michael Peat, it was made clear: '*The Prince of Wales very clearly remembers the revelation relating to there being evidence of sales by Mr Burrell . . . strongly influencing his view.*'

Yet my legal team, because of the case papers we had seen, had tried, two months before the case began, to sound the alarm bells, bang on the palace doors, scream through the loud-hailers, and light the warning beacons. Short of putting up a giant neon sign outside St James's Palace with the words 'PLEASE WILL YOU LISTEN: YOU HAVE BEEN MISLED' there was little more we could do to grab the attention of the royal household.

On 20 August 2002, Lord Carlile met with Fiona Shackleton and her criminal-law specialist Robert Seabrook QC to warn them that '*The decision as to whether the Prince of Wales should support a prosecution had been taken on the basis of unsupported, false information . . .*' One month later, on 30 September 2002, Lord Carlile again met with Mr Seabrook. As the post-trial inquiry stated, Lord Carlile said: '*. . . The essence of the defence was Burrell's unique and very close relationship with the princess . . . their closeness was a ticking timebomb . . . and I suggested the case was a disaster waiting to happen for the Royal Family, and they had been deceived by the police at Highgrove.*'

Outside the door of courtroom number one, a piece of paper was stuck to a board, detailing the case being tried. It said 'Regina v. Burrell', which seemed a warped title for the truth. It wasn't the Queen or the Royal Family who had wanted to see me in that dock. The reality of the trial was that it was 'Spencers v. Burrell'. What had been a sound working relationship between a butler and the princess's family had broken down.

I had been told, by someone who knew the family, that the Spencers 'were sick to the back teeth of hearing how much that bloody butler was a rock to Diana'. In the Old Bailey, they had been offered the perfect chance by Scotland Yard to prove otherwise.

Mrs Frances Shand Kydd shuffled unsteadily into court, two steps at a time, aided by a stick. She was the picture of frailty. A gaunt old lady with white hair whose croaking, rasping voice made it sound like she was incapable of saying boo to a goose. As the jury took in that sympathetic image, I knew better. As she steadied herself into the wooden-framed witness stand, Mrs Justice Rafferty leaned forward to ensure that she was all right. 'Mrs Shand Kydd, which is more comfortable or less comfortable, standing or sitting?'

'I am very happy to stand for a bit.'

'What I suggest, stand until you want to sit, and vary it as you may wish.'

'Thank you, my lady,' said a grateful Mrs Shand Kydd.

William Boyce stood to commence his examination. 'I hope you do not consider us insensitive, discourteous or disrespectful, but during the course of the case, we are referring to your late daughter as Diana, Princess of Wales . . .'

Don't worry about that, Mr Boyce, I thought. She's called her daughter much, much worse.

As she was led through bundles of files by the prosecutor, I didn't take my eyes off her. She never once looked in my direction. I willed her to turn her head and look at me. Why are you doing this to me? I thought. Have you forgotten all those times you spent at our home after her death? The cross and chain you gave me for protection? The kind offer to buy us a home in London? What have I done to deserve this?

But I knew the answer to that one. I had become too close to her daughter, had been regarded as more family than she was, and that pained the Spencers. In her evidence, she sometimes called me 'the defendant' or 'Mr Burrell', never Paul.

Mr Boyce's next question brought me out of my thoughts. 'How would you describe your relationship with your daughter?'

'Loving and trusting,' she replied, and I began to shuffle towards the edge of my seat.

'Was it always? Or were there sometimes ups and downs?'

Mrs Shand Kydd cleared her throat. 'There were sometimes ups and downs. I would suggest to the court that was normal family behaviour, and in every family there are disagreements . . . and those disagreements are irrelevant to the future.'

My mind flashed back to a vivid recollection of a scene at KP, six months before the princess's death, in the spring of 1997. I had been in my pantry when I heard sobbing upstairs.

'Paul! Come here . . . quickly,' shouted the princess, over the banister.

I sprinted up the stairs and was almost behind her. The princess, in her white towelling robe, picked up the telephone receiver, which she had left on the carpet, off the hook, in front of the grey marble fireplace. A voice was rambling at the other end of the line. I had often heard the princess cry with frustration, when she felt sorry for herself, but this was a heartbreak I was witnessing. She sat cross-legged on the carpet, clutching the receiver to her ear, hunched forward. She waved me closer. I knelt beside her, and tilted my head as close as possible to the receiver.

I detected the slurring voice of Mrs Shand Kydd in full flow. The princess was sniffling and shaking her head in disbelief. She was absorbing a volley of verbal abuse from her mother, who was making it quite clear what she thought of her own daughter going on dates and being associated with Muslim men. 'You are nothing but a . . .' She used words that no mother should say to a daughter.

The princess slammed down the telephone, and wept again. I sat with her, and placed an arm round her.

'I am never going to speak to my mother again, Paul, never,' she vowed. They never did speak again, and every time Mrs Shand Kydd sent a letter to KP, the princess recognized the handwriting and sent it back unopened, marked 'Return to Sender'.

Back in the Old Bailey, it was Lord Carlile's turn to begin his cross-examination. He had to tread carefully. 'As far as your relations with your daughter Diana are concerned, I am not going to pry in any detail at all, except to put this aspect of it to you. You and your daughter Diana last spoke to one another in the spring of 1997.'

'That's correct, but it happened with all our family and she made it up with all . . .' and then, in the same breath, she switched the focus on to reducing the importance of my role in the princess's life. Mrs Shand Kydd feared the path my barrister was about to take. '. . . but I think there has been a slight misinterpretation by Mr Burrell . . . that he was referred to as "my rock". This was a term she used regularly and often to many people. She called me her "rock" and "star".'

'But your daughter regarded Paul Burrell as, let us put it this way, a rock?' asked my barrister.

'Yes,' she replied, 'but no more so than other people, which included, of the same vein, her drivers . . . her protection officers . . . her family.'

So the jury heard how everyone, even those who had deserted the princess in service, was her 'rock'. And how Mrs Shand Kydd, who I knew had caused her daughter such heartbreak, was her 'rock'. If only that jury knew the full story as it flashed around inside my head. I so wanted Lord Carlile to let it be known, but the law, as I learned, can be a precarious game when your liberty is at stake.

At that juncture, all the jury saw was a frail, white-haired old lady whose sharp wit had made many in the court smile. She was the mother of the princess and an attack on her at that stage would have been foolhardy. It might have turned some members of the jury against me, said my legal team. Lord Carlile had to skirt round the edges, and the truth would have to wait until *after* the court case. For that moment, Mrs Shand Kydd would trample all over my reputation, putting distance between me and the Boss.

When Lord Carlile asked: 'You knew that Paul Burrell was the person who was there, if required by your daughter, from the time she awoke in the morning to the time she dispensed with his services at night?'

She replied: 'Maybe. She didn't discuss times with me.'

'Do you accept that it is likely?'

'Not really. Because many, many days she was out, away,' and Mrs Shand Kydd felt better to believe that.

I could not believe what I was hearing. But it got worse as she demonstrated her woeful knowledge of life inside KP, and its clear-outs and hand-outs of unwanted royal gifts. Referring to the princess, she said: 'She was very, very careful with all things royal. She was also very careful with gifts from people . . . I can promise you, she gave nothing away other than gifts she usually bought for Christmas and birthdays.'

But, at least, she came clean about the documents she had shredded indiscriminately; the destruction of a history that had led me to raise the handling of the princess's world and memory at my December 1997 meeting with the Queen. As my statement had made clear: '*I feared at the time of the princess's death that there was a conspiracy to change the course of history, and erase certain parts of her life from it. Mrs Frances Shand Kydd spent two weeks shredding personal correspondence and documents.*'

Lord Carlile: 'You spent many hours on many days shredding documents, didn't you?'

Mrs Shand Kydd: 'On many days.'

'How many documents do you think you shredded?'

'Between fifty and a hundred.'

'And you never told Paul Burrell what you were shredding, did you?'

'No, I don't think I did,' she said.

Lord Carlile now focused on my rescue of the princess's world. 'You knew that Paul Burrell was genuinely concerned about the preservation of as good a reputation as possible for your daughter Diana?'

'Yes.'

'You knew that he was concerned that history should not be rewritten in a way which was in any way critical of the princess?'

'Those views were not expressed to me.'

She was being defiant to the end. At the end of her evidence, as she shuffled past me one last time, Mrs Shand Kydd still couldn't look me in the eye.

The last time I had seen Lady Sarah McCorquodale was about six months after my enforced departure from the Memorial Fund. She was walking across Westminster Bridge in London, and we exchanged a few curt words. But the Old Bailey was, essentially, our first proper reunion since that meal with Anthony Julius in the wine bar near Southampton Row.

In the witness stand, she came across as assertive, with the confidence of aristocracy. I never took my eyes off her, hoping my stare would somehow be noticed. Spencer number two had taken the stand to testify against me.

Lady Sarah, out of all the family, had been closest to the princess. The Boss had often said she liked her sense of fun. It was a prime reason why she took her as a lady-in-waiting on foreign tours. After the princess's death, Lady Sarah and I had been great allies, working well together. I remembered the cufflinks she had placed in my hand, the Versace dress she had given to Maria, the £50,000 variation of the will in recognition of my loyalty. Perhaps I had become too close to her sister, raved about her memory too often. But, as she spoke, all I thought was: How did our relationship come to this?

Her words to that court summed up how much she hated the fact that I felt it was my duty to be a keeper of her sister's secrets.

William Boyce asked her: 'What, in your view, might Mr Burrell have had lawfully in his possession?'

She replied: 'Cufflinks, photographs in frames, enamel boxes, tie-pins, ties, and I think that would be all.'

When you sit in the dock of a courtroom, you tend to note the one-time friends or colleagues who suddenly crop up to testify against you. In compiling a defence, you also notice the reticence of those not prepared to raise their heads above the parapet to stand by you.

I had considered the comptroller at KP, Michael Gibbins, to be a friend. I was wrong. This trained accountant had arrived at the palace about a year before the princess died. Yet he took the witness stand for the prosecution, professing to know the true closeness between butler and princess. Which was odd. Because he worked in an office that was completely separate from apartments 8 and 9. He had no idea of life in the princess's sitting room, dressing room, dining room. But because I had once moaned to him about the long, exhausting hours, he felt he was in a position to speak about my feelings of 'insecurity' within my employment.

William Boyce said Mr Gibbins had told police that the relationship was not as strong as I believed. 'There was a closeness but it may not have been entirely as Mr Burrell has described,' said the prosecutor. He even suggested that I was thinking of moving to America. Which was correct – because the princess was, too.

It was Friday 25 October when Michael Gibbins took the stand. That same day, around the corner of St Paul's Cathedral, the Queen, the Duke of Edinburgh and Prince Charles arrived for a memorial service for the victims of the Bali bombings. Her Majesty's Rolls-Royce purred up Ludgate Hill, passing the end of the street leading to the Old Bailey. A few days later, the conversation that took place at that time would have an enormous impact on 'Regina v. Burrell'.

On the following Monday, part-time nanny Olga Powell was another surprise face on the witness stand. She had been a firm favourite of the princess, William and Harry. She was also the last person I expected to see up there. We had shared many aspects of our service at KP. Before the trial, we had spoken and she said she had no intention of becoming a witness for anyone. 'I don't want the fuss and bother at my age,' she told me.

As she stood in court, telling the jury about the tuckbox habits of Prince William, I wondered why she was now turning against me. I could see what she was doing. She was looking out for William and Harry. But, in doing so, she was wielding the prosecution hammer, which was intended to nail me to the wall.

Out of all the numerous dressers I had worked with, Helen Walsh was probably the most spiritual, a practising Catholic like Maria. Perhaps that was why she walked into the witness box and spoke the truth. The moment she took the oath I sensed her reluctance to be part of the prosecution case. Speaking with a candour not expected by the prosecution team, she told how the princess used to tip unwanted clothes into the middle of the floor, or hand unwanted royal gifts or trinkets to staff. She, too, had been given numerous items.

A startled Mr Boyce asked her what she had been given. 'That's really none of your business,' she told him, and I tried to suppress a laugh.

'Didn't know she was rowing in his boat,' one of the prosecution was heard to say by my legal team.

The prosecution case was being held up to scrutiny, and failing on its own questions. The gift-giving culture that had been so prevalent in royal households for so many years was coming to the surface.

Outside the courtroom, I saw Helen in the marbled hallway. Defendant and prosecution witness rushed up to each other and embraced. 'Thank you, Helen, for being so honest,' I told her.

'I just told the truth, Paul. That's all I did.'

Throughout that day, Prince Charles's solicitor Fiona Shackleton had been talking to Commander John Yates of Scotland Yard. We wouldn't know that until the next day.

Tuesday 29 October dawned as any other day. The previous evening, my legal team had surmised that we had gained ground; that, in terms of evidential point-scoring, we had come out on top. My opportunity to give my version of the truth was almost upon me. Lord Carlile had prepared me to take the witness stand the next day. The defence was due to start within twenty-four hours.

None of us had any inkling of the behind-the-scenes activity until we walked into the courtroom. The press, Lord Carlile and the rest of the defence team were asked by the ushers to clear the court. The prosecution were locked in chambers with Mrs Justice Rafferty. The case was adjourned for an hour.

'What's all this about? Is it bad for me?' I asked Lord Carlile. He had no idea.

When Mrs Justice Rafferty re-entered the courtroom, the news stunned everyone. Turning to the jury, she said: 'Ladies and gentlemen, I am sorry, there has been a slight delay. We can't sit today and I am going to send you away now.'

Just like that. She sent the jury home and adjourned the case until further notice. Lord Carlile leapt to his feet. He inquired about the reasons for the unexplained adjournment. Mrs Justice Rafferty declined to inform him. She stood. Everyone rose. And that was the day's court proceedings. It was shortly after eleven o'clock.

'What on earth is going on? Is this normal?' I asked Andrew Shaw.

'Erm, no. It's all a bit strange,' he said.

I didn't know what to think. My head was spinning with speculation. The press crowded outside the courtroom, equally baffled. Mystery hung in the air above the chatter of intrigue. Something was happening, but nobody milling around that hallway knew anything.

In our 'safe room' on the first floor, we pondered the possibilities.

'Could it be more evidence? What if they think they've got more evidence?' I panicked.

'No, Paul. If it was that, we would most certainly know about it.

388

It has to be more serious than that,' said Lord Carlile. He thought for a bit longer. 'Paul,' he said, 'is there anything you can think of, something you haven't told us, which might have relevance to your case? *Anything?*'

We sat there – Lord Carlile, Ray Herman, Andrew Shaw, Shona and I – and raked over old ground in a monotonous recall of the facts, a bit like one of those movie murder squads that have reached a dead end. Lord Carlile knew about the offer of accommodation from a senior royal – everyone knew about the meetings with Mark Bolland. Was there anything about Prince Charles? Anything about Prince William? Anything about my meeting with the Queen?

You see, I had already disclosed *that* meeting with Her Majesty. It was disclosed to the police in a pre-trial statement. It was also mentioned in a sixty-four-page statement that had been intended for my legal team's eyes only. It read: '*It seemed to me that everyone the princess ever knew wanted to relay their own personal grief to me. Even the Queen . . . granted me an audience which last* [sic] *almost 3 hours in her private apartment at Buckingham Palace.*' That was all it said because that was all I thought to write down at the time. I hadn't detailed the actual conversation.

After that sudden adjournment, all I could concentrate on was one question: What is going on? In that safe room, we began to speculate about Prince Charles being called as a witness, and we could all live with that prospect.

But what if Prince William was to take the stand? I couldn't bear the thought of sitting in the dock as the eldest son of the princess stood in front of me, testifying against me. As soon as that seed was planted in my mind, my imagination went into overdrive. In my mind, the talks behind the scenes were all about orchestrating the handling of the evidence of a royal, and that left me fretting endlessly.

Later that day, we were informed that the court would not be sitting for two days, until Friday.

I didn't sleep a wink all night. The more the hours dragged, the more paranoid I became. The not knowing was driving me mad. It was mental torture, and it infuriated me that the legal system was toying with me in such a way.

After pacing around the Harts' home all morning, I needed to get out. After days of thinking the case was going my way, I viewed the adjournment as a blow. I had never felt so down since the first day of the trial. The need for a pint of milk became my excuse to go for a long walk.

I walked and walked and walked, and found myself wandering into the open spaces of Bushey Park. It was raining hard, and the incessant downpour sent men and women scuttling along the footpaths, heads down. In the distance, I could hear the swishing of passing traffic, and the rain bounced off taut umbrellas. The only person who didn't care about getting wet was me. I looked at my watch. I had gone out for that pint of milk three hours earlier. I watched the world go by, thinking that I should be in the Old Bailey clearing my name, not in the park fretting about what was happening. I felt like screaming. I did the next best thing. I rang a journalist friend who was covering the case, and vented my frustration. I rambled on to Steve Dennis for fifteen minutes: 'I don't know how much more I can take – I'm losing my mind. How dare they toy with me like this? What have they got that is taking so long? I know this is bad news. I know it.'

'Paul,' said Steve, 'you don't know what it could be. It could be another witness, it could be the end. This could be anything . . . and it could be good news.'

He was attempting to lift me, but I didn't thank him. 'It won't be, not in my wildest dreams, so don't tell me that.'

The uncertainty was excruciating.

Kevin Hart had been driving around Hampton looking for me. He found me in Bushey Park, placed his arm round me and said, 'Come on, let's go for a pint.'

On Thursday night, we had a legal conference in the London chambers of Lord Carlile. Once more, the team sat around racking its brains. We went back over the letter I had sent to Prince William, then the meeting with the Queen.

'What did you talk to the Queen about?' asked Lord Carlile.

'We talked about many things,' I said, 'Maria and the boys, her family, the princess, William and Harry, and I told her everything that was happening at Kensington Palace. We spoke about lots of things,' I said.

'Did you express your concerns about Mrs Frances Shand Kydd shredding documents?'

'Yes.'

At that point, all the other eyes in the room flashed in my direction.

'Well,' said Lord Carlile, clearly at a loss, 'why didn't you tell us that earlier?'

'It was a private conversation with the Queen. We spoke about a lot of things.'

I'm not sure that even then the significance of that conversation truly dawned on us. It was useful to know, it was an important piece of information for the defence. We could incorporate it into my testimony when I took the stand. That was our thinking at the time. Never did any of us think that we were armed with the capability to destabilize the trial.

There seems to have been a lot of bewilderment, cynicism and conspiracy theories surrounding my meeting with the Queen and what was said. Yes, I had told Her Majesty that I had taken papers for safekeeping. But I had told her no more than I had relayed to Prince William in my letter of 19 April 2001, and the CPS had seen that letter. The CPS had seen the words 'for safekeeping', and it didn't seem to matter. In the light of my declaration to William, the silence from St James's Palace, and the pursuit of a conviction by Scotland Yard merely told me that none of my written pleas was important.

What, after all, is the difference between telling the Queen about retaining items for safekeeping, and telling Prince William? In fact, I had also written a letter to Prince Charles on 5 February 2001, telling him exactly the same thing. It was said that the letter never reached him. But his deputy private secretary Mark Bolland saw it. Therefore, the significance of informing the Queen of my intentions was lost on me.

It is still lost on me, to this day, why it was such a surprise to the CPS, because its officials had known I had told Prince William of my safekeeping intentions. What William Boyce would go on to tell the court would sum up, in my eyes, the farcical nature of the prosecution, and the blindness it had displayed since January 2001.

★

The air was thick with anticipation on Friday 1 November, All Saints Day. There seemed to be more press than ever before. I didn't want to think what the day would bring. Having settled into a legal routine over the previous two weeks, I was back to square one, and trembling inside.

'Something of significance is happening,' Lord Carlile had said the previous evening.

As if to add to the drama, in the middle of the morning the fire alarms went off at the Old Bailey. Everyone was evacuated into the street. It was chaos. I stood on the pavement between Lord Carlile and Andrew Shaw. Television cameras and photographers swarmed around me. I tried to look relaxed, tried to concentrate on the conversation around me, but it was useless. I was distracted and tense.

Then clearance was given to return to court.

A few minutes later, Lord Carlile offered the first reassurance of the morning: 'The police are starting to shuffle around and pack up their boxes. It's a good sign.'

I waited outside courtroom number one. My mobile telephone rang in my pocket.

It was journalist Steve Dennis. His voice was shaking. He was standing at the other side of the double doors near the staircase. 'Paul, it's gonna collapse. No one knows why, but it's coming to an end. There are press officers for the CPS and Metropolitan Police on hand.'

It didn't dawn on me. 'So what does that mean?'

'It means they're here to clear up the mess. Paul, we all know it's going to end. We know!'

I couldn't believe it. 'No – not in my wildest dreams! Look, I've got to go.' I clicked off the phone.

'Paul, it's time to go in,' said Lord Carlile.

All of a sudden, I felt completely detached from myself. I walked into the dock. Michelle, the guard, smiled at me. Three knocks on the door. Mrs Justice Rafferty strode in, and the horrible quiet of a courtroom descended.

William Boyce got to his feet. 'My lady, it has been an important part of the prosecution case that there was no evidence that Mr Burrell informed anyone that he was holding any property belonging to the executors of the estate of Diana, Princess of Wales –'

I was too hooked on his next words to dwell on the inaccuracy of that claim.

'. . . Further, prosecution witnesses have been examined in chief, and cross-examined, on the basis that the prosecution had no evidence to show that he had ever notified anyone that he was holding property of Diana, Princess of Wales . . .'

Wrong again, I thought. The letter to Prince William had been under your noses the whole time.

He continued: 'On Monday of this week, the prosecution was informed by the police that, during a private meeting with the Queen in the weeks following the death of Diana, Princess of Wales, Mr Burrell mentioned . . . that he . . .' Mr Boyce carried on explaining the 'false premise' of his case. It transpired that the Duke of Edinburgh had mentioned to Prince Charles, as they travelled to the Bali bombing memorial service the previous week, that the Queen had been told by me that I had taken documents for safekeeping. Prince Charles informed his private secretary Sir Michael Peat the next day. He then confirmed the account with the Queen. St James's Palace then reported the topic of that conversation to Scotland Yard.

Then I heard William Boyce say: '. . . and the proper course would be to invite no further evidence against Mr Burrell, and invite the jury to find him not guilty.'

I was sitting there, heart thumping, trying to grasp the rushed legal statement he had just delivered. I threw a look at Lord Carlile. He smiled. I looked at Andrew Shaw, who had been with me from when the police had raided my home, and he was sitting back. Relief in the camp. Then she said it. The words I shall never forget. 'Mr Burrell, you are free to go.' Mrs Justice Rafferty smiled warmly.

For a second or two, I didn't move. I looked back at Lord Carlile. He nodded. 'Come on,' he mouthed.

I didn't know if my legs would support me as I got up and stood tall in the hush. A huge swell of emotion rose in my throat. Every noise I made – the chair going back, the shuffling, my footsteps – was heard by everyone watching me. Michelle, the guard, gave me a guiding hand. The press stared at me in silence. I left the dock, turned right, went down three steps into the well of the court and sat down as three not-guilty verdicts were entered against my name in the absence of the jury.

Mrs Justice Rafferty stood, and walked out of court. The press darted out to explain to the world the magnitude of the Queen's historic intervention. The one witness I knew from the outset I could never call had come through for me: the Queen I had served all those years ago had spoken up for me in defence of my memory of another remarkable royal: Diana, Princess of Wales. As reporters and television producers rushed into the street, I walked over to Lord Carlile. 'Is that it?'

'Yes, that's it, Paul. It's over . . . it's all over.'

I couldn't stop the sob that sent me leaning into the shoulder of my defence barrister. The QC who had been brave enough to take on the Crown in a case involving the Crown, and he had done a superlative job in seeing me home. As my tears wet the shoulder of his cloak, he patted me on the back. 'I think we should all go to lunch. I know a nice little place in Covent Garden,' he said.

Then Andrew Shaw passed me his mobile telephone. 'It's Maria.'

I took the phone, and the first thing I heard were her tears of joy.

I think all I managed to say was 'Chuck?' before we started crying together. 'It's the Queen, chuck. It's all thanks to the Queen,' I said, and I was surrounded by my legal team. The rollercoaster ride we had all been on was finally at an end.

Maria was hardly making sense in her euphoria but she told me to listen. She held out the phone, and a mass of cheers broke out. She was in our florist's shop in Holt, and family and customers roared out their support.

Andrew Shaw and I went out into the street. I don't think my feet touched the ground as a scrum of reporters, photographers and television crews swarmed round me, all fended off by shoulder-to-shoulder policemen. I had to steady myself on the backs of the officers in front of me.

'Paul! Paul!' the photographers screamed. 'Paul! Over here.' I tripped over the leg of a newsman who had toppled over. I looked up and faces were pressed against the windows of the buildings towering above me; other office workers hung out of the windows and waved. I tried to wave back, but my arms could hardly move.

Then Andrew Shaw spoke on my behalf to the media. A railed-off pen at the top of the street was a prearranged press conference point. He thanked everyone, told of my relief, and everyone was shouting my name. I was drained and numb, but had I been able to, I would have screamed to the world: 'God, it feels good to be free!'

We all went to celebrate in a restaurant in Covent Garden. It was quiet, save for four other diners sitting round a table. As I walked in, that table broke out in spontaneous applause, and each one of those kind strangers shook my hand.

Two special people joined our celebration, and added to the poignancy of the occasion: Richard Kay and Susie Kassem, friends of the princess. I don't think I've ever hugged Susie so tight. 'Someone is looking down on you,' she said, and that set us both off.

As we sat down, another face walked in: Fiona Bruce, of the BBC. It was raining outside, and she looked soaked but she didn't seem to care. She had come to drop off a bottle of champagne. 'I just wanted to say congratulations, Paul.' She kissed my cheek and left us to toast my acquittal.

That evening, I returned to Cheshire and the sanctuary of a relative's home. Ultimately, despite being denied the opportunity in court, I was able to issue my defence, as it would have been told in court, in the *Daily Mirror*. Then the rest of the newspapers – in Britain and America – turned on me. Having survived the prosecution of the state, I had to survive a two-week persecution by the media. I had sold my soul, they said. I had betrayed the princess and, once more, the ignorance of the many blurred the knowledge of the few.

Even in doing this book, I know I have not betrayed the princess. For to grasp the definition of betrayal, you first need to know the amount of knowledge. It is for that reason that I know I have remained true. The princess would understand that too. It goes some way to answering the question: Where do you go from here?

I walked away from the Old Bailey to begin a new future, and yet I refuse to get rid of the past. It is either a flaw or a strength. But having cleared my name in court, it remains my duty to clear the name of the princess, and ensure she is remembered for the remarkable woman she was. Memories are there to be treasured. People worry about me being obsessed, but I am merely haunted by an exceptionally kind ghost.

I am stronger than I have been in a long while and, despite the actions of the police, I still have faith in human nature and the millions who believe, like I do, that the princess's memory should remain as vibrant and as vivid as the magical mark she left on people's lives.

Will I move on? Of course.

Will I let go? Never.

The princess gave me something special and, in sharing with you some of those warm memories and stories, I hope her personality shines through. For ever and a day, I will continue, in the face of whatever may come my way, to stand in the princess's corner and defend her memory. It is what she would have expected.

I know what we had. I know the depth of what we shared. I know the future we were heading to. And the one thing that people cannot take away from me is her final letter to me, left propped up on my desk in my pantry in the month of her death.

I read it often as a source of immense strength and comfort. It turned out to be a written farewell, and it seems a fitting one to this book:

Dear Paul,

Clearly from your third eye, this coming weekend is an important one!

I know that too, and I wanted to write on paper how enormously touched I am that you share this excitement with me as well. What a secret!

You are marvellous how you cope with my questions day after day and it's quite annoying that you're constantly right!

But, on a serious note, your support, as always, has been invaluable and kept me sane during some of the nightmare times . . .

Now, the tide is changing and we can all now have peace of mind and look forward to happier times and different homes!

Thank you Paul, for being such a tower of strength

love from, Diana.

What's the secret?

Sorry. That's between the butler and the princess.